The Nonverbal Communication Reader

CLASSIC AND CONTEMPORARY READINGS
Second Edition

The Nonverbal Communication Reader

CLASSIC AND CONTEMPORARY READINGS
Second Edition

Edited by

Laura K. Guerrero
Arizona State University

Joseph A. DeVito
Hunter College

Michael L. Hecht
The Pennsylvania State University

WAVELAND
PRESS, INC.
Prospect Heights, Illinois

For information about this book, write or call:
Waveland Press, Inc.
P.O. Box 400
Prospect Heights, Illinois 60070
(847) 634-0081

Contents

Acknowledgments

It is a pleasure to thank the many people who have contributed to this volume. Most importantly we want to thank the people who have allowed their work to be printed in this collection, in particular those who took time from their busy schedules to write original pieces for this volume. They are clearly the writers of this book.

As always Carol and Neil Rowe, and the people at Waveland Press made working on this book a pleasure. We thank them for their cooperation, their wise counsel, and their dedication to providing the field of communication with quality books.

In addition to those already mentioned, we wish to thank Susanne Jones for her help in putting this book together and proofreading galleys.

From Laura Guerrero:
Thanks to my husband, Vico, for putting up with the zillions of articles and chapters that were scattered all over our study as I worked on this.

From Joseph DeVito:
As always, to Boo.

From Michael Hecht:
My thanks to Stan Jones, who first introduced me to the study of nonverbal communication; to Donnie and Lenore, and to Jim and Rebecca for their generational influences, and, eternally, to Ann.

Preface

When the first edition of this reader was published in 1990, nonverbal communication was one of the fastest growing areas in the field of communication. This continues to be the case. More than ever, communication researchers are recognizing that if we are to understand the communication process, both nonverbal and verbal messages must be investigated. Since 1990, many new journal articles and books on nonverbal communication have been published. The second edition of this reader includes many of these contemporary, cutting-edge research articles, as well as some of the classic literature that brought the area of nonverbal behavior to the forefront and continues to inform us today.

OUR GOALS

The selections for this reader were chosen with several goals in mind. First, although there are many excellent textbooks in nonverbal communication, there are few places where students can go to read classic and contemporary research firsthand. We hope that this reader will fulfill this need by giving students access to a wide variety of research, theory, and literature written by various scholars who are experts in nonverbal communication. Second, nonverbal communication is studied by researchers from various disciplines, including communication, psychology, and anthropology, among others. Therefore, although this volume focuses on research in the field of communication, it also includes many readings from scholars who are associated with other disciplines. Third, this reader was designed to give students knowledge about the basic codes of nonverbal communication (such as kinesics and proxemics) as well as the basic functions of nonverbal communication (such as interaction management and persuasion). We believe that a focus on codes and functions is representative of current research trends in nonverbal communication.

The Nonverbal Communication Reader is appropriate for undergraduate students taking a first or second course in nonverbal communication. It is also appropriate for beginning graduate students who would like to see a sampling of classic and contemporary work in the nonverbal area. This reader was designed so that it would work well with any of the excellent textbooks on nonverbal communication. Of course, it can also be used as a primary text.

ORGANIZATION OF THE BOOK

The reader contains four sections: Beginning Perspectives, Nonverbal Codes, Nonverbal Functions, and Contemporary Nonverbal Theories. The first section, Beginning Perspectives, defines the basic terms related to nonverbal communication, describes nonverbal communication skills, and provides an overview of various common nonverbal research methods. Our discussion of methods should be especially informative for students because it will help them understand the methods used in the studies appearing in this reader. The second section of this reader, Nonverbal Codes, describes the "areas" of nonverbal communication, including the body, face, and eyes; appearance and adornment; space and touch; the voice and silence; and the environment and time. Within this section, all of the readings focus on messages within a single area (such as space and touch). The third section, Nonverbal Functions, focuses on how messages from the different codes work together to accomplish goals such as sending emotional or relational messages, managing interaction, or persuading and influencing others. The fourth and final section, Contemporary Nonverbal Theories of Message Exchange, examines five communication theories that focus on how messages are exchanged between interaction partners: communication accommodation theory, expectancy violations theory, discrepancy arousal theory, cognitive valence theory, and interaction adaptation theory. Because the readings in this section are all authored by the scholars who developed these theories, this section should be particularly helpful to students who want to read about theory firsthand. Taken together, the four sections of the reader accomplish the goals of introducing students to the field of nonverbal communication, giving them an in-depth look at each of the nonverbal codes, illustrating how messages from various codes work together to fulfill communication functions, and explaining how people respond to the messages of others.

TEACHING AIDS AND FEATURES

Unlike many readers, this text contains a variety of learning aids and unique features. The introductory material in Section 1 places the field of nonverbal communication in perspective and provides an orientation to the readings which follow. Each of the major parts of the reader begins with an overview to acquaint readers with the selections contained in that part. Each selection is further placed in perspective using introductory headnotes. Another unique feature of this reader is that methods and statistics have been summarized in ordinary language that students can understand. This was done without damaging the integrity of the research and, in all cases, with the approval of the original researcher or publisher. We believe that this will make research studies more accessible to students who are new to the area of nonverbal communication.

Another unique feature of this reader is its emphasis on the practical applications of nonverbal communication. This reader contains many of the most significant research and theory papers by the field's leading contributors and at the same time also provides important practical applications to a wide variety of situations. These include increasing effectiveness in employment interviews, communicating power in an organization, using nonverbal communication to persuade others, sending appropriate messages of liking and attraction, making positive first impressions, communicating effectively with those from different cultures, and being better able to detect deception. These practical applications are firmly based on findings from the very best nonverbal research available.

We enjoy teaching the nonverbal communication course and we want to share our enthusiasm with you. We hope that this reader succeeds in capturing the diverse array of topics and important research findings that make the study of nonverbal communication such an exciting and worthwhile enterprise.

PART I

Beginning Perspectives

Nonverbal communication is all around us. You are expressing yourself nonverbally when you smile, dress in a certain style, lean forward or backward, stand close or far, or talk in a certain tone of voice. Nonverbal messages are important because they are generally more *believable* than verbal communication, and because they are the primary mode of expressing emotion, creating and managing impressions, and communicating messages of attraction, liking, distance, and dominance. However, unlike some popular books suggest, it is difficult, if not impossible, to "read someone like a book." Nonverbal communication can be an illusive and ambiguous form of communication. You will interpret nonverbal messages more accurately if you avoid relying too heavily on a single nonverbal cue (for example, crossed arms as a sign of defensiveness) and, instead, look for clusters or packages of behaviors (for example, look for crossed arms, frowns, rigid posture, and leaning away as signs of defensiveness).

Of course, before you can become more skilled at sending, recognizing, and interpreting nonverbal communication, you need to have a clear idea of what nonverbal communication is. In the first article in this section, we define nonverbal communication and discuss several characteristics of nonverbal messages. You have many ways of communicating nonverbally. You use your body, face, and eyes, clothing and other forms of adornment (such as perfume, jewelry, and briefcases), space and touch, voice sounds and silence, the environment, and even time (such as spending extra time with others or showing up late for a group meeting). These nonverbal messages communicate many different *meanings* and accomplish numerous *functions* or *goals*. These issues are discussed in article 1.

Knowing how to send and interpret nonverbal messages requires a great deal of communication skill. Nonverbal skills are crucial for successful communication. You use nonverbal messages to communicate that you are interested in others, to start and end conversations, to express your feelings, and to impress and influence those around you. In article 2, a group of communicative behaviors that are generally seen as competent are described and explained. A rating scale is also included so that you can see one way in which nonverbal skills can be measured.

Finally, this section looks at common research methods in nonverbal research. Although you observe nonverbal communication all the time, observation is not a simple task when it comes to nonverbal signals. Many of the most important nonverbal behaviors occur quickly and subtly. A slight change in posture, a shuffling of the feet, or a quick facial movement can all communicate valuable information that is difficult to observe and measure. In article 3, several common methods of researching nonverbal communication are discussed so that you can appreciate the sophistication with which nonverbal research is conducted. This article should also help you understand the methods that you read about in the various research articles that are included in this reader.

This article provides an overview of nonverbal communication. Hecht, DeVito, and Guerrero define nonverbal communication as messages other than words that are either sent with intent or typically interpreted by a receiver as meaningful. They also describe the basic characteristics of nonverbal communication, including the basic codes (or types) of nonverbal messages, and the primary functions of nonverbal communication.

1

Perspectives on Nonverbal Communication
Codes, Functions, and Contexts

Michael L. Hecht
Joseph A. DeVito
Laura K. Guerrero

Nonverbal communication occurs in all areas of life. Note the role of nonverbal communication in business and personal relationships in these examples.

> Pat is negotiating to buy an office building owned by Kelly. They have been negotiating for three weeks and now appear ready to complete the deal. "Five hundred thousand is my final offer!" asserts Pat. Kelly looks directly back at the other negotiator. Pat returns the gaze except for a brief glance and smile at the building they are discussing. Kelly also notices Pat's feet move nervously and thinks, "Pat really wants this property and is nervous about leaving without a deal." Kelly answers, "I won't take less than $525,000."

This article was written especially for *The Nonverbal Communication Reader.*

Jamie and Chris met two weeks ago at a party. Last week they went out for lunch and talked for three hours. Tonight they had their first date. After dinner and a drink at a quiet bar, they return to Jamie's apartment. They talk for awhile and hold hands. Chris reaches over and softly touches Jamie's cheek. As their heartbeats quicken, Chris leans forward, slowly closing the distance between them until they kiss softly for the first time.

These descriptions emphasize the nonverbal world in which we live (Frye, 1980). During the negotiation, Pat's words convey one meaning. Kelly, however, relies on nonverbal cues to make the last bid. In the romantic interaction, without speaking a word, a powerful message of attraction passes between two people and is acted upon. While most of our formal education focuses on verbal messages, our nonverbal skills often play the key role in our success or failure.

In this article, we highlight the importance of nonverbal communication in our daily lives. After defining nonverbal communication, we discuss three important characteristics of nonverbal communication: (1) nonverbal communication is organized into codes, (2) nonverbal messages are functional, and (3) nonverbal messages are influenced by context.

THE IMPORTANCE OF NONVERBAL COMMUNICATION

Nonverbal communication plays an important role in our interactions with others. In fact, research suggests that approximately 60–65% of social meaning is derived from nonverbal behaviors (Burgoon, 1994). Studies show that people often interpret messages by relying more on nonverbal than verbal cues. For example, you may infer what your boss is thinking and feeling from facial expressions, stance, and other nonverbal messages. Noller's (1984) research suggests that people also rely more on nonverbal than verbal communication to send positive and negative messages to relational partners, such as spouses, family members, or best friends. From practical experience we know that verbal messages are important too. In fact, verbal messages usually account for most of the meaning when people are interpreting factual or persuasive messages (Burgoon, 1994). However, there are times when the nonverbal messages are more influential. Nonverbal messages are particularly important when expressing emotion, forming impressions, and communicating relational messages, such as intimacy and dominance (Noller, 1984; Patterson, 1983).

Nonverbal communication is particularly powerful because it is usually seen as more believable than verbal messages. People view nonverbal behaviors as spontaneous expressions of internal thoughts and feelings that reveal our "inner selves." This is why nonverbal messages are especially important when inconsistent verbal and nonverbal messages are sent. When interpreting messages, people often pay more attention to the visual channel, which includes facial expressions and body movement, than the verbal channel (Bugental, Kaswan, & Love, 1970; DePaulo & Rosenthal, 1979). The vocal channel, which includes voice tone, pitch, and volume, is also important. Noller (1984) demonstrated that close relational partners, such as spouses, often rely heavily on the voice when sending and interpreting messages. To illustrate the importance of the visual and vocal channels, imagine asking a friend if something is wrong. Your friend says "no" in a muted voice and turns away with arms across the chest. Are you likely to believe the verbal or the nonverbal message? According to the research, when verbal and nonverbal messages contradict, most adults in the United States believe the nonverbal (Zahn, 1973). So if you ignore the nonverbal messages, you will surely be at a disadvantage.

A DEFINITION OF NONVERBAL COMMUNICATION

Now that you recognize the importance of nonverbal communication, you might be wondering what kinds of messages count as nonverbal communication. *Nonverbal communication* includes all the messages other than words that people exchange in interactive contexts. To qualify as a message, a behavior typically must be sent with intent and/or it must typically be interpreted by others. In other words, it must have a social meaning. For example, if you vary your voice tone to make it clear that you are being sarcastic, you have communicated with intent. If you are nervous when you give a public speech, and your hands and voice shake a little bit, you are not intentionally communicating your nervousness. Nonetheless, the audience is likely to attach a meaning to (and therefore to interpret) your shaking hands and voice as signs of nervousness.

Our definition of nonverbal communication takes into account both the receiver and the sender of the message. It also takes into account that the goal of nonverbal communication usually is to create shared meaning. As Frey, Botan, Friedman, and Kreps (1991) state, "Communication is the management of messages for the purpose of creating meaning. That is, communication occurs whenever a person attempts to send a message or whenever a person perceives and assigns meaning to behavior" (p. 28). This doesn't mean, however, that all behaviors constitute communicative messages. Messages stand for something other than themselves. Behavior, in contrast, stands for itself. It just is. For example, consider the distinctions between normal blinking, blinking to hold back tears, and winking at someone. Normal blinking is behavior, not communication. When you blink, you usually do so without conscious thought or intent. In addition, you don't usually pay any attention when someone is blinking, much less attach any meaning to it. However, if you blink rapidly to hold back tears, your action stands for something. For example, you may not want other people to realize how sentimental you are. In this case, the act of rapid blinking is probably intentional (you are trying to hide your internal feelings) and would likely be noticed and interpreted by others. Similarly, a wink is usually an intentional behavior that others interpret as meaningful. You might wink at someone flirtatiously to communicate romantic interest. Or you might wink to signal that you are teasing someone or to let a friend know he or she is doing a good job at something. Thus, winking can stand for a number of different things, including attraction, teasing, or approval.

Although the goal of nonverbal communication is to create shared meaning between a sender and a receiver, misunderstandings can and do occur. In line with our definition of nonverbal communication, we believe that three factors affect the process of exchanging nonverbal messages: (1) whether or not the sender intends to send a message, (2) whether or not the receiver pays attention to and interprets the message, and (3) whether the receiver's interpretation is accurate. The figure below illustrates six possible outcomes based on these factors. With the exception of unattended behavior, we believe that all of these message types can be studied as part of the communication process.

Message Exchange Outcomes

	Message NOT Received	Message Received Inaccurately	Message Received Accurately
Message Sent Intentionally	Attempted Communication	Miscommunication	Successful Communication
Message Sent Unintentionally	Unattended Behavior	Misinterpretation	Accidental Communication

CHARACTERISTICS OF NONVERBAL COMMUNICATION

At this point you should have a general idea of the types of behaviors that qualify as nonverbal communication. In the next section, we will discuss three characteristics of nonverbal communication that should further clarify what nonverbal communication is, what it does, and how it functions in different contexts. We start our discussion by examining the various types of channels (or codes) through which nonverbal communication is sent. For example, nonverbal messages can be sent by the face, the body, the voice, and so forth. Next, we discuss how nonverbal messages work together to fulfill certain functions, such as helping you make a good first impression or showing someone that you like (or dislike) them. Finally, we discuss the role that context plays in helping us decide how best to send and interpret nonverbal messages.

Nonverbal Messages are Organized into Codes

Our definition of nonverbal communication distinguishes between verbal communication (involving words) and nonverbal communication (involving all the rest of the message). Nonverbal communication, therefore, involves all messages other than words or language, including aspects of the voice, body movement, facial expressions, space, time, smell, and the environment. This part of our definition also points to the complexity of nonverbal communication. It reminds us of all the different ways we communicate nonverbally. In interpreting the meaning of a message, therefore, we need to focus on the words and on the various nonverbal messages from the eyes, the face, the body, and so on.

Because there are so many different levels of nonverbal communication, researchers have found it useful to separate nonverbal messages into different *codes* (Knapp & Hall, 1992). Codes are organized message systems consisting of a set of symbols and rules for their use. For example, our verbal language consists of words (a set of symbols) and the rules of grammar (the rules for combining). We define the nonverbal codes by the means of expression we use. Each code is communicated by a different nonverbal channel, such as your body, the environment, or the space between people. Next, we discuss the various nonverbal codes in more detail.

Kinesics. This code includes messages sent by your body, through gestures, posture, body movement, body lean, and so forth. It also includes messages sent by your face, such as smiles, frowns, grimaces, and pouts. The kinesic code also includes eye behavior, which is sometimes referred to as *oculesics*. Eye behavior includes eye movement, eye contact, gaze aversion, and pupil dilation and constriction.

Appearance and Adornment. This code includes physical appearance and olfactic (or smell) cues, such as those used to adorn yourself and create impressions on others. Physical appearance cues include the size, shape, and color of your body, your perceived level of attractiveness, and how you dress, wear your hair, and use cosmetics, as well as what accessories (e.g., briefcases, jewelry) you use to adorn yourself. Olfactic cues deal with how smell or odor communicates. Included here are body smells and perfume/cologne.

Vocalics. This code includes the sounds of the voice as well as silences. In other words, vocalics (sometimes referred to as "paralanguage") refers to *how* you say words rather than *what* you actually say. This includes how you communicate through changes in speaking rate, volume, voice qualities and pitch, accents, pauses, and hesitations. Also included is silence and the meanings attributed to it. Sometimes silence communicates a message more "loudly" than words ever could.

Contact Codes. This code includes both spatial and tactile communication. *Spatial communication*, or *proxemics*, focuses on how you use space and territory. Personal space refers to how far apart people are while engaged in various activities. *Territoriality* refers to fixed or moveable space such as homes, cars, or public spaces that people occupy. *Tactile communication*, or *haptics*, refers to touch and physical contact, such as grabbing, patting, hitting, hugging, kicking, and kissing.

Time and Place Codes. This code refers to the larger context in which communication occurs. Communication through time, which is often referred to as *chronemics*, includes how you use and perceive time. Time preferences, punctuality, and personal perceptions of time are some of many chronemic factors. *Environmental cues* include factors such as architectural design, color, noise, furniture arrangement, and so forth. These cues set the stage for communication with others.

Nonverbal Messages are Functional

In addition to knowing what nonverbal communication is and how nonverbal messages are sent (through the codes), we must also know what the nonverbal message *does* and *why* it is sent. Nonverbal messages are used to send a variety of messages and to fulfill many different functions. In fact, messages from the different codes (such as proxemics, haptics, and kinesics) often work together to send powerful messages. Looking at a single code is not enough. Instead it is important to look at the how the different nonverbal codes work together as a package to fulfill different functions. Several scholars (e.g., Andersen, in press; Burgoon, Buller, &

Woodall, 1996; Patterson, 1983) have developed functional approaches to studying nonverbal communication that focus on what nonverbal messages *do* rather than on what they look like. Although these scholars have forwarded somewhat different lists of functions, they are in general agreement that nonverbal messages are essential in accomplishing the following: (1) creating first impressions and person perceptions, (2) helping people manage interactions, (3) expressing emotion, (4) sending relational messages, such as closeness, intimacy, and distance, (5) enabling people to send mixed or deceptive messages, and (6) sending messages of power and persuasion.

Creating Impressions.   In many cases, people make judgments about you before you begin talking with them. Physical appearance and kinesics are especially important in creating impressions because they are often noticed first. Imagine, for example, deciding who you want to ask to dance at a formal function where you don't know many people. You are likely to "check out" potential partners by evaluating their physical appearance and assessing how friendly and accessible they might be. If a potential partner is appealing to you, but he or she looks defensive (e.g., has arms across the chest and an unpleasant facial expression) or is engaged in conversation with someone else, you might decide not to extend an invitation to dance. On the other hand, if the potential partner is standing alone, smiling, and tapping her or his foot in beat to the music, you would probably be more likely to ask for a dance.

In this book, several readings focus on impression formation and management. For example, in the section on appearance and adornment you'll see how physical appearance and perfume affect your perceptions of other people. Similarly, the article by Semic (article 17) shows how vocal qualities affect your evaluations of others. Clearly, nonverbal communication is a major determinant of first impressions.

Managing Interaction.   Nonverbal messages tell people how to conduct a conversation by regulating the flow of the interaction. This includes when to begin a conversation, whose turn it is to speak, how to get a chance to speak, how to signal others to talk more, and how to end a conversation. For example, head nods can be used to accomplish several interaction management functions. Nods can be used as *backchannels* to signal that a person is listening and wants you to continue talking. But nods can also be used to signal that a person wants to speak or wants to end the conversation. Imagine someone who is nodding very rapidly while you are speaking. This person probably wants you to finish your turn so that she or he can either start a new speaking turn or terminate the conversation, or this person might be very much in agreement with what you are saying. People also often lean forward, gesture, and open their mouths slightly when they want a chance to talk in a group.

Social rhythms, the synchronicity (coordination) and tempo (rate of speed) of conversations, are also significant. Cultures seem to have their own rhythms; individuals and dyads, too, can have their own unique "beats." This is why it is sometimes awkward when you interact with someone for the first time—you are uncertain about their communication style and rhythm. For example, when you attend a sporting event for the first time, you might not understand how to do "the wave." At first you might stand up and sit down at the wrong time. Eventually, however, you will be in sync with the rest of the crowd. In your interpersonal relationships you also learn to be in sync with others. Think about how awkward it is when you are on a first date with someone and there is a long silence or you keep accidentally interrupting your partner. After you get to know your dating partner better, you will become more comfortable with her/his communication style and interaction will probably become more coordinated. Achieving smooth interaction patterns with others requires considerable knowledge and skill.

Expressing Emotion.   As noted earlier, nonverbal communication is the primary means of expressing emotion (Andersen & Guerrero, 1998). For example, smiles and wrinkles alongside the eyes are usually nonverbal displays of happiness. Frowns, on the other hand, are signs of displeasure. Nonverbal researchers have identified *primary* or *basic emotions* such as happiness, fear, anger, sadness, disgust, and surprise. The facial expressions that people show when feeling these basic emotions appear to be universal. In other words, people from different cultures use the same facial expressions to send these emotions. People from different cultures also interpret these facial expressions similarly (Ekman, 1973). So whether you are in Argentina, Australia, Germany, Great Britain, Saudi Arabia, South Africa, or the United States, people are likely to smile when they are happy, frown when they are sad, and furrow their brows when they are angry. You should also be able to do a pretty good job identifying and interpreting these facial expressions no matter which country you are in.

However, *emotional blends*, which occur when more than one basic emotion is experienced at the same time, are expressed more subtly and are therefore more difficult to recognize. Examples of emotional blends include disappointment, which is a blend of sadness and surprise, and jealousy, which is often a blend of anger and fear. Although you often express both basic and blended emotions freely and spontaneously, there are other times when you want to control (or manage) your emotional expression. For example, you might not want your friends to know how hurt and angry you are that they forgot your birthday. Or you might want others to think that you are happy with a gift they bought you, when you are actually disappointed. In article 32, Andersen and Guerrero discuss several *display rules* that people use to help them manage their emotions. Whether you are expressing or managing emotion, nonverbal behavior is a crucial element within the communication process.

Sending Relational Messages.   You use nonverbal behaviors to tell others how you feel about them. You also evaluate the nonverbal communication of others to try to figure out how they feel about you. Many different positive relational messages are communicated nonverbally. You can show others that you like them, are similar to them, and trust them. You can also use nonverbal communication to help define a relationship as formal or informal, and task related or socially oriented (Burgoon et al., 1996). One of the primary ways people communicate closeness, liking, and intimacy is through *immediacy* cues. People communicate immediacy through behaviors such as smiles, close distances, touch, gaze, and forward lean. These behaviors show others that you are interested in them, involved in the conversation, and feel positively toward them (Andersen, 1985). The immediacy principle, developed by Albert Mehrabian (1971), predicts that people will approach individuals, situations, and objects they like and will avoid or move away from those they dislike. Think about the times you have flirted with someone or have tried to subtly let another person know that you were not interested in her or him. Your behavior in these two situations probably illustrated the immediacy principle.

The opposite of immediacy is *nonimmediacy*. Nonimmediacy functions to create distance and cut off communication. Maintaining large distances, leaning and looking away from someone, and engaging in defensive posturing, such as hugging your arms around your body, signal that you are unavailable for communication and possibly dislike someone. Whether nonverbal behaviors are used to signal affiliation or distance, they help us communicate our feelings without necessarily having to verbalize them.

Deceiving and Detecting Deception.   Nonverbal behaviors play a very important role in the deception process. Two kinds of nonverbal cues typically co-occur during deception: strategic and nonstrategic behavior (Buller & Burgoon, 1994). People use *strategic cues* to try and hide the fact that they are deceiving. For example, you might think that people tend to look away from you when they are deceiving you. This, however, is not true. When people are deceiving, they know that one of the behaviors that people look for when they are trying to "catch a liar" is eye behavior. Therefore, many deceivers strategically control their eye contact by looking you "straight in the eye." Deceivers may also smile a lot to try to appear friendly and honest. However, even when a deceiver is trying to control her or his nonverbal behavior, some nonstrategic deception behaviors are probably present. *Nonstrategic cues* are the behaviors that deceivers cannot control. These behaviors "leak" negative emotion, such as guilt and anxiety. For example, when deceivers look you straight in the eye and smile to try to appear friendly and honest, they might also "leak" some negative emotion. Their smiles might look a bit false and their voices might sound a little shaky. In this case, the falseness in the smile and the shake in the voice are nonstrategic cues leaking negative affect and anxiety.

Some research has examined strategic and nonstrategic cues as part of a leakage hierarchy (Ekman & Friesen, 1969). According to the leakage hierarchy, some nonverbal behaviors are harder to control than others during the deception process. These hard-to-control cues leak negative affect and provide clues that a person is deceiving. The leakage hierarchy specifies that the leakiest (and therefore hardest to control) channels are the voice and the lower body. The face and upper body are easier to control. Therefore, if you want to detect deception, you are usually better off listening to the voice and looking at the lower body. Even then, however, your chances of detecting deception accurately are not very good. The mix of strategic and nonstrategic nonverbal behaviors that occur during deception make it very difficult to detect deception (Knapp, Hart, & Dennis, 1974; Miller & Burgoon, 1982; Zuckerman, DePaulo, & Rosenthal, 1981).

Sending Messages of Power and Persuasion.   Nonverbal messages exercise social control (Patterson, 1983). Such messages can be used to control people and events, to establish or exert power, or to dominate others. Think of the strong leaders you know. They probably have a distinctive nonverbal style. Powerful people touch others more than they are touched. They look at others less than they are looked at (except when they use gaze to "stare someone down") and they have control over time and territory. For example, presidents of large corporations have the power to start and stop meetings and to arrive late. They can also control where meetings are held and who is allowed to attend particular meetings. Powerful people also take up more space than less powerful people, and environments can be used to control people by structuring interaction. Take a look at your classroom. If it is like most others, the teacher will have a large share of the space to move around in, and the chairs will be arranged so that the students pay attention to the teacher and not to each other. Desks also prevent students from moving around and taking up too much space. Space is used similarly in business settings, with executives having large private offices protected by territorial markers (such as a secretary who controls who enters), and subordinates working side by side or in small cubbyholes.

Finally, nonverbal messages are used to persuade others. For instance, you might smile and touch your friend on the shoulder when you are trying to get him or her to do a favor for you. Or you might use an authoritative voice to get a child to obey an order, such as not crossing the street without you. In these and other cases, nonverbal communication can be a powerful tool of persuasion.

Nonverbal Messages Are Influenced by Context

Whether you are trying to create a positive first impression, signal that you are attracted to someone, or get someone to do something for you, nonverbal communication does not occur in a vacuum. As our definition of nonverbal communication suggests, nonverbal messages are exchanged within an interactional context. This context includes cultural, relational, and situational elements.

Culture. Culture influences both the performance and the interpretation of nonverbal messages. Moreover, the rules of nonverbal communication vary from one culture to the next (Hecht, Andersen, & Ribeau, 1989). What one culture considers polite, another may consider offensive. For example, in businesses in the United States, it is usually effective to get to the point quickly. The Japanese, however, may view this as rude and unfriendly. Clothing norms also vary by culture. For instance, beach goers are more scantily clad (with men often in speedo-type suits and women often topless) in places in Southern Europe, the Caribbean, and South America. The same beach attire would be considered inappropriate in parts of North America. Similarly, in some parts of the world, people are expected to wear body deodorant. In others, such as parts of the Middle East and Europe, they are not. These are only a few of many examples showing how rules guiding nonverbal behavior vary based on cultural norms. The important point here is that, like verbal communication, nonverbal communication should be viewed as a "cultural event."

Interestingly enough, a booklet was distributed to all 37,000 United States volunteers working the Pan American Games to warn them that nonverbal messages are evaluated differently across cultures:

> Realize that gestures can be significant. Hand motions which are innocent in one culture may be offensive in another. Keep your hands relatively still and refrain from pointing—instead use wide arm motions, turning your head in the desired direction. Avoid scratching your nose, indicating the number two by holding up two fingers, or making the thumbs up or the "O.K." sign. (*Sports Illustrated,* August, 1987, p. 16)

Even though virtually all cultures interpret some nonverbal behaviors similarly (such as smiling), all cultures also differ from one another in interpreting other nonverbal messages. The message is clear. When you are in a different culture, find out the nonverbal rules that influence how your behavior will be interpreted.

The Relational Context.   Relational factors, such as the type of relationship between the interactants (co-workers, friends, spouses) and the stage of the relationship (how long the interactants have known one another), influence how nonverbal messages are enacted and interpreted. A pat on the behind by your employer usually means something completely different than a pat on the behind by your lover. Moreover, the same behavior may be interpreted differently by various receivers. Consider the following example.

> Tina and Tim, who are newlyweds, are together at a big social gathering given by Tim's boss. Tim knows that Tina is really tired. She worked a lot of overtime this week and really didn't want to go to the party in the first place. She only agreed to go because it was important to Tim. While Tim is engaged in conversation with a co-worker, Tina pulls away from the group a bit, waits a minute or so, and then glances at the door several times when she doesn't think Tim's colleague is looking. Tim interprets Tina's nonverbal behavior (moving away and glancing) as a signal that she wants to leave. From past experience, Tim knows that this is Tina's way of signalling that she is bored or tired and wants to go home. Two other observers, however, interpret Tina's behavior differently. Jenny, who doesn't know Tina at all, infers that Tina is expecting someone. She thinks that perhaps her date hasn't shown up yet and she is waiting for him to come through the door. Still another onlooker, George, who only knows that Tina is Tim's wife, infers that Tina and Tim must be in a fight because she looks unhappy and has moved away from him.

In this case, Tim was able to make the correct interpretation of Tina's behavior because he shares a relationship with her and has knowledge about her typical behavior. Jenny and George's interpretations were logical, but they were based on the wrong assumptions. This example illustrates the important role that both relational and situational information plays in helping us interpret nonverbal messages.

Other research has shown that people use different nonverbal behaviors when interacting with different relational partners. For example, studies show that friends are generally more comfortable interacting at very close relational distances than are strangers (Baker & Shaw, 1980), and that women show more pronounced facial expressions of emotion when with friends as compared to strangers (Wagner & Smith, 1991). Guerrero (1997) found that people use more gaze, more touch, and closer proximity when interacting with romantic partners as compared to friends. However, when interacting with friends, people were more fluent and used more nodding, shorter response latencies, and less silences.

Nonverbal behavior also changes as relationships develop. For example, studies by Guerrero and Andersen on touch (see article 23) suggest that serious daters touch each other in public about twice as much as casual daters or spouses. They also found that men are more likely to initiate touch in the beginning stages of dating relationships, whereas women are more likely to initiate touch in married relationships. Taken together, the studies on relationship type and relationship stage differences in nonverbal communication show that relational context affects how people send and interpret nonverbal messages.

The Situation. As seen above in the example with Tina, situational factors also influence the performance and evaluation of nonverbal messages. These factors include the environment in which a person interacts (e.g., public vs. private environments) as well as the type of situation (e.g., a formal vs. informal situation) and the timing of the interaction (e.g., in the morning vs. late at night). Temporary states, such as moods and physical states (e.g., headaches or feeling tired) can also be thought of as situational factors. All of these situational factors influence the types of nonverbal communication that people use and the meanings that receivers give them. For example, your significant other is much more likely to show you affection when you are alone in your home after an evening out than when you are at a business luncheon surrounded by a large group of colleagues. Similarly, you are unlikely to show much vocal and facial pleasantness when you are feeling ill. Situational factors also influence how people *react* to various forms of nonverbal communication. Andersen (1985) noted that if a stranger walks close behind you during broad daylight on a busy sidewalk, you are unlikely to feel any anxiety. However, if the same stranger is close behind you on a dark, deserted sidewalk you are likely to become fearful. Research also suggests that you are more likely to smile and laugh in response to a friend's joke when you are in a good versus bad mood (Guerrero, Andersen, & Trost, 1998).

A SUMMARY AND LOOK AHEAD

In this article we defined nonverbal communication as involving messages other than words that are used in our interactions with others. Such messages are typically sent with intent and/or are typically interpreted by receivers as meaningful. Nonverbal messages play a central role in communication and are particularly important when people express emotions, send and form first impressions, and communicate about their relationships. The remaining articles in Part I of this reader should extend your knowledge of nonverbal communication by focusing on skill acquisition (article 2) and nonverbal research methods (article 3). After reading Part I, you should have a good understanding of what types of behaviors are studied within the field of nonverbal communication. You should also be able to understand the basic ways that researchers go about studying nonverbal communication.

One way that researchers study nonverbal communication is by breaking messages down by codes. As you have learned, nonverbal communication is comprised of various codes that represent different communication channels, such as the body, space, or time. In Part II of this reader, we examine the various codes of nonverbal communication. All of the readings included in Part II focus on a *single code*. Some of the readings in this section describe the code. For example, the reading by Ekman and Friesen (article 4) describes different types of gestures and the reading by Lyman and Scott (article 20) describes different types of territories. Other readings in this section examine how the code functions within a particular context, such as a job interview (article 12), a competitive sporting event (article 13), or an intimate relationship (article 14).

In contrast, the readings in Part III focus on how *multiple messages* from *different codes* work together to fulfill functions such as expressing emotion, managing interaction, and persuading others. For example, Planalp (article 31) shows that the face, voice, and body work together to express emotion. Prager's article (article 35) on intimacy includes behaviors from all of the nonverbal codes, as does Segrin's article (article 38) on compliance gaining. These articles highlight the important functions that nonverbal messages fulfill in our daily lives. They also show that it is useful to examine packages of nonverbal behaviors rather than single codes.

We should note, however, that the separation of the articles into sections focusing on "codes" versus "functions" is somewhat artificial. This is because nonverbal communication is highly functional. Therefore, it is hard to talk about even a single code of nonverbal communication without also talking about its function. For example, you will notice that in the section on kinesics, we include an article discussing the various functions of gaze (article 7) as well as an article discussing how kinesic cues help people make a good impression during employment interviews (article 12). Similarly, in the section on appearance and adornment, we include articles showing that appearance affects first impressions (articles 11 and 14). The key distinction between Parts II and III of this reader is whether the focus is on a single nonverbal code (Part II) or on how messages from various codes work together as a package to fulfill various functions (Part III).

The final section in the reader (Part IV) includes five articles that describe contemporary theories about nonverbal communication. All five of these theories examine patterns of interaction between two or more people rather than simply looking at the nonverbal communication of a single person. These theories all describe processes of *nonverbal adaptation*. In other words, how do you adapt your behavior to be similar or dissimilar to the behavior of your partner? How do you react when someone you like gets close to you or someone you are attracted to moves away from you? Part IV will help you understand the answers to these types of questions.

Nonverbal communication is all around us. We hope that the readings in this book will help you recognize and describe various nonverbal messages as they occur in your daily life. We also hope that these readings will help you to understand how various nonverbal behaviors work together to send messages to others. Although you will never be able to "read everyone like a book," as some of the popular literature suggests, this reader should give you a better grasp of the nonverbal world around you.

References

Andersen, P. A. (1985). Nonverbal immediacy in interpersonal communication. In A. W. Seigman & S. Feldstein (Eds.), *Multichannel integrations of nonverbal behavior* (pp. 1–36). Hillsdale, NJ: Erlbaum.

Andersen, P. A. (in press). *Beside language: Nonverbal communication in interpersonal relationships.* Mountain View, CA: Mayfield.

Andersen, P. A., & Guerrero, L. K. (1998). Principles of communication and emotion in social interaction. In P. A. Andersen & L. K. Guerrero (Eds.), *Handbook of communication and emotion: Research, theory, applications, and contexts* (pp. 49–96). San Diego, CA: Academic Press.

Baker, E., & Shaw, M. E. (1980). Reactions to interperson distance and topic intimacy: A comparison of strangers and friends. *Journal of Nonverbal Behavior, 5,* 80–91.

Burgoon, J. K. (1994). Nonverbal signals. In M. L. Knapp & G. R. Miller (Eds.), *Handbook of interpersonal communication* (2nd ed., pp. 229–285). Thousand Oaks, CA: Sage.

Burgoon, J. K., Buller, D. B., & Woodall, W. G. (1996). *Nonverbal communication: The unspoken dialogue* (2nd ed.). New York: McGraw-Hill.

Bugental, D. E., Kaswan, J. W., & Love, L. R. (1970). Perceptions of contradictory meanings conveyed by verbal and nonverbal channels. *Journal of Personality and Social Psychology, 16,* 647–655.

Buller, D. B., & Burgoon, J. K. (1994). Deception: Strategic and nonstrategic communication. In J. A. Daly & J. M. Wiemann (Eds.), *Strategic interpersonal communication* (pp. 191–224). Hillsdale, NJ: Erlbaum.

DePaulo, B. M., & Rosenthal, R. (1979). Ambivalence, discrepancy, and deception in nonverbal communication. In R. Rosenthal (Ed.), *Skill in nonverbal communication: Individual differences* (pp. 204–248). Cambridge, MA: Oelgeschlager, Gunn, & Hain.

Ekman, P. (1973). Cross-cultural studies of facial expression. In P. Ekman (Ed.), *Darwin and facial expression: A century of research in review* (pp. 169–222). New York: Academic Press.

Ekman, P., & Friesen, W. V. (1969). Nonverbal leakage and clues to deception. *Psychiatry, 32,* 88–106.

Frey, L. R., Botan, C. H., Friedman, P. G., & Kreps, G. L. (1991). *Investigating communication: An introduction to research methods.* Englewood Cliffs, NJ: Prentice Hall.

Frye, J. K. (1980). *Find: Frye's index to nonverbal data.* Duluth: University of Minnesota Computer Center.

Guerrero, L. K. (1997). Nonverbal involvement across interactions with same-sex friends, opposite-sex friends, and romantic partners: Consistency or change? *Journal of Social and Personal Relationships, 14,* 31–58.

Guerrero, L. K., Andersen, P. A., & Trost, M. R. (1998). Communication and emotion: Basic concepts and approaches. In P. A. Andersen & L. K. Guerrero (Eds.), *Handbook of communication and emotion: Research, theory, applications, and contexts* (pp. 3–27). San Diego, CA: Academic Press.

Hecht, M. L., Andersen, P. A., & Ribeau, S. (1989). The cultural dimensions of nonverbal communication. In M. Asante & W. B. Gunykunst (Eds.), *The handbook of international and intercultural communication* (pp. 163–185). Newbury Park, CA: Sage.

Knapp, M. L., & Hall, J. A. (1992). *Nonverbal communication in human interaction* (3rd ed.). Fort Worth, TX: Holt, Rinehart, & Winston.

Knapp, M. L., Hart, R. P., & Dennis, H. S. (1974). An exploration of deception as a communication construct. *Human Communication Research, 1,* 15–29.

Mehrabian, A. (1971). *Silent messages.* Belmont, CA: Wadsworth.

Miller, G. R., & Burgoon, J. K. (1982). Factors affecting witness credibility. In N. L. Kerr & R. M. Bray (Eds.), *The psychology of the courtroom* (pp. 169–194). New York: Academic Press.

Noller, P. (1984). *Nonverbal communication and marital interaction.* Oxford, UK: Pergamon.

Patterson, M. L. (1983). *Nonverbal behavior: A functional perspective.* New York: Springer-Verlag.

Wagner, H. L., & Smith, J. (1991). Facial expression in the presence of friends and strangers. *Journal of Nonverbal Behavior, 15,* 201–214.

Zahn, G. L. (1973). Cognitive integration of verbal and vocal information in spoken sentences. *Journal of Experimental Social Psychology, 9,* 320–334.

Zuckerman, M., DePaulo, B. M., & Rosenthal, R. (1981). Verbal and nonverbal communication of deception. In L. Berkowitz (Ed.), *Advances in experimental social psychology* (Vol. 14, pp. 1–59). New York: Academic Press.

Spitzberg describes nonverbal communication skills. He presents a measure of these skills and summarizes them in four fundamental categories: interaction management, other-orientation, composure, and expressiveness. The article shows how nonverbal communication is used to achieve success in conversations.

2

Perspectives on Nonverbal Communication Skills

Brian H. Spitzberg

For centuries, scholars and laypersons alike have pondered the nature of social skills. Why do some people seem so adept and competent at meeting people, initiating and maintaining conversations, and dealing with a variety of people in appropriate and successful ways? What skills and abilities are involved in socially skilled interaction?

Certainly, the search for these skills is an important one. An examination of over 300 studies and reviews conducted by Spitzberg and Cupach (1988) indicates that people who are less socially skilled are likely to be lower in self-esteem, academic success, occupational success, and higher in levels of loneliness, shyness, depression, mental illness, marital distress, hypertension, stress, and anxiety. There is even some evidence to suggest that less interpersonally skilled persons are more likely to become drug abusers, sexual offenders, and may experience higher mortality rates generally than those higher in social skills.

These conclusions should not be particularly surprising given how much of our everyday lives is centered around interpersonal interaction.

This article was written especially for *The Nonverbal Communication Reader.*

Perlman and Rook (1987) review research indicating that approximately 70% of our waking time is spent in the presence of others. We grow up in family units, are educated in group systems, and some 90% of us will marry in our lifetimes. Many of us also communicate with other people while we work. As Rook's (1984) research reveals, our life satisfaction is strongly influenced by how positive or negative our interpersonal interactions are. Interpersonal skill is not simply a desirable commodity for a well-adjusted and satisfying life. It is virtually indispensable.

While it is impossible at this time to specify a comprehensive list of all the elements of interpersonal skill, there is some sound basis for identifying the most basic skills. For the most part, the basic interpersonal skills involve nonverbal forms of communication.

Many different skills have been associated with interpersonal effectiveness. In an attempt to verify the importance of many of these skills, Dillard and Spitzberg (1984) examined the results of sixteen studies of social skills. By looking at the results of several different studies, they were able to make more reliable and confident conclusions about which behaviors are most consistently perceived to be skillful or competent. Out of twelve behaviors studied, nine were nonverbal: *response latency* (the average or total amount of time it takes after one person stops talking before the other person begins talking), *eye gaze* (the average or total amount of time a conversant spends looking in the general region of the other person's face), *eye contact* (the average or total amount of time spent looking directly at the other person's eyes), smiles (*the frequency or total number of smiles in a conversation*), *head movements* (generally, the number of head nods indicating understanding, agreement, or reinforcement), *adaptors* (e.g., finger tapping, hair-twirling, ring-twisting, etc.), *volume* (the average loudness of talk), and *talk time* (either the total amount of time a person spends talking or the average duration of speaking turns). All of these behaviors were related to perceptions of subject skillfulness; generally speaking, the more of each of these behaviors a person displayed, the more competent the person was perceived to be. The exception was the category of adaptors, such that the fewer adaptors displayed, the more competent the person was considered to be.

After examining this study, and the results of numerous other similar studies, Spitzberg and colleagues (Spitzberg & Hurt, 1987; Spitzberg, Brookshire, & Brunner, 1987) developed a measure of interpersonal skills. Over a thousand college students were asked to rate either a recent recalled conversation or a get-acquainted conversation they had just been involved in as part of an assignment. The ratings were on the questionnaire listed in table 2.1. These behaviors, which are generally nonverbal in

Table 2.1
The Conversational Skills Rating Scale

Person being rated: _____

Person doing rating: _____

Rate the conversant according to the following responses:

1 = INADEQUATE (use was awkward, disruptive, or resulted in a negative impression of communicative skills)

2 = SOMEWHAT INADEQUATE

3 = ADEQUATE (use was sufficient but neither very noticeable nor excellent. Produced neither positive nor negative impression)

4 = GOOD

5 = EXCELLENT (use was smooth, controlled, and resulted in positive impression of communicative skills).

Circle the single most accurate response for each behavior:

1 2 3 4 5	(1) Use of eye contact
1 2 3 4 5	(2) Initiation of topics
1 2 3 4 5	(3) Maintenance of topics and follow-up comments
1 2 3 4 5	(4) Use of time speaking relative to partner
1 2 3 4 5	(5) Interruption of partner's speaking turns
1 2 3 4 5	(6) Speaking rate (neither too slow nor too fast)
1 2 3 4 5	(7) Speaking fluency (avoided pauses, silences, "uh," etc.)
1 2 3 4 5	(8) Vocal confidence (neither tense nor nervous sounding)
1 2 3 4 5	(9) Articulation (language is clearly pronounced and understood)
1 2 3 4 5	(10) Shaking or nervous twitches (weren't noticeable)
1 2 3 4 5	(11) Posture (neither too closed/formal nor too open/informal)
1 2 3 4 5	(12) Fidgeting (avoided swaying feet, finger-tapping, hair-twirling, etc.)
1 2 3 4 5	(13) Asking questions
1 2 3 4 5	(14) Nodding of head in response to partner's statements
1 2 3 4 5	(15) Lean toward partner (neither too far forward nor too far back)
1 2 3 4 5	(16) Speaking about partner (involved partner as topic of conversation)
1 2 3 4 5	(17) Speaking about self (didn't talk too much about self or own interests)
1 2 3 4 5	(18) Encouragements or agreements (encouraged partner to talk)
1 2 3 4 5	(19) Use of humor and/or stories
1 2 3 4 5	(20) Vocal variety (avoided monotone voice)
1 2 3 4 5	(21) Vocal volume (neither too loud nor too soft)
1 2 3 4 5	(22) Expression of personal opinions (neither too passive nor aggressive)
1 2 3 4 5	(23) Facial expressiveness (neither blank nor exaggerated)
1 2 3 4 5	(24) Use of gestures to emphasize what was being said
1 2 3 4 5	(25) Smiling and/or laughing

nature, were rated in terms of their competence or adequacy. Thus, the dimensions that result can be understood as the basic or essential skills of competent behavior.

Extensive analyses indicated that these behaviors can be characterized according to four fundamental dimensions: *interaction management, other-orientation, composure*, and *expressiveness. Interaction management* concerns how well verbal speaking turns are managed, maintaining topical flow, and handling the initiation and termination of conversations. This dimension consists of behaviors such as "initiation of new topics," "maintenance of topics and follow-up comments," "use of time relative to partner," and "speaking fluency." *Other-orientation* represents the extent to which someone shows attention to, concern for, and interest in the other person in the conversation. It is exemplified by behaviors such as "use of eye contact," "nodding of head in response to partner's statements," "lean toward partner," and "speaking about self" and about "partner." *Composure* involves not only anxiety and nervousness, but also level of confidence and assertiveness. Composure (or lack thereof) is most clearly indicated by behaviors such as "vocal confidence," "shaking or nervous twitches," "posture," and "fidgeting." Finally, *expressiveness* concerns the level of animation and activity in the conversation and is identified by behavior such as "smiling and/or laughing," "use of gestures," "facial expressiveness," "volume," "vocal variety," and "speaking rate."

These components of competent interpersonal behavior, comprised as they are of primarily nonverbal behaviors, suggest a simple, understandable, and manageable model. Interactants, it seems, tend to assess and evaluate their own behavior and the behavior of their conversational partners in terms of a relatively small set of skills. Generally speaking, the more *expressive, other-oriented, composed*, and adept at *interaction management* an interactant is, the more likely this person will be viewed as a good interpersonal communicator. Of course, it is likely that there can be too much of a good thing. Obviously, someone who is overly expressive, confident, other-oriented, and smooth is likely to be seen as artificial or manipulative.

Furthermore, there are contextual or situational effects that can often alter this general advice. For example, while laughing and smiling are seen as skillful in most interactions, they are less likely to be seen as competent at a funeral or during a heated conflict. Behavior, to be seen as skillful, needs to be adapted to the cultural, interpersonal, and situational expectations.

These four skills seem intuitively appealing, yet they are not likely to be comprehensive. For example, skills such as self-disclosure, assertiveness, conflict management, deception, meeting people, etc. seem to be higher level abilities that may involve behaviors not represented in these dimensions. Still, the research seems very supportive at this point that the components of *interaction management, other-orientation, composure,* and *expressiveness* provide a useful and valid model of the basic skills of interpersonal behavior.

References

Dillard, J. R., & Spitzberg, B. H. (1984). Global impressions of social skills: Behavioral predictors. *Communication Yearbook, 8,* 446–463.

Perlman, D., & Rook, K. S. (1987). Social support, social deficits, and the family: Toward the enhancement of well-being. In S. Oskamp (Ed.), *Family processes and problems: Social psychological problems* (Applied Social Psychology Annual, Vol. 7, pp. 17–44). Newbury Park, CA: Sage.

Rook, K. S. (1984) The negative side of social interaction: Impact on psychological well-being. *Journal of Personality and Social Psychology, 46,* 1097–1108.

Spitzberg, B. H., Brookshire, R. G., & Brunner, C. C. (1987, November). *The factorial structure of competence evaluations of molecular interpersonal skills in naturalistic conversations.* Paper presented at the Speech Communication Association Conference, Boston, MA.

Spitzberg, B. H., & Cupach, W. R. (1988). *Handbook of interpersonal competence research.* New York: Springer-Verlag.

Spitzberg, B. H., & Hurt, H. T. (1987). The measurement of interpersonal skills in instructional contexts. *Communication Education, 36,* 28–45.

In this article, Hecht and Guerrero provide an overview of research methodology for the study of nonverbal communication. The article summarizes the major approaches to research and describes basic methods, such as naturalistic observations, field experiments, laboratory experiments, and diary methods.

3

Perspectives on Nonverbal Research Methods

Michael L. Hecht
Laura K. Guerrero

This article presents an introduction to nonverbal communication research methods. It is not meant as a substitute for a full course in research methodology. Instead, it will introduce you to some of the topics you need to know to understand nonverbal research. After reading the article, you will better understand the various types of methods used in the studies included in this reader.

People conduct research to learn more about nonverbal communication. You conduct a type of informal research when you collect information to make decisions. How do you know if a classmate likes you enough to go out on a date with you? To answer this question, you might try out a number of different strategies. First, you might observe the other person while interacting, looking for signs of attraction. How close does this person stand? Does the person smile at you? Is there mutual eye contact? Second, you might observe the person interacting with others. Are these in-

This article was written especially for *The Nonverbal Communication Reader.*

teractions the same as those the person has with you? Third, you might observe the person's reaction when you mention the idea of doing things together. Does the person smile when you suggest it would be fun to go to a certain concert together? Fourth, you might ask other people how this person feels about you. All of these examples illustrate informal research strategies that we use in our everyday lives. Other everyday research questions include: How does a salesperson know when to try to get the customer to sign a contract? How do you arrange the furniture in your room? What behaviors should you display during a job interview? All of these involve informal research. More formally, we define research as the use of *systematic methods* to answer important questions or test important predictions.

RESEARCH QUESTIONS AND HYPOTHESES

Research always starts with a question or a prediction. Without a good question or a worthwhile prediction, there is no reason to conduct a study. A research question is generally used when people wish to *describe* nonverbal communication. Description is a necessary part of the research process. For example, we can describe body cues by identifying body lean, posture, and gestures. Think about how you would describe the clothing you are wearing to someone who cannot see you. You might comment on style, color, and material. Is there anything this description would leave out? If so, a better description is possible. Researchers are continually looking for better descriptions when they pose various types of research questions. Most research questions are usually of three types:

1. *Describe a type of nonverbal behavior. For example, what are the different styles of walking?*

    Planalp (see article 32) was interested in describing the various ways that emotion is expressed. Planalp and her colleagues had people fill out questionnaires when they noticed that someone they knew was feeling an emotion. The questionnaires asked them to describe "how they could tell" that the person was experiencing an emotion. The responses to this question were then categorized into various types of emotional cues, such as vocal cues, facial cues, and physiological cues.

2. *Describe how one type of nonverbal behavior is related to another type of nonverbal behavior or to a perception or outcome. For example, do we touch more if eye contact increases? How do people perceive individuals who use very high levels of touch and eye contact?*

    Hall's observations of different conversational distances (discussed by Smeltzer, Waltman, & Leonard in article 22) show that distancing is related to a number of other nonverbal behaviors, such as touch, smell, and gesturing. For example, at close distances, it is easy to touch and smell others, but we might not gesture very much because our arms only have limited space to move and our partner would likely be focused on our face rather than our hands.

3. *Describe how nonverbal behavior differs based on the type of person, group, relationship, or situation. For example, do children behave differently than adults? Do people from different cultures display different amounts of touch? Do people show different levels of eye gaze when with friends as compared to strangers? Do people behave differently in various types of environments (in bright orange vs. soft pink rooms)?*

Guerrero and Andersen (article 24) examined two of these types of questions. They observed the touch behavior of heterosexual romantic couples in movie theater and zoo lines. They found that men tended to initiate touch in casual dating relationships, whereas women tended to initiate touch in married relationships. They also found that couples who were seriously dating touched more than couples who were casually dating or married. Thus, this study answered questions regarding possible differences due the person (female vs. male) and the relationship (casually dating vs. seriously dating vs. married).

Research questions, such as those described above, are typically used when a researcher does not feel comfortable predicting the answer to the question. If there hasn't been very much research on a particular topic, or if the past research on an issue has been inconsistent or contradictory, it is a good idea to ask a research question. Sometimes, however, researchers have enough information to warrant making a *prediction* and testing a *hypothesis*. A hypothesis can be thought of as an educated guess. Two specific types of hypotheses are common in nonverbal studies. These types of hypotheses are related to the second and third types of research questions discussed above.

1. *Predict a specific relationship between a nonverbal behavior and another nonverbal behavior, or between a nonverbal behavior and a perception or outcome. For example, the closer people sit, the more likely they are to touch one another. People who speak at a moderately fast rate will be seen as confident and competent.*

Semic (article 18) summarizes research predicting that the more attractive people's voices are, the more likely they are to be judged as likable, trustworthy, sensitive, and competent. Crusco and Wetzel (article 25) predicted that tips are increased by touching. They observed touching and tipping in restaurants to test and then confirm this prediction.

2. *Predict specific differences between people, groups, relationships, or situations. For example, people from southern areas of the United States touch more than people from northern areas of the United States. Teenagers are more expressive when talking with their friends than with their parents. Students will display more attentiveness when they are in moderately stimulating classrooms as compared to highly simulating or unstimulating classrooms.*

Frank and Gilovich (article 14) tested the prediction that sports teams who wear black uniforms are perceived as more aggressive than sports teams wearing non-black uniforms. They tested this prediction by looking at penalty records and comparing referees' judgments of the same action committed by players in black versus white uniforms.

In addition to describing and predicting, researchers often try to *explain* nonverbal behavior. Explanation focuses on the "how" and "why" questions that people ask. For example, Andersen and Bowman (article 38) summarized studies that explain how people dominate other people in organizations. This study tells us how dominance works and allows us to understand this important process. The final section in this reader focuses on how and why people exchange nonverbal messages that are reciprocal (similar) or compensatory (different). In this section, different theoretical explanations are given for why people act similarly to their partners in some situations, and dissimilar to their partners in other situations.

WHAT IS AN IMPORTANT TOPIC?

Whether you are trying to describe, predict, or explain, your topic or issue must be important. So how do you know when your topic is worthwhile? There are four tests you can apply. First, you can ask if other nonverbal researchers agree that it is a good topic. If an article is published in a scholarly journal, then other researchers have agreed that the topic is at least somewhat important. If many articles have been published, you can feel fairly safe that your topic is seen as worthwhile. Scholars such as Kuhn (1970) argue that this is the most commonly applied standard for judging research.

Second, you can ask how answering your questions and/or testing your predictions advance theory. For example, Floyd, Ramirez, and Burgoon discuss expectancy violations theory in article 49 of this reader. They theorize about the different effects of violating people's nonverbal expectancies. We might ask how well this theory applies to different kinds of relationships, such as those between lovers, strangers, co-workers, and parents and children, to see if the theory can be extended. This provides a better understanding of both the theory and nonverbal communication. You might also design a study to compare different theories. For example, Le Poire and Burgoon (1994) compared expectancy violations theory to discrepancy arousal theory (see Part IV of this reader for descriptions of these theories).

Third, you can ask if your study will lead to other interesting questions for research. If it does, then your study has *heuristic value*. For example, answering the question, "What are the signs of attraction?," allows you to ask what happens if people give off too many signs of attraction. For example, Koeppel, Montagne, O'Hair, and Cody (article 35) identify a number of behaviors that people use to flirt with one another. These behaviors include constant smiling, forward lean, pouting, touch, close proxemic distances, demure gaze, and warm vocal tones. What if someone communicates all of these signs? Will this be more effective than using only one sign? Perhaps it is more effective to use one or two flirting behaviors rather than bombarding the person you are attracted to with too many messages all at once.

Finally, you can ask if the topic or issue under investigation can be applied to the "real world" so that the answers to your questions can help us become better communicators. For example, the Crusco and Wetzel study (article 25) on touch and tipping can be helpful to waiters and waitresses who want to increase their tips. Buslig's summary (article 29) on environmental features related to privacy can teach people how to design their homes and offices in ways that either encourage or discourage interaction. A study by Lee (1998) examined nine different types of touch between co-workers to see which types were seen as the most sexually harassing. Lee found that some touches, such as a soft caress of the face, were perceived as more harassing and inappropriate than others. Certainly, research such as this can inform people about what behaviors they should and should not use if they wish to be effective communicators in the workplace.

Not all research satisfies all four of the tests that are described above. Some researchers believe that some of the tests are more important than others. For example, some researchers believe that advancing theory is the most important goal. Others believe that if our research findings cannot be applied to the real world, they aren't very useful. The key is to prioritize these goals and make sure that your research meets the goals that are most important to you.

SYSTEMATIC METHODS

Good research is systematic. This means that it is planned, organized, orderly, and methodical. Systematic research follows a regular, orderly series of steps in obtaining answers to questions. This allows others to understand how the information was obtained and to repeat the study to see if the same information would be obtained again. The research plan is like the script for a play or a lesson plan for a class. In many nonverbal studies, the research is planned from start to finish before anything else occurs. The researchers decide what types of behaviors they will observe and record before they conduct their study. In other cases, researchers study a particular context or situation and record what nonverbal behaviors they see without knowing beforehand what behaviors will emerge as important. Regardless of which method is used, researchers carefully plan a strategy for gaining insight into their research questions or hypotheses.

TWO GENERAL APPROACHES TO RESEARCH

There are two general research approaches: *the grounded approach* and *the hypothesis testing approach*. Researchers using grounded approaches may start with an idea or a general theory of nonverbal communication, or they may start by determining an important group or setting to study. The researcher then formulates an overall plan and observes nonverbal communication, obtaining detailed descriptions. Next, the descriptions are examined and organized. Sometimes the descriptions are organized into categories. For example, the work on touch categories by Stanley Jones (see article 23) is based on observations made by college students who recorded all of the touches that they observed over a period of several days. Jones was interested in understanding what types of touch people commonly exchange. After collecting detailed observations, Jones and his colleagues organized the descriptions into general categories of touch, such as positive affect touches, playful touches, and control touches. Generally, grounded research is highly descriptive in nature.

The hypothesis-testing approach is different. Here the researcher uses theory to *hypothesize* or make specific predictions about what is expected. Manusov's work (article 44) on cultural stereotypes is a good example of this approach. Manusov used ideas from expectancy violations theory and intercultural communication theories to arrive at her predictions. She then designed an experiment that allowed her to test her hypotheses.

There are two main differences between the approaches. The first difference deals with the starting point of the research. In the grounded approach, the researcher literally works from the "ground up" by starting with description. The specific conclusions emerge out of the study itself and are guided and shaped by what is observed. For example, you might go to parties with the idea of studying flirtation. Through your observations, you might conclude that eye contact, distancing, and touch play the most important roles in the flirtation process. In contrast, a researcher using the hypothesis-testing approach decides beforehand in very specific terms what to look for and examines only the hypothesis. For example, you might read a number of articles claiming that touch is the most important sign of attraction. You might then create a set of three videotaped interactions that feature the same man and woman talking to each other. In each video segment, you could keep the verbal conversation exactly the same but change the nonverbal communication so that touch was used in the first video, excessive smiling in the second video, and constant gaze in the third video. Then you could have different students watch each of the video segments and rate how attracted they thought the man and woman were to one another. If the videotaped interaction that included touch led to the strongest perceptions of attraction, you could conclude that touch is a more powerful signal of attraction than gaze or smiling.

The second difference between the grounded and the hypothesis-testing approaches occurs after the research has been conducted. At this point, the researcher often wants to explain the findings. For example, you might want to explain why gaze, touch, and distancing are the most important cues in the flirtation process. Or you might want to explain why touch and attraction are related to one another. Researchers using the grounded approach generally rely on their own interpretations and the interpretations of the people they observe to explain their data and to generate new theory and ideas. Researchers using the hypothesis-testing approach explain their findings using the theory that guided them in the first place.

METHODS OF NONVERBAL RESEARCH

Once you have chosen an approach, you will need to decide *who* to study. The people you study are sometimes referred to as *participants*, *subjects*, or *respondents*. Some researchers focus on one individual's behavior (for example, what nonverbal behaviors a supervisor uses to display power), others focus on how one person interprets the behavior of another (for example, how people interpret nonverbal cues to determine if someone is lying), and still others focus on the interaction between two people (for example, how one person's behavior affects the behavior of another person). The decision about who to focus on should be based on your research question or hypothesis. For instance, if you are interested in seeing how people use nonverbal communication to make first impressions, you might examine the behavior of people in situations such as job interviews. However, if you are interested in how different types of behaviors are interpreted when people first meet, you would need to observe people's behaviors and see how their partners evaluate them.

Similarly, your research question or hypothesis often guides the method you use. After determining what and who to study, the researcher decides how to collect the information needed to answer the question or test the hypothesis. The researcher needs to choose a setting, decide whether to manipulate or control anything, and determine how to record the behavior and/or reactions to the behavior. The next section of this article looks at five common methods used in nonverbal research. These first four of these methods differ in terms of whether the setting is naturalistic versus controlled, and whether something is manipulated. Naturalistic settings are those that exist in the "real world." When researchers use naturalistic settings, they typically go where their participants are. For example, they might examine behaviors in public parks, libraries, or restaurants. Controlled settings are created by the researcher for the purpose of the investigation. Here, the participants come to a particular setting, such as a research laboratory, rather than the researcher coming to them. By *control* we mean that the researcher attempts to create or structure the situation.

In addition to deciding whether to use a naturalistic or controlled setting, the researcher decides whether or not to *manipulate* anything. When something is manipulated, the researcher makes it different in one situation compared to another. For example, the researcher might purposely make one environment comfortable and another environment uncomfortable. Or a researcher might use a *confederate* to help with the manipulation. A confederate is someone who works for the researcher but whose role is not known to the other participants. Confederates act in a predetermined way to arrange (or manipulate) the situation. For example, the Crusco and Wetzel study in this reader (see article 25) on tipping and touch used a manipulation by a confederate. The waitresses (who were confederates) manipulated their touch behavior so that they either (a) gave the customer a fleeting touch on the hand, (b) gave the customer a more sustained touch on the shoulder, or (c) did not touch the customer at all.

Common Methods in Nonverbal Research

When we take into consideration both the controlled versus naturalistic setting, and whether a manipulation has occurred, four different types of methods emerge: laboratory experiments, controlled observations, field experiments, and naturalistic observations.

Laboratory Experiments. In laboratory experiments, the researcher brings people to a research site, arranges for events to occur, and then measures the effects. Therefore, laboratory experiments occur in *controlled settings with a manipulation*. This type of method gives researchers a lot of control because they keep the setting the same across all their subjects and because they have arranged what will happen during the experiment. This kind of method is well-suited for examining types of nonverbal behavior that would not occur in a natural setting. For example, you might want to study how people react to strangers who either flirt with them or act rudely toward them. If you tried to observe this behavior in natural settings, it might take a long time to find people who act both of these ways. Or you might want to study the nonverbal behaviors of people who are lying and telling the truth, as well as people's ability to tell whether others are lying. To do this, you could bring subjects into a lab and have one person act as an interviewer and the other act as an interviewee. Before the interaction, you could put the interviewer and the interviewee in different rooms. Then you could secretly instruct the interviewee to lie on some questions and tell the truth on others. After the interaction you could ask the interviewer to guess which questions the interviewee lied on. You could also videotape the interactions so you could check for observable differences in people's behavior when they were lying versus telling the truth. Notice that it would be very difficult to do an experiment like this in a natural setting because you wouldn't have enough control of the interaction and the subjects' behavior.

Controlled Observations. Sometimes researchers want to bring subjects into a controlled environment even though they do not need to manipulate anything. This type of method, which occurs in a *controlled setting without a manipulation,* is a controlled observation. This method is especially useful when researchers need to collect specific information that is not readily available or is hard to record in naturalistic environments. For example, it would be difficult to accurately record detailed information about eye contact and facial expressions in a natural setting because such behaviors would be very hard to see. Similarly, if a researcher wants to collect data on a fairly large number of nonverbal behaviors, it would be difficult, if not impossible, to observe them all in a naturalistic setting. Therefore, the researcher might decide to bring subjects into a laboratory setting where they can be videotaped. For example, a researcher might be interested in studying how people hide their emotions while playing poker. The researcher could bring groups of people together and ask them to play poker for a half hour. Cameras could be placed so that the researcher could videotape two of the subjects' faces along with their poker hands. Notice that nothing was manipulated here. Everyone engaged in the same task. But a controlled setting was still necessary so that the researcher could get detailed information (on videotapes) regarding facial expressions. These tapes could then be used to study how people hide their emotions. By using this method, the researcher could keep some things about the interactions consistent across all the participants. In our poker example, the length of time that all groups played poker, the seating arrangement, and the number of players might be kept consistent across all of the interactions.

Field Experiments. Sometimes a researcher is able to conduct an experiment in a naturalistic setting. When an experiment occurs in a *naturalistic setting with a manipulation*, it is called a *field experiment*. In this case, the researcher introduces something into the natural setting. For example, you might predict that jewelry sales clerks will be more attentive to well dressed customers than to shabbily dressed customers. To test your prediction, you could ask your friends to go with you to jewelry stores. You could have half of your friends wear professional attire and the other half wear sweats. You could then record the different reactions they get from the sales clerks. Sigelman, Adams, Meeks, and Purcell (1986) provide another good example of a field experiment. These researchers had a confederate stand outside of discount stores and ask parents if he could interview their children for a couple minutes as part of a study on children's wishes and opinions. For half of the interviews, the confederate wore a leg brace and carried a crutch. An observer stood just inside the store where she could take notes without being noticed. Sigelman et al. (1986) were then able to compare the children's reactions to the confederate when he appeared disabled versus nondisabled. Overall the children seemed more interested and curious (but not more negative) when the confederate appeared disabled. In experiments such as these, the researchers are unlikely to get as much detail about nonverbal behavior as they are with videotapes in a controlled setting. However, these types of experiments provide a sense of realism that is not present in laboratory experiments or controlled observations.

Naturalistic Observation. Another method for studying nonverbal behavior is *naturalistic observation*, which occurs when the study is conducted in a *naturalistic setting without a manipulation*. Typically, naturalistic observation is used when a researcher wants to be able to describe nonverbal communication in great detail but without clearly specifying what causes what. For example, a researcher might want to examine the nonverbal dynamics of corporate meetings. The researcher might go to different organizations to sit in on meetings and observe the various types of nonverbal behaviors that people use. Notice that there is no manipulation and that the researcher goes to the subjects instead of having the subjects report to a research site. Several studies in this reader are also good examples of naturalistic observation. For example, Sigelman and Adams (article 26) went to parks to observe parent-child distance and touch. Guerrero and Andersen (article 24) observed touch behavior as couples waited in zoo and movie lines. After making their observations, they asked couples to complete questionnaires so they could compare the touch behavior of people in different types of relationships. Langan (article 31) made detailed observations of the ways in which environmental features function at various restaurants. An advantage of both naturalistic observations and field experiments is that researchers get a wide variety of different kinds of people in their studies (rather than, for example, college students or people willing to volunteer to come to a research laboratory). In addition, the behavior observed is usually more natural than behavior observed in a laboratory setting. This is especially true for naturalistic observations because the researchers do not introduce anything into the environment. As long as the observer is not noticed, the interaction should be completely natural. However, if you are looking for a specific type of behavior, it might be difficult to find in a noncontrolled setting.

It should be obvious by now that none of these methods is perfect. If you bring people into a laboratory setting, you lose some level of realism. If you go out into naturalistic settings, you lose some degree of control. This is why researchers encourage the use of multiple methods to study the same behavior. If we get similar findings across different methods, we will feel more confident in our results.

Stimulus Materials

Sometimes a researcher is interested in how people interpret and/or evaluate nonverbal behavior. If this is the case, stimulus materials can be an appropriate method. Using stimulus materials usually involves taking photographs, creating videotapes, or making audiotapes that contain different nonverbal behaviors. For example, Ekman's research often used slides of different posed facial expressions. He showed these slides to people from various cultures and found that individuals from all across the globe were able to identify basic emotions from the slides (see Ekman & Friesen, 1975). Burgoon (1991) showed subjects photographs of coworkers engaging in different types of touch. Participants then evaluated the touches in terms of relational messages such as intimacy and dominance. Lee (1998) conducted a similar study using videotapes to compare different types of touch in terms of appropriateness and sexual harassment. Guerrero and Miller (1998) used videotapes from distance education courses as stimulus materials in their study. They found that teachers were evaluated most favorably when they used expressive and pleasant nonverbal behavior. Semic (article 18) reports research showing that when people listen to audiotapes or answering machine messages (the stimulus materials) they evaluate people with attractive voices more favorably than they do people with unattractive voices.

Stimulus materials can also be used as part of a larger experiment or observational study. For example, one research paradigm in the emotion literature involves showing subjects videotapes or slides of peaceful (a beautiful sunset) and disturbing (a car accident) scenes and videotaping their facial reactions. Other studies have used humorous and serious movies as stimulus materials. Researchers might show these movies to people alone and in groups to see if they will show stronger nonverbal reactions (smiling, crying, leaning forward) when with others than by themselves.

RECORDING NONVERBAL COMMUNICATION

Regardless of whether the study uses an experiment, an observation, or stimulus materials, the researcher will have to *record* nonverbal communication or people's reactions to nonverbal behavior. Recording describes nonverbal communication. When a researcher relates this description to descriptions of other nonverbal behavior, emotions, attitudes, people, or situations, we can try to predict or explain nonverbal communication. The five most common methods of recording used in nonverbal research are *surveys*, *coding systems*, *field notes*, *diaries*, and *measures of physiological response*.

Surveys

Most of you are familiar with surveys (in the form of questionnaires and interviews). They have become a common form of gathering information. Surveys are written or oral questions designed to gather information. There are two general types of questions: *open* and *closed* questions. The difference is the type of answer that can be given. Open questions do not specify the type of answer. Examples are: How do you express friendship? What did you find satisfying about this conversation?

Closed questions provide specific choices for the answers. For example, you could have to check a box indicating whether you thought someone was lying or telling the truth after observing their nonverbal behavior. You could have to rank order seven behaviors from the most dominant to the most submissive. Or you could have to choose which of the following distances you prefer when standing and chatting with a friend: (a) 0 to 1 foot apart, (b) 1 1/2 to 4 feet apart, or (c) more than 4 feet apart. You might also use a *scale* to provide a closed-ended answer. For example you might be asked to evaluate a nonverbal behavior using one of the following scales:

My partner's face usually looks: unfriendly 1 2 3 4 5 6 7 friendly

My partner shows me a lot of affection. disagree 1 2 3 4 5 6 7 agree

The choice of either open or closed questions depends upon a number of factors. Basically, open questions provide more information than closed questions but are more difficult to interpret. If you are looking for rich description, open questions are usually the better way to go. If you are looking for precision, closed questions are the way to go.

Surveys can be a useful way of recording nonverbal behavior if certain limitations are kept in mind. First, most people are not aware of nonverbal behavior and, therefore, cannot describe it very well. Asking people if they leaned forward while talking to someone last week is not effective. It is even less effective to ask people how they *would* behave in a hypothetical or imaginary situation. People are very poor at predicting behavior in anything but the most typical situations (for example, where you will sit in class next time). They are also not very good at explaining why they behaved in a certain way because they attempt to rationalize their own behavior.

People can tell the researcher how they interpret behavior, what it means to them, and what they find important. They can also give the researcher information about nonverbal behavior that has taken place very recently, but it is best to observe and record this directly.

Coding Systems

Coding systems allow the researcher to observe nonverbal communication directly. There are two types of coding systems. The first lists various *types of nonverbal behavior* and the recorder (a person or a machine) just checks off the behavior when it is observed. For example, the researcher might have a checklist for smiling, touch, eye contact, and close distance (for example, less than four feet) to use for observing behavior at a party. Every time the researcher sees one of these behaviors a check is recorded next to the category. A researcher who separates the records for males and females would also be able to determine if there are sex differences in these behaviors. An example of a checklist is shown below. This coding scheme was used by Petronio, Bourhis, and Berquist (1987) who examined how families use touch and tie-signs when they are together in public places.

Coding Scheme for Tie-Signs:

Wedding Ring

Male _____

Female _____

Engagement Ring

Male _____

Female _____

Hand Hold _____

Arm Lock _____

Waist Hold _____

Hug _____

The second type of coding system provides symbols to record specific nonverbal behaviors. One of the first systems of this type was created by Ray Birdwhistell (1970). In his system, when we see a blank face we record -0-. A frown is recorded as ⌒. Other examples of his recording system are:

Sidewise look	⌒ ⌒
Focus on auditor	⌒ ⌒
Stare	⊗ ⊗
Rolled eyes	⊚ ⊚
Slipped eyes	⌁ ⌁
Eyes upward	⊖ ⊖
Shifty eyes	–⊖ ⊖–
Glare	``⊗ ⊗ ``

A similar coding system was provided by Edward Hall (1974), as shown below.

Body Orientation

This scale describes the orientation of the subjects' bodies to each other, beginning with back-to-back orientation (0) and opening out through side-by-side (5) and right-angle (7) to face-to-face orientation (9). The shoulders are the reference points to observe in deciding orientation. The most common positions for interacting are 5 through 9, although two persons standing "in line" (4) or backed up to each other (0) in crowds will also be aware of and interact with each other to some extent. Be sure that both subjects in an interaction are rated the same on this scale. (See coding scale opposite.)

Body Orientation

Finally, some coding systems use closed-ended questions to evaluate nonverbal behavior. For example, coders might evaluate how expressive, dominant, and friendly a person appears using seven-point scales similar to those described above under "surveys." The difference here is that coders are rating the behaviors of others as they observe their behavior directly or on videotapes rather than trying to recall behavior or trying to imagine what behavior would look like in a particular situation. Still other methods of recording nonverbal behavior are presented in Scherer and Ekman's (1982) book, *Handbook of Methods in Nonverbal Behavior Research.*

Field Notes

A third recording method is called *field notes.* Field notes may use one of the previous systems or may just involve going into a setting and writing down descriptions of the observations. It is usually best to record the notes while making the observation. If this interferes with the situation (for example, writing notes at a party), then the researcher will record the observations as soon afterward as possible. Some observers will even retreat to the bathroom to record notes as soon as possible! These notes will not be as clear or as descriptive as data gathered by the previous two systems, but they leave the researcher free to observe anything that occurs rather than just what is in the recording system. Sometimes audiotape recorders are used for field notes. Other times researchers use video cameras to record events. These taped or videotaped "notes" can later be coded using one of the systems above, and/or the researchers can use open-ended notes to describe the behaviors they have recorded.

Diaries

A fourth type of recording method utilizes diaries. Diaries are similar in some ways to both surveys and field notes because participants write down detailed observations about their nonverbal behavior or the behavior of others. Researchers can use several different strategies to prompt people to write in diaries. Sometimes people are instructed to write at a particular time, such as every night before going to bed. In other cases, people might be instructed to write after a particular event. For instance, if you are interested in the types of nonverbal messages people send when they are in conflict situations, you might ask subjects to write in their diaries immediately after conflicts. Researchers also can use innovative strategies such as having subjects wear beepers and asking them to write down a detailed description of the last gesture they saw someone use before they were beeped.

While diary methods are likely to produce detailed descriptions, they are also subject to some of the same criticisms as survey data. In particular, it may be difficult for people to write accurate accounts of their own behavior. People are likely to do somewhat better when judging the behavior of others, even though there are still some potential problems and biases here (such as seeing your partner's behavior as more negative than your own during a conflict situation). One special limitation of the diary method is that it might make people more aware of their behaviors. For example, if you knew that you would be writing in your diary about the nonverbal behavior you used in a conflict situation, you might be on your "best behavior." If that is the case, the behavior you would describe in your diary would not be completely natural.

Physiological Responses

A final type of measurement system used in nonverbal research involves recording people's physiological responses. A researcher might be interested in determining whether a hostile stare leads to a rise in blood pressure, or whether a loving touch calms people down or arouses them. Researchers might also want to see if people who hold back emotions experience more internal arousal than people who express their emotions freely. In these cases, it may be necessary to measure physiological responses, such as heart rate, skin temperature, and blood pressure. Several communication studies have used this type of measurement. For example, Le Poire and Burgoon (1994) hooked people up to equipment that measures physiological responses. Specifically, they placed electrodes on participants' fingertips using velcro strips to see how people respond to increases and decreases in friendly, involved behavior. The electrodes measured physiological responses such as skin temperature and heart rate.

Andersen, Guerrero, Buller, and Jorgensen (1998) conducted a similar study. They had opposite-sex friends come to a laboratory and instructed one of them (without the other knowing) to engage in moderately or highly flirtatious behavior. They used measures of skin temperature and heart rate to determine physiological reactions to the flirtatious behavior.

SUMMARY

This article provided a brief introduction to nonverbal communication research. Research was defined as the use of systematic methods to answer questions and/or test predictions. Three types of research questions were identified: (1) questions about one particular type of nonverbal message (for example, what are the types of touch?), (2) questions about how two or more types of nonverbal behaviors are related to each other (for example, do we stand closer to strangers who look and smell good in elevators?), and (3) questions about how nonverbal communication is related to types of people, groups, relationships, and situations (for example, do smells have different meanings in Eastern cultures than in European cultures?). Two general types of hypotheses were also identified: (1) predictions about how two or more behaviors or perceptions are related (for example, the more people smile, the more they tend to lean forward and the more people like them), and (2) predictions about differences in nonverbal communication between people, groups, relationships, or situations (for example, people use more intimate touch in private versus public settings). We also saw that the goals of research are description, prediction, and explanation, and that the importance of research topics should be evaluated in terms of contribution to theory, research, and practice.

Systematic methods were then described. Grounded and hypothesis-testing approaches to research were differentiated based on the specificity of their predictions. Hypothesis-testing approaches make specific predictions while grounded approaches ask more general questions. These approaches were also differentiated based on how they explain behavior. Researchers using the hypothesis-testing approach explain their findings in light of current theory. Researchers using the grounded approach use their findings to generate new explanations and theories. Next, we described several common methods used to collect data in nonverbal research. These included laboratory experiments, controlled observations, field experiments, naturalistic observation, and research using stimulus materials. Finally, we described five common methods used in nonverbal communication research: surveys, coding systems, field notes, diaries, and physiological response measures.

References

Andersen, P. A., Guerrero, L. K., Buller, D. B., & Jorgensen, P. F. (1998). An empirical comparison of three theories of nonverbal immediacy exchange. *Human Communication Research, 24,* 501–535.

Birdwhistell, R. I. (1970). *Kinesics and context: Essays on body motion and communication.* Philadelphia: University of Pennsylvania Press.

Burgoon, J. K. (1991). Relational message interpretations of touch, conversational distance, and posture. *Journal of Nonverbal Behavior, 15,* 233–259.

Ekman, P., & Friesen, W. V. (1975). *Unmasking the face.* Englewood Cliffs, NJ: Prentice-Hall.

Guerrero, L. K., & Miller, T. A. (1998). Associations between nonverbal behaviors and initial impressions of instructor competence and course context in videotaped distance education courses. *Communication Education, 47,* 30–42.

Kuhn, T. (1970). *The structure of scientific revolutions.* Chicago: University of Chicago Press.

Le Poire, B. A., & Burgoon, J. K. (1994). Two contrasting explanations of involvement violations: Expectancy violations theory versus discrepancy arousal theory. *Human Communication Research, 20,* 560–591.

Lee, J. W. (1998). *Relational and emotional interpretations of touch.* Unpublished honors thesis, Arizona State University, Tempe.

Petronio, S., Bourhis, J., & Berquist, C. (1987). Families in public places: But mom you promised! In J. A. DeVito & M. L. Hecht (Eds.), *The nonverbal communication reader* (pp. 425–435). Prospect Heights, IL: Waveland Press.

Scherer, K. R., & Ekman, P. (Eds.) (1982). *Handbook of methods in nonverbal behavior research.* Cambridge, UK: Cambridge University Press.

Sigelman, C. K., Adams, R. M., Meeks, S. R., & Purcell, M. A. (1986). Children's nonverbal responses to a physically disabled person. *Journal of Nonverbal Behavior, 10,* 173–186.

PART II

Nonverbal Codes

Early work on nonverbal communication often focused on describing various types of nonverbal *codes*. Each nonverbal code focuses on messages that are transmitted through different channels—the part of the body or environment that sends the message. For example, some nonverbal messages are transmitted through the face (smiling) and the body (forward lean and gesturing), while others are transmitted through sound (the tone of the voice), silence (a long pause) or how one smells (perfume). Still other messages are communicated through the use of space, touch, or time, or the manipulation of environmental features or personal appearance. The *code approach* to studying nonverbal communication can be thought of as a classification system. Based on the communication channel, researchers classify and describe various types of nonverbal messages.

Different researchers have classified nonverbal messages in different ways. Generally, however, there are eight basic nonverbal codes: (1) kinesics, (2) physical appearance, (3) olfactics, (4) vocalics, (5) proxemics, (6) haptics, (7) chronemics, and (8) environmental features. When most people first think of nonverbal communication, they think of body language. The code that comprises body language, as well as messages that come from the face and the eyes, is called *kinesics*. Within this category, researchers study behaviors such as gesture, posture, eye behavior, and facial expressions. Some researchers separate eye behavior from other types of bodily movements and give it a special name—oculesics.

Researchers have also studied how people look and smell as two related, but different, nonverbal codes that are associated with adorning ourselves. The code of *physical appearance* includes some things that are impossible or difficult to change, such as height, bone structure, and skin color range. Other aspects of physical appearance are easier to change. When you get a new haircut, color your hair, change clothes, put on jewelry, wear make-up, get a tan, and so forth, you are often trying to change your physical appearance in a way that makes a good impression on others. Now people even change their eye color using special contact lenses. And, of course, some people have cosmetic surgery to reduce their noses, enlarge their bustlines, and make other beauty-enhancing changes. Similarly, people use perfume and deodorant to make themselves attractive to others. The use of smell as a communication code is called *olfactics*. This code also includes olfactic elements that are hard to manage or control, such as bodily hormones.

Another nonverbal code is called *vocalics*. This includes *how* you say words as well as pauses, silences, and vocal sounds (such as laughter, sighing, and vocalized pauses such as saying "uh"). There is a popular saying that "It's not always what you say, but how you say it, that matters." This expression captures the importance of the vocalic code. Some forms of communication, such as sarcasm, rely very heavily on the way that you say words. The tone of voice, the stress put on certain words, the voice features (such as breathiness or high pitch), and the tempo and volume of the voice are just some of many vocalic features. Silences can also be important by themselves or within a train of verbal utterances. For example, you would probably feel comfortable sitting in silence with someone you know very well. However, silence between strangers can be quite awkward. Hesitancies and other types of pauses can also affect how you are perceived (as competent and credible, for example) as well as how your words are perceived. Take the following phrase. Woman without her man is helpless. If you believe in equal rights for women, you probably didn't like the "sound" of that statement. Now read the same statement with pauses included: Woman: without her, man is helpless. The sentence now has a completely different meaning.

Two other nonverbal codes are related to space and physical contact. The first of these codes, *proxemics*, deals with how we inhabit and protect our territory, as well as how close or far we stand in relation to other people. The space that you put between yourself and others, as well as the territory you occupy, can send powerful messages. Think about the last time you were at a movie theater. If the theater was half full, did you look for a place to sit where you and your companion(s) would be separated from others by at least a chair or two? Or did you sit down right next to someone? The research on proxemics suggests that there are cultural and social norms guiding our use of space, and that in North American and European cultures you would be most likely to sit so that you'd be separated from others. The amount of conversational distance is also important. When you want to tell a secret or exchange intimate self-disclosure with good friends, you are likely to sit close to them, but with strangers you might back away if they get too close. When two people get so close that they touch, they are communicating using the other contact code—*haptics*. Haptics refers to touch or tactile communication. Behaviors such as hugging, kissing, patting someone's shoulder, pushing, shoving, or hitting would fall here, just to name a few.

Finally, the last two codes relate to the general context in which nonverbal communication occurs. *Chronemics* deals with the use of time as a communication code. Being late for an important meeting, showing up for a date an hour early, spending a lot of time with someone, and trying to do five things at once while talking to someone all can send powerful messages. Research also shows that people have different personal orientations toward time. Some people plan for the future, others dwell on the past, and still others live for the moment. These orientations can affect communication patterns. *Environmental features* can also affect communication patterns. For example, you might dim the lights and use candles when having a romantic dinner, or you might paint your front door green to invite people in. Other environmental features such as temperature, color, noise level, architectural features, and furniture arrangement can also help to set a mood and to structure interaction. Teachers, for instance, might change their room arrangements so that the desks are in traditional rows (rather than in a semicircle or in "pods") if the students aren't paying attention. Sometimes easily moveable environmental features, such as pictures, lamps, and plants are called artifacts. Purses and jewelry, although more related to appearance and adornment than to the environment, are also sometimes called artifacts.

In the following section of this reader, the focus is on these eight nonverbal codes. In each subsection, classic and contemporary research describes these codes and highlights how they are important in your everyday life. We begin with a section on kinesics, followed by sections on appearance and adornment, vocalics and silence, proxemics and haptics, and, finally, chronemics and environmental features.

—Section A—

KINESIC CUES
The Body, Eyes, and Face

The kinesic code includes body, eye, and face behavior. We use our bodies to communicate in many ways. Our *posture* can express our feelings and attitudes. If we *lean* toward someone while talking, this may be a sign of interest and involvement, while leaning away is often interpreted as disinterest. Similarly, we tend to face friends *directly* and this may be a sign of interest, liking, or respect. It is also important to consider *postural relaxation* (more relaxed postures are found in higher-status people), *mirroring* as in two or more people adopting the same or similar posture (this is often a sign of similarity or attraction), and *openness* (crossing of arms or legs may indicate defensiveness).

In addition to these body cues, kinesics include *gestures* or hand movements. The first three readings in this section focus on various types of hand movements. Ekman and Friesen's classic work describes five types of gestures: emblems, illustrators, adaptors, affect displays, and regulators. In this reader, however, their article focuses on the first three of these types of gestures. *Emblems* are gestures that stand for or symbolize something. They have a verbal translation. For example, placing your finger over your lips can mean "be quiet," waving at someone can mean "hello" or "goodbye," and extending your thumb up in the air can mean "way to go!" or "I need a ride." *Illustrators* are usually pictorial representations, such as tracing a spiraling staircase in the air or using your hand to show how tall someone is. *Adaptors* are idiosyncratic gestures that help you feel more comfortable or exert nervous energy. Twisting the ring on your finger, wringing your hands together nervously, or moving a strand of hair out of your eyes or the eyes of a friend are all examples of adaptors. The other two gestures, which are not discussed in the Ekman and Friesen article in this reader, are also important. *Affect displays* help reveal the emotions that someone feels. Giving a high-five to show how happy and proud you are, or clapping your hands together as you smile with joy are examples of gestures that serve as affect displays. Finally, *regulators* help you structure and manage interaction. You might lean forward and put your hand out

46

when you are interrupting someone or want a chance to speak. Similarly, if you are in a student role, you might raise your hand if you want to speak. If you are the teacher or group leader, you might point at people to let them know it is okay for them to take a speaking turn. Regulator gestures help keep conversations running smoothly and efficiently.

Gestures also serve other functions. As you will see from the readings in this section, gestures may help deaf children (and possibly sighted children as well) to acquire language. A special group of gestures called *preening* or *self-grooming behaviors* involve self-touch, adaptor gestures, and posture. As a way of managing impressions, people preen by fixing their hair and clothes and positioning themselves in flattering ways. People are most likely to preen when they are attracted to others. Interestingly, preening is not limited to humans. Animals also preen. Peacocks, for example, display their colorful feathers to one another during the courtship process.

The readings in this section also examine eye behavior and smiling. Eye behavior includes gazing at someone; eye contact, which occurs when two people look one another in the eyes; and even pupil dilation. The reading on eye behavior in this section examines the different meanings of eye behavior. For instance, if you look someone squarely in the eye, it could be a sign of affection or intimidation, depending upon the way that you look at them.

The next two readings in this section focus on smiling. Although there are articles on various types of facial expression, such as frowning and looking angry, smiling has received the most attention in the scholarly literature. (Other facial expressions are discussed later in this reader in the section on "expressing emotion and intimacy.") Both articles on smiling show that the presence or absence of others affects when and to what extent you smile. Studies such as these show that smiling is more than an expression of happiness; it is also an important behavior that is affected by and helps shape our social interaction with others.

Finally, the last reading in this section examines how a number of different kinesic behaviors work together to help people manage impressions during employment interviews. This reading shows that using the appropriate amount of eye contact, smiling and head nodding might help you get the job that you want.

In this classic article, Ekman and Friesen discuss three classes of non-verbal behavior: emblems, illustrators, and adaptors. Although they believe that these three types of behavior characterize a wide range of nonverbal behavior, including facial expression, posture, and leg movement, they concentrate on gestures in this particular article.

4

Hand Movements

Paul Ekman
Wallace V. Friesen

Throughout our studies on nonverbal behavior we have emphasized a comprehensive approach, considering not just one aspect of motor behavior, such as facial expression, or eye contact, or hand movements, or posture, or leg movements, but all of these, if possible, on the same subject in the same settings. This comprehensive approach is based on our assumption that because activities in different areas of the body can serve equivalent or substitutive functions, studies of just one type of activity may provide an incomplete picture of what is occurring.

This may seem to be a strange way to introduce a paper which discusses just one area of the body, hand movements, but we want to emphasize that we are reporting here just part of our work. We are conducting studies with the same materials on facial expression, posture, eye contact, and leg movement. The comprehensive approach, we believe, will provide the most important findings and a theoretical breakthrough in the study of nonverbal communication.

Adapted with permission from Ekman & Friesen (1972), Hand movements. *Journal of Communication 22,* 353–374.

On the basis of their origin, coding and usage, we have described five classes of nonverbal behavior. We will describe here just the three classes which are relevant to distinguishing among most hand movements: emblems; illustrators; and adaptors.

Emblems are those nonverbal acts (a) which have a direct verbal translation usually consisting of a word or two, or a phrase, (b) for which this precise meaning is known by most or all members of a group, class, subculture, or culture, (c) which are most often deliberately used with the conscious intent to send a particular message to the other person(s), (d) for which the person(s) who sees the emblem usually not only knows the emblem's message but also knows that it was deliberately sent to her or him, and (e) for which the sender usually takes responsibility for having made that communication. A further touchstone of an emblem is whether it can be replaced by a word or two, its message verbalized, without substantially modifying the conversation.

People are usually aware of their use of an emblem, just as aware as they are of the words they emit. However, there can be emblematic slips, like slips of the tongue, when the sender apparently does not deliberately choose to make the emblem and may be unaware that he has done so. Emblems most often occur when verbal discourse is prevented by external circumstance (e.g., between pilot and landing crew), by distance (e.g., between hunters spaced apart from each other in the field), by agreement (e.g., while playing charades), or by organic impairment. Emblems of course also occur during conversation, repeating a verbalized message, replacing a word or two, adding a separate message not necessarily part of the verbal discourse, or contradicting the verbalization. Emblems, as we have defined them, are communicative and interactive acts.

The origin of emblems is culture specific learning. Efron (1972) found major differences in the emblems used by Italian and Jewish immigrants to the United States. Saitz and Cervenka (1962) have catalogued differences in emblematic behaviors between Colombia and the U.S. We have found major differences in the emblems used in urban Japan, urban Argentina, and a preliterate culture in New Guinea. As we expected, there are a few emblems which are the same across these groups; these are ones which are similar because of our anatomy—referring to a body part, or to a bodily action which, because of anatomical constraints, can only be performed in one way. We have found the number of emblems in each group to vary, but in each group we discovered more than 50 different emblems, and in some more than 100.

Illustrators are those acts which are intimately related on a moment-to-moment basis with speech, with phrasing, content, voice contour, loudness, etc. Illustrators usually augment what is being said verbally, but they may contradict the verbalization or be used as a substitute for a word.

Illustrators are similar to emblems in that they are used with awareness and intentionality, although the use of illustrators is usually in peripheral, not focal, awareness. Illustrators differ from emblems in a number of ways. Many of the illustrators do not have as precise a verbal definition as the emblems, and for some illustrators there is actually no obvious or agreed upon verbal translation of the act. Also, illustrators do not occur without conversation, or the rehearsal of conversation, while emblems may typically occur when the communicants cannot or choose not to converse. And, illustrators are only shown by the speaker in a conversation, not by the listener, while emblems may be shown by either speaker or listener.

Changes in the frequency of illustrator activity for any given individual depends upon mood and problems in verbal communication. When a person is demoralized, discouraged, tired, unenthusiastic, concerned about the other person's impression, or in a nondominant position in a formal interaction and setting, the rate of illustrators is less than is usual for that person. With excitement, enthusiasm about the topic or process of communication, when in the dominant role in a formal interaction, or in a more informal interaction where there is little concern about the impression being conveyed, a person uses more illustrators. When difficulty is experienced in finding the right words, or when feedback from the listener suggests he is not comprehending what is being said, illustrators increase. Illustrators can fill pauses and maintain a person's speaking turn. While illustrators aid in managing the behavior of the other conversant, and help the speaker explain and the listener understand what is said, illustrators also serve a self-priming function, helping the speaker past an awkwardness in his or her speech or thought, and accelerating the flow of her or his ideas. We should note the qualification that these ideas about changes in the rate of illustrator activity are based on and meant to apply to middle class white Americans, and we do not know how much of this is general to other groups. Certainly we do know that the type of illustrator varies with ethnic background, and it may also vary with social class and age. We distinguish the following eight types of illustrators.

> *batons*: movements which accent or emphasize a particular word or phrase
>
> *ideographs*: movements which sketch the path or direction of thought
>
> *deictic movements*: pointing to an object, place, or event
>
> *spatial movements*: movements which depict a spatial relationship
>
> *rhythmic movements*: movements which depict the rhythm or pacing of an event
>
> *kinetographs*: movements which depict a bodily action, or some non-human physical action

pictographs: movements which draw a picture in the air of the shape of the referent

emblematic movements: emblems used to illustrate a verbal statement, either repeating or substituting for a word or phrase

The eight illustrator sub-types are also not mutually exclusive. Although many illustrators fall neatly into one or another category, others are combinations of sub-types.

Illustrators are socially learned, presumably many of them early in life during language acquisition. Their chief function early in life is probably to command the adult's attention, and to aid in explaining matters for which the child has no words. The self-priming function could also occur early, but probably becomes more important after the child has a moderate vocabulary, when there is verbal material to prime. Like emblems, illustrators may involve any part of the body, although typically they involve the hands, head, facial muscular movement, or postural shift.

Adaptors are movements first learned as part of an effort to satisfy self needs or body needs, or to perform certain bodily actions, or to manage and cope with emotions, or to develop or maintain prototypic interpersonal contacts, or to learn instrumental activities. Emitted in private, or even in public if the individual is alone, not with another person, and not the conspicuous object of anyone's attention, the adaptive act (i.e., nose-picking, head-scratching) will be manifest in its entirety, carried through to completion, so that it is obvious what need is being satisfied. When the person is aware that he or she is being watched, or is with another person, and particularly when he or she is speaking in a conversation, adaptor acts will be reduced or fragmented, so that they are not nearly as conspicuous, nor is it always obvious what need is being met. These fragmented adaptors do not serve completely to accomplish their goal (e.g., the scalp may be touched but the itch not thoroughly scratched).

Adaptors are unlike both emblems and illustrators in intentionality and awareness, having little of either. While emblems and illustrators will almost never be shown when the individual is totally alone, self-adaptors will occur, often with high frequency and in their most complete form, when the person is alone.

In any given conversational setting people differ markedly in their rate of self-adaptor activity. Self-adaptors will increase with psychological discomfort or anxiety, although some people will show a decrease in self-adaptors when discomforted or anxious instead freezing movement in muscularly tense immobility.

In closing, we reiterate that our distinction between illustrators, emblems and adaptors applies not only to the hands, but also to facial behavior and leg movements. In addition, we have proposed two other classes of behavior not described here, *affect displays and regulators* (see Ekman & Friesen, 1969). We believe that progress in the study of nonverbal behavior requires consideration of all five classes of behavior, all parts of the organism's motor activity—in the face, hands, legs, posture—and the interrelationship of these nonverbal behaviors with measures of voice and language.

References

Ekman, P., & Friesen, W. V. (1969). The repertoire of nonverbal behavior: Categories, origins, usage, and coding. *Semiotica, 1*, 49–98.

Saitz, R. L., & Cervenka, E. J. (1962). *Colombian and North American gestures: An experimental study*. Bogota, Colombia: Centro Colombo-Americano.

Research by Laura Ann Petitto shows that deaf babies babble with their hands in a way similar to the vocal babbling of hearing children. Petitto argues that this research shows that speech is not essential to learning language, in that deaf children use hand movement rather than speech to help them acquire language.

5

Deaf Babies Babble with Hands

Natalie Angier

Deaf babies of deaf parents babble with their hands in the same rhythmic, repetitive fashion that hearing infants babble vocally, a new study says.

The deaf babies, who presumably watch their parents use sign language at home, start their manual babbles before they are 10 months old, the same age that hearing children begin stringing together sounds into word-like units. And just as hearing babies experiment with a few key noises such as "dadadada" or "bababada," so deaf infants use several motions over and over, including one gesture that looks like "OK" and another that resembles a hand symbol of the numeral 1.

The gestures of the deaf children do not have real meaning, any more than babble noises have meaning, but they are far more systematic and deliberate than are the random finger flutters and fist clenches of hearing babies. The motions seem to be the deaf babies' fledgling attempts to master language, said Laura Ann Petitto, a psychologist at McGill University in Montreal. She is the principal author of the report, which appeared in the journal *Science*.

The new research strongly suggests that the brain has an innate capacity to learn language in a particular, stepwise fashion, by stringing together units into what eventually become meaningful words, Petitto said. The brain will progress from one stage to another regardless of whether language is conveyed through speaking, hand-signing, or presumably any other method of communication, she added.

The results contradict a widespread assumption among linguists that the maturation of the vocal cords affects language development among infants.

"For centuries, people thought that speech is language, and language is speech," she said. "There's been a whole complicated notion that the structure of the motor apparatus and the unfolding of the mouth muscles actually influenced the structure and development of language." But in showing that deaf babies babble with their hands in a manner that has all the basic elements of vocal babbling," she said, "We've decoupled language from speech. We've torn them apart."

Other researchers in the field of early language development praised the new study as significant and extremely well-designed. "I think this is important work," said Richard P. Meier, an assistant professor of linguistics and psychology at the University of Texas at Austin. "It's been suggested that all children pass through a regular sequence of milestones in speech acquisition, from simple cooing early on, to structured babbling at eight months, to the first word at about 12 months. This work gives us a new dimension of how language matures."

Marilyn M. Vihman, who is doing research on language acquisition at Rutgers University in New Brunswick, New Jersey, said the latest results offer further proof that babbling is a crucial step in language development. "You'll see the emergence of babbling at the same age in any infant who has been exposed to language regardless of other things, including intelligence," she said. "Babies babble regardless of whether the language spoken at home is English, Japanese, French, or, it seems, sign language."

Petitto and her graduate student, Paula F. Marentette, videotaped five infants at ages 10, 12 and 14 months. Two of the infants were deaf children of deaf parents who use American Sign Language to communicate, while the other three were hearing offspring of hearing adults.

The researchers analyzed every hand gesture of the infants and compared the two groups. They found that the hearing children made many hand gestures but that the gestures never became organized or repetitive. By comparison, the deaf babies soon began showing evidence of using about 13 different hand motions over and over again. Nearly all of them were actual elements of American Sign Language: gestures that do not in themselves mean anything, but have the potential to indicate something when added to other gestures.

Sign languages are structured much like any spoken language, Petitto said. Distinct gestures and hand shapes are the equivalent of syllables and, thus, must be presented in a series to assume any sense.

Petitto believes that the deaf parents noticed the nascent efforts of their children to communicate through signs and began reinforcing the gestures, just as normal parents talk back to and reinforce their babbling infants by turning the babble into words, for example, by saying "dadadada . . . daddy."

But there was idiosyncratic taste at work as well. Just as one hearing baby may prefer to say "babababa," while another fastens upon "gagaga," so one of the deaf infants tended to make her gestures in front of her torso, while the other deaf baby performed his hand signs around his head and face.

Petitto said that the new work also supports the theory that the basic rhythm of all languages is the same, building upon a pattern that alternates consonants and vowels. Although the analogy is only approximate in sign language, the deaf babies did alternate between mobile gestures, which are thought to be somewhat vowel-like in their rhythmicity, and static hand shapes, the rough equivalent of the consonant.

*A special group of kinesic behaviors involves preening or self-grooming.
Preening behaviors include fixing one's hair, straightening clothes, and
looking at oneself in a mirror. This study examines how these preening
behaviors differ as a function of sex (women vs. men) and the nature of
the relationship (such as friends vs. spouses). Results show that females
preen more than males and that people who are just beginning a relationship preen more than those in established relationships.*

6

Sex and Relationship Affect Social Self-Grooming

John A. Daly
Elizabeth Hogg
David Sacks
Marcy Smith
Lori Zimring

Given the ubiquity of self-grooming or preening in everyday life it is surprising that the activity receives so little attention from behavioral scientists. While a number of ethological studies of grooming among birds and
primates exist (Eibl-Eibesfeldt, 1975; Lawick-Goodall, 1968; Sparks, 1967,
Yerkes, 1933) only Scheflen (1965) and Given (1978) have directly considered the role of preening in human social activities. Among humans, preen-

Adapted with permission from: Daly et al. (1983), Sex and relationship affect social self-
grooming. *Journal of Nonverbal Behavior, 7,* 183–189.

ing may serve a number of functions including boosting self-esteem, relieving boredom, reducing physical discomfort, and managing positive impressions in the presence of others. This investigation examined some correlates of preening as an impression management activity: a pattern of behaviors oriented towards improving one's physical appearance in social environments. More specifically, two potential mediators of the amount of social preening a person engages in were investigated. The first was the person's sex; the second, who he or she was with in the social setting where observations took place.

The first variable considered in this study was the sex of the person. Women were expected to engage in more preening than men. In many cultures standards for feminine beauty receive more explicit recognition than those for males (Ford & Beach, 1951). Empirical evidence suggests that females emphasize appearance more than males. Adolescent women are more concerned about positive social impressions, one of which may be appearance, than their male counterparts (Rosenberg & Simmons, 1975) and both males and females consider attractiveness more central for females than for males (Williams & Bennett, 1975). This greater emphasis by females on attractiveness may be a function, in part, of the importance it plays in judgments made of them by others. Bar-Tal and Sax (1976) found that appearance serves as a more important cue in evaluations of females than of males. Among college students Stroebe, Insko, Thompson and Layton (1971) demonstrated that physical attractiveness was a more important determinant of opposite-sex attraction for males than for females. Further, while females are comparatively unconcerned with the attractiveness of men, males perceive their roles as being attracted to females' physical appearance (Lerner, Karabenick, & Stuart, 1973) and often consider it more important in dating choices than do females (Berscheid & Walster, 1974).

The sort of relationship between a person and those he or she is with in a social environment was the second mediating variable in this study. The amount of preening was expected to vary as a function of the permanence of the association between the people. As relationships progress from the first meeting to stable, permanent, and enduring associations physical appearance may become less important (Schlenker, 1980). Physical appearance seems to play its most crucial role in initial impression formation; familiarity lessens its impact (Berscheid & Walster, 1974). Consequently, physical appearance has a greater effect on dating choices than on marrying ones with college students (Stroebe, Insko, Thompson, & Layton, 1971). Insofar as physical attractiveness is especially important in initial encounters more preening was expected among people who were involved in relatively new relationships than among those in extended relationships.

The purpose of this study was to explore preening as an impression management technique used by people in a social setting. Two variables were hypothesized to affect the amount of preening that occurs. The first was the sex of the person. Females were hypothesized to preen more than males. The second was the nature of the relationship between the person and those he or she is with. The more established the relationship the less preening was expected.

METHOD

Subjects

Seventy-seven individuals (32 males and 43 females), all in their early to mid-twenties, served as subjects in this study. Subjects were randomly selected from an estimated 500 potential participants available during the observational phase of this investigation.

Procedures

Data collection took place in two stages. The first was the observation of preening behaviors. Preening by subjects (defined as hair grooming, clothes straightening, and gazing at self in mirror) was unobtrusively observed and timed in the restrooms of five restaurants and bars located within the university community.[1] Four different observers were used to time preening activities during various observation sessions. However, only one observer timed the preening of any individual subject. Prior to data collection, high reliability among the four observers had been established in terms of identifying and timing preening actions. The observers worked together in identifying preening behaviors and then practice-coded examples until high reliability (percent agreement > 90 percent) was established. Reliable timing of preening was obtained in the same fashion with a similar level of reliability established during practice sessions. The procedures used in any of the settings by any observer were identical. The observer, positioned in the restroom so that he or she could observe preening behavior but at the same time not be overly noticeable, timed each subject's preening. Observers were trained to avoid standing unusually close to subjects, preening themselves while observing subjects, or engaging in behaviors that would attract undue attention from subjects. These cautions were designed to reduce possible confounding among distraction, facilitation, or modeling.

The second phase was the interview phase. As a subject left the bathroom the observer followed and identified the subject to a person who served as an interviewer. After identifying the subject to the interviewer the observer recorded the subject's sex and amount of preening. The interviewer, unaware of how much preening the subject had done, approached him or her and asked if he or she would mind answering three questions for a class survey. No subject refused. The interviewer proceeded to ask (1) how long the subject had been in the establishment, (2) the nature of the relationship between the subject and the person(s) sitting with him or her, and (3) how long the subject had known the other person(s) with him or her.[2] Responses to the second question were coded into four categories: (1) long-term, stable relationships which included married couples and long-term same sex friends who had no intentions of meeting new people that evening, (2) couples who were dating and who had dated for more than four dates, (3) couples who were in the early stages of the relationship: the date was one of their first four with each other, and (4) individuals and groups who were specifically in the establishment trying to meet new people. After the subject answered the questions the interviewer explained the investigation and asked subject about his or her awareness and reactions to it. No subject reported being aware of the observations that had occurred or experiencing any adverse reactions to the project.

RESULTS

Statistical tests indicated that:
1. Females preen for longer periods of time than males.
2. People who are married or close friends preen less than other groups.
3. Couples on their first, second, third, or fourth date preen more than those who have been dating longer.
4. The longer people know one another, the less time they spend preening.

DISCUSSION

This study is one of the very few investigations to explore self-grooming among humans. It provides an empirical demonstration of human social preening and some of its mediators. The results of the investigation are consistent with an impression management interpretation of social preening. Females, for whom physical appearance may be a more important impression management strategy than it is for males, preened significantly more than males. Further, impression management via preening was hypothesized to be more critical in early stages of relationships than in later ones. The data supported this expectation in two ways. First, there was a significant and inverse correlation between the length of a relationship and the time its member(s) spent preening. Second, a significant main effect for relationship type was found in an analysis of variance of preening as a function of relationship. The pattern of means supported the hypothesis: members of more established relationships preened less than early relationship members. In short, women preened more than men and the more extensive the relationship, the less preening its members engaged in.

Aside from the impression management function, it would be interesting to examine other potential functions of preening among humans and their mediators. Further, it would be interesting to examine the presentation strategies that people choose to use as relationships develop. In this study physical appearance via preening was found to be differentially important as a function of sex and relationship. Simply because appearance may become less salient as a relationship develops doesn't imply that impression management becomes less important. Rather, other strategies gain salience. Research to date has mostly focused on the strategies used in initial encounters. It seems important to identify how strategies people select as central to a positive impression change across the life of relationships.

Notes

[1] Concern might arise about the potential privacy invasion involved in this study. A number of procedures were completed in an attempt to minimize any actual or perceived invasion of privacy. First, a number of undergraduates were polled in a classroom setting about how they would feel if such an activity were to take place and they were to be observed. Not one of over 150 indicated it would be a source of concern. Second, managers of each establishment where observations were completed were asked about the potential reactions of patrons. None indicated any particular concern. Third, when the interviewer explained the project to participants none evidenced any concern. A few, in fact, responded in quite positive ways saying, for example, how "neat" and interesting the project was and they wished they had class projects like this one. Finally, each subject was told that if he or she had any objections to the study his or her data would be excluded.

[2] Both observer and interviewer attempted to estimate how sober each subject was. While reliable ($r=.76$) in their estimates, soberness ratings were not significantly related to any of the other variables.

References

Bar-Tal, D., & Saxe, L. (1976). Physical attractiveness and its relationship to sex role stereotyping. *Sex Roles, 2,* 123–133.

Berscheid, E., & Walster, E. (1974). Physical attractiveness. In L. Berkowitz (Ed.), *Advances in Experimental Social Psychology* (Vol. 7, pp. 158–216). New York: Academic Press.

Eibl-Eibesfeldt, I. (1975). *Ethology: The biology of behavior.* New York: Holt, Rinehart & Winston.

Ford, C. S., & Beach, F. A. (1951). *Patterns of sexual behavior.* New York: Harper.

Given, D. B. (1978). The nonverbal basis of attraction: Flirtation, courtship, and seduction. *Psychiatry, 41,* 346–359.

Kirk, R. E. (1968). *Experimental design: Procedures for the behavioral sciences.* Monterey, CA: Brooks/Cole.

Lawick-Goodall, J. van. (1968). The behavior of free living chimpanzees in the Gombe Stream Reserve. *Animal Behavior Monographs, 1,* 161–311.

Lerner, D., Karabenich, J. A., & Stuart, J. L. (1973). Relations among physical attractiveness, body attitudes, and self-concept in male and female college students. *Journal of Psychology, 85,* 119–121.

Rosenberg, F. R. & Simmons, R. G. (1975). Sex differences in the self-concept of adolescence. *Sex Roles, 1,* 147–160.

Scheflin, A. E. (1965). Quasi-courtship behavior in psychotherapy. *Psychiatry, 28,* 245–251.

Schlenker, B. R. (1980). *Impression management.* Monterey, CA: Brooks Cole.

Sparks, J. (1967). Allogrooming in primates: A review. In D. Morris (Ed.), *Primate ethology.* Chicago: Aldine.

Stroebe, W., Insho, C. A., Thompson, V. D., & Layton, B. D. (1971). Effects of physical attractiveness, attitude similarity, and sex on various aspects of interpersonal attraction. *Journal of Personality and Social Psychology, 18,* 79–91.

Williams, J. E., & Bennet, S. M. (1975). The definition of sex stereotypes via the Adjective Check List. *Sex Roles, 1,* 327–337.

Yerkes, R. M. (1933). Genetic aspects of grooming, a socially important behavior pattern. *Journal of Social Psychology, 4,* 4–25.

In this article, Grumet provides an overview of the important role that eye contact plays in perception and interaction. Grumet explains the physiology of the eye—the nerve and organs associated with vision. Next, Grumet describes how eye contact affects relationships. Finally, the article concludes with a discussion of the functions of eye contact.

7

Eye Contact
The Core of Interpersonal Relatedness

Gerald W. Grumet

> Look into a person's pupils; he cannot hide himself.
>
> —Confucius (551–478 B.C.)

In about 450 B.C. the Greek philosopher Empedocles explained vision as resulting from a stream of fiery corpuscles passing first from the eye to the object of vision and returning to the eye. Plato later wrote, "They set the face in front . . . and constructed light-bearing eyes, and caused pure fire to flow through the eyes" (Siegel, 1970, p. 24). Such ancient theories reflect the sense of power ascribed to sight and bedeviled scientific thought until the 17th century, when Kepler correctly proposed that the eye was an optical instrument able to form an image on its own retina. Vision has always

Adapted from *Psychiatry, 48*, 172–180. Copyright © 1983 by William Alanson White Psychiatric Foundation.

carried with it a sense of graphic truth and authenticity, placing it in a position of prominence among the senses. Soltis (1966) notes, "One of our firmest ordinary beliefs is that whatever objects we take to be visually perceived by us do exist" (p. 111). Gibson (1960) adds, "Visual perceiving often enough does not feel like knowing; instead it feels like an immediate acquaintance or a direct contact" (p. 220). Freese (1977) points out that if discrepant sensory information is received, the influence of sight is likely to predominate: "Visual perception is capable of overriding all other information should any of it conflict with the visual sense" (p. 72).

THE IMPACT OF DIRECT VISION

The old axiom, "I'll believe it when I see it," is readily understood in reviewing the impressive neuroanatomical substrates of human vision. Of the 3,000,000 or so sensory fibers entering the primate brain, about two-thirds arise from the eye, and of the 12 cranial nerves, 6 are involved with ocular performance. The complexity and capacity of the human visual cortex is reflected in its enormous size: about 20 square feet by 1/10 inch if flattened out (Newell, 1978). The extraocular muscles, which have the highest innervation of any muscles of the body, may contract 100,000 times a day. As Llewellyn-Thomas (1981) notes, "We have extraocular muscles which, like the wing muscles of insects, do not fatigue. Muscles that keep my eyes jumping constantly while I'm awake and much of the time I'm asleep, forever seeking information from the world around me or following events in the world of my imagination" (p. 319).

The eyes serve a scanning function, and their inputs are subjected to a variety of secondary perceptual processes by which salient stimuli are differentiated from less important ones. The fovea or point of central vision is directed to scrutinize the most significant. William James wrote in 1892, "The main function of the peripheral parts of the retina is that of sentinels which when beams of light move over them cry 'Who goes there?' and call the fovea to the spot" (p. 73), Excitation of cells within the tiny fovea, $1\frac{1}{2}$ millimeters in diameter, is thought to cause neurons within a region 10,000 times the original area to respond (Kaufman, 1974). If one sees in the retinal periphery a face pointed in his direction, it demands foveal attention and the extraocular muscles move the eyeball so that the image falls upon the point of central vision. Certainly, the visual perception of another individual looking at us carries with it considerable importance for survival and mating behavior. It is reasonable to assume that evolutionary selection pressures developed brains which stored generalized representations of salient environmental stimuli, such as visual interest of other parties, coloring it with rich emotional significance. The critical importance of eye contact for lower animals is quite literally emblazoned on the bodies of butterflies, birds, snakes, fish and peacocks, whose eye-shaped patterns are thought to mimic the eyes of predators and thus induce an avoidance response. In many species a common effect of staring eyes is physiological arousal (Argyle & Cook, 1976). In monkeys with permanently implanted electrodes, a maximum alerting response is elicited when their gaze meets that of the experimenter (Wada, 1961). In human subjects, EEG recordings reveal signs of increased arousal when eye contact is established (Gale et al., 1972), and direct eye-to-eye engagement has been shown to generate significantly more excitation in galvanic skin responses than does unreciprocated gaze (Nichols & Champness, 1971).

Eye contact is usually a first step in interpersonal engagement, beginning a train of action that develops and defines the relationship between the gazer and gazed upon. As Garrison and Arensberg (1976) note, "On eye contact, predator and prey, or rival and rival, or lover and loved, are alerted, tensed for what may come next, and a move follows: predator or rival to the attack, lover to tactile approach . . ." (p. 292).

SURVIVAL IMPLICATIONS

A remarkable feature of ocular contact is its ability to transmit instant and meaningful information within new relationships. A pedestrian, crossing the street in front of an automobile halted for a "Stop" sign, will likely attempt to establish eye contact with the driver before beginning to cross in front of him. In doing so, he makes sure that the motorist is cognizant of his presence and will allow him to cross safely. There are other situations where the opposite rule prevails, and avoiding eye contact is more likely to assure safety. Russell Baker of the *New York Times* writes,

> Veterans of New York's guerilla life know better than to make eye contact with other people on the streets. For the criminal, eye contact is an invitation to produce his knife. . . . The rule of survival is never look anyone in the eye, and it is a hard, hard rule to follow at times. . . . Among outlanders there is an embittered old saying about New York that there are a million people on every street corner and not one of them will give you so much as a glance. Those million people are not being coldblooded. Just surviving. (1981, p. 17A)

The ability of interocular contact to convey menace is an outgrowth of man's instinctive fear of predatory gaze, a sinister legacy of Darwinian evolution. Roberts (1976), in a cross-cultural analysis of 186 past and present societies, found evidence for evil-eye beliefs in 67 cultures. Versions of the evil eye are embedded in legends, folklore, mythology and superstitions from antiquity to the present, dating as far back as the 3rd millennium B.C. (Tomkins, 1963). In European folk versions, themes of oral aggression and oral jealousy predominate, with old women held chiefly responsible for the "hostile devouring glance," which is usually directed at infants, children and nursing mothers (Roheim, 1953). A reversal of the evil-eye superstition is found in the Japanese neurotic disorder *taijin kyofu*, in which a person avoids others for fear he will injure them if their eyes meet (Gutheil, 1979).

It should be noted that there is a difference between "looking" and "staring." The former is dynamically tied to the subject's behavior and is influenced by it, whereas the latter is not responsive to the other person's behavior and persists regardless of it. The fear engendered by a stare was well depicted in a study by Ellsworth and coworkers (1972), who had an experimenter on a motorbike stare at motorists stopped for a red light at an intersection. Not surprisingly, these motorists' departure from the intersection was significantly more rapid when the light changed, paralleling the flight behavior of animals. The authors note that "gazing at a person's face is an exceedingly salient stimulus with interpersonal implications which cannot be ignored" (p. 311). This phenomenon was well demonstrated in the World Chess Championship between Viktor Korchnoi and Anatoly Karpov in 1978. The Russian entourage supporting Karpov included Vladimir Zukhar, a parapsychologist and hypnotist: "His only job seemed to be to sit up front and stare at Korchnoi with his bulging, scary eyes. By the third game, Korchnoi was convinced he was being hypnotized. . . . At game 7, Korchnoi, a nervous wreck by that time—and with Karpov way ahead in the match—started to yell, saying he would descend from the stage and poke Zukhar in the nose. Zukhar was moved to a seventh-row seat." (Schonberg, 1981, p. 37).

COURIERS OF AFFECTION

In amorous behavior, eye contact again plays a pivotal role, this time as a messenger and inspirer of love. As expected, Rubin (1970) found that couples in love spend more time gazing into each other's eyes. Eye imagery in poetry and song has for centuries proven an effective and economical way of describing the power and suddenness of passion and the tyranny which love exercises over its victim. Donaldson-Evans (1980) has made an excursion into what he calls "the dangerous territory of Renaissance love poetry where one glance from a Lady's eye can bring love, suffering and death" (pp. 8, 21). He notes that romantic poets preferred the ancient efflux theory of vision: "the eyes shoot arrows, daggers or swords, project fiery beams which burn the soul and kindle love's flame." Direct eye contact between strangers may, on occasion, be described as "love at first sight," which is implied in the lyrics of "Some Enchanted Evening" by Oscar Hammerstein II:

> Some enchanted evening, you may see a stranger;
> You may see a stranger across a crowded room;
> And somehow you know, you know even then,
> That somewhere you'll see her again and again.

The song suggests that a single glance at an unfamiliar person can produce an enormous emotional impact. While a one-way glance signifies one person's interest in another, a mutual glance signifies the inception of a relationship or what has been variously called "shared interocular intimacy" (Tomkins, p. 157), "participation in a wordless exchange" (Exline, 1963, p. 3), or "consciousness of consciousness" (Sartre, 1953, p. 363).

A naive woman, writing to the medical column of a Philadelphia newspaper, communicates the intense and unexpected amorous impact of an ocular exchange (Steincrohn, 1975, p. 67):

> *Question*: I blame my problem on eyes—mine and those of another. I am a married woman with children and was absolutely not looking for another man. But—BOOM!—there it is. My age is 35. . . . I experience this feeling whenever our eyes meet. . . . Of this feeling, we have never spoken, but I sense that he is experiencing the same as I am. . . . How does one turn this off? This must be the way many extramarital affairs begin. Where does it come from? What sets it off? Please try to explain it medically. Just what is there in the eye contact to produce such a problem?

> *Answer*: . . . I wish I knew the answer. . . . All I can offer as a doctor is the fact that the eyes themselves are not to blame. If you really want the problem resolved, better discuss it with your family doctor or with a marriage counselor. . . .

That romantic love can be obsessional in nature and visually-based is depicted in Al Dubin's 1934 lyrics, "I Only Have Eyes for You":

> My love must be a kind of blind love,
> I can't see anyone but you.
> And dear, I wonder if you find love
> An optical illusion too?
> Are the stars out tonight?
> I don't know if it's cloudy or bright—
> 'cause I only have eyes for you. . . .

THE SEARCH FOR MEANING

Visual perception is an active process in which incoming stimuli are combined with learned information in order to make deductions which go far beyond the immediate sensory evidence. What we "see" is actually a mental construction built upon visual inputs, along with information from other senses and from previous experience. Soltis writes of "successful seeing," i.e., adequately interpreting the optical stimulus. He notes that our knowledge about things in the world is "threaded" into the process of visual perception, and visual inputs are "capped" with interpretations that are both economical and comprehensible to the viewer. An example of how the brain searches for meaning from the visual information presented to it is provided by the transparent "Necker" cube, which spontaneously reverses itself in depth as one looks at it. This reversal results from alternating cerebral explanations of what the ambiguous retinal image represents.

Similarly, in the more complex interpretative tasks of interpersonal communication, eye contact is an essential avenue in the quest for comprehension. In dyadic encounters, people look at their conversational partners a large percentage of the time, especially while listening; in one study, women looked at their partners 94% of the time while they were listening, and men, 82% of the time (Exline & Winters, 1966). Yarbus (1967) notes that experimental subjects direct foveal attention primarily to the eyes and lips of photographed faces, as these provide the most information to the observer. As Argyle and Dean (1965) note, "Without eye-contact, people do not feel that they are fully in communication" (p. 289).

The reliance upon vision for extracting supplementary meaning even in an established personal relationship is exemplified by the Senate testimony of Herbert W. Kalmbach, one of President Nixon's personal attorneys. Kalmbach had been instructed to make secret payments to the Watergate burglars and sought assurance from Nixon aide John Ehrlichman that the payments were proper:

> Kalmbach: I can remember it very vividly because I looked at him, and I said, "John, I am looking right into your eyes. I know Jeanne and your family, you know Barbara and my family. You know that my family and my reputation mean everything to me; and it is just absolutely necessary, John, that you tell me, first that John Dean has the authority to direct me in this assignment, that it is a proper assignment, and that I am to go forward on it."
>
> Dash[1]: And did he look at you in the eyes?
>
> Kalmbach: Yes, he did.

Dash: What did he say to you?

Kalmbach: He said, "Herb, John Dean does have the authority, it is proper, and you are to go forward." (Hearings Before the Select Committee on Presidential Campaign Activities 1973, p. 2106)

Kalmbach, apparently suspicious that he was being drawn into unsavory activities, had attempted to prod Ehrlichman into a truthful disclosure by establishing interocular contact and reminding him of their family ties. He reportedly could never get over the fact that Ehrlichman later denied that this conversation had ever taken place (Miller, 1974). Although it is a general perception that persons with high ocular contact are more sincere than those who tend to avert their gaze (Kleinke et al., 1973), people occasionally reveal increased eye-to-eye contact while being deceptive. This was demonstrated in an elaborate experimental study by Exline and coworkers (1970), who contrasted the visual performance of subjects identified as high or low in "Machiavellianism" while implicated in cheating. They noted that those with high Machiavellian tendencies increased their direct eye contact after being accused of cheating as if to project an image of innocence, whereas those with low Machiavellian qualities tended to avert their gaze, being less able to conceal their shame.

A MULTIPLICITY OF FUNCTIONS

Further evidence of the prominence of vision in interpersonal relations is the exceptional number of psychological influences which impinge upon visual interaction and ocular performance. A few of the main features follow.

Social Position: Persons in positions of leadership tend to gravitate toward locations where they are the visual focus of attention, such as the head of a table (Howells & Becker, 1962; Lott & Sommer, 1967). This is similar to the behavior of lower primates where a single dominant animal attains a position of visual command while subordinate members of the pack remain around him, glancing periodically, but carefully refraining from encroaching upon his territory (Chance & Jolly, 1970).

Positive vs. Negative Emotions: Positive emotions, such as surprise, delight or interest, are associated with increased gaze, while negative emotions, such as horror or disgust, are associated with gaze aversion (Kendon, 1967). During periods of high anxiety, eye movements are deployed in an avoidant manner with shorter eye fixations and shifts of gaze away from threatening areas (Luborsky, Blinder, & Mackworth, 1963). Similarly, pupillometric studies reveal that the pupils enlarge when people look at things they like and get smaller when the subjects viewed are uninteresting or distasteful (Hess, 1975). Both gaze direction and pupil size combine to welcome more positive stimuli and avoid more negative ones.

Willingness to Relate: A person's decision to look back into the eyes of someone who is already looking at him is one of the principal signals by which one denotes a willingness to begin an encounter, for ocular engagement reflects human engagement. Mutual gaze or "catching someone's eye" indicates the entrance into a relationship and may be consciously manipulated toward this end. Common examples are efforts to establish ocular contact with a waiter in a restaurant or to avoid establishing eye contact with a beggar on the street.

Women vs. Men: Women tend to look at their conversational partners somewhat more than men (Exline, Gray, & Schuette, 1965; Exline & Winters, 1966). Women also appear to engage more readily in mutual gazing, while men show a greater tendency toward one-way ("stolen") glances (Exline, 1963).

Cultural Factors: Culturally prescribed norms of visual engagement exert a profound effect on gazing patterns (Hall, 1963). Certain groups— such as Americans, Japanese and Navaho Indians—are taught not to stare at others, whereas Arabs, Greeks and South Americans emphasize intense eye contact as evidence of sincerity and interest.

Synchrony of Speech: Analysis of eye contacts during speech reveals typical patterns for listening and for speaking. Listeners glance more frequently than talkers (Kendon, 1967), and gaze aversion among talkers is more pronounced during periods of unfluent speech, presumably to limit distracting sensory input while difficult verbal production is in progress (Goldman-Eisler, 1961). These patterns are believed to assist conversationalists in synchronizing their speech by supplementing auditory information with an interchange of facial expressions and body kinesics.

Character Traits: A direct gaze is more likely to be returned by the person with aggressive and assertive character traits (Moore & Gilliland, 1921). Extroverts also tend to exchange eye contact more readily than introverts (Argyle & Ingham, 1972), and hysterics have been found to avert their gazes more often than obsessives when confronted by a sexually evocative stimulus (Luborsky et al., 1965). People with a high degree of eye contact are judged by their associates to be more "friendly," "natural," "self-confident" and "sincere," while those with little eye contact are perceived as "cold," "defensive," "evasive," "submissive" or "inattentive" (Kleck & Nuessle, 1968; Kleinke et al., 1993).

Thus, visual interactive styles are a final common pathway for a multiplicity of social, psychological and cultural influences, resting ultimately upon a balance of approach and avoidance forces. With direct eye contact, we allow our ocular partner to witness our emotions as we witness his or hers and to mutually acknowledge affective engagement; in gaze aversion, we indicate a desire to maintain psychological distance and to avoid receiving or sending messages of affective arousal.

Note

[1] Samuel Dash, Chief Counsel for the Senate Watergate Committee.

References

Abraham, L. (1927). Restrictions and transformations of scoptophilia in psycho-neurotics: With remarks on analogous phenomena in folk-psychology (1913). In K. Abraham, *Selected Papers*. Hogarth.

Argyle, M., & Cook, M. (1976). *Gaze and mutual gaze*. Cambridge University Press.

Argyle, M., & Dean, J. (1965). Eye contact, distance and affiliation. *Sociometry, 28,* 289–304.

Argyle, M., & Ingham, R. (1972). Gaze, mutual gaze and proximity. *Semiotica, 6,* 32–49.

Baker, R. (1981, July 26). Survival reflects reflexes. *Sunday Democrat and Chronicle* (Rochester, NY).

Callan, H. M. W., Chance, M. R. A., & Pitcairn, T. K. (1973). Attention and advertence in human groups. *Social Science Information, 12,* 27–41.

Chance, M. R. A., & Jolly, C. J. (1970). *Social groups of monkeys, apes and men.* London: Cape.

Donaldson-Evans, L. (1980). *Love's fatal glance: A study of eye imagery in the poets of the ecole lyonnaise.* University, MS: Romance Monographs.

Ellsworth, P. C., Carlsmith, J. M., & Henson, A. (1972). The stare as a stimulus to flight in human subjects: A series of field experiments. *Journal of Personality and Social Psychology, 21,* 302–311.

Exline, R. (1963). Explorations in the process of person perception: Visual interaction in relation to competition, sex and need for affiliation. *Journal of Personality, 31,* 1–20.

Exline, R., Gray, D., & Schuette, D. (1965). Visual behavior in a dyad as affected by interview content and sex of respondent. *Journal of Personality and Social Psychology, 1,* 201–209.

Exline, R., Thibaut, J., Hickey, C., & Gumpert, P. (1970). Visual interaction in relation to Machiavellianism and an unethical act. In R. Christie & F. Geis (Eds.), *Studies in Machiavellianism.* Academic Press.

Exline, R., & Winters, L. (1966). Affective relations and mutual glances in dyads. In S. S. Tomkins & C. Izard (Eds.), *Affect, cognition and personality.* Tavistock.

Fenichel, O. (1945). *The psychoanalytic theory of neurosis.* Norton.

Freese, A. S. (1977). *The miracle of vision.* Harper & Row.

Freud, S. *Standard edition of the complete psychological works.* (1953–74). The interpretation of dreams (1900) (Vol. 4). On beginning the treatment (1913) (Vol. 12). Hogarth.

Gale, A., Lucas, B., Nissim, R., & Harpham, B. (1972). Some EEG correlates of face-to-face contact. *British Journal of Social and Clinical Psychology, 11,* 326–332.

Garrison, V., & Arensberg, C. M. (1976). The evil eye: Envy or risk of seizure? Paranoia or patronal dependency? In C. Maloney (Ed.), *The evil eye.* Columbia University Press.

Gibson, J. J. (1960). Pictures, Perspective and Perception. *Daedalus, 89,* 216–217.

Goldman-Eisler, F. (1961). The distribution of pause durations in speech. *Language and Speech, 4,* 232–237.

Grumet, G. W. (1979). Telephone therapy: A review and case report. *American Journal of Orthopsychiatry, 49,* 574–584.

Gutheil, T. G. (1979). Anxiety and the eye. In Harvard Medical School, Department of Psychiatry (Ed.), *Differential Diagnosis of Anxiety.* New York: Audio Visual Medical Marketing (audiotape).

Hall, E. T. (1963). A system for the notation of proxemic behavior. *American Anthropologist, 65,* 1003–1026.

Hearings before the Select Committee on Presidential Campaign Activities of the United States Senate, Ninety-third Congress. Watergate and related activities. (1973). July 11, 12, 13, 16 and 17, 1973. Book 5. Government Printing Office.

Hess, E. H. (1975). *The tell-tale eye: How your eyes reveal hidden thoughts and emotions.* Van Nostrand Reinhold.

Hinchliffe, M. K., Lancashire, M., & Roberts, F. J. (1971). A study of eye-contact changes in depressed and recovered psychiatric patients. *British Journal of Psychiatry, 119,* 213–215.

Howells, L. T., & Becker, S. W. (1962). Seating arrangement and leadership emergence. *Journal of Abnormal and Social Psychology, 64,* 148–150.

Hutt, C., & Ounsted, C. (1966). The biological significance of gaze aversion with particular reference to the syndrome of infantile autism. *Behavioral Science, 11,* 346–356.

James, W. (1892). *Psychology.* Henry Holt.

Kaufman, L. (1974). *Sight and mind: An introduction to visual perception.* Oxford University Press.

Kendon, A. (1967). Some functions of gaze-direction in social interaction. *Acta Psychologica, 26,* 22–63.

Kleck, R. E., & Nuessle, W. (1968). Congruence between the indicative and communicative functions of eye contact in interpersonal relations. *British Journal of Social and Clinical Psychology, 7,* 241–246.

Kleinke, C. L., Buston, A. A., Meeker, F. B., & Staneski, R. A. (1973). Effects of self-attributed and other-attributed gaze on interpersonal evaluations between males and females. *Journal of Experimental Social Psychology, 9,* 154–163.

Kramer, M. Anxiety and sleep disorders. In M. Kramer (Ed.), *Anxiety: The therapeutic dilemma, #4.* Chicago: Abbott Laboratories.

Laing, R. D. (1965). *The divided self.* Penguin.

Llewellyn-Thomas, E. (1981). Can eye movements save the earth? In D. F. Fisher, R. A. Monty, & J. W. Senders (Eds.), *Eye movements: Cognition and visual perception.* Hillsdale, NJ: Erlbaum.

Lott, D. F., & Sommer, R. (1967). Seating arrangements and status. *Journal of Personality and Social Psychology, 7,* 90–95.

Luborsky, L., Blinder, B., & Mackworth, N. (1963). Eye fixation and recall of pictures as a function of GSR responsivity. *Perceptual and Motor Skills, 16,* 469–483.

Luborsky. L.. Blinder, B.. & Schimer, J. (1965). Looking, recalling and GSR as a function of defense. *Journal of Abnormal Psychology, 70,* 270–280.

MacCurdy, E. (Ed.) (1983). *The notebooks of Leonardo da Vinci* (Vol. 1). New York: Reynal and Hitchcock.

Miller, M. (1974). *The breaking of a president 1974* (Vol. 2). Los Angeles: Therapy Productions.

Miller, W. (1973). The telephone in outpatient psychotherapy. *American Journal of Psychotherapy, 27,* 15–26.

Moore, H. T., & Gilliland, A. R. (1921). The measurement of aggressiveness. *Journal of Applied Psychology, 5,* 97–118.

Newell, F. W. (1978). *Ophthalmology: Principles and concepts* (4th ed.). St. Louis: Mosby.

Nichols, K. A., & Champness, B. G. (1971). Eye gaze and the GSR. *Journal of Experimental Social Psychology, 7,* 623–626.

Reimer, M. D. The averted gaze. (1949). *Psychiatric Quarterly, 23,* 108–115.

Roberts, J. M. (1976). Belief in the evil eye in world perspective. In C. Maloney (Ed.), *The evil eye.* Columbia University Press.

Roheim, G. (1953). The evil eye. *Year Book of Psychoanalysis, 9,* 283–291.

Rubin, Z. (1970). Measurement of romantic love. *Journal of Personality and Social Psychology, 16,* 265–273.

Rutter, D. R., & G. M. Stephenson. (1972). Visual interaction in a group of schizophrenic and depressive patients. *British Journal of Social and Clinical Psychology, 11,* 57–65.

Sartre, J. (1953). *Being and nothingness.* Washington Square Press.

Schonberg, H. C. (1981, September 27). Cold war in the world of chess. *New York Times Magazine.*

Schooler, C., & Silverman, J. (1969). Perceptual styles and their correlates among schizophrenic patients. *Journal of Abnormal Psychology, 74,* 459–470.

Schooler, C., & Silverman, J. (1971). Differences between correlates of perceptual style and Petrie task performance in chronic and acute schizophrenics. *Perceptual and Motor Skills, 32,* 595–601.

Siegel, R. E. (1970). *Galen on sense perception.* S. Karger.

Soltis, J. F. (1966). *Seeing, knowing and believing: A study of the language of visual perception.* Addison-Wesley.

Steincrohn, R. (1975, October 8). Doctor says. The *Evening Bulletin* (Philadelphia).

Strachey, J. (1953). Introduction to Freud's psycho-analytic procedure. In *Standard edition of the complete psychological works of Sigmund Freud* (Vol. 7). Hogarth.

Sullivan, H. S. (1954). *The psychiatric interview.* Norton.

Tomkins, S. S. (1963). *Affect, imagery and consciousness* (Vol. 2). Springer.

Venables, P. H. (1967). The relation of two-flash and two-click thresholds to withdrawal in paranoid and non-paranoid schizophrenics. *British Journal of Social and Clinical Psychology, 6,* 60–62.

Wada, J. A. (1961). Modification of cortically induced responses in brain stem by shift of attention in monkeys. *Science, 133,* 40–42.

Williams, E. (1974). An analysis of gaze in schizophrenics. *British Journal of Social and Clinical Psychology, 13,* 1–8.

Wolff, S., & Chess, S. (1964). A behavioural study of schizophrenic children. *Acta Psychiatrica Scandinavica, 40,* 438–466.

Yarbus, A. L. (1967). *Eye movements and vision.* Plenum.

Zahn, T. P., Little, B. C., & Wender, P. H. (1978). Pupillary and heart rate reactivity in children with minimal brain dysfunction. *Journal of Abnormal Child Psychology, 6,* 135–147.

*This classic study observed smiling behavior in naturalistic
settings such as bowling alleys and hockey games. Results
showed that people are more likely to smile when in the presence of others than when alone. In addition, people appeared
to smile more often as a way of expressing friendliness and
sociability rather than as a way of expressing inner happiness.*

8

Social and Emotional Messages of Smiling

Robert E. Kraut
Robert E. Johnston

Everyday experience suggests that smiling is one of the most common nonverbal signals used in communication among humans. Despite this, and
despite more than 100 years of research on facial expressions, we still know
relatively little about smiling and its social functions. In this article we
attempt to provide evidence about the cause of smiling in social settings.

THE EMOTIONAL EXPRESSION APPROACH: SMILING AS THE EXPRESSION OF HAPPINESS

According to the emotional expression view, a smile is the major component of a facial display associated with and caused by feelings of happi-

Adapted with permission from Kraut & Johnston, Social and emotional messages of
smiling: An ethological approach. *Journal of Personality and Social Psychology, 37,*
1539–1553. Copyright © 1979 by the American Psychological Association.

ness or joy. Anything that makes a person feel good or happy should produce smiling unless the individual wants to mask or inhibit his display. Laughing is considered to be the expression of either more intense happiness (Darwin, 1872/1965) or a particular type of happiness (Ekman & Friesen, 1975). Cultural and individual differences influence smiling both by determining the interpretation of events, which affects the cause of happiness, and by shaping display rules, which determine when it is socially appropriate to smile. But such differences do not alter people's innate and universal tendency to smile when they are happy. Thus, when a smile does occur, the message is usually happiness (Ekman & Friesen, 1975), although this may be a false message if the sender is masking another emotion with a smile or if the sender is simulating happiness for some other reason.

ETHOLOGICAL STUDIES: SMILING INDICATES FRIENDLINESS

A different paradigm has of necessity been used by ethologists studying nonhuman primates. These researchers have concentrated on the causes of smiling, its consequences for the immediate interaction, and its evolutionary functions.

Many nonhuman primates have a submissive facial display, called a grimace, a grin, or a silent bared-teeth face. The display resembles the human smile, and in all species in which it occurs, it seems to have the function of deflecting hostile behavior of more dominant animals (Hooff, 1962). Hooff hypothesized that the human smile is evolutionarily related to the chimpanzee's bared-teeth displays and serves the same functions of deflecting hostility and maintaining friendly contact. On the other hand, according to Hooff, laughter evolved independently and is related to the primate "play face."

If human smiling does serve a friendliness function, one would expect smiling to occur most in fact-to-face interaction, especially where friendly intent is problematic or where social bonds are being established or renewed. The smiler's motivation may be genuine friendliness or an intent to establish friendly relations. Researchers in this ethological tradition have not been concerned with the emotions or feelings experienced by those doing the smiling.

The two approaches outlined above are not necessarily incompatible. The present article tries to compare predictions based on smiling as the expression of happiness with those based on smiling as an indication of friendliness. We asked about the motivational state of the smiler and the conditions under which smiling is produced.

Method and Results Summary

Method: Four separate naturalistic observations were used to study smiling behavior. The first two studies were conducted at bowling alleys. In Study 1, observers recorded information on the nonverbal behavior of approximately 350 bowlers. In Study 2 a smaller number of bowlers were observed from a different angle. In Study 3, a photographer took pictures of fans' faces at a hockey game. The pictures were taken immediately following important game events, such as goals scored or penalties called. The fourth and final study involved an observer recording whether or not pedestrians on a public walkway in New York smiled as they crossed the street. About half of the pedestrians were observed during pleasant weather. The other half were observed during unpleasant weather.

Results: The observations revealed that bowlers smiled often when they were socially engaged and looking at or talking to others. In contrast, bowlers smiled less after scoring a spare or strike. Similarly, bowlers rarely smiled while facing the pins or when bowling alone. However, they smiled frequently when facing their friends. Overall, bowlers appeared "happier" about their bowling success when their friends were present as compared to when they were alone. At the hockey game, fans smiled both when they were socially involved with others and after events favorable to their team occurred. Finally, pedestrians were much more likely to smile when talking to others than when alone. Pedestrians walking in pleasant weather were only slightly more likely to smile than those walking in unpleasant weather. Taken together, these results suggest that smiling is much more motivated by social interaction and the desire to appear friendly than by internal feelings of happiness.

DISCUSSION

Both the present and earlier research provide strong evidence that social involvement is a major cause of smiling, independent of the smiler's emotional state. In each of the four studies described above, smiling was strongly associated with social interaction: talking to and looking at others in Study 1, facing fellow bowlers in Study 2, orienting toward other fans in Study 3, and talking to another person in Study 4. Other researchers have also found that smiling often occurs in a social context. Almost from its first appearance, smiling is socially produced and has social consequences. Human infants, from the age of 1 to 5 months, smile most in response to the human voice and the human face (Sroufe & Waters, 1976). These smiles seem to be a major determinant of the bond between an infant and its caretaker (Fraiberg, 1977; Spitz & Wolf, 1946). Among nursery school children, smiles are likely to occur in the context of other social behaviors such as pointing, giving, receiving, and talking (Blurton-Jones, 1972). When nursery school children approach a stranger, they often smile, and they are more likely to approach when the stranger smiles and talks to them (Connolly & Smith, 1972). In addition, the smile appears to be a universal component of greetings (Eibl-Eibesfeldt, 1972; Kendon & Ferber, 1973). Even when people smile in response to humorous or other nonsocial stimuli, they smile more in the presence of other people than when they are alone (Leventhal & Mace, 1970; Mackey, 1976).

The existence of smiles in uncomfortable social settings is further evidence that smiling indicates friendliness rather than happiness in some situations. Repeated viewings of some of our bowling videotapes convinced us that some smiling was done to apologize for an especially clumsy performance or for poor bowling, such as dropping the ball before bowling or bowling a gutter ball immediately after bowling a strike. Ekman (1972) also notes that people often smile when experiencing an unpleasant emotion in the presence of others, although he interprets the smile as a mask for a socially inappropriate facial expression that the emotion would cause rather than as an appeasement display.

Through this literature review, we have tried to establish that social involvement is a major cause of smiling and that happiness does not seem to be a necessary mediator. Why do people smile in the presence of others? Drawing on comparisons of humans with other primates, Hooff (1972) argues that most human smiling is affinitive, used in the expression of sympathy, reassurance, or appeasement, that is, that the smiler's motivation is to insure the establishment and maintenance of friendly interaction. The message might be paraphrased "I am friendly" or "I would like us to be friendly for a while." This may occur when friendliness is highly probable, as when two old friends greet each other after an absence, or when friendliness is problematic, as when a client interrupts a conversation between two professionals to ask one of them a question. The smile is an evolutionarily designed signal to smooth interaction among members of a species who must cooperate in group living.

References

Blurton-Jones, N. G. (1972). Categories of child-child interaction. In N. G. Blurton-Jones (Ed.), *Ethological studies of child behavior*. Cambridge, England: Cambridge University Press.

Connolly, K., & Smith, P. K. (1972). Reactions of preschool children to a strange observer. In N. G. Blurton-Jones (Ed.), *Ethological studies of child behavior*. Cambridge, England: Cambridge University Press.

Darwin, C. (1965). *The expression of the emotions in man and animals*. Chicago: University of Chicago Press. (Originally published, 1872.)

Eibl-Eibesfeldt, I. (1973). The expressive behavior of the deaf- and blind-born. In M. Von Cranach & I. Vine (Eds.), *Social communication and movement.* New York: Academic Press.

Ekman, P. (1972). Universal and cultural differences in facial expressions of emotions. In J. K. Cole (Ed.), *Nebraska symposium on motivation* (Vol. 19). Lincoln: University of Nebraska Press.

Ekman, P., & Friesen, W. V. (1975). *Unmasking the face.* Englewood Cliffs, NJ: Prentice-Hall.

Fraiberg, S. (1977). *Insights from the blind.* New York: Basic Books.

Hooff, J. A. R. A. M. van. (1962). Facial expressions in higher primates. *Symposia of the Zoological Society of London, 8,* 97–125.

Hooff, J. A. R. A. M. van. (1972). A comparative approach to the phylogeny of laughter and smiling. In R. A. Hinde (Ed.), *Non-verbal communication.* Cambridge, England: Cambridge University Press.

Kendon, A., & Ferber, A. (1973). A description of some human greetings. In R. P. Michael & J. H. Crook (Eds.), *Comparative ecology and behavior of primates.* New York: Academic Press.

Leventhal, H., & Mace, W. (1970). The effects of laughter on evaluation of a slapstick movie. *Journal of Personality, 38,* 16–30.

Mackey, W. C. (1976). Parameters of the smile as a social signal. *Journal of Genetic Psychology, 129,* 125–130.

Spitz, R. A., & Wolf, K. (1946). The smiling response: A contribution to the ontogenesis of social relations. *Genetic Psychology Monographs, 34,* 57–125.

Sroufe, L. A., & Waters, E. (1976). The ontogenesis of smiling and laughter: A perspective on the organization of development in infancy. *Psychological Review, 83,* 173–189.

This article discusses research findings related to sex differences in smiling. The research suggests that when men are around other men and they see something cute, such as a baby or a puppy, they inhibit smiling. However, when they are alone or with women, they feel free to smile. This research shows that the presence of other people affects when and if men smile.

9

Who Can Resist Smiling at a Baby?

Dick Pothier

Who could resist smiling at cute babies and puppies? Most men, apparently, if there is another man around. A majority of male subjects in a Haverford College research project apparently thought that smiling at a baby or a puppy somehow made them less masculine.

The research, carried out by two Haverford College students under the guidance of psychology professor Sidney Perloe, found that male students smiled much less often and less noticeably at babies and puppies presented in a videotape if there was another man—an experimenter—present in the viewing room. But if there were no other men present, most male subjects smiled "to beat the band," Perloe said.

Reprinted with permission from the *Philadelphia Inquirer* (August 1992).

WOMEN SMILE REGARDLESS

Women tested under the same conditions and with the same video-tape of cute babies or puppies smiled a lot regardless of whether a male experimenter was around during the test, Perloe said.

"We think there are certain cultural rules among men that inhibit some emotional responses in men," Perloe said, "especially a response of tenderness or affection." This may all sound theoretical and academic, but I think there is some practical significance to this finding.

"For one thing, it seems to indicate that you can change the behavior of males in all-male groups—which is often boorish, crude and insensitive—by adding the presence of a woman."

In addition, Perloe said, the human smile is the evolutionary result of facial actions among non-human primates, such as apes and monkeys, "and as such, study of smiles is an important part of studying evolutionary behavior."

"Besides, I just think it's good for people to know about this kind of thing," he said. "if, for cultural and social reasons, many males are showing an inability to express tenderness toward a baby in the presence of another male, it's just useful to know about."

The finding does not include male parents, who probably are as affectionate as they can be toward their children, he said.

SENIOR RESEARCH PROJECT

Perloe, who presented the smile-research project at a meeting of the International Primatological Association in Atlanta a few weeks ago, said that two Haverford students who have since graduated—Gregg Solomon and Samuel Blumberg—designed the experiment as their senior research project.

The concept of "toughness" or "masculinity" or "macho" behavior is almost entirely something that concerns men only in relation to other men, not in relation to women, Perloe said, which is why the presence of a female experimenter did not lead to the suppression of smiles. Indeed, nearly all the male subjects—all students at Haverford—smiled more broadly and more often when there was a female experimenter in the room.

During the experiments, while the test subjects—20 males and 20 females—watched a 12-minute videotape of babies and puppies, an unseen camera recorded their facial expressions, Perloe said.

Then a second group of 50 volunteers was shown films of the first group and was asked to guess what kind of response the test subjects were showing. The second group, which did not know the purpose of the test, found that some men smiled a lot and other men not much at all.

Later the experimenters compared the findings and found that men who were in the presence of another man suppressed their smiles far more often than men who knew they were alone.

JUDGING DEGREE OF SMILING

The experimenters also measured the smiles of both groups using a research method called the "facial action scoring system," a method of judging and scoring the degree of smiling and its frequency.

"Smiles are really a very basic kind of signal," Perloe said. "In fact, most parents report that the first time their baby smiled at them was an ecstatic moment, and we believe smiles are the most communicative facial expression there is."

Forbes and Jackson investigated kinesic behavior in the context of employment interviews. They found that interviewees who were offered positions tended to use more direct eye contact, smiling, and head nodding and shaking than did those who were not offered positions. This study demonstrates that nonverbal communication plays an important role in employment interviews.

10

Nonverbal Behavior and the Outcome of Selection Interviews

Ray J. Forbes
Paul R. Jackson

The interview is widely used in making decisions on selection, placement and appraisal (Antsey, Fletcher, & Walker, 1976; Randell, 1978), despite its well-known predictive deficiencies. Acceptance by researchers of the ubiquity of the interview in selection procedures has led to a large body of research aimed not at establishing the degree of reliability and validity of the interview, but rather at "understanding the mechanism of the interview and improving interview technology" (Carlson, Thayer, Mayfield, & Peterson, 1971, p. 268). Since the pioneering work reported by Webster (1964) and the Life Insurance Agency Management Association program of

Adapted from Forbes & Jackson, Nonverbal behavior and the outcome of selection interviews. *Journal of Occupational Psychology, 53,* 67–72. Used with permission from *British Journal of Medical Psychology,* © 1980 The British Psychological Society.

research led by Carlson and Mayfield, several important strands of research have emerged which contribute toward an understanding of the interview process.

One such strand of research is concerned with the role of nonverbal behavior (NVB) in interviews. Keenan and Wedderburn (1975) and Keenan (1976) have found that an interviewer's communication style (operationalized in terms of head nods, smiling and eye contact) affects both the perception of the interviewer and the performance of the candidate. Similarly, a number of studies (Barber & Keil, 1973; Washburn & Hakel, 1973; Hopper & Williams, 1973; Hopper, 1977; Young & Beier, 1977) have reported that a candidate's nonverbal style significantly affects judgments made by observers; though Sterrett (1978) failed to find such effects.

While the importance of NVB in interviews seems clear cut, there is a major problem with all the studies just cited; not one of them was concerned with judgments made in real-life interviews. Each study used carefully constructed video recordings, and their findings are based on judgments made by observers. The present study examines the impact of NVB on the judgments made by participants in the interview itself—the members of the interview panel. Its purpose is to relate the nonverbal behavior of candidates in selection interviews to the decisions made in those interviews. Before discussing the details of the study, however, it is important to review briefly the considerable body of research on nonverbal communication.

Argyle (1972) suggested that NVB serves several important functions in social interaction. The first is in communicating interpersonal attitudes and emotions. Nonverbal signals are used to establish and maintain relationships by reflecting, for example, dominance or status differences and affiliation or aggression. In a series of experiments, Argyle, Salter, Williams, and Burgess (1970) found that nonverbal signals were given greater weight than the verbal content of statements, and that verbal content was discounted when it conflicted with messages from nonverbal sources. Warr and Jackson (1977) suggested that such discounting may be a function of a general dimension of salience of information from whatever source, but the pre-eminence of nonverbal signals seems certain in many circumstances. Argyle (1972) concludes that "in human social behavior, it looks as if the nonverbal channel is used for negotiating interpersonal attitudes, while the verbal channel is used primarily for conveying information" (p. 49).

The second function of NVB is in supporting and maintaining conversation; as Abercrombie (1968) says, "we speak with our vocal organs, but we converse with our whole bodies." Opening and closing of conversations, turn-taking and interruptions are all negotiated at least partly by nonverbal or paraverbal means. A growing body of research is now concerned with the minutiae of such conversation management; at the level of head nods, shifts of gaze, hand movements, body position, and so on.

Body position. The body position that an individual adopts can communicate important social signals about friendly, hostile, superior and inferior attitudes (Mehrabian, 1969). Ekman (1969) has shown that an individual's body position varies with, and to some extent displays, his or her emotional state.

Head nodding and shaking. These are rather special kinds of gestures and have two distinctive roles. They act as "reinforcers," rewarding and encouraging what has gone before; and they play an important role in the controlling and synchronizing of speech: a nod gives the other permission to carry on talking, whereas a rapid succession of nods indicates that the nodder wants to speak himself.

Facial expression. Facial expression is used to communicate interpersonal attitudes and emotions, and often in close combination with speech. "A speaker accompanies his utterances with the appropriate facial expressions, which are used to modify or frame what is being said, showing whether it is supposed to be funny, serious, important etc." (Vine, 1971).

Eye contact. This is probably the most researched area of nonverbal communication, and also probably the most complex. Participants in a conversation look at each other for between 25 and 75 percent of the time, and such eye gaze serves several functions. Argyle and Dean (1965) postulated that looking is a signal of intimacy, and found that people look more when another person is more distant, suggesting that looking and proximity can substitute for each other as signals for intimacy. Looking is also closely coordinated with aspects of verbal communication: to obtain information about the other, to gain feedback on the other's responses while talking and to provide extra information about what is being said while listening.

Gestures. Argyle (1969) has suggested, "A gesture is a movement of the hands, feet or other parts of the body. Some are intended to communicate definite messages: others are involuntary social cues which may or may not be correctly interpreted by others." Body gestures may be communicating an emotional state: for example, fist clenching (aggression), face touching (anxiety), scratching (self-blame) and forehead wiping (tiredness). They form part of the total communication process.

Method and Results Summary

Method: The researchers used observational methods from real selection interviews. The interviews were conducted at the Apprenticeship Training Center of the Engineering Industry Training Board in Great Britain. There were 101 interviewees for approximately 50 apprenticeships. All of the interviewees were between 15 and 17 years old. Interviews were conducted by a panel. Similar questions were asked across all the interviews, which lasted from 15 to 18 minutes. One of the authors observed these interviews and made observations on a detailed coding sheet. Later, the authors found out which candidates were accepted outright ($n = 43$), which were put on a reserve list ($n = 37$), and which were rejected outright ($n = 21$).

Results: The authors then used statistical analyses to see if there were differences in the nonverbal behaviors observed for the three groups (accept, reserve, and reject). Results showed that there were no differences for body position. However, there were differences for eye, face, and head behavior. These differences showed that:

- Interviewees who were accepted used more direct eye contact and less gaze avoidance than did those who were rejected. Interviewees who were placed on the reserve list fell in between the accept and reject groups on eye contact and gaze avoidance.

- Interviewees who were accepted showed less "wandering" of the eyes than did those who were rejected or put on the reserve list.

- Interviewees who were accepted used more smiling and less neutral facial expressions than did those who were rejected or put on the reserve list.

- Interviewees who were accepted showed more head nodding and shaking than did those who were rejected. Those who were put on the reserve list showed more head nodding and shaking than those in the reject group, but less than those in the accept group.

The accept and reject groups are compared in the table on page 86. The behaviors listed under the "general interview situation" represent those nonverbal behaviors that most interviewees engaged in whether or not they were accepted, rejected, or placed on the reserve list.

DISCUSSION

There are substantial differences between the three groups for three of the four classes of behavior. Taking eye contact first of all, direct eye contact occurs more often in the accept interviews, avoidance gaze occurs more often in the reject interviews, and eye wandering occurs less in accept interviews than in the other two groups of interviews. For facial expression, smiling is associated with accept decisions, and a neutral facial expression is associated equally with the reserve and reject groups and occurs less often in the accept group. Head movement also differentiates between the three types of interview outcome. Shaking or nodding occurs much more often in the accept interview while head static occurs less often in these interviews. Finally, no differences between the groups were found for the body position class of behavior. Leaning forward occurred equally often in the three groups, contrary to prediction.

The typical candidate in these interviews displays an upright position with little body or leg movement. The candidate's legs are uncrossed and he or she sits with hands together on his or her lap. Such behavior, or rather lack of it, suggests that the candidate felt rather ill at ease and accepted the formal nature of the setting. There is some evidence (e.g., Anstey, Fletcher, & Walker, 1976), that panel interviews tend to be rather more formal than two-person interviews, though there is nothing in the findings of the present study to suggest that the candidate's performance was adversely affected by the structure of the situation.

The accept interview is characterized by more direct eye contact, more smiling and more shaking and nodding. Such behaviors show interest in the interviewers and act as positive reinforcers. In contrast, the reject interviews are characterized by more avoidance gaze and eye wandering, more neutral facial expression and less smiling, and by head static. Such behaviors may be seen by the interviewers as indicating lack of interest and enthusiasm on the part of the candidate.

Elements of Nonverbal Behavior Associated with the Interview Situation and with Acceptance and Rejection at Interview

NVB in the accept interview	NVB in the general interview situation	NVB in the reject interview
More eye contact	Upright posture	More avoidance gaze and eye wandering
More smiling	Body still	
More head shaking and nodding	Legs still and uncrossed	More neutral expression and less smiling
	Arms in front, hands together	Head still and less head nodding

While the results are straightforward, their interpretation is more problematic. One explanation is that the candidate's NVB is itself the cue which the interview panel uses to form its judgments. Pre-screening of candidates using tests may well produce a sample at interview who vary relatively little on variables such as aptitude and intelligence, which are likely to be important predictors of success in training. In this context, nonverbal behavior may maintain the range that existed before screening and thus become *more* salient as a means of distinguishing among members of an otherwise homogeneous group. This may particularly affect the interviewers' decisions as the candidates' examination results were not available at the time of interview.

There is, however, another explanation of the results of this study which is more complex. If, as Webster (1964) has suggested, interviewers tend to make their selection decisions soon after the start of the interview, then they may give positive reinforcement to those candidates whom they have decided to accept and negative reinforcement to those whom they have decided to reject. The candidate may respond to this reinforcement with just those NVBs described above. This interpretation does not necessarily conflict with the first since the cues for the initial decision may be nonverbal. These two compatible explanations are supplied by a large body of work showing that behavior of participants in conversations is mutually contingent, each person responding to the other with a behavioral echo effect.

What is needed is research which explores a number of aspects of the problem. We expect candidates, and also interviewers, to have coherent styles of NVB, that is, consistent preferences for particular configurations of nonverbal cues, and work is needed to isolate these styles and to relate them to the interview situation. Research also needs to consider the style of the interviewer(s) and the sequential patterning of behaviors of both candidate and interviewer through the interview.

For the practitioner, NVB offers a rich source of information about a candidate and his or her response to the interview. It seems likely that interviewers' decisions are made at least partly on the basis of NVB whether they are aware of it or not, and attention should be paid to these channels of communication since it is not clear that social adeptness at interview is a good predictor of subsequent job success.

In conclusion, the present study is important in two respects: it shows that NVB may be a critical factor in an important social situation; and it extends the findings of previous simulated laboratory studies to real-life settings.

References

Abercrombie, K. (1968). Paralanguage. *British Journal of Disorders of Communication, 3*, 55–59.

Anstey, E., Fletcher, C., & Walker, J. (1976). *Staff appraisal and development.* London: Allen & Unwin.

Argyle, M., & Dean, J. (1965). Eye contact, distance and affiliation. *Sociometry, 28,* 289–304.

Argyle, M. (1969). *Social interaction.* London: Methuen.

Argyle, M. (1972). Non-verbal communication in human social interaction. In R. Hinde (Ed.), *Nonverbal communication.* Cambridge: Cambridge University Press.

Argyle, M., Salter, V., Williams, M., & Burgess, P. (1970). The communication of inferior and superior attitudes by verbal and non-verbal signals. *British Journal of Social and Clinical Psychology, 9,* 222–231.

Barber, J. F., & Keil, E. C. (1973). Experimental techniques of job interview training for the disadvantaged: Videotape feedback behavior modification and microcounselling. *Journal of Applied Psychology, 58,* 209–213.

Carlson, R. E., Thayer, P. W., Mayfield, E. C., & Pearson, D. A. (1971, April). Improvements in the selection interview. *Personnel Journal,* 286–275, 317.

Ekman, D. (1969). Non-verbal leakage and clues to deception. *Psychiatry, 32,* 88–106.

Forbes, R. J. (1978). The effects of a candidate's non-verbal behavior on interview decisions. MA thesis, University of Sheffield.

Hopper, R. (1977). Language attitudes in the employment interview. *Communication Monographs, 44,* 346–351.

Hopper, R., & Williams, F. (1973). Speech characteristics and employability. *Speech Monographs, 40,* 296–302.

Keenan, A. (1976). Effects of the non-verbal behavior of interviewers on candidates' performance. *Journal of Occupational Psychology, 49,* 171–176.

Keenan, A., & Wedderburn, A. A. (1975). Effects of the non-verbal behavior of interviewers on candidates' impressions. *Journal of Occupational Psychology, 48,* 129–132.

Mehrabian, A. (1969). Significance of posture and position in the communication of attitude and status relationships. *Psychological Bulletin, 71,* 359–372.

Randell, G. (1978). Interviewing at work. In P. B. Warr (Ed.), *Psychology at work* (2nd ed.). Harmondsworth, Middx: Penguin.

Sterrett, J. H. (1978). The job interview: Body language and perceptions of potential effectiveness. *Journal of Applied Psychology, 63,* 389–390.

Vine, I. (1971). Communication by facial-visual signals. In J. H. Crook (Ed.), *Social behavior in animals and man.* New York: Academic Press.

Warr, P. B., & Jackson, P. R. (1977). Salience, importance and evaluation in judgments about people. *British Journal of Social and Clinical Psychology, 16,* 35–45.

Washburn, P. V., & Hakel, M. B. (1973). Visual cues and verbal content as influence on impressions formed after simulated employment interviews. *Journal of Applied Psychology, 58,* 137–141.

Webster, E. C. (1964). *Decision making in the employment interview*. Industrial Relations Center, McGill University.

Young, D. M., & Beier, E. G. (1977). The role of applicant non-verbal communication in the employment interview. *Journal of Employment Counselling, 14,* 154–165.

—Section B—

APPEARANCE AND ADORNMENT CUES

The way you look and smell has both subtle and powerful effects on the way others perceive you and even the way you perceive yourself. Physical appearance has received considerable scholarly attention, with pioneering work on the "body stereotypes" and the "halo effect" leading the way. Smell, or *olfactics*, has received less scholarly attention, but new research in the areas of pheromones (or hormonal odors) and perfume shows that the way you smell may help determine how attractive you are to others.

Classic work on body stereotypes and the halo effect show that people are quick to size others up based on their appearances. Research on body stereotypes has shown that people perceive thin, tall people differently than short, round people, or more muscular individuals. For example, people who are tall and thin are often perceived as nervous and intelligent, people who are short and round as friendly and lazy, and people who are muscular as energetic and ambitious. Of course, people come in all shapes and sizes, and specific body types, like stereotypes, often don't really fit. One contemporary issue related to body stereotypes is how media images of thin, glamorous models affect women's perceptions of themselves. This issue is discussed in the first reading in this section.

The other line of classic or traditional research on physical appearance deals with the "halo effect," which is also called the "what is beautiful is good" hypothesis. This line of research has shown that both adults and young children automatically assume that those who are beautiful have more positive attributes (such as being friendlier, more intelligent, healthier, and so forth) than do those who are less beautiful. Part of this may be due to a self-fulfilling prophecy. If beautiful people are treated better than their less attractive counterparts, they may develop more confidence and social skill. For women, however, beauty can sometimes be like the proverbial two-edged sword. Beautiful women are sometimes put on too high of a pedestal, making it hard for them to meet the expectations of others. In addition, when women executives are too "cute" or glamorous, they may not be taken seriously in the workplace. The reading by Kaiser highlights some of the advantages and disadvantages of beauty for women in the workplace.

The focus on women in the first two readings in this section reflects the state of research on body stereotypes and physical appearance. Like it or not, women still tend to be judged more on the basis of physical appearance than men. This is not to say that appearance is not important for men. In fact, it would be a mistake to think that factors such as facial hair, a good-looking face, and height don't influence how people view men. It is just that this influence is even stronger for women. The first two readings in this section reflect this sex difference.

Similarly, clothing norms are less rigid for women than for men, making it harder for women in the workplace to know how to dress. In business settings, a basic suit or shirt and tie in blue or neutral colors, which is moderately conservative, is the typical, appropriate attire for men. For women, however, there is not really a "typical" type of business attire. Women who want to look professional and still look feminine have myriad fashion choices at their disposal, with some of these choices wiser than others. Kaiser touches on this issue in her article on women's appearance in the workplace.

Another issue related to clothing is the messages that uniforms convey. Uniforms can call attention to someone or, paradoxically, make them inconspicuous. The uniform can also be a source of power. Think of all the people you encounter in uniforms—police officers, mail carriers, soldiers, nurses, surgeons, and athletes, just to name a few. Can you imagine how they would look doing their jobs without uniforms? Color is also an important aspect of clothing and, particularly, uniforms. What would nurses look like in orange uniforms? How would you like to see your neighborhood police officer in a yellow or pink uniform? As the article by Frank and Gilovich suggests, color is also an important part of professional sports uniforms, with teams in black often seen as more aggressive than teams in lighter colors.

As you can see, there has been a lot of research on how people look. The research on smell is less abundant. Yet just as people adorn themselves with clothing and jewelry, they also anoint themselves with perfume and deodorant. Just as people have physical appearance features such as certain body shapes, people also emit subtle hormonal odors. The final two readings in this section address these issues by examining two specific olfactic cues, pheromones and perfume. These readings show that olfactic cues have subtle, yet important effects on attraction and liking.

This article reviews research showing that television, magazines, and other media send young women the message that "thin is in" and that beauty and a thin physique go hand in hand. The authors provide startling statistics showing that thin women dominate the media and that many women, perhaps as a result of these media messages, overestimate how heavy they look. The authors also link media portrayals of the "ideal body image" to health problems such as bulimia and anorexia nervosa.

11

The Effect of Television Advertising and Programming on Body Image Distortions in Young Women

Philip N. Myers, Jr.
Frank A. Biocca

What is the average young woman's perception of her body? When the average young woman looks in the mirror, she sees a fat person. In a society where the ideal body is becoming thinner, women in general have been

Adapted with permission from Myers & Biocca (1992), The elastic body image: The effect of television advertising and programming on body image distortions in young women. *Journal of Communication, 42,* 108–118.

found to overestimate the size of their bodies (Birtchnell, Dolan, & Lacey, 1987; Casper, Halmi, Goldberg, Eckert, & Davis, 1979; Garner, Garfinkel, Stancer, & Moldofsky, 1976; Halmi, Goldberg, & Cunningham, 1977). Women with eating disorders, anorexia nervosa, and bulimia, have been found to make even greater overestimations (Cash & Green, 1986; Slade & Russell, 1973; Touyz, Beumont, Collins, & Cowie, 1985; Wilmuth, Leitenberg, Rosen, Fondacaro, & Gross, 1985).

Do media portrayals of the body contribute to this body size distortion? Content analysis studies reveal that the media portray a steadily thinning ideal body image for women (Garner, Garfinkel, Schwartz & Thompson, 1980; Silverstein, Perdue, Peterson, & Kelly, 1986). This image is represented by models whose curvaceousness fluctuates but whose weights are consistently below average. A thinner ideal body is also being promoted by weight and height standards used primarily by insurance companies (Ritenbaugh, 1982).

From these media and cultural messages emerge positive stereotypes of beauty, success, and health (Downs & Harrison, 1985; Garner & Garfinkel, 1980; Kaufman, 1980) and an image of being in control (Joseph, 1982). These have become synonymous with the socially ideal body. At the same time, negative stereotypes of poor health and a lack of control have become associated with obesity (Ritenbaugh, 1982). Together, these positive and negative stereotypes play a role in the social formation of the ideal body. This ideal body is internalized by young women and becomes a goal in a program to transform their body shape to match their internalized ideal body (Banner, 1986; Spitzack, 1990).

THIN IS IN

The mass media's portrayal of the thin, ideal female body is well documented. Advertisers explicitly target the body image of women in the marketing of food and exercise products (e.g., Lautman, 1991). The effects of this practice are just beginning to be explored (e.g., Kaltenbach, 1991).

Silverstein et al. (1986) examined the body representations and the preoccupation with thinness in various media: (a) television shows and their characters; (b) magazine advertisements and articles dealing with body shape and size, dieting, food and drink, or cooking; (c) photographs of women in two women's magazines; and (d) photographs of female movie stars. In the 33 television shows studied, 69.1% of the female characters were rated as thin while only 17.5% of the male characters were so rated. Only 5% of the female characters were rated as heavy, compared to 25.5% of the males.

In their study of four women's and four men's magazines, the total number of ads for diet foods was 63 for women's and only 1 for men's. For the total number of articles on nonfood, figure-enhancing products, the total in the women's magazine was 96 while the men's total was 10.

The final two studies examined photographs from *Ladies' Home Journal* and *Vogue* between 1901 and 1981, and photographs of movie stars between 1932 and 1978. In both studies bust-to-waist ratios were calculated. In both the magazine and movie star photographs, the bust-to-waist ratios decreased through the years, most significantly since the 1930s. Silverstein et al. conclude that:

> ... present day women who look at the major mass media are exposed to a standard of bodily attractiveness that is slimmer than that presented for men and that is less curvaceous than that presented for women since the 1930s. This standard may not be promoted only in the media and it may not even originate in the media, but given the popularity of television, movies and magazines ... the media are likely to be among the most influential promoters of such thin standards. (p. 531)

In another study, Garner et al. (1980) examined the ideal feminine image as presented by *Playboy Magazine* and the Miss America Pageant from 1959 to 1978. The mean weights of women in these groups were significantly less than the mean weights of the general public (comparison made with the 1959 Society of Actuaries tables, controlling for age and height). In addition, during the 20-year period mean weights for centerfolds and contestants declined, while mean weights for the general population actually increased by several pounds. Furthermore, since 1970, pageant winners weighed significantly less than the other pageant contestants.

Kaufman (1980) found yet another interesting twist to the ideal body image as represented in television commercials and programming. Analyzing 600 minutes of videotape, Kaufman's study rated 48% of the 537 characters viewed as thin or average. Fifteen percent of the men were found to be overweight, as compared to 8% of the women. Teenagers were never depicted as obese, and only 7% were found to be overweight. Of the 537 persons rated, 509 (95%) were presented in situations involving food. Characters were shown with food, eating food, or talking about food. Kaufman points out that the characters "rarely ate a balanced meal, gave full attention to what they ate, or ate explicitly to satisfy hunger" (p. 44). According to Kaufman, "Television presents viewers with two sets of conflicting messages. One suggests that we eat in ways almost guaranteed to make us fat; the other suggests that we strive to remain slim" (p. 45). Not only are viewers presented with an unrealistically thin body image, they are often presented with one that remains thin despite frequent snacking and unbalanced meals.

Examining 4,294 network television commercials, Downs and Harrison (1985) made several findings involving the frequency of "attractiveness-based messages." On the average, 1 out of every 3.8 commercials involved some form of an attractiveness-based message. Based on this frequency and average viewing habits, Downs and Harrison estimate that children and adult viewers are exposed to some 5,260 attractiveness messages per year (an average of 14 messages per day). Of these, 1,850 messages deal directly with beauty. While it was found that food and drink commercials had the greatest share of body and weight messages, Downs and Harrison point out that "attractiveness stereotypes have permeated virtually the entire television advertising market, making television commercials powerful sources of attractiveness stereotypes" (p. 17).

There may be some cumulative effect of all these messages. It is reasonable to imagine that each of these body image messages is just one strike on a chisel sculpting the ideal body inside a young woman's mind.

Television and other media are not the only source of representations of the ideal body. Institutions have canonized the ideal body. According to Ritenbaugh (1982), insurance companies' ideal weight standards for women show a steady downward trend. Comparing revisions of these weight tables, Ritenbaugh found that ideal weights for women have steadily declined while weight standards for men have fluctuated.

The ideal body is also associated with the good life. Revealing findings on weight averages have been detailed in a report by Fulwood, Abraham, and Johnson (1981) from a National Health and Nutrition Examination Survey. In their study, associations were made between height and weight, and socioeconomic and geographic variables. On the average, the heaviest females (ages 18–74) were those with an income less than $4,000 and less than 9 years of education. When the years of education increased to 13 or more, females averaged 10 fewer pounds. The heaviest males (ages 18–74) had an income of $10,000 or more and 12 or more years of education. As income and education levels increased, both males and females were found to be taller. In summary, males in higher social classes with more education are taller and heavier. Women with the same background are taller and lighter. According to Ritenbaugh, changes in weight standards have reflected what is happening in the higher social classes rather than an average across all social classes (p. 357).

We have discussed the media messages that advertise the positive attributes of an ideal body image that is thinner than the average woman. We also have seen how the sociocultural message advocates the health aspects of weight control, and at the same time develops height and weight standards that steadily decline, a decline that automatically increases the number of people who could be classified as overweight. Given the swirl of social influences, it is not surprising that the message "strive to be thin" is also circulated through interpersonal communication channels via parents, lovers, and the "gaze" of others (Spitzack, 1990).

But more importantly we have yet to consider what may be happening to the audience that lives with these messages of the ideal body image. What are the possible psychological and behavioral effects of these messages?

Struggling to Attain the Ideal Body

The personal effects of the thinning of the ideal body image may be illustrated by the high levels of dieting among women (Garner & Garfinkel, 1980). According to a Nielsen survey in 1978, 45% of all U.S. households had somebody dieting that year. Of all the women aged 24 to 54, 56% were dieting. Of this group, 76% said that they did so for cosmetic rather than health reasons (Schwartz, Thompson, & Johnson, 1982).

Studies show that dieting for aesthetic reasons also occurs early in adolescence. In a study of approximately 1,000 students (one entire grade level of a public high school), Huenemann, Shapiro, Hampton, and Mitchell (1966) conducted a longitudinal analysis of the student "body" as it graduated from the 9th to the 12th grades. Both boys and girls were found to be dissatisfied with their bodies. Fifty percent of the girls described themselves as being fat, while objectively only 25% could be classified as obese or somewhat obese. The number of girls describing themselves as fat increased as the girls became older. In contrast, the same percentage of boys described themselves as too thin.

Another study conducted a year later by Dwyer, Feldman, and Mayer (1967) had similar results. Four hundred and forty-six female senior high school students were interviewed, and tricep skinfold measurements were taken to determine their body fat levels. Thirty-seven percent of the girls reported that they were on a diet on the day of their interview, while 61.4% reported they had dieted some time in their lives. Only 15% of the girls were found to be obese. When asked what was their most important reason for dieting, 43% were concerned with beauty and good looks. Dwyer and colleagues concluded, "Many girls who do not need to reduce for health reasons wish to reduce for purposes of appearance and are trying to do so" (p. 1055). It is important to note that the studies by Huenemann et al. (1966) and Dwyer et al. (1967) are more than 20 years old, long before the widespread introduction and use of diet soft drinks and diet foods like Lean Cuisine.

The research indicates that both media messages and the target audience of younger females place a high value on physical attractiveness.

Studying 342 college students (124 males and 218 females), Lerner, Orlos, and Knapp (1976) found that "the females' self-concepts appeared more strongly related to their attitudes about their bodies' physical attractiveness than its effectiveness" (p. 324). For females there were more body parts involved in the attractiveness/self-concept relationship than for the males' attractiveness/self-concept or females' effectiveness/self-concept relationships. Once again we can see the emphasis that young females place on physical attributes, and we see these physical attributes playing an important role in the females' self-evaluations. If media content both reflects and contributes to the apparent pursuit of the ideal body by a large segment of the female population, it suggests that for some this pursuit may become obsessive. Eating disorders, anorexia nervosa and bulimia, often result from a "relentless pursuit of thinness" (Bruch, 1978, p. ix). According to Garfinkel and Garner (1982), weight loss becomes a sign of mastery, control, and virtue:

> Pressures on women to be thin and to achieve, and also conflicting role expectations which force women to be paradoxically competitive, yet passive, may partially explain why anorexia nervosa has increased so dramatically. Patients with anorexia nervosa respond to these pressures by equating weight control with self-control and this in turn is equated with beauty and "success." (p. 10)

Bruch (1974) says that "the feeling of all pervasive ineffectiveness is one of the root problems in the development of anorexia nervosa" (p. 1421). With anorexia, weight loss is an attempt to gain self-control and identity. Success or failure at weight control becomes a symbol of the ability to control life in general (Collett, 1984).

Medical records from more than a century ago show that successful weight loss brought a great deal of self-esteem and satisfaction to patients (Casper, 1983). Weight loss, in an attempt to achieve the ideal body image, is more than inches and pounds to the woman with an eating disorder—it becomes a way of life. Starvation, binge eating, and purging become intensely emotional experiences. As the illness progresses and weight continues to decrease, "anorexics become convinced that they are special and different, that being so thin makes them worthwhile, significant, extraordinary, eccentric, or outstanding; each one has a private word to describe the states of superiority she strives for" (Bruch, 1978, p. 79). Levenkron (1982) explains that for the anorexic, all the fears and concerns of life are reduced and equated with her body weight. Success with the external pressures and internal fears of everyday life is measured in inches and pounds. A hardworking perfectionist and overachiever, the anorexic or bulimic works relentlessly toward a thinner body that promises beauty, success, and happiness. The harder she works to lose weight, the farther she gets from the promise. The obsession with the pursuit of a thinner and thinner ideal body sometimes leads to death.

Because anorexics are often thin by all objective standards, their continued pursuit of a thinner ideal body suggests a distorted image of their present body. For an anorexic, body size distortion is immediately evident (Wilmuth et al., 1985). Despite her emaciated figure she will comment on how heavy she is and insist on a need to still lose more weight:

> Fears that others will become skinnier than she is become a paranoid
> focus for the anorexic. She continually compares her body with the
> bodies of other girls and women and sees herself, delusionally, as
> heavier. (Levenkron, 1982, p. 5)

This type of external/internal conflict has become known as body image or *body size disturbance*. The cause of this condition, just like the definitive cause of eating disorders themselves, is still unknown. It is believed that sociocultural pressures and influences, early interpersonal family relations, and the socialization of women are some of the possible catalysts for eating disorders (Boskind-White & White, 1983; Schwartz et al., 1982).

However, it is not only anorexics and bulimics who overestimate their body sizes. Normal non-eating-disordered women also tend to overestimate their body size (Birtchnell et al., 1987; Casper et al., 1979; Garner et al., 1976; Halmi et al., 1977; Thompson, 1986). Thompson (1986) found that more than 95% of the non-eating-disordered women he studied ($n = 100+$) overestimated their body size on the average by 25%. Two out of five women overestimated at least one of their four body parts (cheeks, waist, hips, thighs) by at least 50%.

SUMMARY

Our review of literature suggests that individuals internalize a social model of the ideal body image, based at least partially on cultural representations of ideals of physical beauty. In our culture the ideal may be represented most forcefully in the mass media. But it is also influenced by each individual's interactions with immediate peers, family, and social reference groups. The review above clearly demonstrated that as far as attractiveness-based advertising and programming is concerned, this socially represented ideal body is increasingly thin, much thinner than the average objective body shape of the population.

References

Banner, L. (1986). *American beauty*. Chicago: University of Chicago Press.

Birtchnell, S. A., Dolan, B. M., & Lacey, J. H. (1987). Body image distortion in non-eating disordered women. *International Journal of Eating Disorders, 6*(3), 385–391.

Boskind-White, M., & White, W. (1983). *Bulimarexia: The binge/purge cycle*. New York: W. W. Norton & Company.

Bruch, H. (1978). *The golden cage*. Cambridge, MA: Harvard University Press.

Cash, T. F., & Green, G. K. (1986). Body weight and body image among college women: perception, cognition, and affect. *Journal of Personality Assessment, 50*(2), 290–301.

Casper, R. C. (1983). On the emergence of bulimia nervosa as a syndrome. *International Journal of Eating Disorders, 2*(3), 3–16.

Casper, R. C., Halmi, K. A., Goldberg, S. C., Eckert, E. D., & Davis, J. M. (1979). Disturbances in body image estimation as related to other characteristics and outcome in anorexia nervosa. *British Journal of Psychiatry, 134*, 60–66.

Collett, B. (1984). Diagnoses applied to women: the evidence, example: Anorexia nervosa. *Women & Therapy, 3*(2), 79–86.

Downs, A. C., & Harrison, S. K. (1985). Embarrassing age spots or just plain ugly? Physical attractiveness stereotyping as an instrument of sexism on American television commercials. *Sex Roles, 13*(1/2), 9–19.

Dwyer, J. T., Feldman, J. J., & Mayer, J. (1967). Adolescent dieters: Who are they? *The American Journal of Clinical Nutrition, 20*(10), 1045–1056.

Fulwood, R., Abraham, S., & Johnson, C. (1981). *Height and weight of adults ages 18–74 years by socioeconomic and geographic variables*. (DHHS Publication No. 81–1674). Washington, DC: U.S. Government Printing Office.

Garfinkel, P. E., & Garner, D. M. (1982). *Anorexia nervosa: A multidimensional perspective*. York: Brunner/Mazel.

Garner, D. M., & Garfinkel, P. E. (1980). Socio-cultural factors in the development of anorexia nervosa. *Psychological Medicine, 10*, 647–656.

Garner, D. M., Garfinkel, P. E., Schwartz, D., & Thompson, M. (1980).4 Cultural expectations of thinness in women. *Psychological Reports, 47*, 483–491.

Garner, D. M., Garfinkel, P. E., Stancer, H. C., & Moldofsky, H. (1976). Body image disturbances in anorexia nervosa and obesity. *Psychosomatic Medicine, 38*(5), 227–236.

Halmi, K. A., Goldberg, S. C., & Cunningham, S. (1977). Perceptual distortion of body image in adolescent girls: Distortion of body image in adolescence. *Psychological Medicine, 7*, 253–257.

Hawkins, R., & Pingree, S. (1990). Divergent psychological processes in constructing social reality from mass media content. In N. Signorielli & M. Morgan (Eds.), *Cultivation analysis: New directions in media effects research*. Newbury Park, CA: Sage.

Huenemann, R. L., Shapiro, L. R., Hampton, M. C., & Mitchell, B. W. (1966). A longitudinal study of gross body composition and body conformation and their association with food and activity in a teen-age population. *The American Journal of Clinical Nutrition, 18*, 325–338.

Kaltenbach, P. (1991). Effects of diet advertising on women at-risk for the development of anorexia nervosa. *Dissertation Abstracts International, 51*(10–B), 5031.

Kaufman, L. (1980). Prime-time nutrition. *Journal of Communication, 30*(3), 37–46.

Lautman, M. (1991). End-benefit segmentation and prototypical bonding. *Journal of Advertising Research, 31*(3), 9–18.

Lerner, R. M., Orlos, J. B., & Knapp, J. R. (1976). Physical attractiveness, physical effectiveness, and self-concept in late adolescents. *Adolescence, 11*(43), 313–326.

Levenkron, S. (1982). *Treating and overcoming anorexia nervosa.* New York: Charles Scribner's Sons.

Ritenbaugh, C. (1982). Obesity as a culture-bound syndrome. *Culture, Medicine, Psychiatry, 6,* 347–361.

Schwartz, D. M., Thompson, M. G., & Johnson, C. L. (1982). Anorexia nervosa and bulimia: The sociocultural context. *International Journal of Eating Disorders, 1*(3), 20–36.

Silverstein, B., Perdue, L., Peterson, B., & Kelly, E. (1986). The role of mass media in promoting a thin standard of bodily attractiveness for women. *Sex Roles, 14*(9/10), 519–532.

Slade, P. D., & Russell, G. (1973). Awareness of body dimensions in anorexia nervosa: Cross sectional and longitudinal studies. *Psychological Medicine, 3,* 188–199.

Spitzack, C. (1990). *Confessing excess.* Albany: State University of New York Press.

Thompson, J. K. (1986, April). Many women see themselves as roundfaced and pudgy, even when no one else does. *Psychology Today,* 39–44.

Touyz, S. W., Beumont, P. J., Collins, J. K., & Cowie, I. (1985). Body shape perception in bulimia and anorexia nervosa. *International Journal of Eating Disorders, 4,* 259–265.

Wilmuth, M. E., Leitenberg, H., Rosen, J. C., Fondacaro, K. M., & Gross, J. (1985). Body size distortion in bulimia. *International Journal of Eating Disorders, 4*(1), 71–78.

Wilson and Nias review the classic literature from the 1960s and 1970s on the "halo effect," which is also called the "what is beautiful is good" hypothesis. Research on the halo effect has shown that whether it's right or wrong, people tend to perceive beautiful people as having all sorts of positive characteristics, such as being more intelligent and friendlier.

12

Beauty Can't Be Beat

Glenn Wilson
David Nias

Grigory Rasputin, the libertine Russian monk who lived during the reign of Czar Nicolas II, liked nothing better than to frolic in the woods with a group of beautiful women. It is said that his pale blue eyes had hypnotic powers that women could not resist. The legend must have some truth in it, for Rasputin was a fiercely ugly man.

Most people find beauty more powerful than they will admit. Ask them what qualities they look for in a lover or friend and they will list honesty, sincerity, intelligence, warmth, a sense of humor. Beauty is rarely mentioned. But there is an impressive body of evidence to say that physical attractiveness is the single most important characteristic in determining peoples' friends, lovers and spouses, not to mention their partners in a woodland frolic. Personality hardly counts at all.

The power of beauty shows clearly in studies of couples on blind dates. For example, psychologist Elaine Walster and her colleagues paired

Adapted from Wilson & Nias, *The mystery of love: The hows and whys of sexual attraction*, C 1976 Quadrangle Books/a division of Times Books. Reprinted with permission.

students on a random basis except that the man was always taller than the woman. Before they first met, each member of a pair was rated for attractiveness. They were also assessed on intelligence, personality, and social skills. Later, after attending a dance together, they were asked how much they liked their partners and whether they wanted to see them again. It turned out that a student's interest in his or her date depended solely upon the date's attractiveness. Personality, intelligence, and social skills played no part. The only thing that mattered—for women or men—was looks.

The importance of appearance is not limited to one's love life. Researchers at the Universities of Minnesota and Wisconsin gave a large group of men and women a series of photographic portraits, and asked them to gauge the personality traits of the people depicted. Attractive people came out ahead on all counts. They were thought to be kinder, stronger, more interesting, poised, modest, sociable, outgoing and sexier than unattractive people. The good-lookers were expected to get prestigious jobs, make good husbands or wives, and have happy marriages.

HOMELY AND AGGRESSIVE

One might assume that beauty becomes important only when one begins to look for a mate and that young children, who are uncorrupted by years of cultural prejudice, perceive that beauty is only skin deep. But the advantages of being attractive start early. Psychologists Karen Dion and Ellen Berscheid went to a nursery school and asked children between the ages of four and six to name the classmates they liked best. Not only did the youngsters prefer the good-looking children, they also thought the homely kids were aggressive and unfriendly.

To add to the burden of unattractive children, other research shows that teachers share children's prejudices. Psychologists Margaret Clifford and Elaine Walster showed report cards to 400 teachers and asked them to evaluate the children involved. Sometimes a card was accompanied by the photograph of an attractive youngster; at other times it carried the photograph of a plain child. When the child was good looking, the teachers guessed that he had a higher IQ, had parents who were interested in his education, and got along better with his peers than when the child was plain.

Karen Dion also came up with more alarming results. She gave female students a written description of a seven-year-old's misconduct. When the report included a photograph of an attractive child, the students excused the misdeed or saw it as an isolated incident. But when the same report came attached to the photograph of an unattractive child, the students assumed the naughtiness was a typical incident and that the child had a basically malevolent character.

It appears that beauty would help women get through college—if only they could attach their pictures to their papers and exams. David Landy and Harold Sigall of the University of Rochester asked male college students to grade an essay, and found that the marks varied according to the attractiveness of the female author. The students gave the same essay higher marks when it was accompanied by the photograph of an attractive woman than when they presumed the author was plain.

The power of beauty extends beyond the classroom; beautiful people are also more likely to have happy marriages than their ugly friends. Sociologists Clifford Kirkpatrick and John Cotton of Indiana University asked students to pick well-adjusted and poorly adjusted married couples from among their friends and acquaintances. Researchers then interviewed the couples and rated them on physical attractiveness. Most of the attractive people turned out to be in the well-adjusted group.

ATTRACTIVENESS AND CRIME

Even in the courts, where justice is supposed to be blind, beauty affects the outcome. Harold Sigall and Nancy Ostrove asked students at the University of Maryland to read the account of a crime and then suggest an appropriate punishment for the offender. Sometimes the guilty woman was depicted in a photograph as beautiful; at other times she was made to look homely. Another group of students dealt out sentences without knowing what the defendant looked like.

At least the lack of beauty didn't *increase* the length of sentence; the homely offender fared no worse than her anonymous counterpart. But the attractive woman got special treatment. When the crime was burglary, she got off easy; but when the crime was a confidence swindle, in which her role was to induce a middle-aged bachelor to invest in a nonexistent company, beauty hurt her case. The attractive woman got a slightly stiffer sentence than either the homely woman or the anonymous defendant. It seems that if attractive people use their looks to help them commit a crime, their beauty will testify against them in court. In other cases, their attractiveness may help shorten their prison stay.

Good looks are important in virtually all aspects of our lives, and people generally agree on standards of beauty. Ratings of "handsome" or "beautiful" aren't good enough for researchers, and so, in the nineteenth century, Sir Francis Galton found out what it takes to make a pretty face. He used a technique called composite portraiture, in which he superimposed a large number of faces on a single photographic plate, using very brief exposure times. The finished picture is a face that averages the features of the group; all irregularities or individual peculiarities are eliminated. Galton tried it with men and with women. "The result," he wrote in 1883, "is a very striking face, thoroughly ideal and artistic, and singularly beautiful. It is indeed most notable how beautiful all composites are." His experiment showed that a good-looking face is one with regular, typical features; an ugly face is one with surprises.

When it comes to sex appeal, attractiveness is based largely on the differences in appearance between male and female. The more exaggerated these differences, up to a point, the more sexually attractive a person is. Cosmetics, in fact, do little more than accentuate sexual differences. Lipstick, for example, emphasizes the fuller lips of the woman, and many women pluck perfectly good eyebrows and replace them with thin pencil lines to avoid a bushy, masculine look. And, while a mustache or beard can add to a man's appearance, the slightest facial hair on a woman is as unappealing as acne. Similarly, a good-looking figure is one that bulges one way in a man, another in a woman. In general, then, men are attractive if they look unlike women, and women are attractive if they look unlike men.

With all the advantages that come with good looks, one might expect those who meet the standards of masculine and feminine beauty to be inordinately happy. But looks do not guarantee contentment. When a large group of college students completed a questionnaire that asked about their happiness, self-esteem, and psychological well-being, handsome men were no better off than ugly ones on any of the three measures. Psychologists Eugene Mathes and Arnold Kahn had outsiders rate the students' attractiveness, so their own feelings about their looks had no effect on the results. Beautiful women had only a slight edge over unattractive women on the three measures, and other research suggests that even that advantage disappears with age.

LEVELS OF BEAUTY

The later disadvantages of beauty became clear when Ellen Berscheid compared the happiness of middle-aged men and women with their attractiveness as shown in photos from college days. She found that women who had been beautiful when young were not as happy as those tho had been ordinary looking. The beauties were also less satisfied with their lives and less well-adjusted than the plain women. Again, happiness in men seemed unrelated to attractiveness.

Perhaps the reason that beauty has so little influence on happiness is that people seek out others at their own level of attractiveness. Ellen Berscheid displayed a set of photographs and asked people to select one person they would like to meet. Beautiful people wanted to meet beauties; ordinary people wanted to meet other ordinary folk, and ugly people chose to meet ugly persons. People apparently seek out partners who are similar to themselves in physical attractiveness.

This finding has been checked in real-life situations. In one study, people were asked to judge the attractiveness of newlyweds without telling the judges who was married to whom. The results showed that husbands and wives tended to be alike in attractiveness, whether handsome, plain or ugly. This is probably for the best, if our behavior in public is any guide. In another study, Irwin Silverman of the University of Florida sent students to watch courting couples in bars, theater lobbies and other places where the observers would not be noticed. Male students rated the attractiveness of the women, while female students graded the men. In 85 percent of the cases, the couple's attractiveness differed only by one point. Silverman's spies also noticed the hand-holding and other public intimacies and found that 60 percent of the highly similar couples made contact, while 46 percent of the moderately similar couples and only 22 percent of the least similar pairs touched. It appears that being neither more nor less attractive than one's mate is more important than being beautiful.

There is little doubt that physical attractiveness has important effects on one's life. It helps shape personality, influences who will be friends, lovers and spouses, limits success in school and career, and may even affect the outcome of a trial. The better looking a person is, the easier life will be; but a plain face does not necessarily mean a miserable life. Homely people who keep attractiveness in perspective and who seek out friendships and intimacy with others who are about as good looking as themselves have as good a shot at happiness and well-being as attractive people. Perhaps the transformation from an ugly duckling into a swan comes with the realization that one does not have to be good looking to be beautiful.

*How does appearance affect an applicant's ability to get a job?
Can you really "dress for success?" This article examines these
questions by summarizing research on the effects of physical
attractiveness and clothing in the workplace. Kaiser points out
that although attractive people may have a general advantage,
too much beauty can sometimes backfire, especially for women.
She also discusses the challenges that women face in trying to
choose professional, yet feminine clothing for the workplace.*

13

Women's Appearance and Clothing within Organizations

Susan B. Kaiser

In the world of job-seeking and interviewing, judgments are made on a regular basis about a candidate's qualifications. How well-qualified an applicant is judged to be is likely to be linked (implicitly or unconsciously, at least) to perceptions of competence. Often, as in an interview context, a perceiver is influenced greatly, especially in the first few minutes, by an applicant's personal appearance. Favorable judgments of his or her appearance are likely to contribute to other positive inferences that may not neces-

Adapted with permission from Kaiser (1997), *The social psychology of clothing: Symbolic appearances in context* (2nd ed., rev.), pp. 260–261, 366–367, copyright © by Fairchild Publications/Capital Cities Media.

sarily be logically related. That is, a halo effect operates, in that when a person is judged to be attractive, then he or she is also evaluated as having other positive traits (for example, competence), and therefore, as being the best person for the job. At a time when women are increasingly striving to move up the corporate ladder and to be taken seriously in the business world, there understandably has been a great deal of research on the role of women's appearances in hiring decisions. This research has followed two lines of inquiry, focusing upon physical attractiveness and clothing, respectively. In this discussion, we will first focus primarily on the dimension of physical attractiveness. Second, the effects of women's clothing choices on first impressions of competence will be addressed.

JUDGMENTS OF BEING QUALIFIED FOR THE JOB: THE EFFECTS OF PHYSICAL ATTRACTIVENESS

Regardless of an interviewer's sex and own level of attractiveness, highly qualified applicants tend to be preferred over poorly qualified applicants. Moreover, males tend to be preferred over females, and attractive candidates are preferred over unattractive ones. Thus, discrimination appears to operate along the lines of gender and physical attractiveness stereotypes. However, bias against female applicants appears to be diminished when they are moderately attractive (which appears to be better than being either highly attractive or unattractive). Also, women with low qualifications who are also unattractive are especially likely to elicit a negative evaluation. Female interviewers appear to be as biased as male interviewers, and unattractive interviewers as biased as attractive interviewers (Dipboye, Arvey, & Terpstra, 1977). This gender effect was reinforced in a later study in which male perceivers tended to ignore appearance altogether, whereas female raters were favorably influenced by candidates with average to above-average appearance (Quereshi & Kay, 1986).

Contextual considerations come into play in hiring decisions. Physical attractiveness has been found to be an advantage for males pursuing either managerial or clerical jobs, whereas it is an advantage for women only in clerical jobs (Heilman & Saruwatari, 1979). It seems that a high degree of attractiveness may "backfire" for a female applicant when the job in question emphasizes the need for instrumental or masculine skills (such as making decisions quickly and accurately under pressure), because highly attractive women are stereotyped as being too feminine for the job. However, in a managerial context requiring a high degree of interpersonal skill, such as managing a furniture department in a large department store, attractiveness appears to be an asset (Cash & Kilcullen, 1985). Similarly, in "appearance-relevant" jobs such as personnel interviewing or counseling, physical attractiveness is more of an advantage in hiring decisions than it is in "appearance-irrelevant" positions such as safety administration or working with personnel records (Beehr & Gilmore, 1982).

One study manipulated the level of female attractiveness and appropriateness of dress for a hypothetical entry-level management position within a large corporation (Bardack & McAndrew, 1985). It found that both attractiveness and being well-dressed are assets, with physical attractiveness being weighted more heavily. An unattractive person could increase her chances of being hired from 68 to 76 percent by dressing well, whereas an attractive woman could enhance her chances from 82 to 100 percent. Female perceivers were especially hard on an unattractive applicant; only 58 percent indicated that they would hire her. In contrast, 80 percent of the men said they would (Bardack & McAndrew, 1985).

Attempts to draw general conclusions from these and other similar studies should be tempered by a few qualifications. Often, students have been the perceivers used in these studies rather than individuals who are especially likely to make the hiring decisions. Some research has suggested that there may be differences between students' and professional interviewers' judgments of candidates (Gilmore, Beehr, & Love, 1986). Also, differences in the ways researchers manipulate physical attractiveness (and the unique physical qualities of the individuals they use) may account for some discrepancies from one study to the next. Additionally, it is difficult to know whether perceptions of photographs (the most common stimulus in these studies) actually simulate what occurs in the everyday business world, where people are influenced by other nonverbal and verbal cues in conjunction with appearance. Nevertheless, some common threads run through these studies and point to the relevance of both physical attractiveness and clothing in the context of hiring decisions. It seems that when physical attractiveness is used as a cue for understanding a person, a variety of inferences can lead to an anticipatory set in the mind of an evaluator. The result may be getting or not getting a job.

FIRST IMPRESSIONS OF WOMEN IN THE ORGANIZATIONAL CONTEXT

Historically, women have not had a straightforward business "uniform" code to follow. As increasing numbers of women have entered the work force, a dilemma of sorts has become evident. Especially in first-impression contexts that become so critical in large organizations, both women and men want to make good impressions on others, especially those tho have control over their futures. Appearance can have an important impact in hiring decisions as well as in other short-term interactions, especially when other information about an individual is minimal or incomplete. Although men have a fairly established code of business attire and are likely to be viewed as both attractive and competent if they follow this code, women seem to be forced in some organizational contexts to make a choice between aesthetics and creativity versus competence.

Thus, during the 1970s and early 1980s, "dress for success" advice for women was rampant in the popular literature, and conservative skirted business suits were prevalent. At the same time, clothing scholars pursued research to identify the personality characteristics associated with different styles of women's attire, so as to determine the implications for the professional context.

Several studies indicated that a woman makes a stronger business-like impression in a skirted suit (Forsythe, Drake, & Cox, 1984; Rucker, Taber, & Harrison, 1981; Workman, 1985). Managerial characteristics such as forcefulness, self-reliance, dynamism, aggressiveness, and decisiveness were found to be associated more with certain suit and blouse combinations than with a feminine dress (Forsythe et al., 1984). The addition of a jacket appears to add a businesslike touch to a woman's appearance (Rucker et al., 1981; Scherbaum & Shepherd, 1987).

Male, but not female, businesspersons associated women in jackets that were dark (as opposed to light) in color with more potency (qualified, expert, powerful, professional, bold, and the like), in a study by Damhorst and Pinaire-Reed (1986). Typically, the researchers noted, women have had more freedom to experiment with color, whereas men have been socialized to recognize and adopt the dark business suit as a sign of corporate power and achievement.

> Clothing meanings . . . change with time. As a greater number of women enter management level jobs, businessmen may become accustomed to a variety of colors in women's dress, and meaning of color value may diminish or change for men. Conversely, women may adopt traditional, darker colors in business dress, and the meanings they assign to color could shift toward agreement with men. (Damhorst & Pinaire-Reed, 1986, p. 96)

Another study documented that the color code is still more rigid for males than it is for females in business attire (Scherbaum & Shepherd, 1987). However, within the latitude in women's business attire there appears to be an emerging aesthetic code, as shown in a study of campus recruiters' perceptions of attire appropriate for retail interviews. In this study, the 26 suit styles rated as most appropriate tended to have classic tailoring, natural to boxy silhouettes, neutral or duller colors, low contrast, skirt length right below the knee, neck emphasis, and limited accessories. On the other hand, the less appropriate suits had at least one extreme element, either a highly clothes- or body-dominant silhouette, an unconventional combination of textures or colors, or attention-grabbing, trendy, or outdated elements (Damhorst, Eckman, & Stout, 1986).

Aside from impressions of competence or being businesslike, it is important to consider other meanings conveyed by clothes in organizational contexts. For example, a woman may be viewed as very serious and capable, yet unfriendly or unimaginative. Some research has suggested that there is a downside to women's adoption of a business "uniform." A blazer may be a good intellectual cue, increasing the respect a perceiver has for a woman; however, the addition of a blazer also tends to decrease likability (Lennon & Miller, 1984). A classic suit tends to convey a conventional and dominant impression, but also may be perceived as contributing to a slightly standoffish or somewhat unapproachable air (Sweat & Zentner, 1985). Moreover, research shows that although a suit with a plain white blouse elicits impressions of competence, a woman wearing a dress may be perceived as creative:

> To be dressed in a suit is to have creativity downplayed. Any observable differences in the total clothing outfit |are| limited to slight variations in color and texture or small details in cut. To wear a dress is to introduce a far greater range in variations from a norm, perhaps cueing inferences to creativity and independence. (Johnson & Roach-Higgins, 1987)

Thus many factors must be taken into account before concluding what type of attire a woman should wear in the organizational context. The extent to which creativity is an important attribute in one's position is important, along with considerations about how critical informal contacts can be in business. Often, consequential decisions are made in informal contexts (for example, in the bar or on the racquetball court), and a woman who tries too hard to make a serious impression may diminish her opportunities to interact on this level. Basically, it seems that women are faced with some tough, double-edged choices in the business world; to some extent it becomes a question of choosing between being taken seriously versus being perceived as creative and sociable. Hopefully, a delicate balance or compromise can be negotiated in everyday organizational contexts, in which women can weigh and assess all of the social variables involved.

The complexity in women's choices is further increased by some differences in the perceptions of males and females concerning women's business attire. Studies focusing more on overall style than on color have suggested that women's business attire influences female perceivers more than it does male perceivers (Rucker et al. 1981). DeLong, Salusso-Deonier, and Larntz (1983) found that males evaluated women's business attire less positively and social attire more positively than did females. Females were also more likely to differentiate between business and social attire. Sweat and Zentner (1985) found that females were more stereotypical in their responses than were males. That is, female perceivers viewed the classic business suit as more conventional and dominant than did male perceivers, suggesting that females may think this style has more of an impact on males than it actually does. It should also be noted that the perceivers in the studies by Rucker et al. (1981), DeLong et al. (1983), and Sweat and Zentner (1985) were college students, and females who are preparing to pursue careers may be more concerned about these cues than women who are well-established in their careers.

A business suit worn in the early stages of a woman's career may represent a kind of compensation symbolism. That is to say, until a woman has become comfortable and established in her career role, a business suit may be adopted in part to complete a professional self-image. Once a woman has become more settled in her career and has less need to complete such a self-image, she is likely to feel freer to experiment with appearance (Solomon & Douglas, 1985). Rather than taking her cue primarily from her work associates (who may be predominantly male) as she did earlier in her career, she is likely to feel freer to pursue fashion ideas in magazines and other media (Rabolt & Drake, 1985).

There is another, deeper interpretation of the practice of women borrowing symbolism from males. By engaging in a form of imitative behavior, women may actually reinforce that the masculine model of business attire is the "right" one. Thus by adopting *the* "authority" look, women may actually be reinforcing their subordinate status in organizational culture (McCracken, 1985).

In a broader cultural context, it had become apparent by the 1980s that the skirted business suit had become an emblem or stereotype. In business and general interest magazines between the 1960s and 1980s, there was a significant increase in portrayals of women in skirted business suits. Still, the suit did not replace all of the other acceptable options for women to wear. And in contrast to changes in the images of women, there were no significant differences in how men have been portrayed in these ads (Saunders & Stead, 1986):

> The skirted suit is perceived as a female equivalent of the suit worn almost universally by businessmen and executives. Possibly, by imitating men, women are conveying the impression that to succeed they must transform themselves into copies of men—not only in terms of behavior, attitudes, values and skills, but also in dress. The impression conveyed may be that women can only succeed if they imitate men. . . .

In the short term, as with men, the use of the business uniform can facilitate acceptance of women by creating the necessary impression of competence. In the long term, women who have become successful may need to seek a form of dress that does not merely ape that of men. (pp. 203–204)

Thus there will be a continuing need for a negotiation of aesthetic codes that signify appropriate business attire for women. As designers, retailers, and consumers create and interpret these codes, the *relational* aspects of male and female interactions will need to be considered along with the organizational realities that they construct in everyday life.

References

Bardack, N. R., & McAndrew, F. T. (1985). The influence of physical attractiveness and manner of dress on success in simulated personnel decisions. *Journal of Social Psychology, 125*, 777–778.

Beehr, T. A., & Gilmore, D. C. (1982). Applicant attractiveness as a perceived job-relevant variable in selection of management trainees. *Academy of Management Journal, 25*, 607–617.

Cash, T. F., & Kilcullen, R. N. (1985). The eye of the beholder: Susceptibility to sexism and beautyism in the evaluation of managerial applicants. *Journal of Applied Social Psychology, 15*, 591–605.

Damhorst, M. L., Eckman, M., & Stout, S. (1986). Cluster analysis of women's business suits. In *ACPTC proceedings* (p. 65). Monument, CO: Association of College Professors of Textiles and Clothing.

Damhorst, M. L., & Pinaire-Reed, J. A. (1986). Clothing color value and facial expression: Effects on evaluations of female job applicants. *Social Behavior and Personality, 14*, 89–98.

DeLong, M. R., Salusso-Deonier, C., & Larritz, K. (1983). Use of perceptions of female dress as an indicator of role definition. *Home Economics Research Journal, 11*, 327–336.

Dipboye, R. L., Arvery, R. D., & Terpstra, D. E. (1977). Sex and physical attractiveness of raters and applicants as determinants of resume evaluations. *Journal of Applied Psychology, 62*, 288–294.

Gilmore, D. C., Beehr, T. A., & Love, K. G. (1986). Effects of applicant sex, applicant physical attractiveness, type of rater, and type of job on interview decisions. *Journal of Occupational Psychology, 59*, 103–109.

Heilman, M. E., & Saruwatari, L. R. (1979). When beauty is beastly: The effects of appearance and sex on evaluations of job applicants for managerial and nonmanagerial jobs. *Organizational Behavior and Human Performance, 23*, 360–372.

Johnson, K. K. P., & Roach-Higgins, M. E. (1987). Dress and physical attractiveness of women in job interviews. *Clothing and Textiles Research Journal, 5*, 1–8.

Lennon, S. J., & Miller, F. G. (1984). Salience of physical appearance in impression formation. *Home Economics Research Journal, 13,* 95–104.

McCracken, G. (1985). The trickle-down theory revisited. In M. R. Solomon (Ed.), *The psychology of fashion* (pp. 39–54). Lexington, MA: Lexington Books.

Quereshi, M. Y., & Kay, J. P. (1986). Physical attractiveness, age, and sex as determinants of reactions to resumes. *Social Behavior and Personality, 14,* 103–112.

Rabolt, N. J., & Drake, M. F. (1985). Information sources used by women for career dressing decisions. In M. R. Solomon (Ed.), *The psychology of fashion* (pp. 371–385). Lexington, MA: Lexington Books.

Rucker, M., Taber, D., & Harrison, A. (1981). The effect of clothing variation on first impressions of female job applicants: What to wear when. *Social Behavior and Personality, 9,* 53–64.

Saunders, C. S., & Stead, B. A. (1986). Women's adoption of a business uniform: A content analysis of magazine advertisements. *Sex Roles, 15,* 197–205.

Scherbaum, C. J., & Shepherd, D. H. (1987). Dressing for success: Effects of color and layering on perceptions of women in business. *Sex Roles, 16,* 391–399.

Solomon, M. R., & Douglas, S. (1985). The female clotheshorse: From aesthetics to tactics. In M. R. Solomon (Ed.), *The psychology of fashion* (pp. 387–401). Lexington, MA: Lexington Books.

Sweat S., & Zentner, M. A. (1985). Attributions toward female appearance styles. In M. R. Solomon (Ed.), *The psychology of fashion* (pp. 321–355). Lexington, MA: Lexington Books.

Workman, J. E. (1985). Effects of appropriate and inappropriate attire on attributions of personal dispositions. *Clothing and Textiles Research Journal, 3,* 20–23.

*The authors use four different studies to investigate the connec-
tion between the color black and perceptions of aggressiveness
in sports. Results suggest that teams wearing black are generally seen as more evil and aggressive, are penalized more, and
may actually act more aggressive than teams wearing other
colors. These results underscore the important role that color
may play within the context of competitive sports.*

14

Black Uniforms and Aggression in Professional Sports

*Mark G. Frank
Thomas Gilovich*

A convenient feature of the traditional American Western film was the ease
with which the viewer could distinguish the good guys from the bad guys:
The bad guys wore the black hats. Of course, film directors did not invent
this connection between black and evil, but built upon an existing association that extends deep into our culture and language. When a terrible thing
happens on a given day, we refer to it as a "black day," as when the Depression was ushered in by the infamous "Black Thursday." We can hurt ourselves by "blackening" our reputation or be hurt by others by being "black-

Adapted with permission from Frank & Gilovich, The dark side of self- and social perception: Black uniforms and aggression in professional sports. *Journal of Personality
and Social Psychology, 54,* 74–85. Copyright © 1988 by the American Psychological
Association.

114

listed," "blackballed," or "blackmailed" (Williams, 1964). When the Chicago White Sox deliberately lost the 1919 World Series as part of a betting scheme, they became known as the Chicago Black Sox, and to this day this "dark" chapter in American sports history is known as the Black Sox Scandal. In a similar vein, Muhammed Ali has observed that we refer to white cake as "angel food cake" and dark cake as "devil's food cake."

These anecdotes concerning people's negative associations to the color black are reinforced by the research literature on color meanings. In one representative experiment, groups of college students and seventh graders who were asked to make ratings of colors were found to associate black with evil, death, and badness (Williams & McMurty, 1970). Moreover, this association between black and evil is not strictly an American or Western phenomenon, because college students in Germany, Denmark, Hong Kong, and India (Williams, Moreland, & Underwood, 1970) and Ndembu tribesmen in Central Africa (Turner, 1967) all report that the color black connotes evil and death. Thus, Adams and Osgood (1973) concluded that black is seen, in virtually all cultures, as the color of evil and death.

The intriguing question is whether these associations influence people's behavior in important ways. For example, does wearing black clothing lead both the wearer and others to perceive him or her as more evil and aggressive? More important, does it lead the wearer to actually *act* more aggressively?

Our investigation of the relationship between color and aggressiveness is divided into four parts. First, we investigated whether different colored uniforms carry the same connotations as the basic colors themselves. Do the uniforms of the black-uniformed teams in the National Football League (NFL) and the National Hockey League (NHL) look more evil, mean, and aggressive than the uniforms of the nonblack-uniformed teams? Next we analyzed the penalty records from these two leagues to test whether the teams with black uniforms are penalized more than their rivals. If the evil connotations of the color black lead those who wear black uniforms to act unusually aggressively, then the teams with black uniforms in the NFL and the NHL should be penalized more than other teams. Finally, we conducted two experiments designed to test whether the results obtained in our analysis of penalty records were due to the uniforms' effect on the referees' judgments (Study 3) or on the players' actual behavior (Study 4).

Method and Results Summary

Study 1: Subjects were shown color slides showing the jerseys, pants, socks, and helmets of various NFL and NHL teams. Subjects then rated the uniforms on scales such as good/bad, nice/mean and timid/aggressive. Results showed that black uniforms, such as those of the Los Angeles (now Oakland) Raiders and the Chicago Black Hawks, were rated as more malevolent than non-black uniforms.

Study 2: The second study involved analyzing penalty records from the NFL and NHL over a 16–17 year period. Statistical analyses showed that teams with black uniforms were penalized more than teams with non-black uniforms. The data also showed that when the Pittsburgh Penguins and the Vancouver Canucks switched from non-black to black uniforms, the number of minutes they spent in the penalty box increased.

Study 3: Subjects who were knowledgeable football fans or referees where shown one of two videotapes depicting a scrimmage between two college football teams. The two videotapes were staged to be the same except for the color of the uniforms. In one videotape the defense wore white and in the other they wore black. The offense wore red in both videotapes. After viewing one of these tapes, subjects were asked to determine how "legal" and "aggressive" the defensive team's actions were. Both the football fans and the referees were more likely to rate the defensive team's actions as illegal and aggressive if they were wearing black.

Study 4: Groups of three subjects participated in an experiment on "competition." When they first arrived, each subject was asked to individually choose and rank 5 games from a longer list of 12 that they would like to play. The 12 games varied in their level of aggression. Groups were then outfitted in either black or white uniforms, supposedly to foster identity and distinguish them from the other team. Then the three subjects re-ranked their game preferences as a group rather than as individuals. Results showed that after the groups were outfitted in their uniforms, those in black chose more aggressive games as a group than they had as individuals. Those in white did not show an increase in aggressive choices.

GENERAL DISCUSSION

Previous research has demonstrated that certain uniforms can influence a person's willingness to harm another individual (Johnson & Downing, 1979). With this in mind, we investigated whether the widespread association between the color black and evil and death (Adams & Osgood, 1973) might lead to elevated levels of aggressiveness on the part of people wearing black uniforms. In particular, we examined whether the teams with black uniforms in two professional "contact" sports tend to be unusually aggressive, as measured by how frequently they are penalized. As predicted, teams with black uniforms in the NFL and the NHL were penalized significantly more often during the last 17 years than their rivals in nonblack uniforms. Furthermore, those teams that switched from nonblack to black uniforms during this time period experienced an immediate and dramatic increase in penalties. The results of our two laboratory experiments indicate that the effect of wearing black uniforms on a team's history of penalties may be attributable to two distinct processes. Study 3 demonstrated that players in black uniforms are judged more harshly than those in white uniforms by nonpartisan judges and thus are more likely to be penalized for actions that would be overlooked if performed by members of another team. In Study 4, subjects wearing black uniforms were more inclined than their white-uniformed counterparts to seek out opportunities for aggressive competition, providing some initial support for the idea that football and hockey players who wear black uniforms actually play more aggressively than their rivals.

The present investigation demonstrates how a seemingly trivial variable, the color of one's uniform, can induce such a shift in a person's identity. This is not to suggest, however, that in other contexts the direction of causality might not be reversed. The black outfits worn by gangs like the Hell's Angels, for example, are no doubt deliberately chosen precisely because they convey the desired malevolent image. Thus, as in the world portrayed in the typical American Western, it may be that many inherently evil characters *choose* to wear black. However, the present investigation makes it clear that in certain contexts at least, some people become the bad guys *because* they wear black.

References

Adams, F. M., & Osgood, C. E. (1973). A cross-cultural study of the affective meanings of color. *Journal of Cross-Cultural Psychology, 4*, 135–156.

Johnson, R. D., & Downing, L. L. (1979). Deindividuation and valence of cues: Effects on prosocial and antisocial behavior. *Journal of Personality and Social Psychology, 37*, 1532–1538.

Turner, V. (1967). *The forest of symbols: Aspects of Ndembu ritual*. Ithaca, NY: Cornell University Press.

Williams, J. E. (1964). Connotations of color names among Negroes and Caucasians. *Perceptual and Motor Skills, 18*, 721–731.

Williams, J. E., & McMurty, C. A. (1970). Color connotations among Caucasian 7th graders and college students. *Perceptual and Motor Skills, 30*, 701–713.

Williams, J. E., Moreland, J. K., & Underwood, W. I. (1970). Connotations of color names in the U. S., Europe, and Asia. *Journal of Social Psychology, 82*, 3–14.

Furlow argues that scientists are beginning to take a second look at the role that olfactics play in the attraction process. Researchers have found that smell can stimulate memory and affect our health and moods. New research shows that human pheromones connected to our immune system may serve a mate-selection function by attracting appropriate mates and repelling inappropriate ones. These pheromones may even be related to fertility.

15

The Smell of Love

F. Bryant Furlow

How do we humans announce, and excite, sexual availability? Many animals do it with their own biochemical bouquets known as pheromones. "Why do bulls and horses turn up their nostrils when excited by love?" Darwin pondered deep in one of his unpublished notebooks. He came to believe that natural selection designed animals to produce two, and only two, types of odors—defensive ones, like the skunk's, and scents for territorial marking and mate attracting, like that exuded by the male musk deer and bottled by perfumers everywhere. The evaluative sniffing that mammals engage in during courtship were clues that scent is the chemical equivalent of the peacock's plumage or the nightingale's song—finery with which to attract mates.

In the following century, a rich array of animal pheromones were documented for seals, boars, rodents, and all manner of other critters. But not for human beings.

Some of Darwin's contemporaries embraced human uniqueness in this regard as evidence of our inevitable ascendance, as if Nature's Plan somehow called for the evolution of a nearly naked two-legged primate with a poor sense of smell to conquer the Earth. The French physician Paul Broca—noting that primates' social olfactory abilities are diminished compared to those of other mammals—asserted that monkeys, apes, and humans represent ascending steps from four-legged sniffing beasts to sight-oriented bipeds.

Recent discoveries suggest, however, that the reports of our olfactory devolution have been greatly exaggerated.

Some suspected as much of the whole time. Smell researchers Barbara Sommerville and David Gee of the University of Leeds in England observed that smelling one another's hands or faces is a nearly universal human greeting. The Eskimo kiss is not just a rubbing of noses but a mutual sniffing. "Only in the Western world," the researchers point out, "has it become modified to a kiss." Hands and faces may be significant choices for these formalities—they are the two most accessible concentrations of scent glands on the human body besides the ear.

SCENT AND SENTIMENT

Curiously, remembering a smell is usually difficult—yet when exposed to certain scents, many people may suddenly recall a distant childhood memory in emotionally rich detail. Some aromas even affect us physiologically. Laboratory researchers exploring human olfaction have found that:

- A faint trace of lemon significantly increases people's perception of their own health.
- Lavender incense contributes to a pleasant mood—but it lowers volunteers' mathematical abilities.
- A whiff of lavender and eucalyptus increases people's respiratory rate and alertness.
- The scent of phenethyl alcohol (a constituent of rose oil) reduces blood pressure.

Such findings have led to the rapid development of an aromatherapy industry. Aromatherapists point to scientific findings that smell can dramatically affect our moods as evidence that therapy with aromatic oils can help buyers manage their emotional lives.

Mood is demonstrably affected by scent. But scientists have found that, despite some extravagant industry promises, the attraction value in perfumes resides strictly in their pleasantness, not their sexiness. So far, at least, store-bought scent is more decoration than mood manager or love potion. A subtle "look this way" nudge to the nose, inspiring a stranger's curiosity, or at most a smile, is all perfume advertisers can in good conscience claim for their products—not overwhelming and immediate infatuation.

Grandiose claims for the allure of a bottled smell are not new. In their haste to mass-market sexual attraction during the last century, perfumers nearly drove the gentle musk deer extinct. In Victorian England, the nicesmelling young lady with financial savvy could do a brisk business selling handkerchiefs scented with her body odor.

So it should come as no surprise that when physiologists discovered a functioning vomeronasal organ (VNO) inside the human nose, it was a venture capitalist intent on cashing in on manufactured human pheromone who funded the team's research. That was less than a decade ago. Using high-tech microscope probes, a team led by Luis Monti-Bloch of the University of Utah found a tiny pair of pits, one in each nostril, snuggled up against the septum an inch inside the nose.

The pits are lined with receptor cells that fire like mad when presented with certain substances. Yet subjects report that they don't smell a thing during such experiments. What they often do report is a warm, vague feeling of well-being.

THE GREAT PHEROMONE HUNT

For an animal whose nose supposedly plays no role in sexual attraction or social life, human emotions are strongly moved by smells. And we appear to be profoundly overequipped with smell-producing hardware for what little sniffing we have been thought to be up to. Human sweat, urine, breath, saliva, breast milk, skin oils, and sexual secretions all contain scent-communicating chemical compounds. Zoologist Michael Stoddart, author of *The Scented Ape* (Cambridge University Press, 1991), points out that humans possess denser skin concentrations of scent glands than almost any other mammal. This makes little sense until one abandons the myth that humans pay little attention to the fragrant or the rancid in their day-to-day lives.

Part of the confusion may be due to the fact that not all smells register in our conscious minds. When those telltale scents were introduced to the VNO of human subjects, they didn't report smelling anything—but nevertheless demonstrated subtle changes in mood.

Get a Whiff of the Myths!

Humans have smaller "smell brains" than the rest of the animal kingdom. Oops. The olfactory bulb has been there all along. It's just that it's hard to find, buried in folds and folds of the frontal cortex.

Okay, but we're above scent-driven socialization. Actually, the body scents important in mate attraction are—this even surprised researchers—aromatic by-products of the immune system.

Each of us has a unique "smellprint" that is equally appealing to all others. How pleasant and sexy our body odors are is a totally relative matter. We smell best to a person whose genetically based immunity to disease differs most from our own.

The notion that animal senses play a role in personal attraction diminishes our humanity. Scientific understanding of the role of smell in our lives leads only to conclusions that our tastes and emotions are highly sophisticated, the product of many inputs.

What could be a source of what might be our very own pheromone?

Humans possess three major types of skin glands—sebaceous glands, eccrine (or sweat) glands, and apocrine glands. Sebaceous glands are most common on the face and forehead but occur around all of the body's openings, including eyelids, ears, nostrils, lips, and nipples. This placement is particularly handy, as the secretions of these glands kill potentially dangerous microorganisms. They also contain fats that keep skin supple and waterproof—and, on the downside, cause acne. Little is known, however, about how sebaceous glands contribute to human body odor.

The sweat glands exude water and salt and are nonodorous in healthy people. That leaves the third potential source of a human pheromone—the apocrine gland. Apocrine glands hold special promise as the source of smells that might affect interpersonal interactions. They do not serve any temperature-managing functions in people, as they do in other animals. They occur in dense concentrations on hands, cheeks, scalp, breast areolas, and wherever we possess body hair—and are only functional after puberty, when we begin searching for mates.

Men's apocrine glands are larger than women's, and they secrete most actively during times of nervousness or excitement. Waiting colonies of bacteria turn apocrine secretions into the noxious fumes that keep deodorant makers in business. Hair provides surface area from which apocrine smells can diffuse—part of the reason why hairier men smell particularly pungent.

Most promising of all, apocrine glands exude odorous steroids known to affect sexual behavior in other mammals. Androsterone—a steroid related to the one that nearly doomed the hapless musk deer—is one such substance. Men secrete more androsterone than women do, and most men become unable to detect the stuff right around the time they start producing it themselves—at puberty.

In 1986, the National Geographic Society organized the World Smell Survey to investigate whether people from all cultures experience odor in the same fashion. They distributed over a million scratch-and-sniff cards and questionnaires about subjects' detection and perceptions of intensity of smells, from banana to the sulfur compounds added to natural gas as a warning agent. Included in the survey was the scent of human androsterone.

The steroid itself is not pleasant to smell. Worldwide, those who could smell it rated it second to last in pleasantness—just ahead of the sulfur compounds put in natural gas. A foul-smelling pheromone? It's hardly what scientists expected to find.

ANTI-PHEROMONES?

Despite the poor showing of androsterone in smell ratings, Karl Grammer of Austria's Institute for Human Biology thought it might be the sought-after human pheromone and studied women's reactions to it. He expected to find that women have a strong, favorable reaction to the smell of androsterone around ovulation, when their sense of smell becomes more acute and when they are most likely to conceive. Changes in their bodies' estrogen levels around ovulation, Grammer suspected, may change how women react to androsterone's smell.

He found that women's reactions to androsterone indeed change around ovulation—but not in the manner he expected. Instead of attraction, Grammer's ovulating volunteers shrugged their shoulders and reported indifference. Androsterone, it seems, offers little hope to men looking for a $19.95 solution to their dating slumps.

OF MICE AND MEN

The empirical proof of odor's effect on human sexual attraction came out of left field. Medical geneticists studying inheritance rules for the immune system, not smell physiologists, made a series of crucial discoveries that nobody believed were relevant to human mate preferences—at first.

A segment of our DNA called the major histocompatibility complex (MHC) codes for some disease-detecting structures, which function as the immune system's eyes. When a disease is recognized, the immune system's teeth—the killer T cells—are alerted, and they swarm the intruders, smothering them with destructive enzymes. MHC genes are "co-dominant." This means that if a lab mouse inherits a version of an MHC gene for resistance to Disease A from its mother and a version lending resistance to Disease B from its father, that mouse will be able to resist both diseases. Interestingly, when a female mouse is offered two suitors in mate choice trials, she inevitably chooses to mate with the one whose MHC genes least overlap with her own.

A team led by Professor Wedekind at the University of Bern in Switzerland decided to see whether MHC differences in men's apocrine gland secretions affected women's ratings of male smells. The team recruited just under 100 college students. Males and females were sought from different schools, to reduce the chances that they knew each other. The men were given untreated cotton T-shirts to wear as they slept alone for two consecutive nights. They were told not to eat spicy foods; not to use deodorants, cologne, or perfumed soaps; and to avoid smoking, drinking, and sex during the two-day experiment. During the day, their sweaty shirts were kept in sealed plastic containers.

And then came the big smell test. For two weeks prior, women had used a nasal spray to protect the delicate mucous membranes lining the nose. Around the time they were ovulating (when their sense of smell is enhanced), the women were put alone in a room and presented with boxes containing the male volunteers' shirts. First they sniffed a new, unworn shirt to control for the scent of the shirts themselves. Then the women were asked to rate each man's shirt for "sexiness," "pleasantness," and "intensity of smell."

SEXY GENES

It was found, by Wedekind and his team, that how women rate a man's body odor pleasantness and sexiness depends upon how much of their MHC profile is shared. Overall, women prefer those scents exuded by men whose MHC profiles varied the most from their own. Hence, any given man's odor could be pleasingly alluring to one woman, yet an offensive turnoff to another.

Raters said that the smells they preferred reminded them of current or ex-lovers about twice as often as did the smells of men who have MHC profiles similar to their own, suggesting that smell had played a role in past decisions about who to date. MHC-similar men's smells were more often described as being like a brother's or father's body odor . . . as would be expected if the components of smell being rated are MHC determined.

Somewhat more surprising is that women's evaluations of body odor intensities did not differ between MHC-similar and MHC-dissimilar men. Body scent for MHC-dissimilar men was rated as less sexy and less pleasant the stronger it was, but intensity did not affect the women's already low ratings for MHC-similar men's smells.

That strong odor turned raters off even with MHC-dissimilar men may be due to the fact that strong body odor is a useful indicator of disease. From diabetes to viral infection to schizophrenia, unusually sweet or strong body odors are a warning cue that ancestral females in search of good genes for their offspring may have been designed to heed. (In the case of schizophrenia, the issue is confounded—while some schizophrenics do actually have an unusually sweet smell, many suffer from delusions of foul smells emanating from their bodies.)

Nobody yet knows what roles MHC may play in male evaluations of female attractiveness. Females' superior sense of smell, however, may well be due to their need to more carefully evaluate a potential mate's merits— a poor mate choice for male ancestors may have meant as little as a few minutes wasted, whereas a human female's mistake could result in a nine-month-long "morning after" and a child unlikely to survive.

Perfumers who really want to provide that sexy allure to their male customers will apparently need to get a genetic fingerprint of the special someone before they can tailor a scent that she will find attractive. But before men contemplate fooling women in this way, they should consider the possible consequences.

FOOLING MOTHER NATURE

The Swiss researchers found that women taking oral contraceptives (which block conception by tricking the body into thinking it's pregnant) reported reversed preferences, liking more the smells that reminded them to home and kin. Since the Pill reverses natural preferences, a woman may feel attracted to men she wouldn't normally notice if she were not on birth control—men who have similar MHC profiles.

The effects of such evolutionary novel mate choices can go well beyond the bewilderment of a wife who stops taking her contraceptive pills and notices her husband's "newly" foul body odor. Couples experiencing difficulty conceiving a child—even after several attempts at tubal embryo transfer—share significantly more of their MHC than do couples who conceive more easily. These couples' grief is not caused by either partner's infertility, but to an unfortunate combination of otherwise viable genes.

Doctors have known since the mid-1980s that couples suffering repeated spontaneous abortions tend to share more of their MHC than couples for whom pregnancies are carried to term. And even when MHC-similar couples do successfully bring a pregnancy to term, their babies are often underweight.

The Swiss team believes that MHC-related pregnancy problems in humans are too widespread to be due to inbreeding alone. They argue that in-couple infertility problems are due to strategic, unconscious "decisions" made by women's bodies to curtail investment in offspring with inferior immune systems—offspring unlikely to have survived to adulthood in the environments of our evolutionary past.

Perfume; daily, soapy showers; convenient contraceptive pills—all have their charms. But they also may be short-circuiting our own built-in means of mate choice, adaptations shaped to our unique needs by millions of years of ancestral adversities. The existence of couples who long for children they cannot have indicates that the Western dismissal of body scent is scarcely benign.

Those who find offensive the notion that animal senses play a role in their attention to a partner need not worry. As the role of smell in human affairs yields to understanding, we see not that we are less human but that our tastes and emotions are far more complex and sophisticated than anyone ever imagined.

Does perfume really make women more attractive as the advertisements claim? This study examines this question by comparing people's perceptions of women who use four levels of perfume, ranging from no perfume to several sprays of perfume. Results showed that women are seen as less attractive when they wear a lot of perfume. However, men's rating of women's attractiveness were highest in the "light" perfume condition, suggesting that a little perfume might be better than none. Taken together, the results suggest that there can be "too much of a good thing" when it comes to applying perfume.

16

The Effects of Perfume Use on Perceptions of Attractiveness and Competence

R. Kelly Aune

Although there is a strong belief that scents play an important role in human social behavior (Baron, 1981), the olfactic channel of nonverbal communication has gone largely uninvestigated by social science research (Levine & McBurney, 1986). Knapp and Hall (1992) point out that Americans do not seem to consciously rely on their sense of smell for very much interpersonal information unless the smell is unusually strong or inappropriate to the situation. Nevertheless, people (at least in many parts of

This article was written especially for *The Nonverbal Communication Reader.*

Europe and North America) do seem to have an ongoing interest in how others perceive and evaluate their olfactory cues.

For instance, in our culture it is quite normal to minimize or mask our bodily odors. Bodily odor that is not minimized or masked is often perceived as offensive. We attempt to cover our odors with various marketed smells found in mouthwashes, deodorants, antiperspirants, perfumes, and colognes. Further, we wash our skin and hair with scented soaps and shampoos, insert "odor-eaters" in our shoes, and check to make sure we have our breath mints before we leave the house in the morning.

A routine manipulation of the olfactic code for women comes in the form of the application of perfume. The New York-based Fragrance Foundation, an organization of major fragrance manufacturers who provide funds for olfactic research, reports that Americans spent $5 billion on fragrance in 1997; world wide sales are about $10 billion.

Perfume advertisements would have us believe that perfume use can enhance one's attractiveness and indirectly contribute to both personal happiness and career success. A perusal of many perfume ads indicates that marketing strategies focus on the strong implication that perfume use can enhance sexual attraction (cf. Largey & Watson, 1972). The billions of dollars spent each year suggest that many consumers believe these claims.

This article reports a study that examines the reality behind these beliefs. Specifically, we will look at the findings of a study that shows how people perceived women wearing four different levels of perfume, ranging from no perfume to several sprays of perfume.

PERFUME USE, IMPRESSION MANAGEMENT, AND ATTRIBUTION FORMATION

Nearly all actions can carry some social meanings that have implications for what a person is like (Schlenker, 1980). We tend to attribute characteristics to people by the way they look, dress, talk, and act. It is likely the case that we make attributions about people according to the natural and artificial scents they emit and the degree to which those scents are noticeable.

It is reasonable to suggest that the quantity of perfume a woman wears would have an effect on what we might think about her. Levine and McBurney (1986) argue that the more an odor departs from normative expectations, the more likely the odor will trigger attributional analyses. If the quantity of perfume exceeds the range considered appropriate for the situation, then negative attributions may result. That is, there may be a curvilinear relationship between the quantity of perfume applied and social judgments such as social attractiveness and competence. In other words, perceptions of a woman wearing perfume may become more positive as the perfume becomes more noticeable, but perceptions may become increasingly *negative* as the quantity of perfume goes beyond normative expectations.

In this study we tested the effect of norm violations in perfume use on respondents' perceptions. Specifically we looked at how varying applications of perfume, ranging from none at all to more than average, would affect perceptions of the wearer's social and physical attractiveness, and competence.

METHOD

The study was conducted at the University of Hawaii at Manoa, in Honolulu. Prior to conducting the study, data were collected from women attending the university to determine which perfumes they used most frequently when on campus and how they applied them. Local retailers provided samples of the three most popular perfumes, which were used in the subsequent study.

The study utilized an interview situation in which women confederates wore varying amounts of perfume while interviewing study participants. After the interview, participants recorded their perceptions of the interviewers' social and physical attractiveness, as well as their competence.

Confederates

Four undergraduate women served as confederates in the experiment. The confederates were similar in height, weight, hair and skin coloring. During data collection each dressed in a manner typical of women university students, wearing a white t-shirt and blue jeans. They applied their makeup in typical fashion and were careful not to wear any distracting or attention-getting jewelry.

Participants and Procedures

Two hundred thirty eight university students served as participants in the study. Participants were individually approached outside one of the university libraries and asked if they could be interviewed regarding their library usage habits. Interviewers explained that they were taking a course in interviewing and the interview was part of an assignment. In each interview, one of the confederates served as the interviewer. Before the experiment, confederates had been instructed as to how they should approach the participants and were provided with a short script to follow in their interactions with the participants. The confederates were to stand approximately two to three feet from the participants during the interview. Confederates also explained that since the interview was part of an assignment, they would be asking the participants to answer a few additional items assessing the interviewers' performance after the interview was completed. These final items constituted the dependent variables for the experiment.

Manipulation

For each interview, confederates wore either no perfume or applied one of the three perfumes identified by, and in a manner consistent with, student input from the initial data collection. The perfume was applied to the neck/chest area prior to the data collection period. Perfume was applied in a "low condition" (one spray), "moderate condition" (approximately two to three sprays), or "high usage condition" (approximately five to six sprays). The moderate condition reflected the approximate normative usage reported by respondents in the earlier data collection, and the low and high conditions were operationalized by spraying approximately one standard deviation above and below the mean usage as reported in the initial data.

For the interviews in which the confederates wore perfume, confederates first applied the low level of one of the perfumes, then proceeded to interview approximately three men and three women. Upon completion of the interviews (approximately one hour), the confederate applied the same perfume at the moderate level and interviewed another round of three men and women. Finally, the confederate applied the high quantity of perfume and completed the round of interviewing.[1] At this point the interviewer would quit interviewing for the day. In this manner each confederate wore each of the three perfumes at low, moderate, and high levels. In addition, in order to assess the responses to the confederates without the influence of perfume, confederates first collected data, following the procedures described above, while wearing no perfume.

Dependent Variables

The first part of the survey consisted of items regarding the interviewee's library usage. These items provided the confederates' cover and were orally presented to the interviewee by the interviewer, who recorded the responses. The second part of the survey, containing the measures of perceived social attraction, physical attraction, and competence, was completed by the interviewee. Each dependent variable was assessed using seven-point Likert-type items bounded by "highly disagree" and "highly agree." Social and physical attraction were assessed using three items and five items, respectively, from McCroskey and McCain's (1974) interpersonal attraction scale. Competence was assessed with five Likert-type items designed for the present study.

RESULTS

Data analysis showed that the quantity of perfume applied was related to perceptions of both social attraction and competence in a negative manner: positive perceptions were highest in the "no perfume" condition, and steadily decreased until they were lowest in the "high perfume" condition. The data showed a slightly different pattern for physical attraction, however. Although roughly the same general pattern of means emerged, the highest ratings were in the "low perfume" condition, rather than the "no perfume" condition. This latter finding seemed to be driven by the men's responses. The patterns of men's and women's responses were remarkably similar except for the finding that men's ratings of physical attractiveness peaked in the "low perfume" condition, while the women respondents' scores generally fell more directly from the "no perfume" condition to the "high perfume" condition.

DISCUSSION

Regardless of the respondent's sex, increasing applications of perfume resulted in steadily increasing negative evaluations of the interviewer's social and physical attractiveness, and competence. However, before throwing out your expensive perfumes we need to consider some possible limitations to our manipulation.

It is obvious to anyone who regularly applies an artificial scent (i.e., most of us) that applications of perfume, cologne, deodorant or antiperspirant, and so forth are always most potent, most noticeable immediately after application. We expect the effect of these scents to lighten through the course of the day. However in this study the confederates collected data immediately subsequent to applying the perfume. Data-collecting sessions at each level of the manipulation lasted approximately one hour, whereupon the confederates prepared for the next level of the manipulation. Consequently data were always collected when applications of perfume were at their most salient. It is likely that even the low perfume condition was still quite obvious to the participants, and perhaps not consistent with expectations for a "light" application of perfume. As mentioned previously, a light application of perfume, as manipulated in this study, produced the most positive perceptions of women for the male participants.

If this study were to be replicated, a more realistic manipulation of perfume application should be tested by introducing a "buffer" period between the application of perfume and data collection.

Nevertheless, the results were remarkably consistent: the more perfume the interviewers wore, the more negative their evaluations were. This is particularly interesting in the case of physical attraction ratings. Ratings of social attractiveness and competence are social and psychological judgments arising from inferences the participants make about the interviewers based on a variety of verbal and nonverbal sources of information. Ratings of physical attractiveness, however, would seem to be based on judgments of directly observable data, not inferences from those data. Yet ratings of physical attractiveness fell consistently with increasing applications of perfume. Baron (1983) found a similar effect in an earlier study. His data showed that judgments of how well groomed and dressed interviewers appeared was affected by whether they were wearing perfume. Perhaps there may be some truth to the implications of the perfume industry advertisements.

Although the present study focuses on women's perfume use, and women are, by far, the more frequent users of artificial scents such as perfume, men are frequent users of aftershave and colognes as well. We would expect to find similar results if male confederates had been used. Yet we also must consider the possibility that men may have more rigid constraints regarding their use of scents. It might be the case that our expectations regarding women's use of scents are more flexible, more elastic, and consequently more difficult to violate. On the other hand, our expectations for men's use of scents may be limited by both context and quantities. Perhaps men's use of scent is expected to be more subtle than women's and is limited to more formal situations. For instance, most women in our classes report applying at least some perfume or cologne before going to class; it is more rare to find men reporting the application of cologne before leaving for campus. University women also claim that they apply perfume differently for time on campus compared to a formal work situation. They report applying their perfume differently as a function of their attraction to a dating partner. We suspect men are more binary in their approach to cologne application—they either apply it or not.

In short, we really do not know a lot yet about the norms and constraints that govern our use of scents. The present study adds to a small body of research in this neglected area of communication. Evidence is mounting that the olfactic channel makes a significant contribution to our social and communicative behavior. Research needs to be conducted to fully articulate the olfactory code before our understanding of its contribution to human communication is on par with other nonverbal codes.

Note

[1] In order to account for residual scent left from the prior application, the interviewers operationalized the moderate and high use conditions as *additions* to the prior conditions. That is, after the low use condition the interviewer would spray approximately one or two *additional* sprays for the moderate condition, for a total of three sprays over the two conditions. In the high use condition the interviewers added 2–3 additional sprays, for a total of about five or six sprays over the three conditions. While there may have been some attenuation of scent over time, this was deemed a lesser problem than an over-accumulation of scent.

References

Baron, R. A. (1981). Olfaction and social behavior: Effects of a social scent on attraction and social perception. *Personality and Social Psychology Bulletin, 7*, 611–616.

Baron, R. A. (1983). "Sweet smell of success"? The impact of artificial scents on evaluations of job applicants. *Journal of Applied Psychology, 68*, 709–713.

Knapp, M. L., & Hall, J. A. (1992). *Nonverbal communication in human interaction* (3rd ed.). Orlando, FL: Holt Rinehart and Winston, Inc.

Largey, G. P., & Watson, D. R. (1972). The sociology of odors. *American Journal of Sociology, 77*, 1021–1034.

Levine, J. M., & McBurney, D. H. (1986). The role of olfaction in social perception and behavior. In C. P. Herman, E. T. Higgins, & M. P. Zanna (Eds.), *Physical appearance, stigma, and social behavior: The Ontario symposium* (Vol. 3, pp. 179–217). Hillsdale, NJ: Erlbaum.

McCroskey, J. C., & McCain, T. A. (1974). The measurement of interpersonal attraction. *Speech Monographs, 41*, 261–266.

Schlenker, B. R. (1980). *Impression management.* Monterey, CA: Brooks/Cole.

—Section C—

VOCALICS
Sound and Silence

The voice carries many messages other than words. Vocalic cues such as pitch, speaking rate, pausing, and volume are all important for understanding nonverbal messages. For example, lower-pitched voices are often seen as more credible and powerful. Listen to radio announcers and hear how both men and women have lower-pitched, deeper voices than most of us. Interestingly, male voices in the United States are among the lowest pitched in the world, and the pitch differences between men and women cannot be explained by physiology alone.

People hear your voice in a particular way because of your *vocal qualities*. Voice quality is the characteristic way a person's voice sounds. Just like fingerprints, everyone has a unique "voice print." Some people have very "flat-sounding" voices. These people do not have much vocal or pitch variety and draw out the sound of the letter "a." Flat-sounding voices are perceived as more masculine. Other people have very clear, articulate voices. When they speak, the words sound crisp and clear. Resonance is yet another vocal quality. If you have a resonant voice, it has a deep, rich sound to it.

As you will see in this section of the reader, some vocal qualities are seen as more attractive than others. Specifically, voices that are pleasant and warm, and have variation in pitch, volume, and tempo, are heard as more attractive than cold, monotone voices. People with attractive voices are often perceived as more friendly, likeable, competent, trustworthy, and dominant than people with unattractive voices, especially when they are heard on the telephone or an answering machine.

Vocalizations, which are specific sounds you make that are not words, are yet another form of vocalics. Examples of vocalizations include "uh huh," "um," and "ugh." These sounds have meaning even though they are not words. For example, you say "uh huh" when you agree with someone and use "ugh" when exerting a lot of effort. You might also use vocalized pauses when you are nervous and are not sure what to say. In public speaking situations, people often say "um" because they are nervous and feel a need to "fill in" empty space. In such cases, silence is a better alternative than a vocalization.

Silence is also a vocalic cue. Think of the times you have been silent with people. You were probably feeling one of three emotions: comfort/security, anxiety, or boredom. Silence is a very significant message, and its meaning varies with the situation, relationship, and culture. Silence also occurs within the stream of conversation. Response latencies, for example, are the amount of time it takes for you to answer a question. Long response latencies and hesitancies might telegraph to others that you are nervous or unsure of yourself. In another case, such silence might indicate thoughtfulness.

Vocalics play an important role in persuasion, deception, and the expression of emotion. People who speak with moderately loud volume and moderately fast pace tend to be seen as more credible and confident that those who speak softly or slowly. This can lead to more persuasion. When people try to deceive others, they typically do a better job controlling their facial cues than their voices. The voice often leaks anxiety during deception, making it a good nonverbal behavior to listen to if you are trying to detect deception. Finally, the voice, along with the face, plays a major role in the communication of emotion. When you are happy or excited, chances are that your voice pitch goes up and your tempo increases. If you are depressed, your voice will probably sound monotone and you might talk more slowly than normal. Later when we discuss the various functions of nonverbal communication, you will learn more about how the voice operates in situations involving persuasion, deception, and emotional expression. In the next section, we focus on some of the basic characteristics of vocalics and silence.

*In this article Michael Argyle provides an overview of
paralanguage. Argyle describes the characteristics of the
voice and its functions in communication. In addition
regional and gender differences are discussed.*

17

Nonverbal Vocalizations

Michael Argyle

Vocalizations consist of sounds, of different frequencies and intensities, put
together in different sequences. Some of these are encoded and decoded as
meaningful speech, while others express emotions or interpersonal attitudes, or convey information about the sender.

PROPERTIES OF VOCALIZATIONS

The most objective way of describing sounds is in terms of their
acoustic properties, which are:

1. Duration, rate of speech.
2. Amplitude (perceived as loudness)
3. F_0, fundamental frequency (perceived as pitch) and pitch range.
4. Spectrum of frequency x amplitude (perceived as voice quality, e.g.,
   robust, hollow, shrill).
5. Pitch contour, i.e., change of frequency with time (Scherer, 1982).

Adapted with permission from: Argyle (1988), *Bodily communication*. Reprinted by permission of the Peters Fraser & Dunlop Group Ltd.

135

Another way of describing sounds is by verbal labels which can be used by listeners, such as breathy, nasal, throaty, resonant, clipped, harsh, warm, etc.

It is useful to distinguish between the sounds which are part of language and those which are independent of it.

Emotional Cries

These include moans and groans, shrieks and screams, crying and laughing, oohs and ahs, even roaring and grunting, and are of interest since they are the most similar to animal vocalizations. They have nothing to do with language.

Language

In terms of evolution, language is a later system which has been incorporated in the vocal channel, superimposed on more primitive vocal messages.

Vocalizations Linked to Speech

Prosodic signals are really part of language—e.g., rising pitch to ask a question, pauses and other aspects of timing to show syntax, loudness to give emphasis. Although prosodic signals appear to be part of language, they also convey emotional information.

Synchronizing signals. The synchronizing of utterances is partly achieved by vocal signals, such as a falling pitch at the end of an utterance.

Filled pauses, ers and ahs, are not emotional sounds, but one of a number of kinds of speech disturbances; others are repetitions, stutters, incoherent sounds, omissions, sentence changes, and incompleteness.

Paralinguistic Aspects of Vocalization

These express emotions and attitudes to other people by the way in which words are spoken; the non-verbal message is given simultaneously with the verbal one. This information is conveyed by speech qualities like pitch, loudness, and speed. Other aspects of paralinguistics overlap with prosodic signals. "Pitch contour" can be a prosodic signal indicating end of utterance; it can also be a paralinguistic cue for emotion.

Information About the Speaker

The way a person speaks can convey information about his or her personality, age, sex, social class, regional origins and, above all, who they are. We can classify these different signals as shown in Figure 1.

Figure 1
Nonverbal Vocalizations

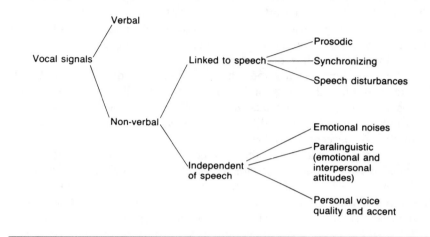

THE COMMUNICATION OF EMOTION

Much research has used posed vocal expressions, where performers have been asked to read something as if they were in some emotional state. Other studies have used role-played scenarios, while some have used mood-induction procedures to produce the required emotions. Here, as elsewhere in bodily communication, posed expressions are not quite the same as the real thing. Posed fearful voices increase raised maximum pitch correctly, for example, but do not raise the minimum pitch (Williams & Stevens, 1972).

Several different methods have been employed to remove the effects of the verbal contents of speech—reading neutral passages or counting, using a band-pass filter which cuts out sounds over 400 or 500 Hz, random splicing of tapes in 2-in. segments, and playing tapes backwards.

Davitz and his colleagues (1964) carried out an important series of studies in which senders posed up to fourteen expressions while reading neutral passages, like "I'm going out now, if anyone calls say I'll be back shortly." They found the range of accuracy of senders and receivers, and which emotions were communicated most accurately.

In these and similar studies, with between four and ten emotions, the average accuracy level is 56 percent versus about 12 percent by chance, which is about the same as the recognition of facial expressions. Some emotions are more easily recognized: negative ones are decoded more easily than positive ones—anger, followed by sadness, indifference, and unhappiness (Scherer, 1981). Joy and hate have been found easier to recognize than shame or love. Some emotions are often confused with each other, because their acoustic properties are similar. Emotions with a high level of activation are confused, e.g., anger, elation, and fear, as are those with a low level, e.g., sadness and indifference.

One problem is that some senders are easier to decode than others; Davitz (1964) found a range of 23–50 percent for different senders. They are easier to decode if they exaggerate, followed by posed performances, with natural ones the most difficult. Receivers also vary in sensitivity—from 20 to 50 percent in the Davitz studies.

In order to separate encoding from decoding, acoustic measurements are needed. An example of encoding research is an experiment by Williams and Stevens (1972) using three male actors as senders, and two acoustic measures of voice quality. In a rare study of real and intense fear, it was found that the pitch range of the pilot of a crashing plane shifted from 168–272 Hz to 288–492; both upper and lower limits of pitch were raised (Williams & Stevens, 1972).

An example of decoding research is a study by Scherer and Oshinsky (1977) who incorporated a wide range of acoustic variables in sounds from a Moog synthesizer, and asked judges to rate the emotions.

Many such studies have now been done on how emotions are encoded. Scherer (1986) reviewed thirty-nine of them. Some of the main findings are as follows:

Joy, elation: raised pitch, pitch range in an utterance, pitch variability, intensity, speech rate, gentle contours.

Depression: lowered pitch, pitch range, intonation, intensity, speech rate, less energy at high pitches.

Anxiety: raised pitch, faster speech, more speech disturbances (except for ah-errors), silent pauses, breathy voice quality, but there is wide individual variation, e.g., some people speak slower when anxious. Nervous public speakers have more and longer silent pauses. Raised pitch speed, and hesitations in speech indicate deception.

Fear: raised pitch, pitch range, variability, high energy at higher pitches, speech rate, special voice quality as in crying.

Anger: raised pitch in rage, lowered in cold anger, raised intensity, harsh voice quality, higher speech rate, sudden increases of pitch and loudness on single syllables (Scherer, 1986).

To what extent are these cues used to encode emotions? The main dimension for both senders and receivers is clearly arousal—communicated by loudness, pitch, and speed, which correlate together. Joy, confidence, anger, and fear all score high. To discriminate between these emotions we have to look at more subtle acoustic parameters. In fact, variables which communicate each emotion are quite similar to those shown above.

The importance of sequential information was shown in an experiment in which tapes were played backwards; this reduced decoding accuracy from 89 percent to 43 percent (Knower, 1941), showing that contour is important. Synthesizing sounds with all components except spectral structure reduced accuracy from 85 percent to 47 percent (Lieberman & Michaels, 1962), so the frequency distribution is important too.

Pitch contour produces some finer differences (Frick, 1985).

happy: gentle contours

angry: sudden increases

surprise: rising pitch

sarcasm: fall on stressed syllable

contempt: fall at end of phrase

coquetry: upward glide on last syllable

question: rise at end of non-ah utterance

The voice is a "leakier" channel than the face, i.e., it is not so well controlled and is more likely to reveal true feelings. Men attend more than women to this leaky channel.

INTERPERSONAL ATTITUDES

There is some overlap here with emotion, since no distinction is made in the voice between anger as an emotional state, and as an attitude directed toward particular individuals. The Davitz studies, for example, did not distinguish between the two and included admiration, affection, amusement, anger, boredom, despair, disgust, dislike, fear, and impatience—all of which can be directed toward others. In a series of studies by the author and colleagues (1970) a number of interpersonal styles were created, using tones of voice (while counting numbers), facial expressions, and head orientations. We had no difficulty in creating tones of voice, corresponding to friendliness, hostility, superiority, and inferiority. Mehrabian (1972) found that tone of voice contributed slightly less than facial expression but much more than the contents of speech to impressions of interpersonal attitudes.

Everyone knows what friendly voices are like: they are like happy ones which, as we have seen, are high pitched, with a lot of gentle upward pitch variation, pure tones, and regular rhythm. Infants produce such sounds very early in life—cooing while smiling. Hostile voices are like the angry ones described before—loud, fast, harsh, sharply rising pitch contours, often lowered pitch—babies make these sounds too (Scherer & Oshinsky, 1977).

Dominance and submissiveness are communicated a little differently. Dominance is expressed by a loud voice, low pitch, broad spectrum, often slow. Submissiveness, like animal appeasement, is higher pitched, sometimes very high, with less resonance, final rising pitch contours, similar to friendly but more tense, anxious, and higher (Frick, 1985).

As with the expression of emotion, the voice is often more truthful, more "leaky" than words. Weitz (1972) rated the voices of eighty supposedly "liberal" white students as they rehearsed the instructions they were to give to another subject, known to be black or white. It was found that tone of voice (rated for friendly and admiring) predicted friendly behavior toward black subjects, e.g., physical proximity and choice of intimate task. On the other hand, verbally expressed attitudes to blacks were *negatively* correlated both with tone of voice and friendly behavior. Those expressing very positive attitudes in fact showed covert rejection of blacks. Tone of voice is leakier than the face, as was shown in connection with the expression of emotion.

Tone of voice is important in social skills and in maintaining relationships. Noller (1984) found that one nonverbal variable which discriminated between happily and unhappily married couples was that the happy couples made more use of the vocal channel for wife-husband communication.

Vocal style has been found to affect persuasiveness. Mehrabian and Williams (1969) found that speakers who spoke faster, louder, and with more intonation were perceived as more persuasive. Later experiments studied the amount of persuasion achieved, and found that the above style is indeed more successful (e.g., Miller et al., 1976). In one experiment tapes were speeded up, slowed down, or altered in pitch. Slower tapes were judged to be less truthful and persuasive, more passive; higher pitched tapes were judged similarly (Apple, Streeter, & Krauss, 1979).

The credibility of a speaker depends on other aspects of vocal style. Pearce and Conklin (1971) found that an actor was judged as more credible when using a serious, scholarly voice (low pitch and volume, small variation in both) than when using a more emotional delivery. Addington (1968) found that throaty, nasal, breathy, or tense deliveries were found low in credibility and competence.

Other research on social skills has found that social influence needs a combination of assertiveness and rewardingness (Argyle, 1983). It is interesting that it is impossible to achieve this combination with the face, since it requires opposed expressions. It is possible to signal this combination with the voice, however.

Accent affects persuasiveness and credibility. In Britain an educated "r.p." (received pronunciation) accent is regarded as more expert and trustworthy, produces more cooperation, and is more likely to be given a job (Giles & Powesland, 1975).

VOICE AND PERSONALITY

If judges are asked to rate the personalities associated with different voices, there is quite a high level of agreement between them. However, there is much less agreement between these judgments and objective measures of personality. We should expect some connection between voice and personality, since people do have some consistency in the emotions and attitudes which they express.

Extroversion is one of the best-established dimensions of personality, and it does correlate with voice—higher pitch (for males), greater vocal affect, faster speech, and fewer pauses (for females). Scherer (1978) produced a "lens" model showing how extroversion, for American males, is encoded as pitch and vocal affect, which are perceived as loudness and (lack of) gloom, and interpreted as extroversion (Figure 2).

A number of experiments have varied the speech style of the same speaker to see how judgments of personality are affected. Rate of speech is one of the most influential variables; faster speech is perceived as potency, extroversion, and competence. Pitch has two effects: raised pitch is judged as extroversion, assertiveness, confidence, and competence, but also as tense and nervous, perhaps because raised pitch is a cue for emotional arousal, which is generalized by perceivers to be a personality trait (Scherer, 1979a).

Anxious people do not have quite the same speech qualities as those produced by anxious situations. They speak fast, but with silent pauses, especially long pauses (over $1^1/_2$ seconds); perhaps they need more planning time, and succeed in controlling other kinds of speech disfluency (Siegman, 1985).

Another group who have been found to have a particular kind of voice are "type A" personalities—those who are competitive, aggressive, impatient, and with a strong drive to succeed. They may succeed, but they are also susceptible to coronary heart disease. Their voices are loud, fast, with explosive emphasis, a lot of variation in speed, and little pause before speaking (Jacobs & Schucker, 1981).

Figure 2
The "Lens" Model for Extroversion

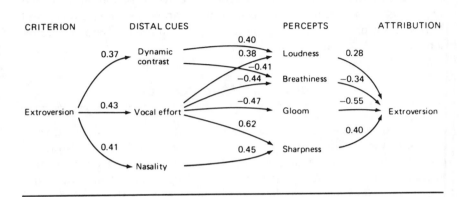

Research on judgments of voices have found three main dimensions—socioeconomic status, pleasing versus displeasing, and active-passive (Mulac, 1976). There is extensive evidence on the stereotypes associated with different voices. Addington (1968) asked male and female performers to speak in nine different ways, and these were then rated by judges on forty scales. There was most agreement on the scales for old-young, masculine-feminine, enthusiastic-apathetic, energetic-lazy, and good-looking-ugly, with interjudge reliabilities of 0.80 or more. Some of the main perceived links with personality were as follows:

breathy: younger, more artistic

flat: more masculine, sluggish, colder, withdrawn

nasal: socially undesirable in various ways

tense: older, unyielding, cantankerous

throaty: older, realistic, mature, sophisticated, well-adjusted

orotund: energetic, healthy, artistic, sophisticated, proud, interesting, enthusiastic

fast: animated, extroverted

varied in pitch: dynamic, feminine, aesthetically inclined.

It is not fully understood what the origins of these stereotypes are. They may be based partly on true associations with personality, partly on the voices of those for different ages, sexes, and cultural groups, partly on analogy—loud, pleasant, shaky, for example.

However, accuracy of judging personality from voice alone is not very great. Judgments from voice have been found to correlate with overall judgments based on voice, face, and contents of speech less well than judgments based on face or verbal contents (O'Sullivan et al., 1985).

Voice and Social Class

Voice is one of the basic cues to social class. This is because in Britain and many other countries there are class differences in accent as a result of historical processes such as the Victorian public schools' propagation of a particular accent and the BBC's of another. A number of experiments in England and the USA have shown that class can be inferred from accent alone. Sissons (1971), at Oxford, found that accent and clothes were the two best single cues to class. Many people try to modify their accent towards that of a higher class, but this is difficult to do. Ellis (1967) found that speakers' real class could still be judged, with a correlation of 0.65, when they were imitating upper-class accents. Harms (1961) found that American students could judge class after the first 10–15 seconds of taped conversation.

Accent varies greatly between situations. Labov (1966) found that with increasingly careful speech, for example when reading lists of words, lower-class Americans shifted not only toward upper-middle-class speech, but on some indices they "hyper-corrected," i.e., they went beyond upper-class speech. In England it has been found that there is a hierarchy of accents of different status. There is some evidence about the vocal characteristics of these accents. Middle-class and educated accents are more clearly articulated, use more intonation, and are less blurred. Consonants are sounded more clearly and there is less stumbling over words. This is not the whole story, though, since there are additional features of accents which are quite arbitrary, and serve solely as indicators of social class.

Regional Accents

Having categorized the speaker by social class, listeners then apply whatever stereotyped beliefs they have about different social classes to the owner of a voice. Giles and Powesland (1975) used the "matched guise" method to study this process. Speakers were used who could simulate the accents of different social groups in Britain, and tape recordings were then assessed by judges. The most prestigious voices in Britain, with "received pronunciation" (r.p.), were judged to be most ambitious, self-confident, intelligent, determined, and industrious. In a study which used thirteen different accents, a single dimension of prestige was obtained: r.p., American and French, north of England, Cockney, and Birmingham. Furthermore, people with less prestigious accents, and from the regions where these are spoken, to a large extent shared these stereotypes. However,

Scots judging Scottish accents and Yorkshiremen judging Yorkshire accents judged the speakers to have greater personal integrity and to be more good-natured and good-humored than r.p. speakers.

Lambert et al. (1961), working in Montreal with English- and French-speaking Canadians, found evidence for similar shared ethnic stereotypes. Annisfeld and colleagues (1962) in America found that a speaker using a Jewish accent was rated as shorter, less good-looking, and lower in leadership—by Jews as well as by Gentiles. They were also rated as higher in humor, entertainingness, and kindness by Jews but not by Gentiles.

Gender

This can be recognized with almost complete success from voice alone. The main difference between males and females is that women's voices are higher pitched, though there is some overlap in the distributions. Women's voices also have greater variation in pitch, especially upward contours (surprise, appeasement), while men use more falling pitch contours. Men talk louder. In addition they try to control conversations and interrupt more. The overall conversational style of men has been characterized as more assertive and less polite (Lakoff, 1973). However, both men and women use more assertive voices when talking to men, despite a common belief that women are more submissive with men than with women (Hall & Braunwald, 1981).

Use is made of gender stereotypes in deciding whether a voice is male or female, and the stereotypes do not entirely correspond to the actual differences between the sexes. For example, the use of tag-questions is regarded as female, whereas in fact there is no difference. But it is widely believed that male speech is loud and aggressive, women's speech friendly, gentle, and trivial (Smith, 1979).

On the decoding side, women attend less than men to the vocal channel, and more to facial expression (p. 286f.). This may be because the vocal channel is leakier, revealing what people want to conceal, or because the vocal channel is more concerned with power and dominance, the face with friendship and attraction.

VOCALIZATIONS RELATED TO SPEECH

The "prosodic" signals of pitch, stress, and timing are able to convey information about emotions and other aspects of the speaker. They are also able to modify the meaning of the message. This is shown by the method used by Noller (1984) in which spouses were asked to send verbally ambiguous messages to give different meanings. Similar effects can be produced by words or nonverbal vocalizations, for example emotions can be aroused by emotive words or emotive expressions, tension can be created by leaving crucial words to the end, or by the manner of delivery. Extra messages can be added by using accents or special intonations, using question intonation for statements, and in other ways.

Pitch

We have discussed pitch changes as a cue for emotions and attitudes. Perhaps the most basic meaning of a raised pitch is emphasis, interest, and excitement, and it is often accompanied by upward movements of mouth, eyebrows, hands, and shoulders. In addition there are standard pitch patterns in every language for different kinds of sentences. In English, for example, questions beginning with "How," "What," etc., are spoken with a falling pitch; but questions with an inversion of subject and verb are spoken with a rising tone. Pitch patterns can be varied to "frame" or provide further meaning for an utterance. "Where are you going?" with a rising pitch on the last word is a friendly enquiry, whereas with a falling pitch it is suspicious and hostile. This expresses more than a paralinguistic attitude to the recipient of the question; it indicates additional thoughts on the part of the speaker, and indicates what sort of answer is needed. Pitch pattern can negate the words spoken, sarcastically, or when the word "yes" is spoken to indicate such unwillingness that it really means "no." Changes of pitch can also be used to accent particular words, though this is usually done by loudness.

Stress

The prosodic system of any language includes rules about the patterns of loudness of words in different kinds of sentences. In English the main nouns and verbs are usually stressed. The same sentence may be given different meanings by stressing different words, as in "they are hunting *dogs*," and "they are *hunting* dogs"; or a sentence may retain the same basic meaning but attention can be directed to quite different parts of the message, as in "*Professor Brown's daughter* is *fond* of *modern music*"—each of the italicized words could be stressed, and this could change the significance of the utterance. In stressing *daughter* there is some implicit reference to a *son*—a case where a nonverbal signal refers or helps refer to an absent object. Speakers can also make soft contrast by speaking some words very quietly.

Duncan and Rosenthal (1968) found that the amount of stress placed on words in the instructions given to experimental subjects had a marked effect on their responses. Subjects were asked to rate the "success" or "failure" of people shown in photographs. There was a correlation of 0.74 between their ratings and the amount of emphasis placed by the experimenter on the words success and failure when describing the scale to be used.

Pauses

Utterances vary in speed, for example a subordinate clause is spoken faster, and a slower speed is used to give emphasis. Pauses are frequent in speech. Pauses of under 1/5 second are used to give emphasis. Longer ones are used to signal grammatical junctures, for example the ends of sentences and clauses. Other pauses occur in the middle of clauses and may coincide with disfluencies, such as repetitions and changes of sentence. About half of speech is taken up by pauses. Unfilled pauses are longer if a speaker has a more difficult task. Most unfilled pauses come at grammatical breaks, before phonemic clauses, often before fluent or complex strings of words, suggesting that the pauses are providing time for planning. However, not all pauses are like this and some may be due to anxiety (Siegman & Feldstein, 1979).

References

Addington, D. W. (1968). The relationship of selected vocal characteristics to personality perception. *Speech Monographs, 35*, 492–503.

Annisfeld, M., Bogo, N., & Lambert, W. (1962). Evaluative reactions to accented English speech. *Journal of Abnormal and Social Psychology, 65*, 223–231.

Apple, W., Streeter, L. A., & Krauss, R. M. (1979). Effects of pitch and speech rate on personal attributes. *Journal of Personality and Social Psychology, 37*, 715–727.

Argyle, M. (1983). *The psychology of interpersonal behavior* (4th ed.). Harmondsworth: Penguin.

Argyle, M., Salter, V., Nicholson, H., Williams, M., & Burgess, R. (1970). The communication of inferior and superior attitudes by verbal and non-verbal signals. *British Journal of Social and Clinical Psychology, 9*, 221–231.

Davitz, J. R. (1964). *The communication of emotional meaning*. New York: McGraw Hill.

Duncan, S. D., & Rosenthal, R. (1968). Vocal emphasis in experimenter's instruction reading as unintended determinant of subjects' responses. *Language and Speech, 11*, 20–26.

Ellis, D. K. (1967). Speech and social status in America. *Social Forces, 45*, 431–451.

Frick, R. W. (1985). Communicating emotion: The role of prosodic features. *Psychological Bulletin, 97*, 412–429.

Giles, H., & Powesland, R. E. (1975). *Speech style and social evaluation*. London: Academic Press.

Hall, J. A., & Braunwald, K. G. (1981). Gender cues in conversations. *Journal of Personality and Social Psychology, 40*, 99–110.

Harms, L. S. (1961). Listener judgments of status cues in speech. *Quarterly Journal of Speech, 47*, 164–168.

Jacobs, D. R., & Schuker, B. (1981). Type A behavior pattern, speech, and coronary heart disease. In J. K. Darby (Ed.), *Speech evaluation in medicine*. New York: Grune and Stratton.

Knower, F. H. (1941). Analysis of some experimental variations of simulated vocal expressions of the emotions. *Journal of Social Psychology, 14*, 369–372.

Labov, W. (1966). *The social stratification of speech in new york city*. Washington, DC: Center for Applied Linguistics.

Lakoff, R. (1973). Language and woman's place. *Language in Society, 2*, 45–80.

Lambert, W. E., Hodgson, R. C., Gardner, R. C., & Fillenbaum, S. (1960). Evaluational reactions to spoken languages. *Journal of Abnormal and Social Psychology, 60*, 44–57.

Lieberman, R., & Michaels, S. B. (1962). Some aspects of fundamental frequency and envelope amplitudes as related to the emotional content of speech. *Journal of the Acoustical Society of America, 34*, 922–927.

Mehrabian, A. (1972). *Nonverbal communication*. Chicago and New York: Aldine-Atherton.

Mehrabian, A., & Williams, M. (1969). Nonverbal concomitants of perceived and intended persuasiveness. *Journal of Personality and Social Psychology, 13*, 37–58.

Mulac, A. (1976). Assessment and application of the revised speech dialect attitudinal scale. *Communication Monographs, 43*, 238–245.

Noller, P. (1984). *Nonverbal communication and marital interaction*. Oxford: Pergamon.

O'Sullivan, M., Ekman, P., Friesen, W., & Scherer, K. R. (1985). What you say and how you say it: The contribution of speech content and voice quality to judgments of others. *Journal of Personality and Social Psychology, 48*, 54–62.

Pearce, W. B., & Conklin, F. (1971). Nonverbal vocalic communication and perceptions of a speaker. *Speech Monographs, 38*, 235–241.

Scherer, K. R. (1978). Inference rules in personality attribution from voice quality: The loud voice of extraversion. *European Journal of Social Psychology, 8*, 46–87.

Scherer, K. R. (1979). Personality markers in speech. In K. R. Scherer & H. Giles (Eds.), *Social markers in speech*. Cambridge: Cambridge University Press.

Scherer, K. R. (1981). Speech and emotional states. In J. K. Darby (Ed.), *Speech Evaluation in Psychiatry*. New York: Grune and Stratton.

Scherer, K. R. (1986). Vocal affect expression: A review and model for further research. *Psychological Bulletin, 99*, 143–165.

Scherer, K. R., & Oshinsky, J. S. (1977). Cue utilization in emotion attribution from auditory stimuli. *Motivation and Emotion, 1*, 331–346.

Siegman, A. W. (1985). Anxiety and speech disfluencies. In A. W. Siegman & S. Feldstein (Eds.), *Multichannel integrations of nonverbal behavior*. New York: Erlbaum.

Siegman, A. W., & Feldstein, S. (1979). *Of speech and time*. New York: Erlbaum.

Sissons, M. (1971). The psychology of social class. In M. Keynes (Ed.), *Money, wealth and class*. Open University Press.

Smith, P. M. (1979). Sex markers in speech. In K. R. Scherer & H. Giles (Eds.), *Social markers in speech*. Cambridge: Cambridge University Press.

Weitz, S. (1972). Attitude, voice and behavior. *Journal of Personality and Social Psychology, 24*, 14–21.

Williams, C. E., & Stevens, K. N. (1972). Emotions and speech: Some acoustical correlates. *Journal of the Acoustical Society of America, 52*, 1238–1250.

Semic discusses the vocal attractiveness stereotype, which is also known as the "what sounds beautiful is good" hypothesis. According to this hypothesis, people with warm, expressive voices tend to be perceived as more likeable, trustworthy, dominant, and competent than people with less attractive voices. The impact of the voice is strongest in contexts such as telephone conversations and voice mail, when the visual channel is not present. Yet, as Semic argues, the voice has some impact even in face-to-face contexts.

18

Vocal Attractiveness
What Sounds Beautiful Is Good

Beth Semic

In business, you can have the finest clothes, looks and credentials, but if you have a weak voice, it considerably lessens the first impression you make. (Farming, 1990, p. 25)

Do certain voices make you cringe or smile? Do some people seem less intelligent or stronger because of the way they sound? Do you like some friends more because of the sound of their voices? Your favorite radio or television personality probably has an attractive voice. For instance, you may enjoy hearing James Earl Jones say, "This is CNN," and you like him, in part, because of the way he talks. We may not always be aware of it, but the voice plays an important role in the impressions we form about other people. According to the vocal attractiveness stereotype, we make judgments about others from their vocal cues. For example, an employer might decide

This article was written especially for *The Nonverbal Communication Reader.*

to bring you in for an interview based partially on the way you sound during a phone interview. Someone you are romantically interested in could be attracted or repelled by your voice. This article will focus on the vocal attractiveness stereotype by describing the attractive voice, explaining the vocal attractiveness stereotype, and summarizing the personality perceptions and attributions associated with this stereotype.

THE ATTRACTIVE VOICE

What makes a voice attractive or unattractive to the human ear? Burgoon, Buller, and Woodall (1996) defined the "good voice" as "maintaining sufficient muscle tone in the vocal folds to produce a highly complex vocal tone at a desired frequency and intensity; positioning the glottis at the correct vertical level; proper horizontal positioning of the tongue for articulation and audibility; proper use of the nasal cavity; and the right amount of sympathetic resonance" (p. 65). In essence, this definition suggests that the attractive voice has two important qualities: pitch and impact (resonance, articulation, and volume) (Zuckerman & Miyake, 1993). Burgoon, Buller, and Woodall (1996) also described vocal qualities that tend to make a voice unattractive. These include voices that are too breathy, husky, nasal, flat, or throaty. Next, let's take a closer look at the two qualities that are present in most attractive voices: pitch and impact.

Pitch

Vocal pitch is how high or low a voice sounds. Some voices may sound deep or husky while others have a squeaky or high sound. As well, a person's pitch may vary or stay the same during a conversation. The attractive voice, in terms of pitch, is one that is neither too high nor too low (Zuckerman & Miyake, 1993) and varies throughout a conversation (Burgoon et al., 1996). A person with these vocal qualities sounds expressive and full of life.

Impact

A voice's impact includes its resonance, articulation, and volume (Zuckerman & Miyake, 1993). Resonance is a vocal quality that can best be described as the fullness of sound in the facial cavity. Resonant voices are smooth and strong. Articulation is the production of crisp and distinct speech sounds. Volume is simply a voice's loudness or softness. The attractive voice is characterized by moderate levels of resonance, articulation, and loudness. In other words, a clear, robust voice conveys vocal attractiveness.

Now that we understand the key features of an attractive voice, we need to understand the effects of that voice on our perceptions of others. The vocal attractiveness stereotype explains many of these effects.

THE VOCAL ATTRACTIVENESS STEREOTYPE

We are all well aware of the importance of how we look and what we do in making first impressions (see the section on appearance and adornment in this reader). From the time we are young we are taught how to manage impressions. We learn to be neat and clean, and speak only when spoken to. We are told how to dress, and how to talk in an interview so as to make a good first impression. It is clear that both our physical and vocal "appearance" affect our lives in various ways.

Before researchers became interested in vocal attractiveness, they were curious about the effects of physical attractiveness on our impressions of others. Dion, Berscheid, and Walster (1972) first explained the link between physical attractiveness and impression formation with their "what is beautiful is good" hypothesis. They believed that attractive people would be viewed more positively by others. For instance, you may see a well-dressed professor as more qualified than one dressed in jeans and a t-shirt. These researchers discovered that people did, indeed, see physically attractive individuals as happier, more well adjusted, and more successful than less attractive individuals.

The physical attractiveness stereotype represents the influence of visual nonverbal cues on first impressions. However, our impressions of other people do not depend solely on how they look. The attractiveness stereotype is a vocal phenomenon as well. We also stereotype people based upon how they sound—the "what sounds beautiful is good" hypothesis (Zuckerman & Driver, 1989). Researchers interested in the impact of the voice on first impressions believed that vocal attractiveness would garner positive impressions (Zuckerman, Amidon, Bishop, & Pomerantz, 1982; Zuckerman & Driver, 1989; Zuckerman & Miyake, 1993). For example, if that well-dressed professor we described earlier also had a clear, robust voice you might see her or him as friendly and pleasant to be around, as well as qualified to do her or his job. But if that same professor spoke with a squeaky, high-pitched voice, or spoke extremely slowly with low volume, you might re-evaluate her or his credibility. This example illustrates the "what sounds beautiful is good" hypothesis by showing that the vocally attractive person has several advantages over the vocally unattractive person.

The first advantage for the vocally attractive person deals with personality perceptions. We tend to see people with "good voices" as good people. This advantage begins early in life and continues throughout one's lifetime. A team of psychologists asked a group of adults their impressions of five-year-old children based on the attractiveness and babyishness of the children's voices (Berry, Hansen, Landry-Pester, & Meier, 1994). Interestingly, these researchers found that we stereotype even the very young. Adults believed that the vocally attractive children were warm, competent, and dominant. As well, adults saw the children with babyish voices as warm and dominant. Consider the impact in the kindergarten classroom. A young child who has a quiet, inarticulate voice may be shunned by his or her peers and considered less intelligent than other children by his or her teacher.

Our urge to stereotype others' personalities based on vocal qualities extends to adults as well. As with children, vocally attractive adults reap the benefits of their attractiveness. Addington (1968) has experimented with the adult voice. He looked at specific vocal qualities and personality perceptions by tape recording two men and two women reading a story using several different voice qualities (breathy, tense, thin, flat, throaty, nasal, and orotund). Individuals gave their impressions of these voices (e.g., feminine-masculine, good looking-ugly, educated-uneducated, kind-cruel, sincere-insincere). Both negative and positive perceptions were obtained for each of the voice qualities. As you can see from the list below, we seem to develop more positive impressions of the male voice (regardless of quality) than the female voice.

Breathy: Male—younger, artistic; Female—feminine, pretty, petite, effervescent, high strung, shallow

Thin: Male—no significant findings; Female—socially, physically, emotionally, and mentally immature

Flat: Male and Female—masculine, sluggish, cold, withdrawn

Nasal: Male and Female—immature, skinny, unemotional

Tense: Male—older, unyielding, cantankerous; Female—younger, emotional, feminine, high strung, unintelligent

Throaty: Male—older, realistic, mature, sophisticated, well adjusted; Female—unintelligent, masculine, lazy, unemotional, ugly, careless, neurotic

Orotund: Male—energetic, healthy, artistic, sophisticated, proud; Female—lively, gregarious, sensitive, proud, humorless

Diane Berry, a psychologist, has also conducted several studies on vocal attractiveness in adults (Berry, 1990, 1992; Berry et al., 1994). She had people listen to attractive adult voices and rate them for certain personality characteristics. Not surprisingly, she found that individuals with attractive voices were seen as powerful, strong, assertive, and dominant. However, the results for vocal babyishness changes slightly for adults. Individuals judged men who had babyish voices negatively. However, the babyish female voice produced positive impressions.

In another personality study, two researchers asked people to rate the attractiveness of 400 voices (Zuckerman & Driver, 1989). They were also asked to give their impressions of the speakers' personalities. Once again, the more attractive voices were rated more favorably than the less attractive voices. For instance, an attractive voice led the hearer to judge the speaker as dominant, industrious, sensitive and warm. Unattractive voices, in contrast, tended to elicit opinions of laziness, timidity, and belligerence. In a related study, Zuckerman, Hodgins, and Miyake (1990) provided even stronger evidence for this stereotype. In terms of the more broad, representative measures of personality (neuroticism, agreeableness, and extroversion) the vocally attractive person wins again. Not only do we attach specific positive personality characteristics to individuals with attractive voices, we also generally give them the "benefit of the doubt." The employer who interviews you for a job will not only see you as competent for the job, but he or she will feel generally you are a good person, especially if your voice fits into an overall package of both physical and vocal attractiveness. If this is the case, you would likely be seen as calm, secure, good natured, flexible, outgoing, and joyful.

Semic, Guerrero, Pulizzi, and Miller (1995) extended this line of research to a practical context. They investigated the attractive voice on business answering-machine messages. In today's highly technical world we often find ourselves talking to machines more than to humans. Therefore, in contexts such as voice mail and answering-machine messages, it is particularly important to understand the impact of the voice. Semic and colleagues looked at the effects of both vocal attractiveness and verbal content on perceptions of personality. Individuals were told to assume that they called a place of business expecting to talk to Chris Miller and instead received a business answering-machine message that included either an internal excuse ("I'm sorry but I do not take calls during this time of the day") or an external excuse ("I have either been called away to a meeting or am on another line and unable to come to the phone right now") for not answering the phone call. Results showed that regardless of the type of excuse given, the vocally attractive message was seen as more trustworthy, competent, likeable, and dominant. Again, the vocally attractive person was given the benefit of the doubt. People believed that he or she was a good person because of the sound of his or her voice.

The power of the attractive voice extends beyond positive perceptions of personality. We also tend to develop a false sense of similarity with vocally attractive others. Why is this important? Think for a moment about people that you believe are similar to yourself. How do you feel about them? You probably like them. If we see someone as similar to ourselves we are more likely to have positive feelings about them. We do not want to be like those we dislike. In one study (Miyake & Zuckerman, 1993), college students listened to vocally attractive and unattractive others read a standard script. These students were then told to decide how similar they were to the person they had just heard reading. They were asked to determine if they and the "reader" were similar in terms of behavior (e.g., taking a course in which the grade depended on a term paper and choosing whether to write an individual or group paper), personality (neuroticism, extroversion, openness, agreeableness, and conscientiousness), and achievement (academic record, and aspirations). The college students saw themselves as similar to the vocally attractive individuals in all areas. For example, you would be likely to judge a vocally attractive person as extroverted or introverted, just like you. Miyake and Zuckerman (1993) gave two reasons for this perceived similarity. First, we feel a need to see ourselves as similar to those we like. Second, we feel a need for validation from those we like.

The power of the voice does not end there. We also tend to see the vocally attractive individual as more socially skilled. Socially skilled people know how to "behave" in social situations. They are able to interact with other people comfortably. Larrance and Zuckerman (1981) examined the relationship between vocal likability and the ability to accurately send vocal cues—a particular social skill. They found that more likeable senders were seen as skillful in conveying the meaning of a message through vocal cues to the listener. So, we not only like the vocally attractive person more, we also think he or she is a more competent communicator.

There is, of course, one important caveat to all of this research. The studies that have found the strongest effects for the vocal attractiveness stereotype have isolated the vocal channel. In other words, the people who made the personality judgments only heard their voices, rather than both seeing them and hearing them. This isn't to say that there are no effects for the voice in face-to-face interactions. Studies that have looked at vocal and physical attractiveness together have found some effect for the voice even then, but the effect is smaller. It is also important to keep in mind that vocal *un*attractiveness may be just as powerful, if not more powerful, than vocal attractiveness. Think of the most irritating voice you have ever heard. Can you imagine spending a lot of time talking to that person? You would probably not perceive this person as someone you would like to get to know better.

So, what does all of this mean? How can we use this information? There should be little doubt that sounding "beautiful" impacts our lives in a number of ways. The voice is a powerful tool. Based on your voice, people might judge your personality, your attitudes, and your skills. Your voice can affect what your professors think about you. It can cause your acquaintances to like or dislike you. It can produce impressions of competence or incompetence in employment interviews. As you interact with others you should be aware of the impressions people may be forming of you, and of the impressions you are creating of them. Just as you should not underestimate the power of a beautiful face, you should no longer minimize the force of an attractive voice.

References

Addington, D. W. (1968). The relationship of selected vocal characteristics to personality perception. *Speech Monographs, 38*, 242–247.

Berry, D. S. (1992). Vocal types and stereotypes: Joint effects of vocal attractiveness and vocal maturity on person perception. *Journal of Nonverbal Behavior, 16*, 41–54.

Berry, D. S. (1990). Vocal attractiveness and vocal babyishness: Effects on stranger, self, and friend impressions. *Journal of Nonverbal Behavior, 14*, 141–153.

Berry, D. S., Hansen, J. S., Landry-Pester, J. C., & Meier, J. A. (1994). Vocal determinants of first impressions of young children. *Journal of Nonverbal Behavior, 18*, 187–197.

Burgoon, J. K., Buller, D. B., & Woodall, W. G. (1996). *Nonverbal communication: the unspoken dialogue* (2nd ed.). New York: Harper & Row.

Dion, K., Berscheid, E., & Walster, E. (1972). What is beautiful is good. *Journal of Personality and Social Psychology, 24*, 285–290.

Farming, D. (1990, Sept. 23). The executive life. The *New York Times*, section 3, p. 25.

Larrance, D. T., & Zuckerman, M. (1981). Facial attractiveness and vocal likability as determinants of nonverbal sending skills. *Journal of Personality, 49*, 349–362.

Miyake, K., & Zuckerman, M. (1993). Beyond personality impressions: Effects of physical and vocal attractiveness on false consensus, social comparison, affiliation, and assumed and perceived similarity. *Journal of Personality, 6*, 411–437.

Semic, B. A., Guerrero, L. K., Pulizzi, J. W., & Miller, T. A. (1995). *Vocal attractiveness as heard in the answering machine: Two tests of the "What sounds beautiful is good" hypothesis.* Paper presented at the 1995 Speech Communication Association convention in San Antonio, TX.

Zuckerman, M., Amidon, M. D., Bishop, S. E., & Pomerantz, S. D. (1982). Face and tone of voice in the communication of deception. *Journal of Personality and Social Psychology, 43*, 347–357.

Zuckerman, M., & Driver, R. (1989). What sounds beautiful is good: The vocal attractiveness stereotype. *Journal of Nonverbal Behavior, 13*, 67–82.

Zuckerman, M., Hodgins, H., & Miyake, K. (1990). The vocal attractiveness stereotype: Replication and elaboration. *Journal of Nonverbal Behavior, 14*, 97–112.

Zuckerman, M., & Miyake, K. (1993). The attractive voice: What makes it so? *Journal of Nonverbal Behavior, 17*, 119–135.

Jaworski discusses the importance of silence in the communication process. In the first two parts of this article, he examines the role of silence in effective communication and in miscommunication. In the last part of this article, Jaworski takes a different approach by discussing the positive and negative functions of silence from a pragmatic communication perspective. For example, silence can function to bond people together or to separate them. Silence may also signal deep thoughtfulness, or it might signal mental inactivity.

19

The Power of Silence in Communication

Adam Jaworski

The awareness of the fact that *how* we say something means at least as much as *what* we say is the central underlying idea of the books by Tannen (1986), and Scollon and Scollon (1987). The authors make their readers aware of the possible and actual miscommunication problems as well as advise them on how to handle situations particularly threatening to their relationships with others.

COMMUNICATION

But what does silence have to do with that? Why should not saying anything be significantly related to speaking? In my view, the main common link between speech and silence is that the same interpretive processes apply to someone's remaining meaningfully silent in discourse as to their speaking. Consider the following example from Polish.

Shortly after the wedding of her daughter, our next-door neighbor visited my wife and me. In order to hear what the purpose of her visit was my wife and I invited her to sit down in the living room and we started chatting. At one point the neighbor turned to me and asked me how much she owed me for a small favor I had done for her in connection with the wedding. I was genuinely appalled at the question so I *did not say anything* and just looked peeved at the woman. After a moment, she said, slightly embarrassed, "*Czy mam wyskoczyc przez okno?*" ("Do you want me to jump out of the window?"). I said, "*Tak*" ("Yes"). Then we changed the topic, and after feeding us some fresh neighborly gossip, she left.

This example clearly illustrates how silence can carry meaning. I did not reply verbally to her question about the money, but she knew that I was offended by her inquiry, and she also realized that I was not going to accept any form of payment for the favor (which would have then turned into a service). I knew she did not intend to be rude to me, but I felt insulted. If I had decided to tell her that I thought she was being rude to me at that moment, I may have hurt her in turn. By not saying anything, I simply allowed her to come up with the most relevant interpretation of my silence and then, because of my indirectness, she was able to turn the situation into a joke, which I accepted.

Or take another Polish example. The scene is a small bathroom and the time is early morning before going to work. The husband is shaving and the wife enters to blow dry her hair.

Wife: *Przeszkadzam ci?* ("Am I disturbing you?")
Husband: [silence]
Wife: [silence, walks out]

In this example, the wife interpreted her husband's silence as a yes. He interpreted her silence as "Okay, I'll come back when you're done." Their exchange was economical, efficient, and to the point.

Our ability to use silence appropriately in our own speech and the adequate interpretation of the silences of others are indispensable for successful communication. Therefore, I believe children acquire the ability to use and understand silence very much in the same manner that they acquire all the other linguistic skills in the acquisition process.

MISCOMMUNICATION

Of course, things do not always go so smoothly as in the "neighbor" and "bathroom" examples. Silence can cause trouble, too. Many teachers should find the following example a familiar one. (The teacher and the students are Polish, but the class is taught in English.) A group of undergraduate students is asked a question of opinion about a theoretical point they have been discussing for some time.

Teacher: So, what do you think of X?

Students: [silence, looking down]

Teacher: Fine. . . . Sure. . . . Yeah, I agree. . . . That's a good
            point you've made. . . .

Students: [giggle]

The teacher's interpretation of the students' silence is open to several possibilities. For example, the silence may signal the students' lack of relevant knowledge to answer the question ("You have not taught us enough about the problem you're asking."), it may indicate their hostility toward the teacher and an uncooperative attitude ("We do not like you and we are not going to talk to you."), or it may mark the students' shyness ("We are afraid of saying something stupid."). Regardless of the accurate interpretation of the ensuing silence, the joking behavior of the teacher (quite successful, judging by the giggling that followed it) functioned as relief for the tension created by the awkward silence. (Note that in the "neighbor" example joking was also used as a strategy to alleviate the effect of silence.)

Another classroom example, this time from a Polish elementary school setting, illustrates how one instance of silence is differently interpreted by two individuals. The teacher asks one pupil to express his opinion on the poem that has been read in class. The boy stands up and remains silent. The teacher interprets his silence as an inability to formulate any opinion on the poem, says nothing to the boy, and asks another one to complete the task. The next boy stands up and says: "I am of the same opinion as my friend." General laughter follows, but it can be safely assumed that the latter boy interpreted the silence of the former as an expression of a negative opinion about the poem.

However, in many cases silence affects human lives more profoundly in a negative way, and mere joking is not a sufficient remedy for the resulting tension. Some people, for example, have the habit of keeping silent more than they are expected to. The so-called strong, silent man is a case in point (Tannen, 1986). His silence may seem quite attractive on stage in the portrayal of fictitious characters or at the beginning of a relationship between a man and a woman, but a woman confronted with a man's silence in a long-term relationship often finds it "like a brick wall against which she is banging her head" (Tannen, 1986, p. 116).

PAUSING

Misjudging someone's use of silence can take place in many contexts and on many levels. Take pausing, for example. One's conversational style may be marked by frequent pausing, thus giving room (or time) for the discourse partner to jump into the conversation by taking his or her next turn. Some speakers, however, may think that the pauses others leave for them are not long enough to claim the floor without being rude, while it may be the feeling of the other party that longer pauses would create awkward silences. Such differences in the perception and valuation of pauses may lead to conflict. The person who does not tolerate long pauses may wonder why the other does not want to talk, whereas the person who needs longer pauses to take a turn may think of his or her interlocutor as intolerably talkative. Says Tannen (1986):

> Such differences are not a matter of some people expecting long pauses and others expecting short ones. Long and short are relative; they have meaning only in comparison to something—what's expected, or someone else's pause. Someone who expects a shorter pause than the person she's speaking to will often start talking before the other has a chance to finish or to start. Someone who is waiting for a longer pause than the person she's speaking to won't be able to get a word in edgewise. (p. 29)

Fighting for the floor can be quite frustrating, especially in a culture that values more talk and faster talk over less talk and slower talk. Anglo-American culture, and probably most Western cultures, subscribe to such evaluative stereotypes (Scollon, 1985). Therefore, we accelerate our conversations with others and avoid pauses at all cost, because we think that whatever silences occur in discourse they inevitably indicate lack of mutual rapport between the interlocutors.

Cultural attitudes to discourse silence and tempo of speech are very important in assessing the perceived success of speakers in getting their point across. When Lech Walesa and Tadeusz Mazowiecki were running for president of Poland, a press article compared the success and effectiveness of their respective campaigns. Among other things, the author of the article contrasted Walesa's and Mazowiecki's discourse styles. Walesa's style—marked by fast tempo, varied intonation, and absence of pauses—

was evaluated more positively (as more effective) than Mazowiecki's style—described as monotonous and marked by long silences:

> Walesa raises his voice, shouts, suddenly slows down, laughs and pulls a face. He does not hesitate for a second, and even interrupts questions which are too long, while sometimes says frankly to somebody from his entourage "I'm lost." There are no longueurs. . . .
>
> If only the prime minister [Mazowiecki] knew that he should speak to the microphone and to the people, not to himself! He talks quietly, slowly, monotonously, with multisecond pauses. (Leski, 1990, p. 3)

The above example shows that in political discourse, fast speech, loudness, and constant shifting between different speech styles are more highly valued than speaking slowly, quietly, and monotonously. This cultural valuation of noise over silence is effectively used by politicians appearing in the media for two purposes. One is when they have nothing relevant to say and the other is when they want to conceal something. In cases like this, the effect is excessive verbiage or gibberish. It may be devoid of any content on the semantic level but gives wide audiences an impression that the communicator is either very knowledgeable or in control of the situation or information or that he or she has all these qualities. The fact that the message may not be at all clear is irrelevant.

POSITIVE AND NEGATIVE VALUES OF SILENCE

When silence is recognized as a possible means of communication, it is typically considered to be able to express a variety of meanings and to perform a range of functions. A number of researchers have pointed out these properties of silence and have indicated that, on a number of planes, silence has two values: positive and negative. For example, Jensen (1973) discusses five functions of silence and assigns a positive and a negative value to each of them. The functions he proposes are the following:

A. *A linkage function*: Silence may bond two (or more) people or it may separate them.

B. *An affecting function*: Silence may heal (over time) or wound.

C. *A revelation function*: Silence may make something known to a person (self-exploration) or it may hide information from others.

D. *A judgmental function*: Silence may signal assent and favor or it may signal dissent and disfavor.

E. *An activating function*: Silence may signal deep thoughtfulness (work) or it may signal mental inactivity.

Tannen (1985) discusses the "positive and negative valuation of silence" in regard to a number of communicative and social processes. Following Allen (1978), Tannen (1985) says "that silence serves two functions in the literature she [Allen] surveyed, one negative—a failure of language—and one positive—a chance for personal exploration" (p. 94). Furthermore, Tannen lists different types of situations in which silence may function in such an ambivalent manner: either as an expression of good or bad rapport and either as comfortable or clumsy communication.

A similar ambivalence of silence is observed in the cultural communicative uses of silence in Japanese (Lebra, 1987). The value of silence in Japan derives from the conceptualization of the self as split into two parts: the *inner* and the *outward*. The inner is associated with truthfulness and is located symbolically in the heart and belly. The outward is associated with the face, mouth, and spoken words and with deception, disguise, falsity, and so on, whereas silence expresses inner truth. Reticent individuals are trusted as honest, sincere, and straightforward. Thus silence is an active state, while speech is an excuse for delaying activity.

On the other hand, silence is associated with concealing the truth. When the speaker wants to "gain social acceptance or to avoid social penalty" (Lebra, 1987, p. 347) he or she may refrain from speaking and avoid revealing the outward truth expressed by the spoken word. Social relations with others are governed by complex norms, which depend on social discretion. In sum, as far as inner truth is concerned, silence is the best way of expressing and maintaining it, whereas when the outward truth of the spoken word may be socially harmful and bring about criticism, hatred, or humiliation, silence is the best means of concealing it.

Two other dimensions in the use of silence in Japanese also stand in a type of functional opposition to one another. The first dimension is embarrassment in intimate relations. Young spouses who are deeply in love, for example, often express their affection for each other by nonverbal means and in silence. On the other hand, silence is used as an expression of social defiance in disagreeing with someone, objecting to what has been said or done, or as a signal of anger and hatred.

The ambiguity of silence may be confusing to an outsider trying to make sense out of the silent behavior of others. It may even be difficult for native speakers to interpret and rationalize their own and others' silence in an appropriate manner. Of course, the ambivalent nature of silent communication may often cause misunderstandings. Further ambivalence regarding the nature of silence is demonstrated in English by two common expressions attributing to silence two extremely different qualities: "Silence is golden" and "Silence is deadly." Sometimes, silence may be regarded as a sign of someone's power or control over others, or it may be a sign of a person's weakness and submission. Silence may be a state in which one gains knowledge, or it may be a state of idle ignorance or *unlearning*. In love and friendship silence may function as an expression of bondage, or it may be a sign of a disintegrating relationship.

References

Allen, C. (1978). Failure of words, uses of silence: Djuna Barnes, Adrienne Rich, and Margaret Atwood. *Regionalism and Female Imagination, 4*(1), 107.

Jensen, V. (1973). Communicative functions of silence. *ETC., 30,* 249–257.

Lebra, T. S. (1987). The cultural significance of silence in Japanese communication. *Multilingua 6–4,* 634–657.

Leski, K. (1990, October 16). Mazowiecki i Walesa czyli dwie kampanie [Mazowiecki and Walesa: Two campaigns]. *Gazeta Wyborcza, 241,* p. 3.

Scollon, R. (1985). The machine stops. Silence in the metaphor of malfunction. In D. Tannen & M. Saville-Troike (Eds.), *Perspectives on silence* (pp. 21–30). Norwood, NJ: Ablex.

Scollon, R., & Scollon, S. (1987). *Responsive communication.* Haines, AK: Black Current Press.

Tannen, D. (1986). *That's not what I meant: How conversational style makes or breaks your relations with others.* London: J. M. Dent & Sons.

This article examines how silence is used and interpreted across several different cultures. Using an ethnographic comparative analysis, Braithwaite forwards two warrants or conclusions. The first warrant is that silence tends to occur in social situations in which the relationship of participants is uncertain, unpredictable, or ambiguous. The second warrant is that silence tends to occur in social situations in which there is a known and unequal distribution of power among participants. Examples from several different cultures are given to support these claims.

20

Cultural Uses and Interpretations of Silence

Charles A. Braithwaite

Silence in human communication has been examined from a variety of perspectives: as an act of contemplation (Dauenhauer, 1980; Mazzeo, 1962; Picard, 1952), as a "speech" disorder (Griffin, 1970; Johnson, 1973; Philips, 1968; Weisman, 1955); as a process of encoding and decoding speech (Bruneau, 1973; Jensen, 1973), and as the origin of speech (Scott, 1972). But few writers have treated silence as a *communicative act*. Communicative silence refers to those instances where the actor, given the option to speak or not to speak, *chooses* not to speak, and thereby makes a strategic or goal-directed choice. Silence is usually viewed as a private, inward act, not as communication. Although several attempts have been made to catalogue the "functions" of silence (Baker, 1955; Bruneau, 1973; Johannesen, 1974), no study has produced sufficient evidence to make any general

This article was written especially for *The Nonverbal Communication Reader.*

ization concerning the communicative function of silence beyond one's own speech community. According to Bruneau (1973), interactive (communicative) silence is highly variable from person to person and "highly bound to the nature of the message sharing process and especially to communicative situations and circumstances" (p. 28).

This article is an attempt to examine communicative silence in a variety of speech communities with the intent to discover some generalizations concerning the use and interpretation of silence *across* cultures. Before this examination begins, it is necessary to explain the significance of a study of silence for the field of *speech* communication. The study of silence in a speech community is important for at least three reasons. First, the use of silence can be seen as one among a range of strategies or options that can itself be part of, or constitute, a "way of speaking." Way of speaking refers to the association of modes of speaking, topics or message forms with particular settings and activities in a speech community. Accordingly, silence can be viewed in much the same way talk is viewed, as an important symbolic resource that can be used by any member of a speech community. Therefore, silence is interesting to study in its own right. In any description of speaking, silence is potentially something of importance.

Second, the use and interpretation of silence can also be a central part of the "foundations" of a speech community. Because silence is a significant communicative resource, and because it, like talk, is patterned in culturally specific ways, the detailing of the patterning of silence, in use and in cultural evaluation, can imply a larger pattern in human communication. According to Hymes (1972), "the distribution of required and preferred silence, indeed perhaps most immediately reveals in outline form a community's structure of speaking" (p. 40). One of the basic building blocks of competence, both linguistic and cultural, is knowing when not to speak in a particular community. Therefore, to understand where, when, and how to be silent, and the meanings attached to silence, is to gain a keen insight into the fundamental structure of communication in that world. Silence is not just the absence of behavior. As Samarin (1965) notes, "Silence can have meaning. Like the zero in mathematics, it is an absence with a function" (p. 115).

A third and most compelling reason for examining silence in a speech community is that it has been posited that some communicative functions of silence are "universal" and can be found in all cultures. That is, the way silence is used as a strategy and the meaning attached to that particular use does not seem to vary crossculturally. Basso's (1990) study of the Western Cibecue Apache and several other Arizona communities of Native Americans has led him to propose as universally true that "the absence of verbal communication is associated with social situations in which the status of focal participants is ambiguous" (p. 225). In other words, in social relationships characterized by uncertainty and unpredictability, silence is the appropriate behavior. But Basso admits that adequate cross-cultural descriptions are insufficient either to support or refute his hypothesis.

Given that silence is such an important feature of communicative behavior, and given that studies to date have not produced sufficient empirical evidence as to how silence is patterned in its use and interpretation across cultures, an important research question is: What are the interactive and cultural uses and meanings of silence?

The perspective and method adopted to answer this question is the ethnography of speaking. The ethnography of speaking is a rules based perspective that focuses on an explication of the knowledge one must share in a particular speech community in order to "use language appropriately in any role in any scene staged in a particular community" (Philipsen, 1977, p. 44). As a method, the ethnography of speaking involves the use of a descriptive framework to identify various components of speech in order to develop a descriptive theory of speech in a community. To an ethnographer of speaking, a community is defined as a group that shares "rules for conduct and interpretation of at least one linguistic variety" (Hymes, 1972, p. 54).

Hymes said, "since one human group's theories of speaking can best be isolated by contrast with those of another, the comparative approach to field work is probably the most useful at this stage" (p. 36). For Hymes, the primary concern for the ethnographer of speaking is to focus on descriptive, comparative analysis from a variety of communities. Therefore, to approach the research question concerning the uses and meanings of silence across cultures, accounts from nineteen speech communities were examined. These ethnographic accounts were studied with the intent of juxtaposing their descriptions of the uses and interpretations of silence in their particular communities to discern where they are similar, where they are different, and where they are *systematically* related.

In each of the studies selected, the when, where, and how of silence, and the meanings attached to silence, were explored. There is special significance to seventeen of the accounts in that they all used a similar descriptive framework for the study of a community's pattern of speaking. Each was concerned, to varying degrees, with those elements central to an adequate descriptive theory of a speech community (c.f. Hymes, 1972, pp. 52–71). Those include an examination of the settings or *scenes* for talk, the *participants* and their roles and relationships, the *ends* or purposes for talk, the *act sequence* or order of talk, the *keys* or tones that accompany talk, the various *instrumentalities* or linguistic varieties in a community, the *norms* for interpretation of talk, and the various *genres* or "types" of talk, i.e., jokes, curses, greetings, etc.

Each study, again to varying degrees, found patterns of conduct and of normative behavior in regard to the use and interpretation of silence in the particular speech community. Although other accounts mentioned the use of silence, those using the descriptive framework of Hymes, or covering those elements outlined by Hymes as adequate for a descriptive theory, revealed the most comprehensive data on when silence was used and how it was interpreted.

A basis for comparative analysis exists in that a similar descriptive framework was used in various studies; therefore the investigators had similar starting points. A comparative analysis of these particular studies makes possible the study of many diverse groups, and the comparison of their communicative behavior will reveal common features of silence. Such a comparative analysis would permit a partial test of Basso's hypothesis concerning the universal patterning of silence. Again to refer to Hymes, "mankind cannot be understood apart from the evolution and maintenance of its ethnographic diversity. A satisfactory understanding of the nature and unity of men must encompass and embrace, not abstract from, the diversity" (p. 41).

Each ethnography was then examined for details of *communicative* silence. Although many accounts contained information regarding places where silence was expected, i.e., church, hospitals, etc., the focus of this study was on those instances where silence occurred as the result of the *actor's choice.* Because the ethnography of communication perspective holds that communication is a decision-making activity, the accounts were analyzed to discover the concepts and premises used by a particular actor to make a decision to use silence in a manner appropriate and understandable to other members of the actor's speech community.

The examination of each ethnographic account reveals two "themes" or warrants for the use and interpretation of silence. The term warrant is used because each provides a framework or a template through which any actor in a particular speech community can determine whether silence, as a communicative code, would be appropriate and/or understood in any interaction in that community.

> **Warrant One.** Silence as a communicative action is associated with social situations in which the relationship of the focal participants is uncertain, unpredictable, or ambiguous.

In other words, the use of silence will increase, and will more frequently be interpreted as appropriate, when greater uncertainty in the relationship of the focal participants is present. This warrant "instructs" the actor that, once an assessment of the status relationship of the other has been made, *if* the relationship is unknown, vague, or allows for little prediction of the behavior of the other, *then* silence is the appropriate and understandable "response." This warrant was found to apply to the use and interpretation of silence in five of the cultures examined: Western Apache (Basso, 1990), Warm Springs Indians (Philips, 1970, 1990), Japanese-Americans in Hawaii (Johnson & Johnson, 1975), Japanese (Fisher & Teshida, 1968), and rural Appalachians (Ray, 1987). The accounts in these ethnographies support that this warrant is the necessary and sufficient condition for silence to occur in those particular speech communities. In each of these communities, it was the *perception* of the relative uncertainty, unpredictability, or ambiguity of the status or relationship that preceded the use of silence. It was the same perception that allowed the native to determine the appropriateness of silence when used by others.

Although it is beyond the scope of this article to give detailed summaries of all the accounts examined, several representative examples will be cited to illustrate the warrant. The account of the Western Apache by Basso (1990) provides the clearest illustration of how this warrant affects communicative behavior. The presence of strangers provides the Apache with a clear situation where silence is appropriate because no information is available regarding the status of the other. This is similar to the admonition American parents give to their children, "Don't talk to strangers," since the child cannot be sure if the stranger is friendly. Apache courtship is also marked by silence since familiarity is necessary for talk to occur even among those who intend to marry. In sharp contrast to the form of greeting behavior common in American families, the Apache remain silent when encountering friends or relatives who are returning from a long absence. This silence occurs due to the possibility that the long absence from the community may have resulted in "changing" the person. The parents of children returning from Anglo schools keep silent to see if the long contact with the Anglos has turned the child away from the community and Apache beliefs. The parents let the children do the talking until it is clear how, if at all, the children have changed. People who are angry, drunk, or in mourning are also responded to with silence because their behavior is very unpredictable. This is true also for those individuals who are part of a curing ceremony. Because it is possible for a spirit to enter a person at the ceremony, those who might be affected by the spirit remain silent, and others also remain silent since the power of the spirit is unpredictable.

Two accounts of the Warm Springs Indians (Philips, 1970, 1990) illustrate that this community also requires a high degree of knowledge regarding the status and relationship of the other for talk to occur. The Indian children in particular are subjected to strange and unfamiliar people and environments when placed in Anglo schools, which results in extreme reticence on their part and frustration on the part of the Anglo teacher, who requires a high level of orality in order to function as a teacher.

The two accounts of Japanese patterns of communication (Fisher & Teshida, 1968; Johnson & Johnson, 1975) demonstrate that silence fosters as well as responds to ambiguous relationships. Hundreds of years of Japanese proverbs reflect the view that silence is appropriate and should be expected when it is not possible to predict how someone will respond to talk, particularly if the talk is during a conflict situation. And conflict invariably results when Japanese-Hawaiians interact with Caucasians since, if status and relationship is vague or unknown, the Japanese-Hawaiian remains increasingly silent, and the Caucasian gets increasingly talkative.

However, this link between silence and uncertainty in role relationships was not the only account discovered in the ethnographies. Other explanations were posited for the use and interpretation of silence in various cultures that did not center on uncertainty, ambiguity, or unpredictability among focal participants. Instead, it was the perception of an unequal distribution of power that was the key to understanding the communicative use of silence.

Warrant Two. Silence as a communicative action is associated with social situations in which there is a known and unequal distribution of power among focal participants.

This warrant states that it is not ambiguity in the perceived status or relationship of the other that will "cause" a participant to use silence; rather, it is the perception that the other is of a *recognizably* different status. Knowledge that there is a discrepancy in relative power or social control provides the necessary and sufficient condition for silence. There is evidence that this warrant applies in the following communities: the Anang of South Western Nigeria (Messenger, 1960); the Wolof of Senegal (Irvine, 1974); the Maori in New Zealand (Salmond, 1975); the Malagasy in Madagascar (Keenan, 1975); some urban American black women (Abrahams, 1974, 1975; Mitchell-Kernan, 1972;) the La Have Islanders (Bauman, 1972); Bear Lake Athapaskan (Rushforth 1981); 17th century Quakers (Bauman, 1970, 1983); and some American white working class (Philipsen, 1975, 1976). In each of these speech communities the presence of perceived differentiation in power, e.g., adult vs. child, friend vs. enemy, king vs. subject, etc., provides the condition on which decisions to speak or to be silent are made. Again, space does not allow for detailed summaries of all these communities. However, examples from the Anang, the Wolof, the Maori, the Malagasy, and the urban Americans in "Teamsterville" should provide sufficient information on which to judge the efficacy of the warrant.

The ethnographic account of the Anang (Messenger, 1960) indicates they place a great value on verbal skills. He notes that the "neighboring Ibo gave the Anang their name, the term denoting 'ability to speak wittily yet meaningfully upon any occasion'" (p. 235). Even young children are encouraged to develop their verbal skills as early as possible, but they are also appraised when silence is preferable to talk. Anang proverbs warn that silence, or cautious speech at the most, is appropriate and expected in the presence of enemies. Enemies include most persons outside the tribal community. The account given is that enemies among the Anang distort a person's words to ruin their reputations. Therefore, among the Anang, the presence of enemies, or the possibility of being overheard by enemies, is considered a sufficient condition for silence to be prescribed.

Ethnographic accounts concerning other African and South Asian communities also point to perceived differences in status as a sufficient condition for the appropriate use and interpretation of silence in interaction. This perception is evident in the descriptions of the various forms of greeting behavior and oratory.

Greeting behavior of the Wolof (Irvine, 1974) places considerable emphasis on the determination and manipulation of status among the interactors. For the Wolof, silence is used as a strategy to take the higher status role in an interaction. Irvine reports that if a person perceived himself or herself as having greater status than the other, it would be inappropriate for that person to initiate a greeting with speech. Silence is used to signal to the other that, as the person of lower status, they must initiate the interaction. Difficulties in greeting behavior arise when each participant perceives him- or herself as higher in status than the other. A period of silence ensues until one of the participants performs a brief ritualistic greeting and then asks the other to account for not being the first to initiate the greeting.

The oratory of the Maori in New Zealand (Salmond, 1975) is marked by elaborate rules for interaction, among which are those rules that specify who can speak and who must remain silent. For the Maori, in oratory as well as other social interactions, the age and seniority of the focal participants is of prime importance in deciding when to speak and when not to speak. For example, younger brothers or sons of living fathers should not speak when at the *marae*, the ancestral speaking ground. Silence is prescribed for those of that lower rank as well as for all women. If this rule for the use of silence for those of lower status is violated, Salmond notes, "the power of public opinion makes itself felt in audible comments from the margins of the *marae*, in devastating silences" (p. 47).

As with the Maori, the Malagasy of Madagascar view the lower status of women as a sufficient condition warranting their silence (Keenan, 1975). This is true for oratory as well as for most other social situations where men *and* women are present. Women are excluded from most talk because, by their own account, "they tend to be hotheaded and openly express anger or hostility" (p. 96). But for situations and relationships that call for that "style" of discourse, it is the men whose talk is proscribed.

According to Keenan (1975), indirectness, politeness, and the saving of face are all highly valued by the Malagasy men. Direct confrontation is avoided at all costs and fights are almost nonexistent. Therefore, when a man is insulted, injured, or harmed in any fashion, it is still prescribed that indirectness and politeness be maintained. No matter what the provocation, men are expected to keep silent about their feelings of injury. But women do not have this rule for the use of silence when it comes to direct confrontation. Men keep silent after an injury, but respond by having "their" women verbally confront the offending party, thereby allowing the man to retain his image of politeness and power. In Malagasy society, silence is appropriate for women in most social situations because of their perceived lower status. But in situations where the status of the man is threatened because of confrontations with others, men keep silent and women speak.

Although half a world away, the working-class speech community known as "Teamsterville" has similar rules for the use and interpretation of silence as those described above (Philipsen, 1975, 1976). According to Philipsen (1975),

> A high quantity of speaking is considered inappropriate in situations in which the participants' identity relationship is asymmetrical. Such relationships are, for the adult man in Teamsterville, those with a wife, child, boss, outsiders to the neighborhood or a man of different ethnicity. (p. 15)

For a male resident of Teamsterville, speech is only appropriate when interacting with others who are similar in status and power. Philipsen states, "speech purchases an expression of solidarity or assertion of status symmetry" (p. 18). On the other hand, nonverbal communication, physical violence, or silence "purchases an assertion of distance, difference, or status asymmetry" (p. 18). In asymmetrical relationships, residents of Teamsterville use and interpret silence as an appropriate and expected actional strategy.

The two warrants discussed can be seen to cover all the accounts for the use and interpretation of silence reported in this study. The particular cultural patterning for the use and interpretation of silence in each community can be subsumed under one or more of the warrants. While it is possible that the particular behavioral manifestations of these themes will vary within a culture over time, it is believed that the underlying concepts and premises from which these behaviors emerge will remain consistent within that culture. The analysis of centuries-old Japanese proverbs provides evidence of the uniformity in concepts and premises over time. Therefore, this study has not provided an etiquette manual for culturally appropriate behavior in a variety of speech communities. This study has provided an outline of the conceptual criteria used in a variety of cultures through which the natives make *understandable* the use of silence.

References

Abrahams, R. D. (1974). Black talking on the streets. In R. Bauman & J. Sherzer (Eds.), *Explorations in the ethnograhy of speaking*. London: Cambridge University Press.

Abrahams, R. D. (1975). Negotiating respect: Patterns of presentations among black women. *Journal of American Folklore, 88*, 58–80.

Baker, S. (1955). The theory of silences. *Journal of General Psychology, 53*, 145–167.

Basso, K. (1990). "To give up on words": Silence in Western Apache culture." In D. Carbaugh (Ed.), *Cultural communication and intercultural contact* (pp. 303–320). Hillsdale, NJ: Erlbaum.

Bauman, R. (1970). Aspects of 17th century Quaker rhetoric. *Quarterly Journal of Speech, 63*, 67–74.

Bauman, R. (1972). The La Have General Store. *Journal of American Folklore, 85*, 330–343.

Bauman, R. (1983) *Let your words be few: Symbolism and silence among seventeenth-century Quakers*. Cambridge: Cambridge University Press.

Braithwaite, C. (1981) *Cultural uses and interpretations of silence*. Unpublished Master's Thesis. University of Washington.

Bruneau, T. J. (1973). Communicative silences: Forms and functions. *Journal of Communication, 23*, 17–46.

Dauenhauer, B. (1980). *Silence: The phenomenon and its ontological significance*. Bloomington: Indiana University Press.

Fisher, J., & Teshida, T. (1968). The nature of speech according to Japanese proverbs. *Journal of American Folklore, 81*, 34–43.

Griffin, K. (1970). Social alienation and communication denial. *Quarterly Journal of Speech, 56*, 347–357.

Hymes, D. (1972). Models of interaction of language and social life. In J. Gumperz & D. Hymes (Eds.), *Directions in sociolinguistics: The ethnography of communication*. New York: Holt, Rinehart, and Winston.

Irvine, J. T. (1974). Strategies of status manipulation in the Wolof greeting. In R. Bauman & J. Sherzer (Eds.), *Explorations in the ethnography of speaking*. London: Cambridge University Press.

Jensen, J. V. (1973). Communicative functions of silence. *Review of General Semantics, 30*, 249–267.

Johannesen, R. (1974). The functions of silence: A plea for communication research. *Western Speech, 38*, 25–35.

Johnson, C. (1973). *Speech reticence: Sounds and silence.* Fort Collins, CO: Schields.

Johnson, C. L., & Johnson, F. A. (1975). The Japanese and Caucasians in Honolulu. *Social Forces, 54*, 452–466.

Keenan, E. (1975). A sliding sense of obligatoriness: The polystructure of Malagasy oratory. In M. Block (Ed.), *Political language and oratory in traditional society.* London: Academic Press.

Mazzeo, J. (1962). St. Augustine's rhetoric of silence. *Journal of the History of Ideas, 23*, 175–196.

Messenger, J. (1960). Anang proverb-riddles. *Journal of American Folklore, 73*, 225–235.

Mitchell-Kernan, C. (1972). Signifying and marking: Two Afro-American speech acts. In J. Gumperz & D. Hymes (Eds.), *Directions in sociolinguistics: The ethnography of communication.* New York: Holt, Rinehart, and Winston.

Philips, G. (1968). Reticence: Pathology of the normal speaker. *Speech Monographs, 35*, 39–49.

Philips, S. (1970). Acquisition of rules for appropriate speech usage. In J. Alatis (Ed.), *Reports of the 21st roundtable meeting. [Monograph series]. Language and Linguistics, 23*, Washington, DC: Georgetown University Press.

Philips, S. (1990). Some sources of cultural variability in the regulation of talk. In D. Carbaugh (Ed.), *Cultural communication and intercultural contact* (pp. 329–344). Hillsdale, NJ: Erlbaum.

Philipsen, G. (1975). "Speaking like a man" in Teamsterville: Culture patterns of role enactment in an urban neighborhood. *Quarterly Journal of Speech, 61*, 13–22.

Philipsen, G. (1976). Places for speaking in Teamsterville. *Quarterly Journal of Speech, 62*, 15–25.

Philipsen, G. (1977). Linearity of research design in ethnographic studies of speaking. *Communication Quarterly, 25*, 42–50.

Picard, M. (1952). *The world of silence.* Chicago: Gateway Press.

Ray, G. (1987). An ethnography of nonverbal communication in an Appalachian community. *Research on Language and Social Interaction, 21*, 171–188.

Rushforth, S. (1981). Speaking to "relatives-through-marriage": Aspects of communication among Bear Lake Athapaskan. *Journal of Anthropological Research, 37*, 28–45.

Salmond, A. (1975). Mana makes the man: A look at Maori oratory and politics. In M. Bloch (Ed.), *Political language and oratory in traditional society.* London: Cambridge University Press.

Samarin, W. (1965). The language of silence. *Practical Anthropology, 12*, 115–119.

Scott, R. (1972). Rhetoric and silence. *Western Speech, 36*, 146–158.

Weisman, A. D. (1955). Silence and psychotherapy. *Psychiatry, 18*, 241–260.

—Section D—

CONTACT CODES
Proxemics and Haptics

The contact codes include both *proxemics* and *haptics*. Proxemics is concerned with the perception and use of space. This includes how space is organized, how territory is used and defended, and distances between and among people. Haptics refers to touch behavior, which is sometimes called tactile communication.

The use of space involves the complicated balancing of *affiliative* and *privacy* needs. People have the need to affiliate or be in contact with other people. Very few people can survive in isolation for extended periods of time. People offer us the stimulation, support, and contact needed for psychological and physical health. On the other hand, people also need privacy. People prefer to have space around them and to be alone for certain periods of time.

Because of these conflicting needs, people strive to balance affiliation and privacy. This is done through controlling our *territories* and *personal space*. Territory is a geographic area. Animals exhibit an innate need for territory called *territoriality*. Some territories are clearly private. These include your home, your room, and your office. Other territories are more public and may include your seat in a classroom, a table in the library, or a booth in a restaurant.

People *mark* their territory by placing personal objects there to communicate to others that the space is taken. For example, you may enter a classroom, place your books on a chair to mark your place, and then go out for a drink of water before class begins. You would probably be surprised and disturbed to return and find your books moved and someone else occupying your marked space.

While territory refers to a geographic area, personal space refers to the area around you. This area moves with you and is sometimes referred to as your *personal space bubble* because it involves a "bubble" of space on all sides of you. Your personal space will expand and contract depending upon the situation. It will be larger in a formal situation among strangers.

173

Here you want more space between you and others. Your personal space will contract, however, when a close friend approaches.

Proxemics play an important role in your life. You refer to developing relationships as "getting close" to someone. You use space to dominate and manipulate people, or to put them at ease. Space is used in many different ways in our lives and its effects, while subtle, are profound. In the following readings, you will learn about different types of territories and reactions to territorial invasion. You will also learn how space functions in organizations and in interactions between parents and children.

Haptics, or touch, also plays an important role in your life. In fact, touch is one of the most basic human needs. Even in today's modern world, *touch deprivation* is a problem. Research shows that people need touch for physical and psychological health. However, we touch and are touched less and less as we grow older. Except for "licensed touchers" such as a nurse or a massage therapist, some people are rarely touched by others.

Touch *rules* are very strong and guide who is allowed to touch whom. In general, people with more power and status are free to touch those with less power and status. Some areas of the body, such as the hands, arms, shoulders, and upper back may be touched by almost anyone. Other areas such as the head, face, neck, torso, buttocks, chest, legs, and feet may only be touched by a select few. There are also differences in the type and amount of touch used at various relational stages. For example, serious daters appear to use more touch than casual daters or married couples.

Some touches are *ritualized*. Ritualized touches are those that occur as part of ceremonial practice and other rigid behavioral patterns. Handshakes are a part of the greeting ritual, and patting someone on the back at an athletic contest is part of the congratulatory ritual. Other touches are not part of rituals, and these may communicate many different meanings, such as control or liking. There are, of course, many cultural differences in touch.

Touch is a powerful channel of communicating, in part because it is so commonly associated with three of the strongest messages we send: sexual interest, emotional intimacy, and dominance. The readings in this section illustrate the powerful role that touch plays in your life. Jones describes may different types of touch, which demonstrates that touch is used to send a variety of messages. Other research reported in this section examines touch in specific contexts, such as in the workplace, within family and romantic relationships, and even within restaurants.

In this classic work, Lyman and Scott provide us with a category system for classifying territories: public, home, interactional, and body territories. Each type of territory has its own rules guiding the type of activity, degree of ownership, and response to territorial invasions. While many people now use the term personal space instead of body territory, this system is frequently used to describe spatial communication.

21

Territoriality
A Neglected Sociological Dimension

Stanford M. Lyman
Marvin B. Scott

All living organisms observe some sense of territoriality, that is, some sense—whether learned or instinctive to their species—in which control over space is deemed central for survival. Although humanity's domination over space is potentially unlimited, in contemporary society it appears that people acknowledge increasingly fewer free territories for themselves.

Free territory is carved out of space and affords opportunities for idiosyncrasy and identity. Central to the manifestation of these opportunities are boundary creation and enclosure. This is so because activities that run counter to expected norms need seclusion or invisibility to permit unsanctioned performance, and because peculiar identities are sometimes impossible to realize in the absence of an appropriate setting. Thus the opportu-

Adapted with permission from *Social Problems*, Vol. 15, No. 2, pp. 236–249, copyright © 1967 by the Society for the Study of Social Problems.

nities for freedom of action—with respect to normatively discrepant behavior and maintenance of specific identities—are intimately connected with the ability to attach boundaries to space and command access to or exclusion from territories.

THE TYPES OF TERRITORIES

We can distinguish four kinds of territories, namely, *public territories, home territories, interactional territories* and *body territories*.

Public Territories

Public territories are those areas where individuals have freedom of access, but not necessarily of action, by virtue of their claim to citizenship. These territories are officially open to all, but certain images and expectations of appropriate behavior and of the categories of individuals who are normally perceived as using these territories modify freedom. It is commonly expected that illegal activities and impermissible behavior will not occur in public places. Since public territories are vulnerable to violation in both respects, however, police officers are charged with the task of removing lawbreakers from the scene of their activities and restricting behavior in public places.

Public territories are thus ambiguous with respect to accorded freedoms. First, the official rights of access may be regularly violated by local custom. Second, status discrepancy may modify activity and entrance rights. For example, the ambiguity in the distinction between minors and adults is a source of confusion and concern in the regulation of temporal and access rights to those whose status is unclear. Finally, activities once forbidden in public may be declared permissible, thus enlarging the freedom of the territory; or activities once legal may be proscribed, thus restricting it. Hence display of female breasts is permitted in San Francisco nightclubs, but not on the streets or before children. Nude swimming enjoys police protection at certain designated beaches, but watching nude swimmers at these same beaches is forbidden to those who are attired.

Home Territories

Home territories are areas where the regular participants have a relative freedom of behavior and a sense of intimacy and control over the area. Examples include makeshift club houses of children, hobo jungles, and homosexual bars. Home and public territories may be easily confused. In fact, the areas of public places and the areas of home territories are not always clearly differentiated in the social world and what may be defined and used as a public place by some may be defined and used as a home territory by others. Thus, a home territory that also may be used as a public one is defined by its regular use by specific persons or categories of persons and by the particular "territorial stakes" or "identity pegs" that are found in such places.

Home territories may be established by "sponsorship" or "colonization." An example of the former is found in the merchant emigrants from China who established caravansaries in certain quarters of Occidental cities which served as public trading establishments but also as living quarters, employment agencies, meeting places, and courts for their *Landsmänner*. Colonization occurs when a person or group lays claim to a formally free territory by virtue of discovery, regular usage, or peculiar relationship. Thus certain restaurants become home territories to those who are impressed with their first meal there; to those who eat there on specific occasions, such as luncheons, birthdays, or after sporting events; and to those who are intimate with the waitress.

It is precisely because of their officially open condition that public areas are vulnerable to conversion into home territories. The rules of openness are sufficiently broad and ambiguous so that restrictions on time, place, and manner are difficult to promulgate and nearly impossible to enforce. Armed with a piece of chalk children can change the public sidewalk into a gameboard blocking pedestrian traffic. Despite building codes and parental admonitions youngsters convert abandoned buildings or newly begun sites into forts, clubs, and hideaways.

But children are not the only colonizers on the public lands. Beggars and hawkers will stake out a "territory" on the sidewalks or among the blocks and occupy it sometimes to the exclusion of all others similarly employed. The idle and unemployed will loiter on certain streetcorners, monopolizing the space, and frightening off certain respectable types with their loud, boisterous, or obscene language, cruel jests, and suggestive leers. Members of racial and ethnic groups colonize a portion of the city and adorn it with their peculiar institutions, language, and rules of conduct.

Among the most interesting examples of colonizing on the public lands are those attempts by youths to stake out streets as home territories open only to members of their own clique and defended against invasion by rival groups. Subject always to official harassment by police and interference by other adults who claim the streets as public territories, youths resolve the dilemma by redefining adults as non-persons whose seemingly violative presence on the youth's "turf" does not challenge the latter's proprietorship. Streets are most vulnerable to colonizing in this manner and indeed, as the early studies of the Chicago sociologists illustrated so well, streets and knots of juxtaposed streets become unofficial home areas to all those groups who require relatively secluded yet open space in which to pursue their interests or maintain their identities.

Interactional Territories

Interactional territories refer to any area where a social gathering may occur. Surrounding any interaction is an invisible boundary, a kind of social membrane. A party is an interactional territory, as are the several knots of people who form clusters at parties. Every interactional territory implicitly makes a claim of boundary maintenance for the duration of the interaction. Thus access and egress are governed by rules understood, though not officially promulgated, by the members.

Interactional territories are characteristically mobile and fragile. Participants in a conversation may remain in one place, stroll along, or move periodically or erratically. They may interrupt only to resume it at a later time without permanently breaking the boundary or disintegrating the group. Even where "settings" are required for the interaction, mobility need not be dysfunctional if the items appropriate to the setting are movable. Thus chemists may not be able to complete a discussion without the assistance of a laboratory, but chess players may assemble or disassemble the game quite readily and in the most cramped quarters.

Body Territories

Finally, there are body territories, which include the space encompassed by the human body and the anatomical space of the body. The latter is, at least theoretically, the most private and inviolate of territories belonging to an individual. The rights to view and touch the body are of a sacred nature, subject to great restriction. For instance, a person's rights to his or her own body space are restricted where norms govern masturbation, or the appearance and decoration of skin. Moreover, rights of others to touch one's body are everywhere regulated, though perhaps modern societies impose greater restrictions than others.

Body space is, however, subject to creative innovation, idiosyncrasy, and destruction. First, the body may be marked or marred by scars, cuts, burns, and tattoos. In addition, certain of its parts may be inhibited or removed without its complete loss of function. These markings have a meaning beyond the purely anatomical. They are among the indicators of status or stigma.

The human organism exercises extraterritorial rights over both internal and external space. In the latter instance the space immediately surrounding a person is also inviolate. Thus conversations among friends are ecologically distinguishable from those between acquaintances or strangers. A person who persists in violating the extraterritorial space of another of the same sex may be accused of tactlessness and suspected of homosexuality, while uninvited intersex invasion may indicate unwarranted familiarity and accusations of harassment. Moreover, eye contact and visual persistence can be a measure of external space. Thus two strangers may look one another over at the proper distance, but as they near one another, propriety requires that they treat one another as nonpersons unless a direct contact is going to be made.

Control over "inner space" is the quintessence of individuality and freedom. Violations of "inner space" are carried out by domination, ranging in intensity from perception of more than is voluntarily revealed to persuasion and ultimately hypnosis. Demonstration of idiosyncrasy with respect to "inner space" is exemplified by the modifications possible in the presentation of self through the uses of the several stimulants and depressants.

TERRITORIAL ENCROACHMENT

We can distinguish three forms of territorial encroachment: violation, invasion, and contamination.

Violation of a territory is unwarranted use of it. Violators are those who have repulsed or circumvented those who would deny them access. Violators are also, by virtue of their acts, claimants in some sense to the territory they have violated. Their claim, however, may vary in scope, intensity, and objective. Children may violate the graves of the dead by digging "for treasure" in the cemetery, but unlike ghouls, they are not seeking to remove the bodies for illicit purposes. Some territories may be violated, however, merely by unwarranted entrance into them. Among these are all those territories commonly restricted to categorical groups such as toilets, harems, nunneries, and public baths—areas commonly restricted according to sex. Other territories may not be necessarily violated by presence but only by innovative or prohibited use. Thus some parents regard family-wide nudity as permissible, but hold that sexual interest or intercourse among any but the married pair is forbidden. Interactional territories are violated when one or more of the legitimate interactants behaves out of character.

Invasion of a territory occurs when those not entitled to entrance or use nevertheless cross the boundaries and interrupt, halt, take over, or change the social meaning of the territory. Such invasions, then, may be temporary or enduring.

Contamination of a territory requires that it be rendered impure with respect to its definition and usage. Cholera may require that a portion of the city be quarantined. Home territories may be contaminated by pollution or destruction of the "home" symbols.

Contamination of bodily territories occurs whenever the immediate space of or around the body is polluted. The removal by bathing of material involuntarily attached to the skin constitutes a ritualized purification rite of considerable importance in industrial societies.

However, body space may be contaminated in many ways, by smell, look, touch, and by proximity to contaminated persons or things. The sensitivity with respect to touch illustrates the complex nature of this contamination and also its peculiarly social character. The rules regarding touch are highly developed in American society and are clear indicators of social distance between individuals and groups. Typically, older people can touch younger ones, but suspicions of sexual immorality modify such contacts. Women who are friends or relatives may greet one another with a light kiss (commonly called a "peck") on the cheek, but not on the lips. Men who are long absent may be greeted by male friends and relatives with a hearty embrace and a touching of the cheeks, but the embrace must not be overlong or tender. Indeed, "rough-housing," mock-fighting, and pseudo-hostility are commonly employed in masculine affective relationships. Touch which would otherwise be contaminating is exempt from such designation when it takes place in situations of intense social action, e.g., on a dance floor, or in situations when the actors are not privileged to interact, e.g., crowded buses. At other times bodies contaminated by impermissible contacts are restored to their pure state by apologies.

Body space may be contaminated by a kind of negative charismatic contact whereby objects which, though neutral in themselves, carry contaminating effect when transferred directly to the body. Thus a comb or toothbrush may not be lent or borrowed in certain circles since to use someone else's tools of personal hygiene is to contaminate oneself. Typically, when clothing, especially clothing that will directly touch the skin, is lent, it is proper for the lender to assure the borrower that the apparel is clean, and that it has not been worn by anyone since its last cleaning.

REACTION TO ENCROACHMENT

We have already suggested that something of a reciprocal relation exists between the territorial types. For example, a public swimming pool—while officially open to all persons—might be conceived by certain regular users as an exclusive area. Strangers seeking access by virtue of their diffuse civic rights might be challenged by those whose sense of peculiar propriety is thus violated. Such a confrontation (sometimes called "when push meets shove") could result in retreat on the part of the party seeking admittance, flight on the part of those favoring denial, or strategy and tactics on the part of the contending parties to expand the area of legitimate access on the one hand, and withhold entirely or restrict the meaning of entry on the other.

Of course, the occupants of a territory may extend its use to others whose presence is not regarded as a threat. The most common situation is that in which common usage will not destroy or alter the value of the territory. When public territories have been colonized by users who do not fully monopolize the space, who embroider it by their presence, or whose occupancy still allows for other public and colonizing usages, the colonists will not be seriously opposed. Delinquent gangs who often define the streets of a neighborhood as a home territory do not usually regard the presence of local adults and children as an encroachment on their own occupancy. Unwarranted intrusion on interactional territories may be countenanced if the unwelcome guest indicates his or her willingness to be present on this occasion alone with no future rights of reentry, or to listen only and not to interrupt the proceedings. Bodies usually invulnerable to feel and probe by strangers may be violated if circumstances render the act physically safe, socially irrelevant, or emotionally neutral. Thus female nurses may massage their male patients with mutual impunity, and striptease dancers may perform unclothed upon a raised stage out of reach of the audience. However, all such contacts will tend to be defined as territorial encroachment when the claimants threaten obliteration, monopoly, or fundamental alteration of a territory. Under these conditions, the holders of territory are likely to react to unwelcome claimants in terms of *turf, defense, insulation*, or *linguistic collusion*.

Turf Defense

Turf defense is a response necessitated when the intruder cannot be tolerated. The animal world provides a multitude of examples which are instructive with respect to the human situation. Here we may be content, however, to confine ourselves to the human scene. When Chinese merchants sought "colonizing" rights among the urban merchants of San Francisco, they were welcomed and honored. A few years later, however, the appearance of Chinese miners in the white Americans' cherished gold fields called forth violent altercations and forced removals. In contemporary American cities delinquent gangs arm themselves with rocks, knives, tire irons, and guns to repel invaders from other streets. Among the "primitive" Kagoro the choice of weapons is escalated in accordance with the social distance of the combatants; poison spears and stratagems are employed exclusively against hostile strangers and invaders.

Turf defense is an ultimate response, however. Other more subtle repulsions or restrictions are available to proprietors wishing to maintain territorial control.

Insulation

Insulation is the placement of some sort of barrier between the occupants of a territory and potential invaders. The narrow streets, steep staircases, and regularized use of Cantonese dialects in Chinatowns serve notice on tourists that they may look over the external trappings of Chinese life in the Occidental city but not easily penetrate its inner workings. Distinct uniforms distinguishing status, rights, and prerogatives serve to protect military officers from the importunities of enlisted men and women, professors from students, and doctors from patients. Bodily insulation characteristically takes the form of civil inattention and may be occasioned by a subordinate's inability to repel invasion directly. Another common form of insulation involves use of body and facial idiom to indicate impenetrability. It may be effected by the use of sunglasses, or attained accidentally, by dint of culturally distinct perceptions of facial gestures, as, for example, often happens to Asians in Western settings. It can also be attained by conscious efforts in the management and control of the mouth, nostrils, and especially the eyes.

Linguistic Collusion

Linguistic collusion involves a complex set of processes by which the territorial integrity of the group is reaffirmed and the intruder is labelled as an outsider. For example, the defending interactants may engage one another in conversation and gestures designed to confuse invaders so they feel excluded. In one typical strategy the defending interactants will speak to one another in a language unfamiliar to the invader.

In another recognizable strategy, the participants continue to engage in the same behavior but in a more exaggerated and "staged" manner. Mood and tone of the voice are sometimes regulated to achieve this effect. Thus persons engaged in conversation may intensify their tone and include more intra-group gestures when an outsider enters the area. Professors may escalate the use of jargon and "academese" in conversations in the presence of uninvited students or nonacademics.

CONCLUSION

The concept of territoriality offers a fruitful approach for the analysis of freedom and situated action. Although the early school of ecology in

American sociology provided a possible avenue for this kind of exploration, its practitioners appear to have eschewed the interactionist and phenomenological aspects of the subject in favor of the economic and the biotic. Nevertheless, much of their work needs to be examined afresh for the clues it provides for understanding the nature and function of space and the organization of territories. Similarly the work done by the students of nonhuman animal association provides clues to concept formation and suggestions for research.

Proxemics and haptics send important messages to your clients, co-workers, and supervisors in the workplace. Smeltzer, Waltman, and Leonard provide useful information on how managers should use personal space and distances in their interactions with others. They also discuss the impact that cultural differences in proxemic norms can have on business interactions. Finally, the authors caution that touch can sometimes be an ambiguous and dangerous form of communication in the workplace because of implications for sexual harassment.

22

Proxemics and Haptics in Managerial Communication

Larry Smeltzer
John Waltman
Donald Leonard

Proxemics, a category of nonverbal signals, can be defined both narrowly and broadly. In this context, it means the space around us and how we relate to it. Managers should be aware of the twofold value in proxemics. To others, the manager's relationship to the environment says much about the manager. To a manager, another's use of the environment can say a great deal about the person.

Adapted from Smeltzer et al. (1991), *Managerial communication: A strategic approach* (2nd ed.). Needham Heights, MA: Ginn Press.

Hearing the word "proxemics," most people probably think only of personal space, the personal "bubble" surrounding a person, and that is a good place to start. But, as we shall see, the concept proxemics encompasses far more than just that. Edward Hall (1966) studied our use of personal distances and determined that we have four arbitrarily established proxemic zones in which we interact. Managers should be aware of these zones both to understand their own reactions to others when their spaces are invaded, and to use the proxemic zones of others to best advantage.

That all are aware of personal space to some degree is readily apparent from some of the verbal usages in our language. We talk about someone "keeping his or her distance," or complain when we perceive others "invading our territory," or say "they are crowding me on this issue" when in fact what they are doing has little to do with territory. When someone is pressing another on an issue, the other may (impolitely) respond, "Keep out of my face," or (certainly more politely), "Give me breathing room."

In the North American culture, businesspersons generally operate within four zones: intimate, personal, social, and public. In the discussion that follows, keep in mind that the figures are averages. They reflect the culture in general as well as the relationship between the parties. A number of other factors enter into any interpersonal relationship to change the details. These can include personal appearance, physical attractiveness, gender, and age, not to mention pathology and deviance. Thus, we may react differently to a tall than a short person, and may draw nearer to an attractive than an ugly individual (Malandro & Barker, 1983).

The intimate zone ranges from physical contact out to roughly eighteen inches to two feet. It is reserved for those closest to us. If it is invaded by others, especially for more than a moment, we usually feel uncomfortable and are likely to react, although often without knowing why. We either attempt to put more space between us, or we put up some kind of barrier between us. To test the almost tangible nature of this zone, stand close to someone you don't know too well. If from a North American culture, the person will likely react as suggested above to achieve a more comfortable distance.

The personal zone goes from the edge of the intimate zone out to roughly four feet. It is reserved for our close friends only, although during introductions we may permit others to enter it, albeit temporarily. Even then, watch as two strangers draw together for an introduction. As they shake hands, they will often stand with one leg forward and the other ready to back up. Then, when the handshake is completed, both will often quickly retreat into the next zone.

This area they retreat into is the social zone. It extends from about four feet to about twelve feet and is the space in which we would like to conduct much of our daily business. Relationships between managers and their employees might begin in this area and continue for a time, but will often move into the personal zone from the social once trust has developed, but this takes time (Hunsaker, 1981).

Our public zone extends beyond twelve feet. It reflects the distance at which most would like to keep strangers. Very little communication of a business nature takes place in this zone. Perhaps the only spoken communication that occurs would be the public speech. For example, photographs taken from above the recent dedication of a public building showed a sizeable, empty gap between the speaker's podium and the audience. This formal occasion dictated the distance people felt was appropriate, yet no formal demarcation was made to set people back at that distance. We can see a permanent institutionalized reflection of this distance in the arrangement of public auditoriums or even in the layout of many political rallies. Even if the latter is not too crowded, the audience will often "keep its distance."

For managers, the value of understanding proxemic zones is clear. An observant communicator can gauge the warmth (or lack of warmth) that exists in a relationship by the distances that the individuals keep during interactions. As trust grows, distances should predictably diminish. If they do not, then some other factor may be entering in. Let's consider some of these.

Keep in mind that proxemic zones vary from culture to culture (and even between the genders). Thus, for example, South Americans and Arabs typically interact with people at far closer ranges than do North Americans. Often when people from North America interact with individuals from either of these two cultures, the varying proxemic zones expected by the two groups create confusion unless one of the participants is aware of the need to adapt to the needs of the other. That is, either the North American gives up some of her ground, or the others keep their distance. Frequently, when two people from such varying cultures interact, a curious backwards "dance" develops as the one invades and the other evades the other.

Studies have shown that men tend to maintain larger personal space bubbles than women do. Women are more likely to allow other men or women to come closer than men typically will and will be more tolerant of temporary violations of their own space (Cohen, 1983). Some of the adverse reactions these (and other) differences in gender-specific behavior create will be explored later.

Naturally, circumstances may artificially affect our use of zones. An example of this is a crowded elevator. Here, people with a clearly defined set of proxemic zones will allow total strangers to invade personal and even intimate zones. Here, though, people will try to adapt to the invasion by other nonverbal means including blocking, that is, by folding their arms across the chest or putting up their briefcases as a sort of shield. Others will stare at the numerals showing the progression of the floors. In doing so, the passengers ensure that no one can easily invade their field of vision. This phenomenon has been called "stimulus overload" and affects city dwellers who become aloof and isolate themselves whenever the opportunity arises (Malandro & Barker, 1983). When one cannot stake out real, tangible, personal space, one can create it in the mind.

Similarly, when the barriers between the proxemic zones our culture typically uses need to be ignored for an extended period of time, people will do what they can to stake out some "territory." One way that is not totally satisfactory is by even spacing (as when seated around a meeting table with moveable seats). Thus, when one of the present authors was teaching an extension course in a state prison, he noted that the prisoners sat at almost precisely even distances from one another at their long classroom tables as they sought to achieve as much personal space as the situation would allow.

In other situations people will erect some sort of barrier to signal the limits of their own space in that situation. Watch at meetings around a conference table as people unconsciously arrange agenda materials, notebooks, pencils, coffee cups and other business artifacts around the outer perimeters of their territory. They are signalling where the boundaries of their limited personal space lie in that crowded environment.

Students can identify with this phenomenon. When they have settled into a routine in a class, they typically occupy the same seat day after day throughout the term. Should someone take that seat one day, the person feels uncomfortable, even slightly violated; his or her space has been invaded.

Scholars studying these phenomena divide territoriality, which is our tendency to defend an area of space as our exclusive preserve (Ardrey, 1966), into fixed-feature and semifixed-feature territory. Fixed-feature territory is that with clear, unmovable boundaries. Probably the most obvious example is the office. On the other hand, semifixed-feature space is what one bounds with movable objects as in the example of the meeting room above. While it is easy for the "owner" to defend (and to justify defending) fixed-feature space since it has clearly been labeled as belonging to that person, semifixed-feature is less so. Being there physically or having others recognize and respect the ownership interest are about the best defenses.

The ramifications for managers are clear. Intruding into another's territory without invitation can be an annoyance or even a threat no matter what one's rank. Recognizing the boundaries of both fixed- and semi-fixed-feature spaces communicates respect for the individual. Similarly, artifacts belonging to another individual should be regarded as personal. The use of another's chair or telephone without permission can be perceived as an arrogant act. The traditional advice to job interviewees, to keep their hands off of the things on the interviewer's desk, derives from this same notion.

Good managers recognize that those with little territory of their own should have that space respected as well. While one may have relatively little power within an organization, one still needs to have a place that is his or her own. Secretaries are probably the most obvious example of this (although many secretaries wield tremendous power and others' cautious treatment of their territory shows that). Talk to many secretaries about territoriality, and they will share their annoyance at having their desk drawers rifled for writing implements, or having the edge of their desk serve as a sort of couch for people stopping to chat. Similarly, many will express annoyance at having people use their telephone or word processors without checking first. Managers would do well to respect these needs.

But proxemics deals with far more than zones and territorial bounds. One of the skills possessed by experienced workers in any area is the ability to read the environment for nonverbal cues. With just a little training, one can quickly scan an area and tell much about the rank of the individual holding control over the territory, the personal habits he or she practices, as well as his or her attitudes about others with whom she or he interacts. The value for managers is twofold. Not only can they read the environmental messages being sent by subordinates and fellow workers, but they can understand what others read into their environment and adapt as needed.

A. G. Athos' work (1975) is relevant here. While many of his findings will come as little surprise to seasoned businesspersons, their value lies in their being brought together into one study. A great deal can be read about a person's status in the organization from the amount of space allotted to him or her, the amount of privacy that space entails, and where in the building that space is located.

Thus, provided a person has a rough idea of how others in the organization are housed, he or she could fairly easily gauge rank from the private office space allocation a person enjoys. "The bigger, the better" is a cliché that usually holds true here. Of course, the amount of privacy afforded to a manager includes more than just the office space allotted. The traditional joke about rising in the organization and having a key to the executive washroom is taken seriously by those who have that key and the additional privacy it affords. The top executive may not even need a key; she may have a private washroom off of her own office. Similarly, status comes with a private parking space rather than mere access to a reserved parking area or even a general parking lot. And the traditional climbing images that are used to describe promotions often go with the new office assignments as well. Typically, the higher one goes in the organization, the higher the office in the building.

If the office of the C.E.O. is not on the top floor, some other factor might have entered in. Thus, for example, the offices of the president of the University of Texas at Austin are on only the fourth floor of a skyscraper. However, they are housed in the wood paneled area once occupied by the rare books library and they open out onto a large roof garden. Here height is traded for size and the antiquity of the appointments.

One can also read much by relative distance from the center of power, so-called propinquity. Generally, the closer one is to the organization's leaders, the more power one enjoys (or is perceived to enjoy). In fact, some will even sacrifice space for propinquity in order to gain what they see to be closeness to power.

What one does in the environment also can speak volumes. The more "things" that one has, generally, the more power enjoyed. Thus, if the head of the department has two telephone lines (while subordinates have one), the division chief might have four and the C.E.O. even more. Unfortunately, even secretaries are often impersonally "counted" either in terms of the number of people they serve or, inversely, the number of secretaries there to serve one person.

The size of the artifacts that fill the environment also matter. Anyone familiar with United States Civil Service regulations knows the elaborate rules guiding what furniture goes with what rank. Individuals new to a job may find the furniture in their offices suddenly replaced by smaller (even cheaper) versions that suit the lower rank of the new occupant. New managers are also often surprised to find that the organization has a cleaning hierarchy that goes with the organizational hierarchy. While a manager may have her office cleaned once a week, the person she reports to might have daily service. Similarly, neat is read by visitors as better than messy. The manager who receives visitors in an environment cluttered with papers sends a signal of disorganization. They might read the confusing clutter as belonging to someone who cannot find the time to attend to details.

HAPTICS

Nonverbal communication is far more than just space and proxemic zones. Another relevant area is haptics. The curious term "haptics" refers to the study of touching behavior. Seasoned managers know that touching is sometimes a necessary part of interpersonal relations. But with the growing awareness of sexual harassment, the significant questions have become who, when, how much, and how often. Of course, haptics is not necessarily affectionate; watch a group of children for any length of time to support that. All the same, haptics typically focuses on affectionate behavior and Heslin (1974) gives five categories it falls into:

1. functional/professional
2. social/polite
3. friendship/ warmth
4. love/intimacy
5. sexual/arousal

Each level in this progressive series leads to the next, and not always in a clear way. Professional touching can lead to social touching which can lead to friendship, and so on. Anyone aware of the sensitive issue of sexual harassment can see that the divisions between the categories must be scrupulously respected if one is to retain a professional relationship.

Subconsciously, most managers realize that when what is permissible within a haptic category is exceeded, it is done to communicate a message about the state of the parties' relationship. It is either warmer than it had been, or one of the parties wishes it so. Unfortunately, conflict can arise when the two parties involved do not agree on an acceptable haptic level for the relationship (Borisoff & Victor, 1989).

Judging where one category of haptics ends and the other begins is not always an easy task. Here, clearly, the cultural aspect is crucial. The functional level of haptics that would be appropriate in the southern United States would likely be judged to be a higher level in the Midwest. Similarly, the touching among friends of the same gender in the Midwest might seem downright frigid in the South. The key is to use discretion and common sense.

As with any learned communication behavior, it would probably be wise to watch respected leaders from within that culture, and follow their behavior. At the same time, keep in mind Henley's (1977) observations that haptics and dominance are often related. Her research found that the person in power is more likely to touch a subordinate than s/he is to be touched by subordinates. As Borisoff and Victor (1989) note, this can lead to confusion; is the touch motivated by intimacy or by dominance? Is it a blend of both? The implications for potential sexual harassment are clear.

References

Ardrey, R. (1966). *The territorial imperative.* New York: Dell.

Athos, A. G. (1975). Time, space, and things. In A. G. Athos & R. E. Coffey (Eds.), *Behavior in organizations: A multi-dimensional view* (pp. 69–81). Englewood Cliffs, NJ: Prentice-Hall.

Borisoff, D., & Victor, D. A. (1989). *Conflict management: A communication skills approach*. Englewood Cliffs, NJ: Prentice-Hall.

Cohen, A. L. (1983, January–February). Nonverbal (mis)communication between managerial men and women. *Business Horizons*, p. 15.

Hall, E. T. (1966). *The hidden dimension*. New York: Doubleday.

Henley, N. M. (1977). *Body politics: Power, sex and non-verbal communication*. Englewood Cliffs, NJ: Prentice-Hall.

Heslin, R. (1974, May). *Steps toward a taxonomy of touching*. Paper presented to the annual meeting of the Midwestern Psychological Association, Chicago, IL.

Hunsaker, P. L. (1981). Communicating better: There's no proxy for proxemics. In R. C. Huseman (Ed.), *Readings in business communication* (p. 52). Hinsdale, IL: Dryden Press.

Malandro, L. A., & Barker, L. (1983). *Nonverbal communication*. Reading, MA: Addison Wesley.

This article discusses meanings of touch. Jones found that touch is used to communicate positive affect, playfulness, and control, and is part of rituals and tasks. He also presents exercises for understanding the tactile communication that you experience.

23

Communicating with Touch

Stanley E. Jones

Touch is our most intimate and involving form of communication and helps us to keep good relationships with others. That is why we use expressions like "Let's stay in touch," "I'll contact you when I get back," and "I was touched" (by what another person said or did). Most people say touching makes them feel good about themselves and that they would like to touch more than they do. It is important, however, to know how to touch appropriately, and this involves knowing how to communicate each of the many meanings of touch.

My colleague Elaine Yarbrough and I asked college students to act as "participant observers" by recording all of their touches with others over several days. A participant observer is a person who participates in the communication being studied but also observes and records the events. In this study, participant observers used the Touch Observation Form provided in Figure 1.

Data were collected from nearly 1,500 touches. Two kinds of events were separately analyzed: (1) touch sequences, consisting of a series of touches (139 cases), and (2) individual touches, consisting of single instances of contact (1,069 cases).

This article was written especially for *The Nonverbal Communication Reader* and is based in part on Jones & Yarbrough (1985), A naturalistic study of the meanings of touch. *Communication Monographs, 52*, 19–56.

Figure 1 **Touch Observation Form**

Name _____ Date _____

Use arrows to link entries which are part
of the same interaction. Ex. 1.
         ↓
         2.

Indicate where applicable: BM—Best Male Friend;
BF—Best Female Friend; MO—Mother; FA—Father

1.
Initiator of touch
A. Me
B. Other
C. Mutual
D. Unclear
(1 letter)

1. _____
2. _____
3. _____

2a.
*Parts of body when ini-
tiated*
(1 or more letters @
blank: note 2-handed
touches)
Initiator   Receiver
touched   touched
with: on:

2b.
*Parts of body when mu-
tual or unclear*
(1 or more letters per
blank)
Me: Other:

3.
Place
A. Mine
B. Other's
C. Neutral
(Specify bldg. and
room)

4.
Time of day
(Include a.m. or
p.m.)

5.
Accompanying verbal statement
(Paraphrase if necessary)
When:
A. Immediately prior to touch
B. Immediately after touch
C. During
By: (M) Me; (O) Other

1. _____
2. _____
3. _____

6.
*Touch translated into verbal state-
ment*
(Make into short sentence if possible;
note voice tone or facial expression if
critical to meaning)

7.
(Mark "Psych" for touches you reject
internally only)
Acceptance/Rejection
A. Touch accepted by me
B. Touch rejected by me
C. Touch accepted by other
D. Touch rejected by other
(Spec. with letter; explain how & why
t. is rejected)

8.
Type of touch
A. Caressing/holding
B. Feeling/Caressing
C. Prolonged holding
D. Holding/pressing ag.
E. Spot touching
F. Accidental brushing
G. Handshake
H. Pat I. Squeeze J. Punch
K. Pinch L. Other
(1 or more letters)

1. _____
2. _____
3. _____

9.
Purpose of participants
A. Give/get info (spec.)
B. Ask/give favor
C. Persuading
D. Persuaded
E. Casual talk
F. Deeptalk
G. Greeting
H. Departing
I. Any other (specify)
Me   Other

10.
Others present
(Male & /or female)
(Specify relation to you us-
ing letters from Category
11)

11.
Relationship to other
A. Relative (spec.)
B1. Close Friend
B2. Not close friend
C. Acquaintance
D. Co-worker
E. Superior
F. Subordinate
G. Stranger
H. Other (spec.)
Spec. if intimate

12.
*Nature of social occa-
sion*
A. Work
B. Class
C. Party
D. Informal meeting
E. Other (spec.)
For public places, spec-
ify function (bar, etc.)

1. _____
2. _____
3. _____

13.
Status of other
A. Higher   1. Formal
B. Lower   2. Informal
C. Equal
(1 letter and 1 no.)

14.
Age of other
(Approximate)

15.
Sex of other
(M/F)

16.
Race of other
A. Anglo
B. Black
C. Chicano
D. Asian
E. Other (spec)

17.
Standing or sitting
Me: Other:

1. _____ _____
2. _____ _____
3. _____ _____

18.
Any other contextual factors you think influenced your touches:
_____
_____
_____

TOUCH SEQUENCES

Touch sequences are two or more touches communicatively related to one another within the same interaction. A touch sequence occurs when one person touches another and the second person touches back, or when one person touches another more than once. Two basic types of sequences were found: repetitive and strategic.

Sometimes one touch is not enough, and repetition intensifies the meaning. In repetitive sequences, each of the touches has the same meaning. In the overwhelming majority of cases, the touches are all strictly positive (not playful or controlling). For example, in the "support" sequence, one person comforts and reassures another. If you are tucking someone in bed when they are sick, just pulling the covers up to the chin is not sufficient. You also need to fluff up the pillow, gently brush the forehead, pat the shoulder or chest, and so forth. As another example of a type of repetitive sequence, opposite-sex "best friends" who are not romantic partners tend to use a version of "repetitive affection" by exchanging pats, caresses, or spot touches back-and-forth. This "ping-pong" trading of touches seems to symbolize the equality of this kind of relationship.

Strategic sequences are touches which move from one meaning to another, usually with a "surprise" at the end. For example, in the affection-to-control sequence, one person "softens up" the other with one or more affection touches, and then touches while asking the other person to do something (a control touch, even though it resembles earlier touches). In one case when a couple was watching television together on a couch, the female first cuddled against the male; a minute later, the male kissed the female; several minutes later, the male put his arm around the female and said, "Will you get me some water?" There is a "gamey" quality about strategic sequences because they imply an ulterior or hidden motive. If overused in a relationship, they might undermine the impact of other, more straightforward touch messages.

INDIVIDUAL TOUCHES

Individual, single touches are more common than sequences. If done at the right time to convey an accurate meaning, they can have considerable effect. Touches are oftentimes subtle and hard to interpret unless you understand the language of touch. The same touch can have different meanings. For example, a simple contact of a hand to a shoulder or elbow can convey "Hi, how are you?", "I want to comfort you," "Do this for me," or a variety of other meanings. Also, different touches can have the same meaning (a kiss, a hug, or just a pat can communicate affection). The secret to understanding touches is to read them in the total context, including such things as what is said, the nature of the relationship, and the social situation.

A blueprint for touching. The research revealed 18 different meanings of touch which can be grouped into 7 overall types: Positive affect (emotion), playfulness, control, ritual, hybrid (mixed), task-related, and accidental touches. These are summarized in Table 1, which can be read as a blueprint for how to touch. On the left-hand column of the table are the names of each type with a definition of the meaning. In the next column, on the right, is a description of the "key features" of the meaning, the way the touch is done or elements of the context which must ordinarily be present for the meaning to come across clearly. In the far right column are examples of each kind of touch. Sometimes "enactment types" are described, distinctively different ways the same meaning can be conveyed. If you imagine what the touch would look (and feel) like, or act out the touches with someone else, the way each meaning is communicated becomes clearer.

In the table, the abbreviation "NVBP" means "non-vulnerable body parts" (hand, arm, shoulder, and upper back). "VBP" means "vulnerable body parts" (all other body regions). "Close relationships" refers to romantic intimates, close friends, and immediate family members.

EXERCISES FOR UNDERSTANDING TOUCH

1. Keep a record of your own touches for one or more complete days using photocopies of the Touch Recording Form and writing down the specifics immediately after each touch. (Tell other people it's a class assignment if they ask, but don't go into detail.) There will be space to record three touch events on each copy (lines 1, 2, and 3 throughout the form). Record every contact; indicate if it was initiated by you or someone else, mutually initiated (like a hug or handshake), or whether the initiator was unclear (accidental touches). When you're done, analyze the results by counting up the touches:

   a. Were you more of a toucher or a "touchee?" How many touches did you experience per day? (Average is about twelve for females, eight for males.)

   b. With whom did you have touches most (kinds of relationships, category eleven on the form)?

TABLE 1   Characteristics of Meaning Categories for Individual Touches

Category (definition, # of cases)	Key Features	Typical Examples and Enactment Types
A. Positive Affect Touches		
1. Support — serves to nurture, reassure or promise protection (39 cases)	(1) Situation calls for comfort or reassurance (100%) (2) Hand (100%), and sometimes an arm, directed to 1-2 body parts (89.7%) (3) Initiated by person who gives support (84.6%)	(1) Knowing from a conversation the night before that a roommate is worried about a test, the toucher pats him on the shoulder when he sees him in the morning and says, "You'll do O.K." (2) After a friend expresses sadness about an event, the toucher silently reaches out and squeezes her arm. (3) Cuddling a crying child who is injured. (Hugs are rare events, reserved for a person who expresses strong distress.)
2. Appreciation — expresses gratitude (16 cases)	(1) Situation: receiver has performed service for toucher (100%) (2) Touch initiator verbalizes appreciation, usually some version of "thanks" (87.5%)	(1) A boss touches a subordinate on the shoulder at the end of a day's work and says, "Thanks for the way you handled things." (2) A woman kisses a close male friend on the cheek after a meal he prepared and says "Thanks a lot."
3. Inclusion — draws attention to act of being together; suggests psychological closeness (32 cases)	(1) Sustained touch (100%) (2) Close relationship (90.6%), mainly sexual intimates and close friends; only 2 cases involve immediate family members other than spouses	(1) A couple walks down the street holding hands or with arms around one another. (2) A couple sits on a couch watching television with one person leaning against the other. (3) A male and a female who are close friends talk in a restaurant with knees touching.

4. *Affection* — expresses generalized positive regard beyond mere acknowledgement (56 cases)	(1) Close relationships (85.7%) (2) A residual category; absence of a more specific positive affect meaning suggests affection	(1) (Highly intense form) Spontaneously hugging a romantic partner or close friend and saying words of endearment ("Hi, sweetheart," "I love you," etc.). (2) (Less intense, but more common type) Patting or caressing a close person when passing by in the room. (3) (Examples are varied and include hugs, kisses, and less involving, simple contacts.) The lack of a specific situation calling for touch — such as a sad event or a greeting — defines pure affection. (Rare between men.)
5. *Sexual* — expresses physical attraction or sexual interest (21 cases)	(1) Sexually intimate relationships (100%) (2) Holding and/or caressing (100%) (3) VBP (95.2%), including or restricted to "sexual" body parts — chest (women), pelvis, and/or buttocks (85.7%)	(1) Movement from one to another type of holding and/or caressing (e.g., lovers embracing and caressing; multiple kinds of touching distinguish it from affection). (2) A simple hand touch to a sexual body part (e.g., reaching over and touching an intimate on the buttock).

B. Playful Touches

1. *Playful Affection* — serves to lighten interaction; seriousness of affection qualified (26 cases)	(1) Affectionate or sexual messages with play signal (100%)	(1) A male saying "How's about a kiss?" (I'm just kidding around) to a close female friend or romantic partner, followed by a quick kiss. (2) With others present, a male puts his arm around his male roommate, who is doing the dishes, and says, "You'd make a good wife" (I'm teasing about being affectionate).
2. *Playful Aggression* — serves to lighten interaction; seriousness of aggression qualified (26 cases)	(1) Aggressive message with play signal (100%) (2) Initiated, not mutual (100%)	(1) Aggressive touch with a comment which clarifies the intent as play (e.g., saying "Let's wrestle," and then performing a mock half-nelson to the other person — notice the importance of the early verbal warning). (2) Aggressive comment with a touch play signal (e.g., a customer says to a waitress, "No, we don't want the check and tear it up," with a smile and light touch to her arm).

C. Control Touches

1. *Compliance* — attempts to direct behavior and oftentimes also attitudes or feelings of another (75 cases)

   (1) Initiated by person attempting influence (92%)
   (2) Verbalization occurs (states or implies requested action) (90.7%)

   (1) A boss touches an employee on the shoulder and says, "Could you get this done by 5 o'clock?" (Touch translation: "I really want you to do it.")
   (2) Grabbing a companion by the upper arm and saying, "Let's hurry across the street."

2. *Attention-getting* — serves to direct the recipient's perceptual focus (66 cases)

   (1) Initiated by person requesting attention (100%)
   (2) Initiator verbalizes (clarifies purpose) (100%)
   (3) Brief touches (spot, pat, brush) directed to 1-2 body parts (84.8%)

   (1) Patting a companion on the shoulder and saying, "Look at this!"
   (2) Spot touching a stranger on the arm to say, "Excuse me, do you have the time?"

3. *Announcing a Response* — calls attention to and emphasizes a feeling state of initiator; implicitly requests affect response from another (46 cases)

   (1) Initiated by person announcing response (91.3%)
   (2) Verbalization by toucher(s) announces feeling directly or indirectly (97.8%)

   (1) A woman touches her female friend and says, "Can you believe he did that?" (Translation: "I hope you feel the same way about him.")
   (2) A woman touches her male companion and says, "I'm so excited about today!" (Translation: "Get psyched!")
   (3) A man slaps another man on the shoulder and says "Congratulations!" (I'm happy for you). (Or, an exchange of hand-to-hand slaps — mutual congratulations.)

D. Ritualistic Touches

1. *Greeting* — serves as part of the act of acknowledging another at the opening of an encounter (43 cases)

   (1) Situation is beginning of interaction (100%)
   (2) Verbalization of standard greeting phrase (93%), before or during touch, not after (88.4%)
   (3) Hand to one body part (90.6%)
   (4) (Near to key feature) Minimal form of contact (handshake, spot touch, pat or squeeze) (83.7%)

   (1) (Formal) handshake greeting (mainly used between males).
   (2) (Slightly more informal) Hand to body part greeting, usually to shoulder or arm (mainly female-male or female-female touches).

2. *Departure* — serves as part of the act of closing an encounter (20 cases)

   (1) Situation is end of an encounter (100%)
   (2) Verbalization of standard departure phrase (90%), before or during touch, not after (85%)
   (3) Hand to one body part (85%)

   (1) Male pats male friend on shoulder when leaving.
   (2) Female touches lower back of female friend when leaving.

E. Hybrid Touches

1. *Greeting/Affection* — expresses affection and acknowledgement at the initiation of an encounter (79 cases)

   (1) Situation is beginning of interaction (100%)
   (2) Verbalization occurs (88.6%)
   (3) Close relationships (86.1%)
   (4) VBP touches (86.1%)

   (1) Hug and/or brief kiss between male and female (usually close friends, romantic partners, or parent and son or daughter).
   (2) Hug between female friends.
   (3) (Most common after a period of absence — most of a day or longer; rare between men.)

2. *Departure/Affection* — expresses affection and serves to close an encounter (72 cases)

   (1) Situation is end of interaction (100%)
   (2) Verbalization occurs (94.4%)
   (3) Close relationships (94.4%)
   (4) VBP touches (91.6%), principally hugs and/or kisses (84.7%)

   (1) Opposite-sex prolonged hug with a kiss (at the airport, for instance; same relationships as greeting/affection).
   (2) Hug between female friends when one is leaving.
   (3) (More common and more extensive the longer the expected separation; rare between men.)

F. Task-Related Touches

1. *Reference to appearance* — a touch which points out or inspects a body part or artifact referred to in a verbal comment about appearance (11 cases)

   (1) Words accompany and justify the touch (100%)
   (2) Spot touch by a hand to a VBP (100%)
   (3) Close relationships (90.1%)

   (1) A woman inspects a female friend's necklace and says, "This is pretty."
   (2) A woman brushes a male friend's hair with her hand and says, "I like your haircut."
   (3) (Males rarely use this touch, although they could, saying "Nice suit," while feeling the material at the lapel.)

2. *Instrumental Ancillary* — a touch which occurs as an unnecessary part of the accomplishment of a task (56 cases)

   (1) Hand-to-hand contacts (91.1%)
   (2) Instrumental act is clear in itself, but task doesn't require touch (100%)

   (1) Most common is handing an object to someone and allowing hand-to-hand contact (e.g., a clerk returning change to a customer).

3. *Instrumental Intrinsic* — touch which accomplishes a task in and of itself (54 cases)

   (1) Instrumental meaning is clear from the touch itself — a helping touch (100%)

   (1) Assisting a person in putting on a coat.
   (2) Placing a hand on a person's forehead to check for a temperature (implies support, but mainly accomplishes a task).
   (3) Putting suntan lotion on a person's back (may imply flirtation or affection).

G. Accidental Touches

1. *Accidental* — touches which are perceived as unintentional (86 cases)

   (1) Touches consist of single, momentary contacts, principally brushes (89.5%), with a few spot touches (9.3%)
   (2) Touches seem to be mistakes (100%), although a secondary message (like flirtation or attention-getting) might be implied.

   (1) Brushing a person when passing by, getting up to go, etc.
   (2) (Bumps or brushes between strangers are usually rejected, unless an apology is given.)

   c. What meanings did you communicate? Were there some rejected touches and why? Are there other meanings you would like to communicate?

2. Observe and record touches of others in some likely location. Airports, railway stations, or bus terminals are good places for observation, especially at departures. (Or, for observing touches between parents and children, preschools at the beginning or end of the day are good locations.) The same categories as in Exercise 1 may be used (although you may have to guess about relationships between adults). Analyze the results:

   a. What differences in touching did you observe for men with men, women with women, and men with women? (Or, what were the differences in the way mothers or fathers touched daughters or sons?)

   b. Did you notice any other nonverbal behaviors which preceded goodbyes (or hellos) like waving, extending arms for a touch, etc.?

Suggestions for Further Reading

1. For more details on touch meanings and sequences, see:

Jones, Stanley E., & Yarbrough, A. Elaine (1985). A naturalistic study of the meanings of touch. *Communication Monographs, 52,* 19–56.

2. For information on male and female differences in touching, see:

Greenbaum, Paul E., & Rosenfeld, Howard M. (1980). Varieties of touching in greetings: Sequential structure and sex-related differences. *Journal of Nonverbal Behavior, 5,* 13–25.

Jones, Stanley E. (1986). Sex differences in touch communication. *The Western Journal of Speech Communication, 50,* 227–241.

3. For a discussion of the importance of touch, especially with infants and young children, see:

Montagu, Ashley (1971). *Touching: The human significance of the skin.* New York: Harper & Row.

Touch is a powerful form of communication in romantic relationships. Guerrero and Andersen examined public touch behavior between men and women who were romantically involved. Results showed that couples touched more when they were seriously dating than when they were either casually dating or married. Results also showed that even though men and women tended to use similar amounts of touch overall, men were more likely to initiate touch in casual dating relationships, whereas women were more likely to initiate touch in married relationships.

24

Public Touch Behavior in Romantic Relationships between Men and Women

Laura K. Guerrero
Peter A. Andersen

The considerable power of touch in close relationships is well documented. Research has shown that touch can send strong messages of intimacy or hostility. For example, a loving touch can show affection and comfort, whereas a harsh slap can show anger and violence. Because of the powerful messages touch sends, tactile communication helps individuals define their

The results reported here are from: Guerrero, L. K., & Andersen, P. A. (1991). The waxing and waning of relational intimacy: Touch as a function of relational stage, gender, and touch avoidance. *Journal of Personal and Social Relationships, 8,* 147–165; and Guerrero, L. K., & Andersen, P. A. (1994). Patterns of matching and initiation: Touch behavior and touch avoidance across romantic relationship stages. *Journal of Nonverbal Behavior, 18,* 137–153.

relationships. In fact, interpersonal touch has been labeled the primary nonverbal behavior that "influences the nature and quality of the relationship" and "directly and immediately escalates the balance of intimacy" (Thayer, 1986, p. 8). Our research on touch has focused on tactile behavior in romantic relationships between men and women. Specifically, we have investigated how public touch differs across three relational stages: casually dating, seriously dating, and married.

In this short report, we focus on three of the ideas we have tested. First, we were interested in seeing whether public touch differs depending upon the stage of a romantic relationship. Second, we examined the extent to which romantic partners used similar amounts of touch. Finally, we investigated sex differences in two areas: (1) the total amount of touch men and women displayed, and (2) whether men or women initiated touch more across various relational stages.

RELATIONAL STAGE DIFFERENCES IN TOUCH

Positive forms of touch are used to send messages of affection and attraction. They also decrease both the physical and psychological distance between people (Andersen, 1985). In romantic relationships, touch is especially instrumental because it can convey sexual interest and commitment (Johnson & Edwards, 1991). Public touch can also serve as a *tie sign* that shows others that your partner is "taken" (Morris, 1977). For example, couples who hold hands or have their arms around one another in public settings are signalling to others that they are a couple. When these tie signs bring couples especially close together, they also signal that a couple would prefer to be alone, and that they are therefore unavailable for communication with "outsiders."

It is clear, then, that public touch is used as both an affectionate message and a tie sign in romantic relationships. But who uses public touch more—couples who are trying to develop their relationships and increase intimacy, or couples who have already developed highly intimate, committed relationships? Some research and theory suggests that people will show increasing levels of intimacy (including more touch behavior) as their relationship moves from impersonal to personal. For example, social penetration theory (Altman & Taylor, 1973) predicts that people will become more self-disclosive and more nonverbally intimate as they move through various relational stages and become closer. In contrast, research and theory on courtship and flirting suggests that touch will be used more in intermediate stages of a relationship. Burgoon, Buller, and Woodall (1996) summarize this research by stating that "tie signs are more prevalent among dating and courting couples than among marrieds. Once a relationship is well established, the need for public displays of affection and [bondedness] are no longer necessary" (p. 324). Therefore, our first question addressed *how relational stage affects public touch within romantic relationships between men and women.*

MATCHING

When two people use similar positive behaviors, they feel more attracted to one another and more satisfied with their relationship. This similarity between partners is often referred to as *behavioral matching* (Burgoon, Dillman, & Stern, 1993). Behavioral matching occurs when a particular behavior is similar between relational partners. So if both partners use large or small amounts of touch, behavioral matching has occurred. If one partner uses no touch while the other partner engages in a lot of touch, no matching has occurred. Cappella (1994) suggested that people tend to evaluate others who act similarly to them favorably. Street (1982) also showed that behavioral matching can increase attraction and perceptions of communication competence.

Because both matching behaviors and touch communicate intimacy, we felt that partners in romantic relationships would match levels of touch behavior. We also expected that married partners would show the most matching because they have probably negotiated rules about how much public affection is appropriate. Their communication with one another is also likely to be synchronized. Cappella and Palmer (1990) found a similar pattern for gaze, illustrators, and smiles/laughter. They found that these behaviors were used similarly between partners in developed relationships, but not between strangers. Therefore, we predicted that *the amount of public touch used by heterosexual romantic couples would be similar, especially for people in married relationships.*

SEX DIFFERENCES

Studies on sex differences in touch behavior have tended to measure touch in one of two ways. Some studies compare the overall frequency of touch used by men versus women. Other studies examine whether men or women initiate touch more often. Our study examined both of these issues.

Past research on sex differences in touch has produced contradictory results. Some studies have found women to use slightly more touch than men in opposite-sex relationships (Jones, 1986). Other studies have found no differences in overall touch between men and women (Stier & Hall, 1984). Henley (1973, 1977) and Major (1981) reported that men *initiate* more touch in opposite-sex dyads, perhaps because touch initiation is a dominance move. A similar explanation is that men, who often attach more sexual connotations to touch than do women (Eakins & Eakins, 1978; Fromme et al., 1986), feel it is their role to initiate contact. Blumstein and Schwartz (1983) argued that in American culture, sexually escalating the relationship is seen as more of the man's prerogative. However, some researchers have failed to find overall sex differences in touch initiation (Stier & Hall, 1984) or found that females initiate opposite-sex touch more than males (Willis, Rinck, & Dean, 1978).

Based on these inconsistent findings, we thought that relationship stage might influence sex differences in touch frequency and touch initiation. Specifically, we thought that touch may be used to communicate power and social control more often during the beginning stages of a romantic relationship between men and women. In developed relationships, we thought touch would usually be used to communicate intimacy. This idea is related to Patterson's (1983) argument about relationship development and the meanings of touch. Patterson argued that social control may be most influential in early relationships when couples are on their best behavior and follow socially prescribed gender roles. In contrast, Patterson (1983) argued that intimacy is most important in developed relationships. Based on past research on sex differences, Patterson's work led us to speculate that men would feel a need to show social control when relationships first develop, whereas women would feel a need to express intimacy as the relationship develops and becomes committed. Therefore, we predicted that *men would touch more and initiate more touch in casual dating relationships, but that women would touch more and initiate more touch in serious dating and married relationships.*

Method and Results Summary

Method: Under our supervision, student research assistants observed 154 opposite-sex couples as they waited in movie theater and zoo lines in a large metropolitan city. Each couple was observed for exactly two minutes. Observations started when couples began standing at the end of the line. Couples were unaware that they were observed. The research assistants recorded their observations on coding sheets that contained body drawings of a man and a woman. They noted who initiated the first touch (the female, male, mutually initiated, or "can't tell"). For each touch they observed, the research assistants placed a mark in the corresponding area of the body drawings. After the observations were concluded, the assistants approached the couple and asked them to complete a short questionnaire that asked them if they would classify their relationship as "not dating," "on a first date or casually dating," "seriously dating or engaged," or "married." Each person completed the questionnaire separately. After completion, couples were asked not to share any information about the experiment with people who would be entering the line behind them.

Results: Statistical analyses compared touch across three relational stages (casual daters, serious daters, and marrieds). The results showed that serious daters touched each other over twice as much as casual daters or married partners. In particular, serious daters used more touch to the hand and waist than did casual daters or spouses. Spouses showed the least touch in the shoulder and butt areas. Results also showed that men and women used similar amounts of touch across all relational stages. Similarity was especially prominent in married couples, with marrieds showing more behavioral matching than casual daters or serious daters. The analyses for sex differences showed that although there were no sex differences for overall touch frequency, there were sex differences for touch initiation. As predicted, men tended to initiate touch more in casual dating relationships, whereas women tended to initiate touch more in married relationships.

DISCUSSION

This research shows that touch behavior changes as heterosexual romantic couples move through different relational stages and become more committed to one another. The amount of public touch appears to peak when couples are in the serious dating stage. However, the matching of touch behavior appears to be highest for married couples. Men appear to be more likely initiators of public touch in the beginning stages of relationships, whereas women appear to be the initiators more often in married relationships. These three findings are discussed in more detail below.

Differences across Relational Stages

Our results strongly support the prediction that relational stage influences public touch. Seriously dating couples touched each other more than twice as much as casually dating and married couples. Seriously dating couples also touched each other more often in the hand and waist areas. This may be because seriously dating couples use a lot of tie-signs, such as holding hands and putting their arms around one another's waists. Touch in the shoulder and buttocks areas was lowest for those in married relationships, perhaps because spouses engage in these types of touch more often in private than public. It is also interesting to note that hand touching was the most common form of touch, with 61 percent of seriously dating couples touching hands at least once during the two minutes they were observed. Of the casual daters, 33 percent touched hands. Similarly, 35 percent of the married couples touched hands.

There are several reasons why serious daters may touch more than casual daters and spouses. First, casually dating couples may be uncertain about their relationships and their feelings toward one another. Touch is a highly intimate behavior that may be somewhat risky in uncertain or ambiguous relationships. Unwanted touch may lead to rejection and/or feelings of discomfort. Second, serious dating couples may use touch to escalate intimacy, show bondedness (through the use of tie signs), and signal availability to one another. Givens (1978, 1983) described touch as one of the key behaviors used when couples flirt with or "court" one another. Third, married couples may show a decrease in public touch behavior because they no longer feel a need to display their relationship to others or to show public affection to one another. Givens (1978, 1983) noted that flirting behaviors, which include touch, may function to show availability for sexual encounters. Therefore, after couples become sexually intimate on a regular basis, flirting behaviors become less necessary. Similarly, Patterson (1988) noted that highly intimate couples have less pressure to give their partners attention. In fact, he observed that "it is as though relationship intimacy gives individuals some license to ignore their partner" (Patterson, 1988, p. 53). Of course, displays of intimacy may be less necessary in secure, committed relationships. In other words, married couples may feel close to one another without touching. Married couples may also use much more private than public touch.

Another possibility is that married couples feel less relational closeness than seriously dating couples, and, therefore, they touch each other less. Our results, however, show that this is not the case. The married couples we observed indicated that they were just as close to one another as did the seriously dating couples.

Behavioral Matching of Touch Behavior

Our research suggests that dating and married partners tend to touch each other with similar frequency regardless of their relational stage. Behavioral matching, however, was highest for married couples who were likely to be highly committed to one another and to share a relational history. This finding supports previous research and theory suggesting that nonverbal communication becomes more similar and synchronized as a relationship moves from an impersonal to a personal level (Altman & Taylor, 1973; Knapp & Vangelisti, 1992). Spouses, who displayed the most matching behavior, may have adapted to one another's nonverbal communication styles because of the unique combination of stability and intimacy within their relationships.

When the results for matching are combined with the results showing that serious daters touch most (see above), an interesting picture emerges. It appears that touch behavior becomes more similar between partners as a relationship develops, even though the frequency of touch may decline. Therefore, it appears that couples who are in serious dating relationships display the most touch, whereas married couples show the most behavioral similarity. Interestingly, the highest levels of *behavioral matching* may be reserved for long-term, committed relationships like marriage while the highest *frequency* of touch may be used in intermediate-level relationships as a way to escalate intimacy and display bondedness. Both types of touch behavior are undoubtedly important.

Sex Differences in Touch Initiation

Because we found romantic partners in cross-sex relationships to use similar amounts of touch, it is not surprising that there were no sex differences in the total frequency of touch used. We did, however, find sex differences for touch initiation. As we predicted, men initiated touch more often in casual dating relationships, whereas women initiated touch more in married relationships. No sex differences in touch initiation were found for those in serious dating relationships. These findings are similar to those found by Willis and Briggs (1992), who showed that men tend to initiate touch in dating relationships, but women tend to initiate touch once the "honeymoon period" is over. These results can be explained in terms of needs for social control and intimacy. Social control and social appropriateness may be more important in early stages of relationships, with men seen as having the prerogative to initiate touch. This reasoning fits with research showing that social norms in American culture may still dictate that males "make the first move" in dating relationships (Blumstein & Schwartz, 1983). Once a relationship has developed, intimacy may become more important than social control. Women, who tend to be somewhat more nonverbally expressive and intimate than men (LaFrance & Mayo, 1979), may then begin to initiate touch more often once relationships are established.

LIMITATIONS AND CONCLUSIONS

Before concluding it is important to point out that these results cannot be generalized beyond the context of public touch in heterosexual, romantic couples. Private touch may be different. Perhaps married couples do not feel a strong need to show public affection even though they show a lot of affection in private. Gay and lesbian couples may follow similar patterns in terms of touching each other more when they are in the serious dating stage. However, social norms may prevent them from touching each other as much in certain public environments, such as in the movie theater and zoo lines that we observed for this study. Sex differences in touch patterns may also emerge for gay versus lesbian couples, but such differences have yet to be tested. It would also be interesting to see how touch initiation is accomplished in gay and lesbian relationships. In heterosexual relationships, social rules dictate that the man should initiate the first tactile move. In gay and lesbian relationships, a more symmetrical pattern of touch initiation may occur. Finally, touch patterns between friends have not been examined very much and are a worthy area for future study. We know that female friends and cross-sex friends touch one another more than do male friends, but the types of touch they use have not been investigated in detail. More research on touch patterns between different types of relational partners, including friends, family members, and gay and lesbian couples, will help us understand how touch is used to develop and maintain good relationships with others.

References

Altman, I., & Taylor, D. A. (1973). *Social penetrations: The development of interpersonal relationships.* New York: Holt, Rinehart & Winston.

Andersen, P. A. (1985). Nonverbal immediacy in interpersonal communication. In A. W. Siegman & S. Feldstein (Eds.), *Multichannel integrations of nonverbal behavior* (pp. 1–35). Hillsdale, NJ: Erlbaum.

Blumstein, P., & Schwartz, P. W. (1983). *American couples.* New York: Pocket Books.

Burgoon, J. K., Buller, D. B., & Woodall, W. G. (1996). *Nonverbal communication: The unspoken dialogue* (2nd ed.). New York: McGraw-Hill.

Burgoon, J. K., Dillman, L., & Stern, L. A. (1993). Adaptation in dyadic interaction: Defining and operationalizing patterns of reciprocity and compensation. *Communication Theory, 3,* 295–316.

Cappella, J. N. (1994). The management of conversations. In M. L. Knapp & G. R. Miller (Eds.), *Handbook of interpersonal communication* (2nd ed., pp. 380–419). Newbury Park, CA: Sage.

Cappella, J. N., & Palmer, M. T. (1990). Attitude similarity, relational history and attraction: The mediating effects of kinesic and vocal behaviors. *Communication Monographs, 57,* 161–183.

Eakins, B. W., & Eakins, R. G. (1978). *Sex differences in human communication.* Boston: Houghton-Mifflin.

Fromme, D. K., Fromme, M. L., Brown, S., Daniell, J., Taylor, D. K., & Rountree, J. R. (1986). Attitudes toward touch: Cross-validation and the effects of gender and acquaintanceship. *Rassegna di Psicologia, 3,* 49–63.

Givens, D. B. (1978). The nonverbal basis of attraction: Flirtations, courtship, and seduction. *Psychiatry, 41,* 346–359.

Givens, D. B. (1983). *Love signals.* New York: Crown Books.

Henley, N. M. (1973). Status and sex: Some touching observations. *Bulletin of the Psychometric Society, 2,* 91–93.

Henley, N. M. (1977). *Body politics: Power, sex, and nonverbal communication.* Englewood Cliffs, NJ: Prentice-Hall.

Johnson, K. L. & Edwards, R. (1991). The effects of gender and type of romantic touch on perceptions of relational commitment. *Journal of Nonverbal Behavior, 15,* 43–55.

Jones, S. E. (1986). Sex differences in touch communication. *Western Journal of Speech Communication, 50,* 227–241.

Knapp, M. L. & Vangelisti, A. L. (1992). *Interpersonal communication and human relationships* (2nd ed.). Boston, MA: Allyn & Bacon.

LaFrance, M. & Mayo, C. (1979). A review of nonverbal behavior of women and men. *Western Journal of Speech Communication, 43,* 96–107.

Major, B. (1981). Gender patterns in touching behavior. In C. Mayo & N. M. Henley (Eds.), *Gender and nonverbal behavior* (pp. 15–37). New York: Springer-Verlag.

Morris, D. (1977). *Manwatching: A field guide to human behavior.* New York: Abrams.

Patterson, M. L. (1983). *Nonverbal behavior: A functional perspective.* New York: Springer-Verlag.

Patterson, M. L. (1988). Functions of nonverbal behavior in close relationships. In S. W. Duck (Ed.), *Handbook of personal relationships.* New York: Springer-Verlag.

Stier, D. S. & Hall, J. A. (1984). Gender differences in touch: An empirical and theoretical review. *Journal of Personality and Social Psychology, 47,* 440–459.

Street, R. L., Jr. (1982). Evaluation of noncontent speech convergence. *Language and Communication, 2,* 13–31.

Thayer, S. (1986). Touch: Frontier of intimacy. *Journal of Nonverbal Behavior, 10,* 7–11.

Willis, F. N., Jr. & Briggs, L. F. (1992). Relationship and touch in public settings. *Journal of Nonverbal Behavior, 16,* 55–63.

Willis, F. N., Jr., Rinck, C. M., & Dean, L. M. (1978). Interpersonal touch among adults in cafeteria lines. *Perceptual and Motor Skills, 47,* 1147–1152.

Crusco and Wetzel conducted a study to determine the effect of touching on restaurant tipping. Results indicate that touch increases tipping even if the customer is not aware of it. This study demonstrates that touch can be used as a persuasive tool.

25

The Midas Touch
The Effects of Interpersonal Touch on Restaurant Tipping

April H. Crusco
Christopher G. Wetzel

Interpersonal touch is a form of nonverbal behavior in which meaning is derived from a myriad of environmental and personal cues. Touch as a source of information feedback can be decoded as an expression of affiliation, love, or sexual interest; it can signal dominance or aggression; and it can guide the recipient's attention as part of a greeting/parting process (Knapp, 1978).

Touch research has frequently demonstrated positive effects from the innocuous touch of another. Tactile contact has increased positive affect or liking ratings of another (Alagna, Whitcher, & Fisher, 1979; Fisher, Rytting, & Heslin, 1976; Florez & Goldman, 1982; Hubble, Noble, & Robinson, 1981; Jourard & Friedman, 1970; Silverthorne, Noreen, Hunt, & Rota, 1972; Whitcher & Fisher, 1979); it has influenced the purchasing

Adapted from Crusco & Wetzel, The Midas touch: The effects of interpersonal touching on restaurant tipping. *Personality and Social Psychology Bulletin, 10,* (4), pp. 512–517, copyright © 1984. Reprinted by permission of Sage Publications, Inc.

behavior of shoppers (Smith, Gier, & Willis, 1982); and it has increased compliance to legitimate requests (Kleinke, 1977).

Research has also revealed sex differences in touch interactions and reactions to touch. Females are touched more than males; males touch females twice as much as females touch males; and males generally respond less positively to being touched than do females (Fisher et al., 1976; Goldberg & Lewis, 1969; Henley, 1973; Sussman & Rosenfeld, 1978; Cowen, Weissberg, & Lotyczewski, 1983; Whitcher & Fisher, 1979). Touching generally flows from a high status toucher to a lower status touchee, and being touched can signify inferiority or dependency. Sex effects have thus been interpreted as males' expression of dominance over females (Henley, 1973). For example, Whitcher and Fisher (1979) examined whether therapeutic touch could reduce patient anxiety. Nurses, during the course of a routine preoperative instruction, touched some of their patients on the arm for one minute while they examined a pamphlet with them. Females who were touched reacted more favorably than did control patients on affective, behavioral, and physiological (blood pressure) measures, whereas touched males reacted more negatively than controls. Whitcher and Fisher hypothesized that the nurse-patient relationship led males to interpret the touch as conveying a message of relative inferiority and dependency.

The purpose of this study was to determine the effects of touch in a previously unexamined, nonreactive, natural setting where experimental control could be exercised. Diners in a restaurant were administered one of two types of touch by a waitress just before the diners left their tips. A brief touch on the hand was expected to produce positive affect toward the waitress for both male and female customers and hence increase the amount of tip. However, a touch on the shoulder, often used as a sign of dominance by high status individuals, might not be viewed as positively, especially by males. Servants, after all, are not expected to dominate their employers. Hence, the shoulder touch condition may reduce tipping compared to the hand touch condition, and more so for male than for female customers.

METHOD

Subject Selection

Subjects were 114 diners, 79 males and 35 females, from two restaurants. Any customer who was a friend of the waitress/confederate was eliminated. Teen-aged males and college-aged females dining in groups greater than two were not selected as subjects because they generally do not tip. Approximately 25% of the participants were excluded because they either tipped before the touch manipulation was executed, or because the tip left on the table could not be definitely linked to them.

Procedure and Setting

A majority of the data (79 subjects) were collected in one restaurant by one waitress who was blind to the experimental hypotheses. A second waitress collected data on an additional 17 diners. A third waitress collected 18 observations in a second restaurant. All three waitresses were in their early to mid-twenties. Both restaurants were located in a small college community; they served lunch, dinner and cocktails; and they were frequented by business people, college students, and permanent residents of Oxford, Mississippi. A large majority of the participants were college students.

In both restaurants, the waitress was responsible for collecting the bill, and she randomly assigned diners to the experimental condition after she had collected the customer's money but before she returned with change. The touch manipulation was carried out during the change-returning transaction. Thus the waitress was blind to the touch manipulation when she was serving her customer. After returning change, the waitress asked the subjects to fill out a restaurant survey, seal it in an envelope, and leave it on the table.

Touch Manipulation

Participants were randomly assigned to one of three levels of touch. In the Fleeting Touch condition, the waitress twice touched the diner's palm with her fingers for one-half second as she returned the diner's change. In the Shoulder Touch condition, she placed her hand on the diner's shoulder for one to one and one-half seconds. In the No Touch condition, there was no physical contact with the customer. The waitresses were carefully trained to behave consistently during the change-returning transaction. The waitress approached the customers from their sides or from slightly behind them, made contact but did not smile as they spoke "Here's your change" in a friendly but firm tone, bent their bodies at an approximately 10 degree angle as they returned the change, and did not make eye contact during the touch manipulation.

Dependent Variables

The percentage of bill gratuity (tip) left for the waitress served as a behavioral measure of the diners' reactions to being touched; a restaurant attitude survey assessed the diner's affective reactions. The survey consisted of nine, seven-point semantic differentials that assessed the goodness, pleasantness and comfortableness of the dining experience, the helpfulness, friendliness, and quality of the waitressing, and the positivity, attractiveness, and comfortableness of the restaurant's atmosphere. Because all nine items intercorrelated .50 or higher (with many in the .90s), they were summed to form a single attitudinal measure.

RESULTS

Statistical analyses indicated that:

1. Tipping was higher if the weather was sunny, it was later in the week, and there were more people in the party.
2. The Shoulder Touch and the Fleeting Touch increased tipping an equal amount. This finding is not influenced by gender, weather, day of the week, number in party, or the individual waitress.
3. Touch did not influence perceptions of the pleasantness of the restaurant.
4. Males tipped more than females, and also rated the restaurant as more positive.
5. There was no relationship between tipping and perceptions of the restaurant.

DISCUSSION

This study employed a novel behavioral measure (tip percentage) to assess the effects of two types of touch in a field setting, something not previously done in the literature. We found that males did not significantly differ from females in their reactions to both types of touches, and in fact showed a tendency to be less negatively influenced by the shoulder touch than did females. (As all the touchers were female, any sex differences would have been difficult to interpret.) Our failure to find males reacting more negatively to being touched than did the females may have occurred because male diners felt secure enough about their role and status that they benevolently viewed the waitress' innocuous touch as playful endearment or affiliation. Males' status may have been secure because (1) in a restaurant there are few contextual cues present that signal lowered status or dependency, or (2) the waitress-diner relationship may have the status lines clearly drawn. Whether similar results would occur with male waiters needs to be addressed by future research.

Although there was a trend in that direction, the shoulder touch did not significantly decrease tipping compared to the hand touch. It may be that the shoulder touch, preceded as it was in this experiment by a notification that change was coming, was justified and unambiguous; both factors have been shown to facilitate positive reactions to touch (Kleinke, 1977; Sussman & Rosenfeld, 1978).

Our failure to find touch effects on the restaurant attitude survey is not terribly disturbing given that other researchers have frequently obtained significant behavioral effects without obtaining significant effects on cognitive, evaluative, or self-report ratings (Pattison, 1973; Smith et al., 1982; Whitcher & Fisher, 1979). Pattison's hypothesis, that survey and self-report data are unreliable, seems unlikely because we obtained a much larger sex main effect on our survey than on the tip percent. Thus the survey was sensitive enough to detect sex differences and apparently was more sensitive than our behavioral measure. A second explanation, that innocuous touches like ours have short-term effects, seems unlikely given the contiguity of the tipping and the survey. Most customers filled out the survey immediately after leaving the tip, and a few may have completed the survey before placing their tip. A third possibility is that the customers were unaware of the touch or, even if aware, it did not affect their conscious, verbal explanatory system (Nisbett & Wilson, 1977, Wilson, 1983). Although the unobtrusive nature of our experiment precluded our asking our subjects if they were aware of being touched by the waitress, Fisher et al. (1976) and Silverthorne et al. (1972) have found that many of their subjects were unaware that they had been touched. Thus brief, fleeting, unobtrusive touches like ours may have subliminal effects.

References

Alagna, F. J., Whitcher, S. J., & Fisher, J. D. (1979). Evaluative reaction to interpersonal touch in a counseling interview. *Journal of Counseling Psychology, 26*, 465–472.

Cowen, E. L., Weissberg, R. P., & Lotyczewski, B. S. (1983). Physical contacts in interactions between clinicians and young children. *Journal of Consulting and Clinical Psychology, 51*, 132–138.

Cunningham, M. R. (1979). Weather, mood, and helping behavior: Quasiexperiments with the Sunshine Samaritan. *Journal of Personality and Social Psychology, 37*, 1947–1956.

Fisher, J. D., Rytting, M., & Heslin, R. (1976). Hands touching hands: Affective and evaluative effects of an interpersonal touch. *Sociometry, 39*, 416–421.

Florez, C. A., & Goldman, M. (1982). Evaluation of interpersonal touch by the sighted and blind. *Journal of Social Psychology, 116*, 229–234.

Freeman, S., Walker, M. R., Borden, R., & Latane, B. (1975). Diffusion of responsibility and restaurant tipping: Cheaper by the bunch. *Personality and Social Psychology Bulletin, 1,* 584–587.

Goldberg, S., & Lewis M. (1969). Play behavior in the year-old infant: Early sex differences. *Child Development, 40,* 21–31.

Henley, N. M. (1973). The politics of touch. In P. Brown (Ed.), *Radical psychology.* New York: Harper & Row.

Hubble, M. A., Noble, F. C., & Robinson, E. F. (1981). The effect of counselor touch in an initial counseling session. *Journal of Counseling Psychology, 28,* 533–535.

Jourard, S. M., & Friedman, R. (1970). Experimenter-subject distance and self- disclosure. *Journal of Personality and Social Psychology 15*(3), 278–282.

Kleinke, C. L. (1977). Compliance to requests made by gazing and touching experimenters in field settings. *Journal of Experimental Social Psychology, 13,* 218–223.

Knapp, M. L. (1978). *Nonverbal communication in human interaction* (2nd ed.). New York: Holt, Rinehart & Winston.

Nisbett, R. E., & Wilson, T. D. (1977). Telling more than we can know: Verbal reports on mental processes. *Psychological Review, 84,* 231–259.

Pattison, J. E. (1973). Effects of touch on self-exploration and the therapeutic relationship. *Journal of Consulting and Clinical Psychology, 40*(2), 170–175.

Silverthorne, Noreen, C. C., Hunt, T., & Rota, L. (1972). The effects of tactile stimulation on visual experience. *Journal of Social Psychology, 88,* 153–154.

Smith, D. E., Gier, J. A., & Willis, F. N. (1982). Interpersonal touch and compliance with a marketing request. *Basic and Applied Social Psychology, 3*(1), 35–38.

Sussman, N. M., & Rosenfeld, H. M. (1978). Touch, justification and sex: Influences on the aversiveness of spatial violations. *Journal of Social Psychology, 106,* 215–225.

Whitcher, S. J., & Fisher, J. D. (1979). Multidimensional reaction to therapeutic touch in a hospital setting. *Journal of Personality and Social Psychology, 37,* 87–96.

Wilson, T. D. (1983). *Strangers to ourselves: The origins and accuracy of beliefs about one's own mental states.* Unpublished manuscript, University of Virginia.

In this study, 207 families were observed in park settings. The obser-
vations showed that as the child's age increased, there was more
distance and less touching between the parents and the child. Results
also showed that the size of the family mattered. When two parents
were present, the average distance between the parents and the child
was larger than when only one parent was present. There was also
more distance between parents and children when more than one
child was present. This study shows how age and family
dynamics affect touch patterns among parents and children.

26

Family Interactions in Public
Parent-Child Distance and Touching

Carol K. Sigelman
Robert M. Adams

The study of parent-child interactions has progressed well beyond the stage of focusing almost exclusively on mother-infant interactions (e.g., Belsky, 1981; Feiring & Lewis, 1978). Researchers are now examining the complex ways in which mothers, fathers, and children reciprocally affect one another's behavior. Based on this new perspective, the present study addresses a deceptively simple question: How do mothers and fathers interact with girls and boys of different ages in a natural setting?

Adapted with permission from Sigelman & Adams (1990), Family interactions in public: Parent-child distance and touching. *Journal of Nonverbal Behavior, 14*(2), 63–75.

More specifically, we focus on factors that influence degree of parent-child interactional involvement, as reflected in close physical proximity and touching. We observe the behavior of family groupings in public parks to move the study of parent-child interaction beyond the laboratory and into a naturalistic setting.

What do family interaction studies reveal about factors affecting parent-child interaction? They suggest, first of all, that a child's age influences parent-child interactional involvement. Generally, physical distance increases and touching decreases as the child becomes older or more behaviorally independent (e.g., Burgess & McMurphy, 1982; Rheingold & Eckerman, 1970). Because most studies have involved infants or very young children, a special interest in the present study was to determine whether this age trend continues into the school years.

A child's sex may also influence interaction patterns, for boys have often been found to range farther from parents than girls do. Goldberg and Lewis (1969) and Brooks and Lewis (1974) found that infant girls maintain closer proximity to mothers than infant boys do. In addition, Block (1979) reported greater parental supervision of girls, and Hart (1978) reported that boys range farther from home in their neighborhoods. Moreover, Ginsburg and Miller (1982) observed greater risk-taking by boys than girls in a zoo setting. Finally, in a field observational study in parks, Anderson (1972a,b) found that boys up to age three explored at greater distances from their mothers than girls did, and that these were child-determined distances; the mother's behavior had little effect on the child's comings and goings. However, Ley and Koepke (1982) and Martinsen (1982) failed to replicate Anderson's finding of sex differences. Thus not all previous research agrees, and much of it has used only infants and mothers as subjects. This raises questions about whether such findings are generalizable to older children and to children interacting with their fathers.

Some researchers also find that same-sex parent-child dyads maintain closer distances and engage in more touching than opposite-sex dyads do (Belsky, 1979; Weinraub & Frankel, 1977). Mackey (1979) detected a male adult-male child "bond" when he examined the gender composition of adult-child groups in public settings, and Hoffman and Teyber (1985) found both man-boy and woman-girl pairs to be more prevalent than opposite-sex pairs in public settings. However, overrepresentation of same-sex pairs was only partially confirmed by Adams and Lockard (1982) at shopping centers and a zoo. Liddell, Henzi, and Drew (1987) observed more father-son than mother-son vocal exchanges in a field observational study of playground behavior; yet there was no such outcome for other behaviors, and mothers did not vocalize more frequently with daughters than fathers did. By contrast, Stettner et al. (1978) found greater *father-daughter* and *mother-son* interaction in their playground study. Thus, the data are inconsistent, but hint at more intimate same-sex than opposite-sex parent-child interaction, particularly between fathers and sons.

Finally, researchers have also examined how the presence of a second parent or a sibling alters the interaction between parent and child (Feiring & Lewis, 1978). The presence of a second parent generally reduces a given parent's interaction with his or her child (Belsky, 1981). It also has the potential to alter the quality of that interaction. Liddell et al. (1987) found that interactional behavior when both parents were present differed from mother-child, but not father-child, interactions. The second parent effect has also been documented by Adams and Lockard (1978): A child walking with a single parent was more likely to be in physical contact with a parent, usually holding hands, than the child accompanied by both parents.

The effect of the presence of one or more siblings is much less well established. However, Samuels (1980) found that the presence of an older sibling was associated with greater infant distance from mothers, largely because infants often followed their older siblings. Adams and Lockard (1978) also observed reduced parent-child contact in most age and sex groups when a sibling was present.

Based on these previous studies, the hypotheses for this naturalistic study of family distancing and touching were that there would be: (1) increased parent-child distance and decreased touching with increasing age of child, (2) greater distance and less touching for boys than for girls, (3) reduced distance and greater touching in same-sex parent-child dyads than in cross-sex dyads, and (4) greater distance and less touching in the presence of a second parent and/or a sibling than in a dyadic family grouping.

Method and Results Summary:

Method: Six trained observers went to two public parks in the late afternoon and evening hours on weekdays and all day on weekends. They observed 207 family groups containing at least one adult and three or less children. The observers plotted the distance of the family members from one another every 20 seconds for a total of 15 observations. Observers also recorded whether or not people touched one another.

Results: The observations showed that parent-child distance increased and touching decreased as children got older. Children stood closer to their parents when there were no siblings present. When two parents were present, the average distance between a parent and a given child was larger than when only one parent was present. However, in the two-parent groups, children were just as close to the parent standing nearest them as were children in one-parent groups. Thus, it appears that when families are in groups with two parents present, the parents stand close to different children. For example, the mom might stand close to her toddler and far from her kindergartner, but the dad might compensate by standing close to the kindergartner and far from the toddler.

DISCUSSION

The observational methodology used in the present study proved to be a highly reliable source of data regarding proximity and touching between parents and children in parks. As in previous studies (e.g., Rheingold & Eckerman, 1970), parent-child distance increased with age. Previous work has tended to focus on young infants and on mother-child dyads; our data suggest that this age trend levels out after the preschool years, but applies to touching as well as to distance and to father-child interactions as well as to mother-child interactions. It seems likely that two things happen as children get older: They become more independent, willing and able to launch out on their own, and their parents feel less need to supervise their every movement. Our casual observations suggested that parents often trail closely behind young toddlers so that they can help them on and off park equipment and protect them from moving swings and other hazards, and that they touch these youngsters primarily in the course of facilitating their play.

Although parent-child interactional involvement was clearly influenced by a child's age, it was largely unaffected by the sex of the parent. Although mothers were more likely than fathers to accompany children to parks in the first place, this may reflect no more than the fact that most single-parent families are headed by mothers. The more important finding was that mothers and fathers played virtually interchangeable roles once in the park. This finding may not be unique to child-oriented and play-promoting settings such as parks. Observations in the home also suggest that mothers' and fathers' styles of interacting with children are far more similar than different, even though mothers typically devote more time to child care (Belsky, 1979; Clarke-Stewart, 1978).

Similarly, differences between boys and girls were minimal. Like Ley and Koepke (1982) and Martinsen (1982), we found little support for the hypothesis that boys achieve earlier independence from parents than girls do. Girls stayed closer to their mothers and fathers than boys did only when average distance from mothers and fathers, rather than distance from the closer of the two parents, was examined in two-parent families.

Moreover, the only support for the hypothesis that same-sex parent-child pairs are especially close came from a comparison of rates of touching in solo-mother and solo-father families.

However we did find that the presence of other family members affects a given parent-child pair. As predicted, the presence of one or more siblings generally increased parent-child distance and decreased parent-child touching. This effect is readily interpretable. An adult accompanied by multiple children simply cannot direct as much attention to any one child as he or she can when the dyad interacts in isolation. The presence of a brother or sister may also reduce the demand on mother or father to serve as a child's playmate.

By contrast, the presence of a second parent generally did not reduce a child's experience of parental closeness and physical contact below the levels observed in solo-parent families, as indicated by measures of distance from the closest parent and physical contact with one or the other parent. This occurred despite the fact that the average parent-child distances maintained by both mothers and fathers were larger in two-parent groupings than in one-parent groupings. Thus, couples apparently managed to ensure that one or the other of them remained close to any particular child in the family, even if it meant distancing himself or herself from another child. Very possibly, the negative effects of a second parent's presence have been overestimated in previous studies because attention has been focused on changes in the behavior of one parent (typically the mother) when the other (typically the father) is present. Our analysis suggests that the child can still experience a high level of parent-child closeness through the combined efforts of two parents even though, on average, each parent is likely to be more distant from children when two parents are present than when only one parent is present.

The touching data for two-parent families reinforce this interpretation. In the solo-parent families we observed, the probability that parent and child would touch was .55. Assuming for the moment that each of the parents in a two-parent family had an independent probability of .55 of touching a child, the probability that a child accompanied by two parents would be touched by either parent or both parents would be .79. Yet the actual proportion of children in two-parent families who were touched was only .41, significantly below .79. Thus, even though the proportion of children touched was not significantly lower in two-parent families than in one-parent families, the presence of a second parent apparently reduced the odds that an individual parent would touch the child.

In sum, a child's experience of physical closeness and contact with parents in a natural setting is partly influenced by the child's own characteristics, particularly his or her age. Moreover, parents and children are influenced by the family context in which they interact, a finding that underscores the importance of viewing the family as a complex system and of appreciating that what holds true of mother and child interacting in a vacuum does not necessarily hold true of mother and child accompanied by father and little brother or sister.

References

Adams, R. M., & Lockard, J. S. (1978, June). *Parent-child interactions in recreational settings.* Paper presented at the meeting of the Animal Behavior Society, New Orleans, LA.

Adams, R. M., & Lockard, J. S. (1982). Age and sex composition of family groups in shopping and recreational settings. *Ethology and Sociobiology, 2,* 131–134.

Anderson, J. W. (1972a). Attachment behaviors out of doors. In N. Blurton Jones (Ed.), *Ethological studies of child behavior.* London: Cambridge.

Anderson, J. W. (1972b). On the psychological attachment of infants to their mothers. *Journal of Biosocial Science, 4,* 197–225.

Belsky, J. (1981). Early human experience: A family perspective. *Developmental Psychology, 17,* 3–23.

Belsky, J. (1979). Mother-father-infant interaction: A naturalistic observation study. *Developmental Psychology, 15,* 601–607.

Brooks, J., & Lewis, M. (1974). Attachment behavior in thirteen-month-old, opposite-sex twins. *Child Development, 45,* 243–247.

Burgess, J. W., & McMurphy, D. (1982). The development of proxemic spacing behavior: Children's distances to surrounding playmates and adults change between six months and five years of age. *Developmental Psychobiology, 15,* 557–567.

Clarke-Stewart, K. A. (1978). And daddy makes three: The father's impact on mother and young child. *Child Development, 49,* 466–478.

Feiring, C., & Lewis, M. (1978). The child as a member of a family system. *Behavioral Science, 23,* 225–233.

Goldberg, S., & Lewis, M. (1969). Play behavior in the year-old infant: Early sex differences. *Child Development, 40,* 21–31.

Hart, R. (1978). *Children's experience of place.* New York: Irvington.

Hoffman, C. D., & Teyber, E. C. (1985). Naturalistic observations of sex differences in adult involvement with girls and boys of different ages. *Merrill-Palmer Quarterly, 31,* 93–97.

Ley, R. G., & Koepke, J. E. (1982). Attachment behavior outdoors: Naturalistic observations of sex and age differences in the separation behavior of young children. *Infant Behavior and Development, 5,* 195–201.

Liddell, C., Henzi, S. P., & Drew, M. (1987). Mothers, fathers, and children in an urban park playground: A comparison of dyads and triads. *Developmental Psychology, 23,* 262–266.

Mackey, W. C. (1979). Parameters of the adult-male-child bond. *Ethology and Sociobiology, 1,* 59–76.

Martinsen, H. (1982). A naturalistic study of young children's explorations away from caregivers. *International Journal of Behavioral Development, 5,* 217–228.

Rheingold, H. L., & Eckerman, C. C. (1970). The infant separates himself from his mother. *Science, 168,* 78–83.

Samuels, H. R. (1980). The effect of an older sibling on infant locomotor exploration of a new environment. *Child Development, 51,* 607–609.

Stettner, L. J., Templin, T., Kobson, K., & French, S. (1978, June). *Adult-child playground visits: A naturalistic study.* Paper presented at the Animal Behavior Society Meeting, Seattle.

Weinraub, M., & Frankel, J. (1977). Sex differences in parent-infant interaction during free play, departure and separation. *Child Development, 48,* 1240–1250.

—Section E—

TIME AND PLACE CODES
Chronemics and Environment

When most people think about nonverbal communication, they are likely to think about messages that are sent with the body, face, or eyes, or communication through space and touch. In contrast, most people don't tend to think about time or the environment as forms of nonverbal communication. However, the way that we perceive and use time, and the way that the environment is structured, help set the stage for communication. Imagine being late for an employment interview. Do you think that your lack of punctuality will affect the interview? It probably would. Look around the room that you are in now. Is it a pleasant place to read? Would it be a good place to get together and chat with friends? If the furniture is comfortable, the lighting is adequate, and the colors around you are soft and attractive you probably said "yes." But if you are sitting on an uncomfortable chair, the lighting is too dim or bright, or the walls of the room are painted in a "loud" color such as orange, you probably answered "no."

The way that people perceive and use time is referred to as *chronemics*. As an area of communication research, the study of time is still in its infancy. Yet it is obvious that time plays a major role in our everyday lives. This role is reflected in watches, calendars, appointment books, and schedules. You also have your own *individual* sense of time and your own rhythm and sense of pacing. You might be a morning person, or perhaps you perform better in the evening. Maybe you like to do things quickly, or maybe you'd rather move along more slowly and methodically. You also have a specific *time orientation*. You might always be thinking about the past or planning for the future. In contrast, you might live for the moment.

When two or more people are together their senses of time must be coordinated. This is called *interactional* time. Will they get together in the morning or the afternoon? Will it be a short conversation or a long one, and how will each person know when the conversation is over? Will it be a fast-paced interaction? Will they arrive late to the party or on time? These are all questions of interactional time. When people violate rules of interactional time (such as forgetting to call at a specified time), the relationship can be threatened.

Institutions and *cultures* have their own ideas of time. Some jobs require the employee to be in the office from nine to five, while others have more flexible hours. The nine-to-five timing of traditional jobs has caused major problems in large cities where rush-hour crowding has reached critical proportions. Cultures also have different time systems. Latin American countries, for example, operate at a much slower pace than the United States.

So time plays a role in many areas of your life. It may be useful to figure out your own personal timing system by keeping track of when you feel the most energetic, how you schedule your activities, and on what days of the week you are most successful. For example, some research suggests that people are most likely to be in bad moods and to get into arguments on Wednesdays because it is the middle of the work week.

The environment also plays an important role in your life. At a basic level, our environment provides us with shelter and protects us from the elements. Environments also provide us with privacy and a place to relax. The way that an environment is structured can impact communication. Think about the classroom environment. Some classrooms have the desks all arranged in rows, whereas other classrooms have desks in a circle or semicircle. In many elementary school classrooms, the desks are arranged in "pods" of four desks together in square formations. Such an arrangement allows students to work together cooperatively in small groups. The more traditional rows, in contrast, are designed to keep the students' attention focused on the teacher.

Sometimes you purposely arrange your environment in a certain way to encourage a particular type of communication. For example, if you are having a party at your house, you might place chairs in various places to encourage people to sit down and interact with others. If you are planning a romantic dinner for two, you might dim the lights, use nice place mats and napkins, light candles, place flowers on the table, and turn on soft music. You might also start a fire if you have a fireplace. In these types of situations, the environment can be manipulated to create a particular mood or atmosphere.

The moveable, changeable features of the environment are called *semifixed elements*. These elements include how you arrange things (such as the classroom desks), how you use artifacts or objects (such as the place mats, candles, and flowers) and how you use light, color, temperature, and noise (such as dimming the lights, lighting the fire, and turning on music). Other elements in the environment are harder to change. These elements, which are called *fixed elements*, include architectural features such as the size and volume of space and the materials used in the environment. Think about all the different styles of homes in which you have been. Some have low ceilings, others have cathedral-style ceilings. Some homes have a lot of open space; others have more defined barriers between different rooms. Some homes are long and rectangular; others are square. Some homes use brick; others use wood or stone. All of these features help set the stage for the interaction that occurs within a given environment.

Environmental features have been found to be important in a variety of settings. As the readings in this section show, environmental features can lure you into frequenting a certain restaurant or help you maintain your privacy. Environmental features may also deter crime and help neighborhoods create a sense of community. A good example of this is the use of neighborhood watch signs. Research on crime and the environment has also shown that when a community works together to make their neighborhood look better, it instills pride in the community members and helps to combat problems like drug use, delinquency, and violence. So whether you are trying to make your neighborhood a better place to live, or just trying to create a cozy environment for a dinner party, environmental cues can make a big difference.

*Gonzalez and Zimbardo explain the role of time in people's
lives. They surveyed over 11,000 people in the United States
and around the world and identified 7 different ways of
experiencing time. They call these time perspectives.*

27

Time in Perspective

*Alexander Gonzalez
Philip G. Zimbardo*

There is no more powerful, pervasive influence on how individuals think
and cultures interact than our different perspectives on time—the way we
mentally partition time into past, present and future. Every child learns a
time perspective appropriate to the values and needs of his society. Where
religion stresses ancestor worship, for example, the past is sacred and of
primary significance. Nomads and others who live on a subsistence level
develop a keen sense of the present and a limited sense of the future.

As industrialization, capitalism and technology flourished in Western
society, thinking became dominated by a preoccupation with the future.
Savings banks and insurance agencies, important institutions in our society, became viable only after people had developed a sense of an extended
future.

Our temporal perspective influences a wide range of psychological
processes, from motivation, emotion and spontaneity to risktaking, creativity and problem-solving. Individual behavior is regulated by subjugat-

ing the urgencies of the present to the learned demands of past and future. Without an articulate sense of the future, the force of obligations, liabilities, expectations and goal-setting is diminished.

Without a time perspective in which the past blends into the present, how could we establish a sense of personality—a sense of self that is stable through time—or extract causality and consistency from possibly coincidental, random events in our lives? George Orwell recognized the importance of time perspective when in 1984 he created a Ministry of Truth to destroy it. By deliberately rewriting the past to "say of this or that event, *it never happened*," governments can reconstruct what was to fit more acceptably into what ought to have been, given what is.

But we do not need a Ministry of Truth to bias our time perspective. Many people today have abandoned the past as irrelevant to achieving future objectives. Some have gone a step further, giving up the present time as an equal waste of time—a concern that interferes with the delay of gratification and task perseverance necessary to "make it" in their jobs. Others have never developed a meaningful sense of the future; they cannot shift focus away from the concrete reality and sensory temptations of the present to consider abstract future goals. Their temporal bias gives precedence to events that can be directly experienced here and now.

To see how these different time perspectives relate to characteristics such as age, sex, income and occupation, we asked *Psychology Today* readers in February last year to complete a two-page questionnaire called "The Times of Your Life," a version of the Stanford Time Perspective Inventory. Respondents provided demographic information and indicated, on a 5-point scale from "very characteristic" to "very uncharacteristic," how well each of 31 statements described them. They also selected from among six time perspectives the one that best matched their own.

The box below summarized the demographic data. Most of the 11,892 people who returned the survey came from the United States—all 50 states. Five percent came from Canada, Mexico, Puerto Rico, the Virgin Islands, four European countries and as far away as Saudi Arabia. Many teachers sent in batches of surveys filled out by their students in junior and senior high schools, colleges and adult-education classes.

The diverse sample included an 8-year-old boy and a 93-year-old great-grandmother, many ministers and prisoners (one on death row), a self-reported millionaire, others living at the poverty level, professional athletes and retired military officers. A surprising 72 percent of the sample consisted of those who were firstborn (46 percent) and secondborn (26 percent). Three out of four indicated a willingness to discuss their answers in a follow-up and provided their phone numbers.

The most statistically "typical" respondent was a 34-year-old white woman, firstborn, a college graduate in a skilled occupation, earning more

Profile of Respondents

Sex		Occupation	
Men	33%	Artist, writer, designer,	
Women	67%	craftsperson	5%
Age		Homeworker	5%
8-19	12%	Manager, administrator,	
20-29	27%	businessperson	17%
30-39	26%	Professional with advanced	
40-49	19%	degree	9%
50-59	11%	Teacher, counselor, social	
60 and over	5%	worker, nurse	17%
Education		Technician, skilled worker	4%
High school graduate or less	21%	Semiskilled or unskilled worker	2%
Some college	27%	White-collar worker	10%
College graduate	24%	Student	20%
Some graduate school	3%	Retired	3%
Master's degree	18%	Unemployed	1%
Professional degree (doctor,		Others (farmer, military, prisoner)	6%
lawyer, engineer)	2%		
Ph.D.	5%	*Percentages add up to less than 100	
Income		because they were rounded off.	
Less than $10,000	28%		
$10,000 to $15,999	14%	**Ethnic Background**	
$16,000 to $25,999	23%	Caucasian/white	89%
$26,000 to $35,999	17%	Black	3%
$36,000 to $45,999	8%	Hispanic	3%
$46,000 to $60,999	5%	Asian American	1%
$61,000 to $99,999	3%	Native American, Pacific	
$100,000 or above	2%	Islander and other	4%

than $25,000, living in California or New York. Because respondents are self-selected, findings from this *Psychology Today* reader survey cannot be generalized beyond this sample. Nevertheless, the size and variability of the sample are desirable qualities in exploratory stages of research such as ours.

SELF-RATED PERSPECTIVES

Asked to select one phrase from among six that best characterized their personal time perspectives, 57 percent of our respondents choose a "balanced orientation of present and future," and another 33 percent feel they are primarily "future oriented." Only 9 percent are "present oriented," and a mere 1 percent report that they focus mainly on the past. Among those who are future oriented, more focus on short-term rather than long-term goals (20 percent versus 13 percent). And twice as many of those with a present orientation describe themselves as "enjoying the moment" rather than "avoiding planning or thinking ahead" (6 percent versus 3 percent).

Perhaps a balanced orientation is the most popular choice because it seems more socially desirable than the other options. In any case, the percentage of respondents who rate themselves as balanced increases steadily with age, from 50 percent of the teenagers to 63 percent of those 40 or older. More women than men feel they have a balance orientation; this is especially true among homemakers and teachers.

Men are more likely than women to report a future focus, a tendency that increases as income goes up. The focus on short-term goals is most apparent among those in professional occupations, and least for the retired, homemakers and semiskilled or unskilled workers. Students are the most preoccupied with long-term future orientation; retired people are the least.

Professionals, managers and teachers are least likely to enjoy living for the moment. Unskilled and semiskilled workers, younger people and the less affluent are most likely to focus on the present.

A past orientation, rare for all groups, is found mostly among the retired, homemakers and blue-collar workers. Because we knew from previous research with our survey that few people in our society have a past orientation, we excluded items that explored this perspective from the questionnaire that ran in *Psychology Today.* Instead, we focused on items that would reflect different aspects of present and future orientations.

Seven Time Perspectives

We began our current research by analyzing the psychological aspects of what it meant to be future or present oriented. For each of these perspectives, we prepared a specific statement that seemed to capture its essence. Thus "delaying gratification," an aspect of a future time sense, was represented by the statement "I am able to resist temptations when I know there is work to be done." Similarly, the "action-without-reflection" feature of a present orientation was represented by "I do things impulsively, making decisions on the spur of the moment."

We reduced an initial pool of about 70 such items to the 31 used in this survey through a statistical technique called factor analysis. This method enables one to identify a set of underlying factors that contribute

Seven Time Zones

(All items are listed in order of their significance within each factor.)

Factor 1: Future, work motivation—perseverance

 A. Meeting tomorrow's deadlines and doing other necessary work comes before tonight's partying.

 B. I meet my obligations to friends and authorities on time.

 C. I complete projects on time by making steady progress.

 D. I am able to resist temptations when I know there is work to be done.

 E. I keep working at a difficult, uninteresting task if it will help me get ahead.

The items that make up this factor were the ones noted highest as a group by the Psychology Today *sample. The factor embodies a positive work motivation and a stereotypically Protestant work ethic of finishing a task despite difficulties and temptations.*

Factor 2: Present, fatalistic, worry-free, avoid planning

 A. If things don't get done on time, I don't worry about it.

 B. I think that it's useless to plan too far ahead because things hardly ever come out the way you planned anyway.

 C. I try to live one day at a time.

People with this orientation live one day at a time, not to enjoy it fully but to avoid planning for the next day and to minimize anxiety about a future they perceive as being determined by fate rather than by their efforts.

Factor 3: Present, hedonistic

 A. I believe that getting together with friends to party is one of life's important pleasures.

 B. I do things impulsively, making decisions on the spur of the moment.

 C. I take risks to put excitement in my life.

 D. I get drunk at parties.

 E. It's fun to gamble.

In contrast with the present-oriented people described by Factor 2, hedonists fill their days with pleasure-seeking partying, taking risks, drinking and impulsive action of all kinds. Many teenagers fall into this category. Among older hedonists, gambling is often an important element.

Factor 4: Future, goal seeking and planning

 A. Thinking about the future is pleasant to me.

B. When I want to achieve something, I set subgoals and consider specific means for reaching those goals.

C. It seems to me that my career path is pretty well laid out.

Compared to future Factor 1, the items here center less on work per se and more on the pleasure that comes from planning and achieving goals.

Factor 5: Time press

A. It upsets me to be late for appointments.

B. I meet my obligations to friends and authorities on time.

C. I get irritated at people who keep me waiting when we've agreed to meet at a given time.

This factor doesn't fall neatly into a present or future orientation (although it does correlate positively with the future factors). It centers on a person's sensitivity to the role time plays in social obligations and how it can be used as a weapon in struggles for status.

Factor 6: Future, pragmatic action for later gain

A. It makes sense to invest a substantial part of my income in insurance premiums.

B. I believe that "A stitch in time saves nine."

C. I believe that "A bird in the hand is worth two in the bush."

D. I believe it is important to save for a rainy day.

These people act now to achieve desirable future consequences. We had thought that the item "A bird in the hand is worth two in the bush" would be characteristic of present orientation. Instead, our respondents saw it as advice to do or have something concrete now rather than gambling on an uncertain outcome. Thus it is a conservative strategy to safeguard future options.

Factor 7: Future, specific, daily planning

A. I believe a person's day should be planned each morning.

B. I make lists of things I must do.

C. When I want to achieve something, I set subgoals and consider specific means for reaching those goals.

D. I believe that "A stitch in time saves nine."

Factor 7 describes individuals obsessed with the nitty-gritty of getting ahead. They adopt a somewhat compulsive attitude toward daily planning, make lists of things to do, set subgoals and pay attention to details.

to a complex ability or trait and to measure the relative importance of each factor. We then factor-analyzed data from the *Psychology Today* survey to assess how the 31 items were perceived by the sample as a whole, and by various subgroups selected by age, sex, income and occupation.

By analyzing the statistical correlations among the items, we found that 25 of them clustered together in different combinations to form seven distinctively different factors: four future-oriented, two present-oriented and one that is a measure of time sensitivity or emotional reaction to the pressure of time. We gave each of the factors a name (see the "Seven Time Zones" table) based on what we felt were the distinctive characteristics of its cluster.

As part of our analysis, we established four age categories—19 years old and younger; young adults, 20 to 39; middle-aged, 40 to 59; and elders, 60 years and older. When we compared the scores for each of the seven time factors on the basis of age, gender, income level and occupation, we uncovered a number of consistent patterns among them.

Age and Gender

Both men and women become more future oriented as they age—with one exception, goal seeking and planning. Women 20 to 39 years old are the least preoccupied with goal seeking. Sensitivity to time pressures is also age-related, with older people indicating more emotional reactions to lateness and time pressure.

Those 19 and younger are significantly lower than any of the other age groups in their work motivation, daily planning and time sensitivity. We would expect them to be the most present oriented of any group, and they are, if you combine both present Factors 2 and 3, fatalism and hedonism. However, people 60 and older are as fatalistic as those 19 and younger, with older women being the most fatalistic of all. The dubious honor of being most hedonistic goes not to teenagers, who come in second, but to young male adults. Among women, young adults are the most hedonistic.

Income and Gender

How much money one makes relates closely to temporal perspective. Annual income goes up as future orientation increases, and down as present orientation becomes more dominant. Those with incomes of less than $16,000 differ from wealthier people in a variety of ways. They report less motivation to work, goal seeking, pragmatic action and daily planning, and they are much more fatalistic as well as hedonistic. This present-oriented bias is at its strongest among the men with the lowest incomes.

The mixture of factors that best predicts high income is future-oriented work motivation, goal seeking and daily planning, coupled with low scores on fatalism. Pragmatism does not vary among women with different incomes, and very little among men, although men with low incomes focus least on pragmatic action. Women become less hedonistic as income goes up. Among men, those with the lowest incomes are the most hedonistic, followed by those with the highest incomes. Men of every income level are considerably more hedonistic than are women.

Women score significantly higher than men across all income levels on three of the four future factors: work motivation, pragmatic action and daily planning. On goal seeking, the top-income men score higher than the top-income women. The generally stronger future orientation of women on these survey items contrasts with what the respondents said when we asked them directly to choose their personal time perspective from among six options. In answer to that question, as mentioned earlier, more men than women rated themselves as being future oriented.

Occupations

As the "Time-Bound Occupations" table shows, different kinds of jobs best represent each of the future and present factors. It seems likely that two processes are at work here. Individuals select certain occupations because they already have the time orientation called for. Once in the job, success and satisfaction depend on intensifying the orientation further.

The time orientation that individuals develop early in life depends chiefly on their socioeconomic class and their personal experiences with its values, influences and institutions. A child with parents in unskilled and semi-skilled occupations is usually socialized in a way that promotes a present-oriented fatalism and hedonism. A child of parents who are managers, teachers or other professionals learns future-oriented values and strategies designed to promote achievement.

We have found in other studies that present-oriented people, especially fatalists, tend to see their world as one in which rewards are controlled by others. Men and women who are future oriented, especially those high in work motivation and goal seeking, see themselves as in charge of their own destinies. In an industrial, technologically based society such as ours, a present-oriented time sense dooms most people to life at the bottom of the heap. There is no place for fatalism, impulsivity or spontaneity when the marketplace is run on objectives, deadlines, budgets and quotas.

We believe that many of the explanations that have emphasized motivation or ability in accounting for differences among individuals, groups or cultures can be more accurately understood in terms of differing time perspectives. If so, what we need is remedial time-perspective training rather than another round of programs based on incentives and education concerned only with the acquisition of knowledge. Chronic problems, such as delinquency and the high incidence of unwanted pregnancies among teenagers, historically have resisted change through these latter approaches, but might be vulnerable to time-perspective modification.

Time-Bound Occupations		
	*Most**	*Least**
F_1-Future **Work Motivation**	Manager White collar	Student Semiskilled/ unskilled
F_2-Present **Fatalism**	Semiskilled/ unskilled Homemaker	Professional Manager
F_3-Present **Hedonism**	Student Semiskilled/ unskilled	Homeworker Retired
F_4-Future **Goal Seeking**	Professional Teacher	Semiskilled/ unskilled White collar
F_5-**Time Sensitivity**	Retired Manager	Student Farmer/Military/ Prisoner
F_6-Future **Pragmatic Action**	Retired Homemaker	Artist Student
F_7-Future **Daily Planning**	Teacher Professional	Semiskilled/ unskilled Student

LEARNING TO SHIFT GEARS

The clash of time perspectives also accounts for some of the misunderstandings between us and people from Latin American and Mediterranean countries. From their strong present and past perspectives, they see us as obsessed with working, efficiency, rationality, delaying gratification and planning for what will be. To us, they are inefficient, lazy, imprudent, backward and immature in their obsession with making the most of the moment.

It is probably unrealistic to expect either type of culture to accept, or even fully understand, the other's time perspective. But by acknowledging how our temporal perspectives direct our thinking, feeling and behavior into narrow channels, we can choose a more balanced, situationally appropriate orientation. When it is time to work, a future orientation is needed to determine the best means to the ends you have chosen. But when it is time to play, to consume food, to enjoy social relationships and other pleasures, it makes sense to suspend work motivation, daily planning, pragmatic action and goal seeking. Then is the time to adopt a measure of hedonism. To live a life in but one time zone diminishes the richness of human experience and limits our options.

Can you easily handle multiple tasks at one time, or do you prefer to concentrate on a single task and then move on to the next one? Does it bother you when you are talking to someone who is doing something else, like watching television, while they are listening to you? According to Hall and Hall, your answers to these questions might depend at least partially on your culture. Monochronic cultures focus on one thing at a time, whereas polychronic cultures do many things all at once.

28

Monochronic and Polychronic Time

Edward T. Hall
Mildred Reed Hall

There are many kinds of time systems in the world, but two are most important to international business. We call them monochronic and polychronic time. Monochronic time means paying attention to and doing only one thing at a time. Polychronic time means being involved with many things at once. Like oil and water, the two systems do not mix.

In monochronic cultures, time is experienced and used in a linear way—comparable to a road extending from the past into the future. Monochronic time is divided quite naturally into segments; it is scheduled and compartmentalized, making it possible for a person to concentrate on one

Reprinted with permission of the authors, from *Understanding cultural differences: Germans, French, and Americans* (pp. 3–31). Copyright © 1990.

thing at a time. In a monochronic system, the schedule may take priority above all else and be treated as sacred and unalterable.

Monochronic time is perceived as being almost *tangible:* people talk about it as though it were money, as something that can be "spent," "saved," "wasted," and "lost." It is also used as a classification system for ordering life and setting priorities: "I don't have time to see him." Because monochronic time concentrates on one thing at a time, people who are governed by it don't like to be interrupted. Monochronic time seals people off from one another and, as a result, intensifies some relationships while shortchanging others. Time becomes a room which some people are allowed to enter, while others are excluded.

Monochronic time dominates most business in the United States. While Americans perceive it as almost in the air they breathe, it is nevertheless a learned product of northern European culture and is therefore arbitrary and imposed. Monochronic time is an artifact of the industrial revolution in England; factory life required the labor force to be on hand and in place at an appointed hour. In spite of the fact that it is *learned*, monochronic time now appears to be natural and logical because the great majority of Americans grew up in monochronic time systems with whistles and bells counting off the hours.

Other Western cultures—Switzerland, Germany, and Scandinavia in particular—are dominated by the iron hand of monochronic time as well. German and Swiss cultures represent classic examples of monochronic time. Still, monochronic time is not natural time; in fact, it seems to violate many of humanity's innate rhythms.

In almost every respect, polychronic systems are the antithesis of monochronic systems. Polychronic time is characterized by the simultaneous occurrence of many things and by a *great involvement with people.* There is more emphasis on completing human transactions than on holding to schedules. For example, two polychronic Latins conversing on a street corner would likely opt to be late for their next appointment rather than abruptly terminate the conversation before its natural conclusion. Polychronic time is experienced as much less tangible than monochronic time and can better be compared to a single point than to a road.

Proper understanding of the difference between the monochronic and polychronic time systems will be helpful in dealing with the time-flexible Mediterranean peoples. While the generalizations listed below do not apply equally to all cultures, they will help convey a pattern:

Monochronic People	*Polychronic People*
do one thing at a time	do many things at once
concentrate on the job	are highly distractible and subject to interruptions
take time commitments (deadlines, schedules) seriously	consider time commitments an objective to be achieved, if possible
are low-context and need information	are high-context and already have information
are committed to the job	are committed to people and human relationships
adhere religiously to plans	change plans often and easily
are concerned about not disturbing others; follow rules of privacy and consideration	are more concerned with those who are closely related (family, friends, close business associates) than with privacy
show great respect for private property; seldom borrow or lend	borrow and lend things often and easily
emphasize promptness	base promptness on the relationship
are accustomed to short-term relationships	have strong tendency to build lifetime relationships

THE RELATION BETWEEN TIME AND SPACE

In monochronic time cultures the emphasis is on the compartmentalization of functions and people. Private offices are soundproof if possible. In polychronic Mediterranean cultures, business offices often have large reception areas where people can wait. Company or government officials may even transact their business by moving about in the reception area, stopping to confer with this group and that one until everyone has been attended to.

Polychronic people feel that private space disrupts the flow of information by shutting people off from one another. In polychronic systems, appointments mean very little and may be shifted around even at the last minute to accommodate someone more important in an individual's hierarchy of family, friends, or associates. Some polychronic people (such as Latin Americans and Arabs) give precedence to their large circle of family members over any business obligation. Polychronic people also have many close friends and good clients with whom they spend a great deal of time. The close link to clients or customers creates a reciprocal feeling of obligation and a mutual desire to be helpful.

POLYCHRONIC TIME AND INFORMATION

Polychronic people live in a sea of information. They feel they must be up to the minute about everything and everybody, be it business or personal, and they seldom subordinate personal relationships to the exigencies of schedules or budgets.

It is impossible to know how many millions of dollars have been lost in international business because monochronic and polychronic people do not understand each other or even realize that two such different time systems exist. The following example illustrates how difficult it is for these two types to relate:

> A French salesman working for a French company that had recently been bought by Americans found himself with a new American manager who expected instant results and higher profits immediately. Because of the emphasis on personal relationships, it frequently takes years to develop customers in polychronic France, and, in family-owned firms, relationships with customers may span generations. The American manager, not understanding this, ordered the salesman to develop new customers within three months. The salesman knew this was impossible and had to resign, asserting his legal right to take with him all the loyal customers he had developed over the years. Neither side understood what had happened.

These two opposing views of time and personal relationships often show up during business meetings. In French meetings the information flow is high, and one is expected to read other people's thoughts, intuit the state of their business, and even garner indirectly what government regulations are in the offing. For the French and other polychronic/high-context people, a tight, fixed agenda can be an encumbrance, even an insult to one's intelligence. Most, if not all, of those present have a pretty good idea of what will be discussed beforehand. The purpose of the meeting is to create consensus. A rigid agenda and consensus represent opposite goals and do not mix. The importance of this basic dichotomy cannot be overemphasized.

The need for privacy is basic to all human beings. Buslig discusses the role that the environment plays in helping people protect their privacy. She discusses several different environmental strategies for maintaining privacy, such as putting a "do not enter" sign on your door, choosing the room in your dorm that is farthest from the entryway, or soundproofing a room in a noisy environment.

29

"Stop" Signs
Regulating Privacy with Environmental Features

Aileen L. S. Buslig

The issue of privacy is one that spans many boundaries and many disciplines. While many theories and models emphasize the separation of self to "be alone" as the goal of privacy (e.g., Hammitt & Patterson, 1991; Werner & Haggard, 1992), not all instances of privacy necessarily preclude the presence of others, as when we seek intimacy with another person, or anonymity in a crowd (e.g., Inness, 1992; Westin, 1970). Also, within most conceptions of privacy, there is an acceptance that the environment and architecture can and often does play a key role in the achievement of privacy. For example, Duvall-Early and Benedict (1992) claim that perceptions of privacy are highly related to architectural privacy. Similarly, Archea (1977) proposes that the appropriateness and effectiveness of any behavior used to gain privacy is dependent on one's architectural and spatial circumstances.

This article was written especially for *The Nonverbal Communication Reader.*

241

While much communication research has looked at the verbal and nonverbal behaviors or "mechanisms" that people use to regulate their privacy, less systematic attention has been paid to the use of environmental features for the same purpose. However, we shall see in the coming paragraphs that the environment can be an indispensable first line of protection against unwanted privacy intrusions.

ENVIRONMENTAL PRIVACY MECHANISMS

Environmental privacy mechanisms are features of the physical environment, including architectural elements, spatial arrangements, and furnishings, which people either choose or manipulate to their advantage when seeking privacy. Both the natural and the built environment afford people many ways to achieve privacy. When it is possible, people can and will choose to utilize certain features of their environment to manage their privacy before resorting to more overt verbal or nonverbal actions.

There are two basic types of environmental privacy mechanisms. People can either take *flight*, literally or figuratively, from situations that threaten their privacy, or they can *fight* by asserting their right to, or desire for, privacy. Flight responses allow people to remove themselves from interactions nonconfrontationally. These fall into four basic categories: (1) withdrawing; (2) distancing; (3) separating; and (4) masking. In contrast to flight mechanisms, fight responses help people to stand their ground as they protect their claim to privacy and involve a more assertive or confrontational approach. Fight responses are referred to as rejecting mechanisms.

Let us look at some examples of the wide-ranging forms of environmental privacy mechanisms.

Withdrawing

When people use withdrawal as a mechanism for gaining privacy, they retreat or remove themselves from interaction, by shutting off one or more channels of communication, refusing to continue their participation, or by actually physically leaving the scene. When withdrawal is used to prevent anticipated privacy invasions, the mechanism may be more appropriately called avoidance.

One way that people may withdraw for privacy is by retreating to a *remote space*. For example, the farther away a room is from the front door of the home, the more privacy it provides (Lawrence, 1987). Deasy (1985) suggests that parents' part of the home be remote from the children's area so that intimate behavior is protected. This might help explain the popularity of "split" floor plans, where the master bedroom is on the opposite side of the house than the smaller bedrooms. Hammitt and Patterson (1991) found that many people seek the remoteness of the wilderness when they want privacy.

Furniture arrangement or orientation can be used to withdraw or avoid interactions, such as positioning one's desk so that it faces away from the door or traffic areas (Miller & Schlitt, 1985; Werner & Haggard, 1992). Students sharing quarters in dormitories indicated that they could arrange their room for privacy to avoid contact with others (Vinsel, Brown, Altman, & Foss, 1980). *Room shape* can also be used to withdraw from others. Cloverleaf and L-shapes create pockets of spaces which block the line of sight and lessen visual distractions (Miller & Schlitt, 1985).

Architectural elements can also help a person withdraw from unwanted interactions psychologically through the use of *visual escape*. Interesting window views allow people to focus their attention on something other than others nearby (Miller & Schlitt, 1985). For example, Stern and Buslig (1992) found that architecture students sometimes preferred a desk near a window overlooking the street as a diversion from their always crowded studio.

At first glance it might seem contrary to privacy needs, but *adjacencies* can also provide the ability to withdraw, especially for intimacy or group seclusion. Stone (1991) points out that by locating the master's and mistress' rooms adjacent to one another, rather than at opposite ends of the house as was previously practiced, intimate privacy was greatly increased in English manors. In a case such as this, a "block" of rooms together might be considered "off limits." Gauvain and Altman (1982) also note that women in India are separated from others into kinship groups in a courtyarded building with a single entrance, while in Indonesia relatives often occupy adjacent apartments. Although convenient as well, Kennedy (1953) explains the importance of a bathroom in the master bedroom for sexual privacy needs.

Distancing

The use of physical or mental space to put distance between oneself and others for privacy is called distancing. If used as a pre-interactional mechanism, distancing delays intrusions, allowing a person a moment to gain his or her composure (Archea, 1977). If used during an interaction, distancing allows a person to create greater distance either physically or psychologically, to lessen the intimacy or involvement of an interaction without actually completely withdrawing from the interaction.

Of course distance can be created through pure *physical space*. The use of space is often a conscious choice not only on the part of the designer but also the user of privacy. In Kenya, the homes of co-wives are separated from one another by an entire agricultural field (Gauvain & Altman, 1982). To create a private office, Deasy (1985) suggests putting distance between the office and areas where traffic flows. Duvall-Early and Benedict (1992) found that one of the best predictors of co-workers' perceived privacy was the maintenance of at least a ten-foot distance between workers, even if visual separation was not possible.

A related feature of the environment that can increase privacy is the *enlarging of space* so that more distance is created between people in an area (O'Reilly & Sales, 1987). For those who can afford the cost, larger distances between the self and others can be created through architectural or landscape design. To meet an increasing desire for privacy, the surrounding gardens of eighteenth-century English country houses were expanded to monumental proportions (Stone, 1991).

Distance can also be achieved *vertically*. It is not uncommon for the more private portions of a house, such as personal bedrooms, to be located on the second (or other upper level) floor of a multilevel home (Gauvain & Altman, 1982; Hanson & Hillier, 1982; Miller & Schlitt, 1985; Stone, 1991). Similarly, ground-level houses or apartments are considered less private than their more remote counterparts. Gauvain and Altman (1982) note that in India, men's houses are located on platforms.

Transition spaces, such as porches, foyers, and front yards, are suggested both inside and outside the home in order to regulate access and control visibility (Kennedy, 1953; Lawrence, 1987). Lack of a transitional feature as simple as an entrance hall reduces the separation of public and private space, thereby reducing the ability to control what the casual visitor sees of one's private life. A study of English country houses (Stone, 1991) found that some of the largest had processions of eight different, carefully controlled rooms through which a guest or family member must pass to get to the most private, master's "closet."

Environmental distancing may also be used to create psychological distance by limiting the amount of information someone can gather about another person from the environment. Stern and Buslig (1992) found that some architecture students regulated private information about themselves through the *control of personalization*, by displaying only classroom-related material, or nothing at all, at their studio desks.

Separating

Separation is used to divide oneself from others through the use of real or symbolic obstacles to intrusions. Environmental features can help people to deny access of themselves to others by acting as a "wall" that discourages privacy violations, setting off an area as distinct from others.

Barriers to visual and auditory inputs or outputs are often the first suggestions of architectural design guides. Barriers can be walls but can also be objects, furnishings, partitions, or more substantive features, like chimneys or closets (Kennedy, 1953; Miller & Schlitt, 1985). For added auditory privacy, soundproofing is often accommodated into barriers (Miller & Schlitt, 1985). One of the most cited, manipulable barriers is the *door* (e.g., Churchman & Herbert, 1978; Duvall-Early & Benedict, 1992; Hanson & Hillier, 1982; Kennedy, 1953; Werner & Haggard, 1992). Keeley and Edney (1983) found that houses designed for privacy had more doors than houses designed for either security or interaction. Keeping doors and windows shut or covered for privacy is common in the Middle East (El-Rafey, 1992) and many other cultures.

Symbolic barriers can also help to create private areas in places that must be shared. Symbolic barriers convey messages of ownership and protect personal space, increasing the chance that others will respect one's privacy (Churchman & Herbert, 1978; Miller & Schlitt, 1985). There are a number of ways of symbolically defining private space: partial partitions, objects, shape, lighting, color, pattern, and/or elevation (Miller & Schlitt, 1985; Sommer, 1970). Researchers have observed that students who *personalized their space*, indicating ownership (Mehrabian, 1976), reduced the use of their territories by others (Spencer & Banerji, 1982/84; Stern & Buslig, 1992). *Thresholds* are symbolic barriers at doorways or other openings which also deter the crossing of boundaries (Lawrence, 1987).

The use of booths or other *enclosures* can serve to isolate oneself from distractions (Miller & Schlitt, 1985). For example, phone booths are a type of enclosure specifically designed for privacy. Mack (1976) observed that many of his pre-adolescent students created complete or partial (three-sided) enclosures within the classroom to make their own private spaces. Today, novel ways of enclosing privacy are still being developed. For example, an issue of *Progressive Architecture* ("Office," 1994) reports that an encapsulated workspace for "nonterritorial offices" has been designed to allow office workers a high-tech, comfortable, and private place in which to work.

Providing unique spaces that can be used for different functions also facilitates separation. When privacy is necessary for one's activities or communication, it is often necessary to provide *duplicate facilities* for people who must otherwise share an area (Kennedy, 1953). For example, providing double sets of furnishings for dormitory residents permits the separation of private areas without the need for negotiation (Spencer & Banerji, 1982/84). *Separate facilities*, such as providing more rooms or distinct spaces in general, can also increase one's ability to achieve privacy (Keeley & Edney, 1983; O'Reilly & Sales, 1987). The maintenance of a formal living room or guest area, separate from the rest of the house, is seen in multiple cultures (e.g., El-Rafey, 1992; Hanson & Hillier, 1982). Functional separation can also be aided by the insertion of *corridors*, which link individual rooms together, while simultaneously allowing the separation of spaces. In English country homes, as privacy became more important, corridors were inserted so people did not have to pass through others' rooms to get to their own (Stone, 1991).

Masking

Masking is used as a privacy mechanism when some exposure of the self to others is unavoidable or actually desired. Masking generally gives the privacy-seeker the upper hand, by allowing one to survey one's own situation while giving only a limited and vague view of oneself to others. Environmental masking involves the use of features to hinder visual, auditory, or other access of others to oneself, or to disguise private behaviors so that one may act more freely in the presence of others.

The use of *ambient sound* to mask intrusive noises or one's own private conversations or actions has been suggested in various architectural guides. White noise, the sound of waterfalls or fountains, and background music can all help to cut down on the distractiveness of other noises and the audibility of one's own vocalizations (Deasy, 1985; Miller & Schlitt, 1985; Vinsel et al., 1980). Listening to music on headphones helps to mask outside noises without disturbing others (Miller & Schlitt, 1985; Spencer & Banerji, 1982/84; Stern & Buslig; 1992). People also use *ambient smells* such as incense or perfume to mask undesirable odors coming from an outside source, or their own odors that could betray private activities.

Archea (1977) also suggests that masking can be achieved through the use of well placed *lighting*, either through low lighting that makes one's activities hard to see, or through placement of the light source between oneself and potential intruders. Lighting can also be used to mask potential distractors by placing them in areas of low illumination (Miller & Schlitt, 1985).

High density and *public settings* may also help people to achieve privacy by limiting their visibility and allowing them to get lost in the crowd (Archea, 1977; Westin, 1970). For example, Taylor and Ferguson (1980) found that students sometimes seek solitude by escaping to public places. In either high-density or public-setting conditions, privacy stems from the ability to be unrecognized and, therefore, unconstrained by the prior expectations of friends and acquaintances.

In mental institutions, O'Reilly and Sales (1987) found that many patients strongly desired at least *partial barriers* so that privacy could be increased, specifying the need for curtains around the patients' beds, partitions around sinks and toilets, and so forth. Unlike complete barriers, partial barriers only mask oneself or one's behaviors, rather than completely separating and denying access of oneself to others. Some more novel partial barriers mask private behaviors or conditions in other ways. For example, Kennedy (1953) cites the common use of opaque glass in bathrooms. Churchman and Herbert (1978) also emphasize that properly located door swings can provide masking when being opened.

Rejecting

The only environmental fight mechanism, rejecting is the most direct and unambiguous method of preventing invasions of privacy. While more aggressive strategies for preventing or combating privacy invasions exist in verbal and nonverbal forms, environmental rejecting strategies are typically considered more polite or tactful assertions of one's desire for privacy.

Hanging a "do not disturb" sign on the door handle of a motel room is one example of the use of *prescriptive signs* to regulate privacy, and functions just as actually speaking the words might. Haggard and Werner (1990) found that subjects pointed out a sign (indicating the need for privacy) on the door of the lab when trying to regain privacy. The Buginese often display a sign in their houses reading that the back part of their homes is "off limits to guests" (Gauvain & Altman, 1982). Americans often put "no solicitors" signs on their front doors. Mack (1976) found that students in an elementary school classroom erected their own signs to prevent others from entering their private spaces, even though such infringements were uncommon.

One form of rejecting, the *flag*, apparently has been overlooked by most studies of privacy but is illustrated in numerous movies and television shows. Tying a flag such as a bandanna (or some other pre-arranged object) on one's dormitory room is often portrayed as a signal between roommates that one is claiming the room for private or intimate behavior at the time. This type of rejecting depends on prearranged agreement that when a physical marker is used, one's privacy is not to be disturbed, and therefore it requires that all involved are aware of the meaning of the flag in order for it to work effectively. Flags must surely exist in real life, the form and use of which is limited only to the imagination of the user and his or her confidants.

A type of flagging that does appear in the literature is the use of *symbolic indicators* to signify settings for privacy. Using colored lighting discriminately, putting up or unfolding screens, or unrolling area rugs have all been suggested as somewhat unusual ways to signal a space is being used for privacy at a particular time (Miller & Schlitt, 1985). Indicators such as these can serve several purposes—to keep others out, to symbolize to those present that the setting is considered private, or to allow cohabitation of a setting as long as the significance of the indicator is observed. They are rejecting mechanisms in that they are considered clear, pre-arranged, indications that privacy is required.

CONCLUSION

It should be obvious now that people can and do use many different environmental mechanisms to achieve privacy. While environmental mechanisms are not as flexibly used as behavioral mechanisms, they nonetheless can contribute greatly to one's sense of privacy and control over interactions in many instances. The specific types of mechanisms preferred may be influenced by one's cultural norms, but all regulating mechanisms are expected to help one to: (1) withdraw from privacy invasions; (2) distance oneself from invasions; (3) separate oneself from others; (4) mask private information from others; or (5) reject the invasions of others. An added benefit of using the (appropriate) environmental features to regulate privacy is that in most cases once they are in place their maintenance needs little attention. Using the environment to protect one's privacy does so with a minimum of contact with others, reducing the very actions and intrusions from which one may be seeking privacy in the first place. Furthermore, if one's environment supports privacy regulation, one may feel more free to use nonverbal or verbal mechanisms when violations do occur (Haggard & Werner, 1990). As this article shows, the role of the environment should not be underestimated in the fulfillment of privacy.

References

Archea, J. (1977). The place of architectural factors in behavioral theories of privacy. *Journal of Social Issues, 33*, 116–137.

Churchman, A., & Herbert, G. (1978). Privacy aspects in the dwelling: Design considerations. *Journal of Architectural Research, 6*, 19–27.

Deasy, C. M. (1985). *Designing places for people: A handbook on human behavior for architects, designers, and facility managers.* New York: Whitney Library of Design.

Duvall-Early, K., & Benedict, J. O. (1992). The relationship between privacy and different components of job satisfaction. *Environment and Behavior, 24*, 670–679.

El-Rafey, M. (1992). Housing and women's needs: Emerging trends in the Middle East. *Architecture and Behavior, 8*, 181–196.

Field, D. J. (1939). *The human house.* Boston: Houghton Mifflin.

Gauvain, M., & Altman, I. (1982). A cross-cultural analysis of homes. *Architecture and Behavior, 2*, 27–36.

Haggard, L. M., & Werner, C. M. (1990). Situational support, privacy regulation, and stress. *Basic and Applied Psychology, 11*, 313–337.

Hammitt, W. E., & Patterson, M. E. (1991). Coping behavior to avoid visitor encounters: Its relationship to wilderness privacy. *Journal of Leisure Research, 23*, 225–237.

Hanson, J., & Hillier, B. (1982). Domestic space organization. *Architecture and Behavior, 2*, 5–25.

Inness, J. C. (1992). *Privacy, intimacy, and isolation.* New York: Oxford University.

Keeley, R. M., & Edney, J. J. (1983). Model house designs for privacy, security, and social interaction. *The Journal of Social Psychology, 119*, 219–228.

Kennedy, R. W. (1953). *The house and the art of its design.* New York: Reinhold.

Lawrence, R. J. (1987). *Housing, dwellings, and homes.* Chichester: John Wiley.

Mack, D. (1976). Privacy: A child's need to be alone in the classroom. *Teacher, 93*, 52–53.

Mehrabian, A. (1976). *Public places and private spaces: The psychology of work, play, and living environments.* New York: Basic Books.

Miller, S., & Schlitt, J. K. (1985). *Interior space: Design concepts for personal needs.* New York: Praeger.

Office in a capsule. (1994, August). *Progressive Architecture*, p. 27.

O'Reilly, J., & Sales, B. (1987). Privacy for the institutionalized mentally ill: Are court-ordered standards effective? *Law and Human Behavior, 11*, 41–53.

Sommer, R. (1970). The ecology of privacy. In H. M. Proshansky, W. H. Ittleson, & L. G. Rivlin (Eds.), *Environmental psychology: Man and his physical environment* (pp. 256–266). New York: Holt, Rinehart, and Winston.

Spencer, C., & Banerji, N. (1982/84). Strategies for sharing student accommodation. *Architecture & Behavior, 2*, 123–135.

Stern, L. A., & Buslig, A. L. S. (1992). *Conflict and privacy management in architectural studios.* Unpublished manuscript, University of Arizona.

Stone, L. (1991). The public and the private in the stately homes of England, 1500–1990. *Social Research, 58*, 228–251.

Taylor, R. B., & Ferguson, G. (1980). Solitude and intimacy: Linking territoriality and privacy experiences. *Journal of Nonverbal Behavior, 4*, 227–239.

Vinsel, A., Brown, B. B., Altman, I., & Foss, C. (1980). Privacy regulation, territorial displays, and effectiveness of individual functioning. *Journal of Personality and Social Psychology, 39*, 1104–1115.

Werner, C. M., & Haggard, L. M. (1992). Avoiding intrusions in the office: Privacy regulation on typical and high solitude days. *Basic and Applied Social Psychology, 13*, 181–193.

Westin, A. (1970). *Privacy and freedom.* New York: Atheneum.

It is difficult to turn on the evening news nowadays without seeing a story on urban crime. Can environmental features be manipulated to deter some of this crime? Krupat and Kubzansky argue that they can, at least to some extent. They argue that the environments that convey a sense of privacy and make criminals feel more detectable can help deter crime.

30

Designing to Deter Crime

Edward Krupat
Philip E. Kubzansky

No matter what city you live in, it is impossible to open the local paper without being bombarded by stories of fear and crime. Evidence of public vandalism and concerns about being mugged or robbed are part of daily life in the city. The causes of urban crime and its possible remedies have been debated endlessly by social reformers, from politicians to philosophers, but few have been able to do anything significant to reduce this critical social problem.

Based on the premise that slums were the breeding ground of crime, planners in the 1950s and '60s tore down entire neighborhoods of old, decaying buildings and replaced them with new high-rise housing developments. They also improved street lighting and hired extra police to patrol problem areas. Yet, to their surprise and disappointment, crime still flourished. Police presence and better lighting did little to reduce either crime or fear. In fact, people seemed more afraid to use the newly created open spaces of their housing projects at night than they had been to walk the streets of their old slum neighborhoods.

Architect Oscar Newman looked at these efforts in his controversial book, *Defensible Space*, and labeled them misguided. He claimed that crime occurred because of this new design, not in spite of it, and concluded, "the new physical form of the urban environment is possibly the most cogent ally the criminal has in his victimization of society." Better lighting, more police and stronger locks could not deter crime, Newman said, unless residents became the critical agents in their own security.

Newman believed that the proper design, one that fostered "defensible space," could arouse the strong, but latent, territorial feelings of city dwellers and stir them to action. First, it should generate opportunities for people to see and be seen continuously. Knowing that they are, or could be, watched makes residents feel less anxious, leads them to use an area more and deters criminals by making them fear being identified and caught.

Second, people must not only watch but also be willing to intervene or report crime when it occurs. Newman proposed reducing anonymity and increasing territorial feelings by dividing larger spaces into zones of influence. This can be accomplished on a small scale by clustering a few apartments around a common entrance or a common elevator. On a larger scale individual yards or areas can be demarcated by having paths and recreational areas focus around a small set of apartment units or by having each building entry serve only a limited number of apartments.

Newman and his followers tested these ideas by studying housing developments in cities across the country, from New York to San Francisco, and concluded that rates of crime, vandalism and turnover were lower in places that conformed to the principles of defensible space. In a variety of large and small cities, housing projects and urban neighborhoods have been redesigned in accord with defensible space principles. While the results have not been consistent, reductions in crime and fear and increases in a sense of community have been found in several places.

Still, many disagreed. Some have argued that the principles are too mechanistic and narrow to account for the complex issues of fear and crime. Other critics object to the concept of territoriality that forms the basis of the theory, while still others believe that Newman and his colleagues did a poor job of picking matched sites for comparison and analyzing their data.

More recent studies have looked at crime from the opposite perspective, that of the criminal. Social psychologists Ralph Taylor and Stephen Gottfredson of Temple University and other researchers believe that criminals form mental images of potential target sites in deciding where to commit a crime. They read the nonverbal cues given off by the target to pick up messages about the opportunities, risk and convenience involved.

Social psychologists Irwin Altman and Barbara Brown of the University of Utah have expanded on this idea. They suggest that burglars ask themselves five kinds of questions:

- How detectable am I? For instance, where are windows and doors positioned, and how far is it from the street to the house?
- Are there any real barriers present? Does the place have strong locks, a gate or an alarm system?
- Are there any symbolic barriers present? Are there any nameplates, "Neighborhood Watch" signs or similar indicators of territoriality and vigilance?
- Are there traces of presence or activity on the part of the residents? Is the newspaper still in the driveway, and are the lights on?
- What is the social climate of the area? Are people staring at and questioning me, or can I go about my business ignored by others?

In 1984 sociologist Stephanie Greenberg, then of the University of Denver, and urban planner William Rohe of the University of North Carolina at Chapel Hill tested this "criminal opportunity" theory in three pairs of Atlanta neighborhoods. They were matched on racial and socioeconomic makeup but differed greatly in their levels of crime. The researchers found that the low crime neighborhoods were more residential, had less public parking and had fewer through-streets.

To get a closer look into the mind of a burglar, Altman and Brown went right to the scene of the crime. The Salt Lake City Sheriff's Office gave them the locations of 102 suburban middle-class homes that had been broken into over the previous 15 months. The researchers compared these homes to similar homes that hadn't been burglarized. Their research team walked along the block coding each home—or should we say, casing it—for the presence or absence of 200 specific environmental cues that might give off a special scent of criminal attractiveness.

Several differences were clear. Burglarized homes were more likely to be on a street with signs revealing it was a public thoroughfare, where strangers might commonly be found. Nonburglarized blocks had a more private sense about them: They looked hard to enter, were clearly set off from public areas and often had large names or numbers on them. These cues, all suggesting the owners' presence, activity and territorial commitment, apparently signaled criminals to keep away.

The Southland Corporation, owner of the 7-Eleven convenience chain, has redesigned its stores with a special eye toward the criminal's aversion to surveillance. The chief architect of this plan, Ray D. Johnson, has excellent credentials. Before working for 7-Eleven, Johnson served 25 years for robbery and burglary in the California state penitentiary system.

Now working on the other side of the law as a consultant on crime prevention, Johnson and his colleagues rearranged the physical design of 60 7-Elevens in southern California.

Knowing that robbers like concealment, they provided just the opposite. To allow clear sightlines from the street into the store, they moved cash registers up front and removed all advertising from the front windows. They also put bright floodlights outside the entrance, forcing potential robbers to perform where any passerby could look in and see.

They also installed special cash drawers that make it impossible to get at more than $10 every two minutes. This gives the would-be robber the choice of getting away with very little cash, waiting "onstage" to make the payoff worthwhile or simply going elsewhere. As Johnson says, "It takes too much time. With the register so visible from the street, no robber would hold a gun on anyone that long. When you're worried about getting caught—and every robber is very worried every time—two minutes is an eternity. Its just not worth it to wait that long for another $10."

Johnson's insights proved to be right on the money. The Southland Corporation found that robberies were 30 percent lower in the 60 redesigned stores than in 60 similar stores that had not been redesigned. "Our experience has been that robbers frustrated by small takes don't shoot; they leave," says Richard Nelson, security manager for Southland.

The new design has proven itself over time against other convenience stores, as well. While the average loss at convenience store holdups was $607 and the number of robberies rose 47 percent in the late 1970s and early 1980s, 7-Eleven's losses averaged $45 and its number of robberies went down 56 percent.

Anthropologist Sally Merry of Wellesley College combined the resident and criminal perspective during 18 months as a participant-observer in a low-to-moderate-income housing project in Boston, which Merry refers to as "Dover Square." Merry got to know many of her fellow residents and interviewed several young men who were responsible for much of the street crime in the neighborhood. The section Merry studied consisted of four-story buildings, built in 1965, that reflected several of the design factors later recommended by Newman. Yet it had the highest per capita robbery and assault rates in the city.

More than half Chinese and one quarter black, with a sprinkling of whites and Hispanics, Dover Square is, in Merry's words, "a neighborhood of strangers." It is a pot that simmers and boils but rarely melts or blends. Few friendships stretch across racial or cultural lines, and each of the groups harbors strong and often negative stereotypes of the others.

In Merry's interviews and surveys, she found several differences between the residents' perspective and that of the criminals. The places the residents considered most dangerous were not necessarily those where the most crime took place. They felt safest when they were familiar with an area and the people who used it, and felt unsafe if the turf was unfamiliar. And although they did identify a number of architectural features that they associated with danger, these were not major concerns.

The criminals, on the other hand, equated the safety of a place with the number of crimes that took place there, and they were particularly conscious of an area's architectural features. Several of them spontaneously mentioned that they looked for places with poor surveillance, such as narrow, enclosed pathways or where windows were obstructed by fences.

One of the young criminals had a favorite spot where no one could hear or see his victims. Describing it, he explained, "Someone can back you in there, and if you scream, all you can hear is the echo." Another young robber mentioned that he carefully avoided one spot because there are "so many eyes there."

Merry's research on criminals and residents helped make a critical distinction between space that is defensible and space that is defended. She notes that a neighborhood may be architecturally designed to encourage defense against crime but still not be defended because there is little or no social cohesion. Even when buildings are low and the entrances and public spaces focus around a small set of families, people will not react to crime when they believe that they are on someone else's turf, when they do not consider the police effective, or when they fear retribution.

Designing defensible space is neither the panacea that some proponents have hoped, nor is it as irrelevant to crime and fear as some detractors have contended. Environmental design does address the when and where of crime and can make people feel more secure even when they live in dangerous circumstances. But it can never eliminate crime, because it does not attack its root causes; design, as some critics have suggested, may only move crime from one place to other, more vulnerable areas. It remains easier to remodel buildings than to create opportunities for teenagers who live in poverty, and until that is done the motivation for crime will not disappear.

Design also cannot generate a social environment in which people of different races and cultures understand, care for or share responsibility for one another. As Merry says, "Design can provide preconditions for effective control, but it cannot create such control if the social fabric of the community is fragmented." Environmental design is hardly the ultimate solution to the puzzle that we call urban crime, yet it does add some new and important pieces that make the picture a good deal clearer.

*When you want a cheeseburger do you go to a fast-food restaurant
or to a more expensive place that has ambiance and interesting
surroundings? According to Langan's observational study, you
might be willing to pay more for that cheeseburger if the restaurant's environment is entertaining. Langan examines the environmental features that lure people into "theme restaurants"
such as the Hard Rock Café and Planet Hollywood.*

31

Environmental Features in Theme Restaurants

Emily Jane Langan

*London, August 8, 1993. For dinner, Christie and I decided to splurge
and go out to dinner at Planet Hollywood—the Hard Rock Café for
movies. We waited an hour and a half for a table (and this on a Sunday
night!) but had a great time anyway. It was rather pricey, but we both
thought it was really worth it. It was just kind of cool to be around tons
of movie memorabilia. I thought it was fun—Tom's suitcase from* Top
Gun, *Han Solo frozen in carbonate, Indiana Jones' whip, Chaplin's
cane, etc. I had fun as a last hurrah and figure the price included dinner and entertainment.*

—entry from a college student's journal

In 1971, Robert Earl began Hard Rock International by opening the first
Hard Rock Café near London's West End district. Even the most hopeful
entrepreneur might not guess that the corporation would blossom into a

This article was written especially for *The Nonverbal Communication Reader.*

business grossing $400 million annually. Seventy-six Hard Rock Cafés later, Earl's idea has spread around the globe and brought him one step closer to fulfilling his chain's motto: "Love all—serve all—all is one" (Jermanok, 1997, p. E1). But in 1997, Hard Rock Café has stiff competition. In 1992, Earl left HRI to start a new chain which would spotlight movie memorabilia: Planet Hollywood. These two forerunners in theme restaurants are closely followed by myriad other establishments. Competitors include the All-Star Café (another Earl enterprise), Harley-Davidson Café, The House of Blues, Fashion Café, Marvel Mania, Michael Jordan's and Bay Watch Café, just to name a few. With this much competition, successful restauranteurs need to understand their audience.

David Rush, consultant for Kurt Salmon and Associates, believes that the artifacts are the reasons people come in: "The key attraction to consumers is that [the restaurant] is a theme they can get into. The food is passable . . . But that's not the reason people go. The big driver is the atmosphere" (Roush, 1997, p. E1). Rush's assertion highlights the question guiding this project: How are the environments of theme restaurants structured to attract and sustain interest in eating at a particular restaurant? In other words, what are the structural elements behind the "driving force" of the atmosphere in theme restaurants? This paper uses an ethnographic analysis to answer this question.

THE ROLE OF THE ENVIRONMENT

Burgoon, Buller, and Woodall (1996) argue that nonverbal environmental codes mediate behavior in three ways: (1) the occurrence of interaction, (2) indications of expected behaviors, and (3) "staging" the current situation. Goffman (1967) suggests that the environment provides implicit and explicit rules for the interaction. Although individuals may not constantly or consciously attend to these elements, nevertheless the "place" influences the "action." Social interaction both influences and is influenced by the context in which it takes place. Peterson (1992) puts it more strongly: "People cannot be understood outside of their environmental context" (p. 154).

The underlying assumption of this environmental approach is that different situational factors change the nature of the interaction. In other words, people act differently in different settings. Mehrabian (1976) suggests that this is a result of the emotional reactions triggered by the setting. As people approach or avoid the environment, the person's interactions are changed. In the context of theme restaurants, the emotional reaction (or lack thereof) sparks an approach or avoid response in the individual. The individual either chooses to further interact with the setting or to avoid the environment.

This investigation examines the effect the environment of theme restaurants has on the social interactions that occur there. Ethnographic observations took place during the fall of 1997 at six theme restaurants, with three restaurants in the southwestern United States and three in the Midwest. As the forerunners in the field of theme restaurants, Hard Rock Café and Planet Hollywood were observed in both locations. Additionally, one local (nonfranchised) restaurant was included in each location. Both Majerle's Bar and Grill and Harry Caray's Restaurant maintain celebrity status in their respective locations. Observations were conducted on both weekdays and weekends, at the lunch and dinner hours. All observations lasted between one and three hours.

While in the field, notes were taken by the researcher either on paper or on a laptop computer. Notes included both observations and information gathered from key informants (Taylor & Bogdan, 1984). These informants included members of the waitstaff, management, and patrons. Although none of the restaurants were informed beforehand of the observations, information was not withheld when the researchers were present in the restaurant.

Immediately after exiting the field, the notes were expanded and thick description was generated from the observations. The descriptions and notes were coded using an open coding technique to reveal labels and categories. A technique called axial coding was used to examine the codes and to places them into categories and subcategories based on connections in the data (Strauss & Corbin, 1990). The information presented in this paper represents the central themes of the codes which describe a particular category or subcategory. In particular, this article will focus on two critical categories of environmental features: (1) the restaurant's *motif*, which includes artifacts and decorations, and the restaurant's *environment*, which includes spatial arrangement and layout.

THE MOTIF: ARTIFACTS AND DECORATIONS

The restaurant's motif describes the presentation of artifacts and decorations. By definition, theme restaurants have a central theme or subject matter. Hard Rock Café showcases music and musicians while Planet Hollywood spotlights movies, actors, and actresses. Both Harry Caray's and Majerle's feature local sports celebrities, from baseball and basketball, respectively. The artifacts within the collections are displayed throughout each restaurant, and many collections are obviously large. For example,

Bernstein (1997) reports that each Planet Hollywood restaurant has an estimated 200 pieces of memorabilia, with the other restaurants keeping that pace.

The artifacts run the gamut of possibilities, depending on the restaurant's theme. The artifacts at both Hard Rock Café locations center around the restaurant's signature guitar collection. One location showcases its guitars by mounting the instruments over the bar area. In the other location, the guitars line the inside walls. Both locations label each guitar with a small black plaque naming the musician. Other artifacts include costumes (e.g., John Lennon's shirt or Stevie Nicks's cape) and concert posters. The restaurants also have extensive collections of sales awards, mounted on plaques displaying the type of record award (gold, silver or platinum sales) and the album's or single's cover design.

At Planet Hollywood, decorations include movie props (e.g., The Flying Nun's scooter and Spock's phaser), the yearbooks of celebrities, and costumes (e.g., Batman and Robin, and Demi Moore's dress). One common element among the diverse items on display is their documentation. Next to or inside of every item's case is a plaque identifying what movie the item appeared in, whose high school picture a yearbook page is opened to, or who wore the costume. In the cases of props or costumes, often a picture is also displayed showing the people or item from the movie (e.g., Kevin Costner *carrying* the gun on display or Arnold Schwartzenegger *wearing* the terminator costume). Each location has a room which designer David Rockwell calls the "diorama room" (Bierman, 1995, p. 102). This central room displays a montage of busts of movie stars, as well as having Hollywood-esque spotlights and technicolor lighting. Finally, each site has a room significant to the restaurant's location. This room contains artifacts from movies shot locally (e.g., a costume from the movie *Tombstone*, displayed in the Southwest location) or movies about the city (e.g., gangster movie memorabilia at the Midwest location).

Both Harry Caray's and Majerle's spotlight the sport of the celebrity owner. At Harry Caray's, the baseball announcer is shown in photos with players, coaches, and other public figures. As befits the long-standing announcer for a major league baseball team, Harry Caray's displays baseball artifacts in general (photos of baseball stadiums and players throughout the game's history and artifacts specifically from his team (e.g., signed balls, uniforms). The restaurant's entryway is lined with press photos of celebrities (local and national) signed to Harry or to the restaurant.

The majority of items at Majerle's are from Dan Majerle's career in the NBA. Items include jerseys from each team for which he has played (including a wall display that progresses chronologically through his career from college through his current location), photographs, and team banners. Other sports memorabilia are also displayed, including an extensive autographed baseball collection, football helmets, and hockey jerseys.

In each location, the artifacts come together to form a collection and create a motif. Siegal (1996) refers to theme restaurants as "museums of popular culture . . . that provide chairs and sell beer" (p. 17). However, unlike like most highly documented museums, theme restaurants vary in the degree to which items are identified. These variations can be understood as high- or low-context environments (Hall, 1966). Hall describes cultures as being either high- or low-context depending on how much knowledge is implicit or explicit. He describes the differences:

> A high-context communication (HC) or message is one in which most of the information is either in the physical context or internalized to the person, while very little is in the coded, explicit, transmitted part of the message. A low-context (LC) communication is just the opposite: i.e., the mass of the information is vested in the explicit code. (Hall, 1981, p. 91)

This distinction between cultures is also applicable to the restaurant's motifs. The context (high or low) is dependent on the amount of documentation given and the amount of knowledge that must be implicit in the participant. Harry Caray's restaurant exemplifies a high-context situation. Few items are explained and meaning must be generated by the viewer's tacit knowledge of the sport. On the other end of the continuum, Planet Hollywood restaurants are prototypically low-context. Extensive documentation is provided, requiring very little of the viewer. Majerle's and Hard Rock Café represent less extreme examples of high- and low-context communication. Some documentation is provided at Majerle's, but much is still left to the sports fan's knowledge. When asked if people inquire about items, my informant at Majerle's said, "No, they can see it [pointing to the signature]. They can read." Ironically, I *couldn't* decipher the signature. At the Hard Rock Cafés, most items are labeled. However, many items are displayed high above the viewer, and, therefore, the signage become nearly invisible.

THE ENVIRONMENT:
SPATIAL LAYOUT AND STRUCTURAL ORGANIZATION

While motif describes the artifacts and decorations of a location, environment focuses on the spatial layout or structural organization of the location. Hall (1966) distinguished between fixed- and semi-fixed elements of the environment. Fixed-feature elements are largely stable and impervious to change, including architectural style, building materials, and spatial organization. Rapoport (1990) suggests that fixed features provide cues to the culture of the inhabitants. Semifixed elements "can and do change fairly quickly and easily" (Rapoport, 1990, p. 89). These mobile features can alter and personalize the environment according to the people present. The elements at the restaurants comprise some middle ground between fixed and semi-fixed features.

Most of the artifacts have become fixed-feature elements in their environments. At Planet Hollywoods, Hard Rock Cafés, and Majerle's, the items are displayed in cases, oftentimes mounted on the wall or arranged within the floorplan. The task of reorganizing would be very cumbersome. Key informants at both Planet Hollywood locations described the fluctuation of individual items within the collection, but the grouping is largely stable. One Hard Rock location was in the process of completely revamping their collection, with new items displayed and current items moved or replaced. My informant said this was the first time the entire restaurant had been remodeled in its six-year history. Items at Harry Caray's were more movable than those at the other restaurants, perhaps demonstrating more semi-fixed elements. The pictures were displayed in individual frames and could be removed or reordered without much difficulty.

One semi-fixed element present in multiple locations was seasonal decorations. Three locations displayed holiday wreaths and two restaurants had decorated Christmas trees. In one case, even the tree gave evidence of its location. The ornaments of the tree at Majerle's were basketball-playing Santas, and the lights were in the shape of basketballs. These seasonal imports suggest that some elements in the environments change regularly or at least seasonally.

The organization or layout of each restaurant also differs. Osmond (1957) and Sommer (1969) examined spatial layouts and seating arrangements in various locations, including hospitals, jails, and public spaces such as bus terminals and airports. Osmond argued that there are two basic designs in seating arrangements: sociofugal and sociopetal:

> By *sociofugality* I mean a design which prevents or discourages the formation of stable human relationships . . . *Sociopetality* is that quality which encourages, fosters, and even enforces the development of stable interpersonal relationships such as are found in small, face-to-face groups. (p. 28)

Although Osmond's comments were directed chiefly at seating arrangements, this concept emerged from my observations in regard to both seating and artifact arrangement.

Seating arrangements tended to be a combination of both sociofugal and sociopetal elements. Most tables were rectangles or squares, a style that would foster interaction between the people at individual tables. At one location, the Hard Rock Café had larger circular tables to encourage interactions even among large parties. Likewise, booths along the edges of both Planet Hollywood locations were circular. However, both Majerle's and Harry Carey's had tables and booths that were all rectangular to square. In all except the Planet Hollywood locations, the bar area was also designed in a rectangular arrangement. Mehrabian (1976) suggests that this arrangement is sociofugal: "Our experiments have shown that such side-by-side seating along a straight line discourages conversation among strangers. This is why, when all bar stools are occupied, most of the animated conversation usually goes on at the corners" (p. 248). Although the bar area at both Planet Hollywood locations was arranged semicircularly, the bar was a standard rectangle against one wall.

The seating arrangements of the tables and booths, while creating conversation within groups, did not foster interaction between groups. At each location, tables on the floor had movable chairs, and booths provided more private seating. Tables at both Harry Caray's and Majerle's were arranged symmetrically, while the other locations appeared to have more random patterns. The location of the tables and booths were almost entirely sociofugal. An extreme example of a sociofugal arrangement was observed at one Hard Rock Café location. All the tables and booths were pushed to the extreme outside parameters of the restaurant. At this location, all sides of the restaurant had seating. At the other Hard Rock location, a lunch counter (which utilizes the same noninteractive principles of a standard bar) filled the majority of one wall.

The arrangement of the artifacts fell more neatly into the two categories. Four out of six restaurants were entirely sociofugal in their artifact displays. The two Planet Hollywood locations were the exceptions, being more sociopetal than sociofugal. For the majority, all the artifacts were displayed on the walls, usually behind a customer table or booth. Costumes, record awards, pictures, and jerseys were placed against a wall and typically higher than the eye level of the patrons seated in front of the display.

The Planet Hollywood locations had a decidedly different arrangement style. Architect and planner of over 30 of the locations worldwide, David Rockwell describes his rooms as a "swirling collage of space in which variously treated places overlap" (Bierman, 1995, p. 102). Two major differences were apparent between Rockwell's creations and the other locations. First, both Planet Hollywood locations incorporate an arched walkway through the main section of the restaurant. This arch creates a main eating area (in both cases, the "diorama room") that is semicircular. Along the inside of this arch, circular booths are placed and visible from both inside and outside the archway. This archway is lined with artifacts. In both locations, major displays are set in plexiglass along the path with documentation on both sides of the case. Displays included the costume from the *Terminator*, a *Ninja Turtles* costume and Demi Moore's dress worn in *Indecent Proposal*. These large displays allowed customers to walk right next to the item, without having to lean over a table or booth of people.

The second noticeable difference between Planet Hollywoods and the other establishments was the location of the artifacts throughout the restaurants. Unlike the sociofugal design of the other four locations, Planet Hollywood restaurants have a definite sociopetal arrangement. Showcases of displays and costumes are distributed around the restaurant, including some centrally placed in the room. All the displays are encased in transparent plexiglass so that they can be seen from any angle. At one location, a display formed the walls between two rooms and the bar area. These displays (of costumes from the *Untouchables* and *The Blues Brothers*) provided a semiobstructed view into the rooms.

THE PRODUCT OF MOTIF AND ENVIRONMENT

Taken together, the elements of the motif and the environment create the restaurant's sense of "place." Each restaurant's place elements were established by being either high- or low-context, having fixed- or semi-fixed elements, and being either sociofugal or sociopetal in design. Table 1 provides a summary of these elements for each restaurant.

The elements of the place combine to create a setting. As Sommer (1969) describes the influence of place on social interaction, "Drinking

Table 1
Theme Restaurants' Elements of Place

	Context High vs. Low	Feature Elements Fixed vs. Semi-Fixed	Design Sociopetal vs. Sociofugal
Hard Rock Café #1	primarily low	fixed**	sociofugal
Hard Rock Café #2	primarily low	fixed	primarily sociofugal
Planet Hollywood #1	low	fixed	sociopetal
Planet Hollywood #2	low	fixed	sociopetal
Harry Carey's	high	semi-fixed & fixed	sociofugal
Majerle's	primarily high	primarily fixed	sociofugal

** While the artifacts at Hard Rock location #1 are fixed, they are currently in transition and hence, semi- to nonfixed.

establishments establish their own unique character, which will determine who will be attracted to the premises, how they will act, what they will drink, and how long they will stay" (p. 126). If Sommer's assertion is true, then the social interaction at a theme restaurant should be affected by its motif and environment. Perhaps this explains why people willingly pay up to five or six times more for a cheeseburger than at a fast-food restaurant. After all, the journal entry at the beginning of this article stated that the price does include both food and entertainment.

References

Bernstein, C. (1997, April 1). Hard Rock and Planet Hollywood: Head to head. *Restaurants and Institutions, 107*(8), 84, 90.

Bierman, M. L. (1995, December). David Rockwell, Vox Populi: Hooray for Planet Hollywood! *Interior Design,* 98–102.

Burgoon, J. K., Buller, D. B., & Woodall, W. G. (1996). Nonverbal communication: The unspoken dialogue. New York: McGraw-Hill.

Goffman, E. (1967). *Interaction ritual: Essays on face-to-face behavior.* Garden City, NY: Doubleday.

Hall, E. T. (1966). *The hidden dimension* (2nd ed.). Garden City, NY: Anchor/Doubleday.

Hall, E. T. (1981). *Beyond culture.* New York: Doubleday.

Jermanok, S. (1997, April 13). Theme eats: Care for some kitsch with your quiche? *The Washington Post,* pp. E1, E13, E14.

Mehrabian, A. (1976). *Public places and private spaces: The psychology of work, play, and living environments.* New York: Basic Books.

Osmond, H. (1957). Function as the basis of psychiatric ward design. *Mental Hospitals, 8,* 23–32.

Peterson, D. R. (1992). Interpersonal relationships as a link between person and environment. In W. B. Walsh, K. H. Craik, & R. H. Price (Eds.), *Person-environment psychology.* Hillsdale, NJ: Erlbaum.

Rapoport, A. (1990). *The meaning of the built environment: A nonverbal communication approach.* Tucson: University of Arizona.

Roush, C. (1997, September 17). Celebrity cafes: Is the market's plate too full? *The Atlanta Constitution,* p. E1.

Siegal, S. M. (1996, April 29). Officially licensed burgers and fries. *Brandweek, 37*(18), 17.

Sommer, R. (1969). *Personal space: The behavioral basis of design.* Englewood Cliffs, NJ: Prentice-Hall.

Strauss, A. L., & Corbin, J. (1990). *Basics of qualitative research: Grounded theory procedures and techniques.* Newbury Park, CA: Sage.

Taylor, S. J., & Bogdan, R. (1984). *Introduction to qualitative methods: The search for meanings* (2nd ed.). New York: John Wiley.

PART **III**

Nonverbal Functions

The early work on nonverbal communication tended to focus on various codes of nonverbal communication. Increasingly, however, nonverbal scholars have focused on how various nonverbal messages work together as *packages* to fulfill various functions. Psychologist Miles Patterson was one of the first researchers to propose a functional view to the study of nonverbal communication, as was communication researcher Judee Burgoon. Although different scholars have different "lists" of nonverbal functions, some functions appear to be particularly important within the context of human interaction.

One such function is creating and managing impressions. So far, you have already learned quite a bit about impression management. For example, in the readings on physical appearance and adornment, you learned that how you look and smell can have a great impact on the way other people see you. You also learned that in the workplace, attractiveness can either help or hurt as you try to impress people with your competence and skill. In the section on vocalics, you learned that an attractive voice can help you make a good impression on others. In this section, you will learn about several other functions of nonverbal communication.

The first group of readings in this section looks at how nonverbal communication is used to express emotions and relational intimacy. Imagine trying to determine what kind of emotion someone was feeling without having access to nonverbal cues such as the face or voice. You can probably think of times when people denied feeling an emotion, but you could tell that something was wrong. For example, your friend might tell you that she isn't mad at you, but her tone of voice and cold facial expression tell you otherwise. Similarly, nonverbal communication is instrumental in communicating your feelings of intimacy or disinterest in others. When you like someone, you usually signal your liking with smiles and a warm voice. When you dislike someone, you might move a few steps away and avoid engaging in eye contact. In the sections on expressing emotion and intimacy, you will learn how people use nonverbal communication to express a wide variety of emotions and relational messages.

Power is another important relational message. In fact, many scholars regard intimacy and power (or dominance) to be the two key messages that people send using both verbal and nonverbal communication. In the second group of readings in this section, you will learn how people convey power using nonverbal cues. You will also learn how people can influence or persuade others, as well as deceive others, using nonverbal communication.

Finally, the last group of readings in this section will look at how people manage interaction with one another. Nonverbal communication works alongside verbal communication to help people engage in smooth, efficient interaction. Nonverbal communication is also used to help people initiate and end conversations. Think about the last time you unexpectedly ran into someone you know. You probably looked over at the person, recognized her or him, and then waved and called out the person's name. When you end conversations with other people, you also use a lot of nonverbal communication. When you say "I have to get going" you might take your car keys out of your purse or pocket, or you might take a step toward the door.

Hopefully, this section of the reader will get you to start thinking about all the different ways that nonverbal messages work together to *do* things in your life. The next time you express an emotion, signal that you are attracted to someone, or try to persuade or deceive a friend or stranger, think about the way you use nonverbal communication. In addition, the next time you find yourself greeting someone or saying "good-bye," imagine how hard it would be to regulate interaction without the help of nonverbal communication.

—Section A—

EXPRESSING EMOTION AND INTIMACY

Nonverbal communication is an important part of messages about emotions and relationships. In fact, research has shown that people rely more on nonverbal than verbal messages when they are trying to determine the emotions you feel. Similarly, people rely heavily on nonverbal messages when they send and interpret messages about relationships, such as signs of interest, attraction, and liking. For example, when you want to comfort a friend, you might use a hug or a pat on the shoulder. If you are romantically interested in someone, you might use nonverbal flirtation to send subtle messages of attraction. Think about all the different ways that you show people how you feel about them without uttering a word.

Research on emotion has shown that people rely heavily on the face and the voice when sending and interpreting emotional messages. Some emotional messages, such as smiling when you are happy and frowning when you are sad, are easily understood. In fact, research suggests that happiness, sadness, anger, and fear tend to be communicated in similar ways across different cultures. However, research has also shown that emotional displays vary depending on the individual and the context. Most people use a variety of cues to display a single emotion. For example, you might raise your voice, furrow your brow, clench your fist, and turn red when you are very angry. In other instances, you might simply raise your voice. People can also display multiple emotions within short periods of time. You might be surprised, disappointed, and then angry when you find out that you did poorly on an exam for which you studied really hard. This complexity can make it difficult to pinpoint how someone really feels at a given moment.

In this section, you will learn how different nonverbal messages work with each other and with contextual and verbal cues to send emotional messages. You will also learn how nonverbal communication is used to send spontaneous messages of happiness, pride, anger, fear, sadness, embarrassment, and love. Sometimes, however, people decide to alter or manage their emotional expression. For example, you might act like you love the purple and yellow polka-dotted sweater that your grandma knitted for you, even though you really hate it. Or you might curb your anger when a child spills something all over your important paperwork. As these examples show, the way that you manage your emotions is a significant part of the communication process.

Nonverbal communication is also used to help people manage their relationships with others. As you will see in this section, nonverbal communication plays an important role in initiating, maintaining, and ending interpersonal relationships. Messages such as interest, disinterest, intimacy, and love are often sent nonverbally. Think of all the ways that you use nonverbal communication to *establish* interpersonal relationships. Imagine meeting someone new at a party. You might use nonverbal cues such as eye contact and smiling to let this person know you are interested in meeting her or him. Distance cues are important too. When people want to meet each other they move closer. Nonverbal flirting and courtship behaviors may also be considered. People who do not know when other people like them are at a tremendous disadvantage in meeting people and are often quite lonely. People are also at a disadvantage if they misread nonverbal cues. For example, you might perceive that someone is flirting with you when they are really just being nice.

Nonverbal cues are also used to *develop* and *maintain* relationships. On dates, sexual intimacy is regulated by nonverbal cues, and increasing intimacy is marked or indicated through more intimate physical contact. Lovers express their feelings through eye contact, touch, and special gifts. In all kinds of relationships, intimacy or closeness can be displayed through a variety of nonverbal cues such as closer distances, forward lean, and smiling, which signal involvement and interpersonal warmth. In this section, Marston and Hecht's article looks specifically at how love is communicated using nonverbal cues. Prager's article takes a look at how both emotional and sexual intimacy are communicated. As you will see, many of the same cues used to communicate love also communicate intimacy.

Finally, nonverbal cues are involved in relationship *disengagement.* There are many nonverbal signs that a relationship is ending, including decreased time together, less touching and mutual eye contact, colder voices, and fewer smiles. At the very end, some people just walk away without saying anything at all. Others will provide a verbal message to clarify that the nonverbal behaviors mean that the relationship is over.

The nonverbal signs of emotions and relationships are quite powerful and are often intertwined. You probably feel the most intense emotion in your relationships with others. It is no surprise, then, that nonverbal communication is a potent force in showing those we care about how we feel. A friendship is reinforced through spending time together and engaging in joint activities, such as the weekly card game or the annual trip to the lake. The most intimate friendships are often marked by hugging, close distance, and presents. Similarly, romantic relationships are expressed non-verbally. Think of the most common symbols of romance—flowers, rings, kisses, and loving glances. The nonverbal side of our relationships cannot be ignored.

How can you tell when someone is feeling an emotion? This is the question that Planalp and her colleagues tried to answer. Planalp's research suggests that emotion is expressed through a complex combination of different behaviors that unfold over a period of time. Vocal cues, including volume, tempo, and duration of talk, appear to play a sizable role in emotional expression, as do facial cues. Other nonverbal cues found to express emotion include activity cues (such as smoking, touching, or throwing things), body cues (such as clenched fists), and physiological cues (such as blushing).

32

Varieties of Emotional Cues in Everyday Life

Sally Planalp

My colleagues and I asked the simple question—How can people tell when someone is feeling an emotion? To be consistent with earlier research, we focused on categories of cues (voice, face, body, etc.) that people use to detect standard emotions (like anger, joy, and sadness). But breaking from tradition in a way we did not consider particularly radical, we simply asked people, assuming that people could tell us something valid about how they interpret other people's emotions. Details of the study can be found in Planalp, DeFrancisco, and Rutherford (1996). We asked college students and working adults to monitor a person they knew well (preferably someone with whom they lived). They were asked to fill out a brief question-naire the first time they noticed the other person experiencing an emotion. One format asked them to list the cues they detected; the other told them to describe in their own words "how they could tell" that the other was feeling an "emotion." Their responses were coded for the types of cues and other relevant information.

Quantitative analyses showed some interesting patterns. First, almost everyone reported using multiple cues. Figure 1 shows a plot of the number of cues used (as bars) and the number of cues from different cate-gories that were used (on the line). The modal number of cues reported was 4, although it was not uncommon for people to report using 6 or 7. A few people said they used just one, but an equal number said they used more than 10. The line above the bars indicates that cues came typically from 3 to 5 different categories (for details, see Planalp et al., 1996).

Figure 1
Number of Observers Using Multiple Cues

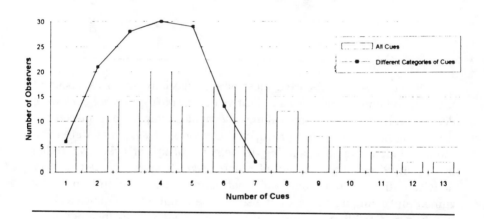

Figure 2 shows the percentage of all respondents who used at least one example of each category of cue (on the line), the percentage of all cues reported that were in each category (the open bars), and the percentage of cues identified as the "single most important cue" in each category (the shaded bars). There were no statistically significant differences when com-paring the frequencies of all cues and of "most important" cues with one exception; context cues were identified less often as the most important cue than they were overall.

Figure 2
Uses of Cues in Different Categories

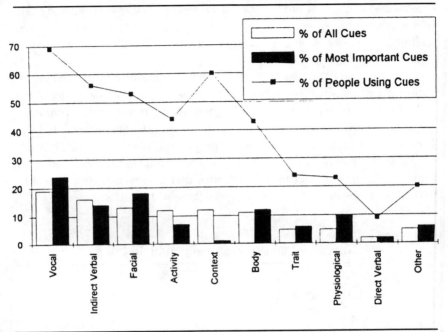

Legend:
- % of All Cues
- % of Most Important Cues
- % of People Using Cues

Vocal cues were reported most often, especially loudness, speed of talking, and amount of talking (talkative/quiet). *Indirect verbal* cues were diverse, ranging from name-calling and apologizing to long discourses describing the incident that provoked the emotion. *Facial* cues were common, including eye gaze, smiling, movements of lips or eyebrows, rolled eyes, puffy eyes, and a variety of others. *Activity* cues included solitary activities such as going for a walk, eating, drinking, smoking, throwing things, and changing putters, but also interpersonal activities such as kissing, hugging, tickling, hitting, and touching. *Context* cues included facts that were relevant to understanding the emotion, such as knowing that the person had just received a letter or phone call, was getting married, had a school assignment due, was attending a hearing, and so forth. Because context cues were unlikely to be considered the "most important" cue and because they often came first in the sequence, we suspect that context alone is not sufficient to identify an emotion, but it provides background information and alerts the observer to a possible (even likely) emotion. *Body* cues were cited frequently and include clenched fists, walking heavily, stamping feet, throwing arms up, stomping around, and the like. *Trait* cues made reference to the other person's typical behaviors and took two forms. One was that the other person typically shows this expression when emotional (e.g., John's face always gets red when he's angry). The other was when the person behaves atypically (John didn't criticize my driving like he usually does). Neither type was used frequently. Physiological cues were rare and referred most often to crying, although other examples were blushing and changes in breathing. Direct *verbal* cues were very rare (e.g., saying directly "I'm happy" or "He pissed me off"). Finally, *other* cues fell outside all the categories above and referred most often either to qualities of behaviors rather than behaviors themselves (e.g., looked worried, acted irritable) or to timing (took a while to calm down). No two categories were more likely to occur together than any other, and there was no pattern to their order, except that context cues and to a lesser extent trait cues were more likely to be first in the reports. Thus, these cues appear to provide a backdrop for interpreting emotional messages.

To appreciate these findings, however, one must look at examples of our respondents' reports in their own words. The following are more or less typical:

Example A: I heard my friend arguing on the phone with her boyfriend. Her voice was raised above its usual pitch. She had a red face and her eyes were glazed. When she hung up she sat down on the couch not speaking. I asked her if she was all right. She did not answer me; however, tears started to run down her face. Her way is to contain her feelings until she is ready to talk. However, her face changed as if she was reviewing or reliving the conversation.

Example B: He was feeling remorse and sadness. We have broken up and he would like to make up and marry. He was talking nonstop—he's usually monosyllabic. His voice was quavering. He started crying. He talked about deep feelings he had for me—something he never did prior. He hugged me and was quivering. He apologized. He repeated himself over and over. He expressed fear of the future.

Example C: My mother's attitude became increasingly upset when she found out I was going down to Colorado Springs to see my boyfriend instead of studying. Her face began to get flustered and the tone of her voice became bitchy. She began to bring up irrelevant mistakes I'd made in my past as a way of eliciting response. She gave me that motherly disappointed face and finally . . . the silent treatment.

One gets the sense here, not of an array of cues that might be added up or averaged, or even of one important cue that might dominate others, but rather of a complex combination of cues that often unfold over a period of time. The observations are subtle and seem to be grounded in knowledge of the situation and the other's typical patterns of interacting. And the emotion messages do appear to be at least partially goal-oriented, at least in the eyes of the observers. In Example A, the observer interprets the roommate's behavior as trying to suppress emotional expressions until she is ready to talk. In Example B, the man's expressions of sadness and remorse suggest that they are at least partially an attempt to get his girlfriend to reconsider marrying him. In Example C, the mother seems to persuade or perhaps even coerce her daughter into staying home by expressing "upset" (what we would call some version of anger).

Another notable finding in this study was that when asked to identify the emotion that they observed, respondents usually used more than one word (*even though* they were prompted by the question, "What emotion did you observe [e.g., anger, happiness, fear, etc.])?" Some used one word (33%), but many used two (45%), and some used three or more words (22%). Many of the uses of multiple words were within basic emotion categories or prototypes (Shaver, Schwartz, Kirson, & O'Connor, 1987, e.g., anger and frustration or sadness and loneliness). But many combinations were across categories (24%), and the overwhelming majority of across-category emotions were negative (e.g., fear, sadness, and anger). This is consistent with Oatley and Duncan's (1992) finding that mixed emotions are common, especially anger and fear, or anger changing to sadness.

References

Oatley, K., & Duncan, E. (1992). Incidents of emotion in daily life. In K. T. Strongman (Ed.), *International review of studies on emotion, Vol. 2* (pp. 249–293). Chichester, UK: Wiley.

Planalp, S., DeFrancisco, V. L., & Rutherford, D. (1996). Varieties of cues to emotion in naturally occurring situations. *Cognition and Emotion, 5,* 435–465.

Shaver, P., Schwartz, J., Kirson, D., & O'Connor, C. (1987). Emotion knowledge: Further explorations of a prototype approach. *Journal of Personality and Social Psychology, 52,* 1061–1086.

*Research has shown that emotions are often expressed nonverbally.
Andersen and Guerrero discuss how nonverbal behavior is used to
communicate six different emotions: happiness, pride, anger, fear,
sadness, and embarrassment. They also discuss how people use
display rules to manage their emotional expressions. For example,
you might pretend to feel an emotion when you don't, or you might
cover up one emotion with another.*

33

Expressing and Managing Emotion with Nonverbal Communication

*Peter A. Andersen
Laura K. Guerrero*

Research supports the commonsense notion that people tend to communicate emotions on a variety of levels with different nonverbal and verbal cues. Planalp (article 32, this volume) demonstrates that people overwhelmingly use multiple cues to send emotional messages. Vocal cues, including volume and rate, were frequently reported, as were indirect verbal cues such as name calling and apologizing; facial cues such as gaze, smiling, and rolled eyes; activity cues such as going for a walk alone or hug-

Adapted with permission from pp. 54–56 and 74–81 in Andersen & Guerrero (Eds.), *The handbook of communication and emotion*, copyright © 1998 by Academic Press, Inc.

ging the partner; and body cues such as clenching one's fists or throwing one's arms in the air. Direct verbal cues, such as telling the partner, "I'm mad at you" or "I feel really happy," were also reported, but with less frequency (see Planalp, article 32, this volume). These results suggest that communicators have a wide array of strategies at their disposal for communicating emotion.

In the following pages we will show that several selected emotions are inherently interactive and typically shared through interpersonal communication, especially nonverbal communication. Then we will discuss five ways that people manage emotion using display rules.

HAPPINESS/JOY

Because happiness is one of the most positive emotions its sharing is usually a reinforcing and pleasant experience for both parties. Unless another envies one's happiness, this emotion usually results in positive contagion, reciprocity, and affect sharing. Happiness is communicated via positive facial displays, particularly smiling (Ekman, Friesen, & Ellsworth, 1972). Research shows that people smile more commonly in the presence of friends and acquaintances than when alone (Kraut & Johnston, 1979). Shaver, Schwartz, Kirson, and O'Connor (1987) showed that, prototypically, "the happy person is socially outgoing; he or she seeks contact with others (acts friendly, hugs people, etc.) and tends to communicate his or her good feelings" (p. 1078). According to this research, joy is portrayed as energetic, active, and bouncy, and is expressed by laughing, smiling, and talking enthusiastically (Shaver et al., 1987). Since people are rarely violent or dangerous when experiencing happiness, the sharing of happy states may have functioned through the ages as positive relational overtures or appeasement displays (Van Hooef, 1972). Today, of course, people who exude happiness are viewed as more attractive and popular (Sommers, 1984), making the communication of happiness a rewarding experience for most people.

PRIDE

Pride is an emotion associated with a person's success or creation of a socially valued outcome. While little research has been done on pride, some research suggests that it is associated with particular types of interpersonal communication. Proud individuals often stand taller or seek to become larger or stronger as signs of success, triumph, or esteem. They also display their worthy self to others, produce celebratory gestures like the high-five signal, and smile broadly (Mascolo & Fischer, 1995). Children are especially prone to seek eye contact with significant others when feeling proud of accomplishments, which indicates their desire to seek and share social approval (Leary & Meadows, 1991). Shaver et al. (1987) reported a man's account of sharing pride after he successfully produced and directed a musical at his high school. The man recounts his communicative response this way: "I just kept saying, 'We did it, and we did it great!' I had the biggest smile on my face, and I was hugging all of the cast members" (p. 1073). This example illustrates that although pride certainly has internal components, people frequently engage in proud nonverbal displays and share their pride with significant others (see also Mascolo & Fischer, 1995). Communicating pride probably has a central role in self-esteem development and is a way of interactively receiving recognition for one's accomplishments.

ANGER

Anger has numerous nonverbal manifestations, starting with the angry facial expression (see Ekman et al., 1972) and including angry tones of voice, breaking things, slamming doors, making threatening gestures, staring at someone in a hostile fashion, decreasing distance and/or leaning forward to intimidate, giving someone the "silent treatment," holding a grudge, and walking out on another (Canary, Spitzberg & Semic, 1998). Yet anger is not always communicated in an aggressive or threatening manner. Sometimes individuals disclose anger in a nonthreatening manner in order to talk about problems. Other times, individuals simply internalize their feelings and deny being angry (Buck, 1979; Guerrero, 1994). Even in these cases, some angry cues are likely to be leaked despite attempts to suppress them. For example, a person's face and body may appear tense despite her or his best attempts to look relaxed.

FEAR AND ANXIETY

Shaver et al. (1987) reported that prototypical fear expressions, including screaming, crying, and pleading, are presumably used to avert an impending disaster. Similar fear reactions such as running or hiding probably have the same function. Likewise, freezing, an effort to become invisible or inconspicuous, involves an attempt to curtail all behavior, including interaction. Another function of fear displays may be to warn friends and allies of impending danger. While little research has documented this function, Bavelas's research (e.g., Bavelas, Black, Lemery, & Mullet, 1986) suggests that motor-mimicry displays function to communicate danger quickly and effectively.

Interestingly, the fear of expressing nervousness or interacting in inappropriate ways that harm one's interpersonal image can lead to social anxiety or communication apprehension. Research indicates that people experiencing this form of anxiety may display their fear through nervous cues such as vocalized pauses, hesitancies, and long response latencies, or they may withdraw from social interaction, remain silent, or decrease eye contact (see Leary & Kowalski, 1995; McCroskey, 1982; Siegman, 1985).

SADNESS AND DEPRESSION

Sadness is communicated in a variety of ways. Whereas most sad reactions, especially extreme grief and chronic depression, are involuntary, communicative responses to sadness may function to gain sympathy or to seek help. Paradoxically, sadness and depression often involve withdrawal from social contact (Shaver et al., 1987). This may involve efforts at face saving, the inability to function interpersonally, or passive help-seeking behaviors. Guerrero and Reiter (1998) discuss several responses to sadness that involve social withdrawal. The first *immobilization*, involves behaviors such as staying in bed, moping around the house, and skipping work or school. These strategies focus on ceasing normal activity. The second withdrawal strategy, *solitude*, comprises behaviors such as spending time alone and avoiding other people. Guerrero and Reiter (1998) also discuss a passive help-seeking strategy, which they termed *dependent behavior*. Waiting for others to help, trying to get the attention of others, and relying on friends for help are examples of dependent behaviors.

Numerous nonverbal behaviors display sadness, including frowning, sad or sober facial expressions, crying, whimpering, slouching, moping, a monotone voice, a sad voice, reduced smiling, less eye contact, longer response latencies, and indirect body positions (Ekman et al., 1972; Magai & McFadden, 1995; McCann & Lalonde, 1993; Segrin, 1998). Overall, depressed or sad communication is manifested in negative tone and poor, inept communication. Moreover, the sad individual often has difficulty focusing on others during conversations (McCann & Lalonde, 1993; Segrin, 1998).

SHAME AND EMBARRASSMENT

Shame is associated with feelings of inferiority and low self-worth, and therefore tends to produce avoidance rather than active communication. As Tangney (1995) stated: "The shamed individual seeks to hide the self from others, and to escape from the overwhelming pain of the situation. Thus, shame motivates behaviors that are likely to sever interpersonal contact" (p. 119). The negative affect experienced by a shamed individual is intensified by the presence of others, leading to avoidant responses. These avoidant behaviors include face hiding, gaze aversion, burying the face in one's hands, body slouching, head lowering, and fleeing from social contact (Barrett, 1995; Keltner, 1995; Mascolo & Fischer, 1995; Scheff, 1995). Some nonavoidant nonverbal responses have also been observed. Blushing is a typical response to shame, although less so than to embarrassment (Leary & Meadows, 1991; Roseman, Wiest, & Swartz, 1994). Control behaviors, such as biting or licking the lips, wrinkling the forehead, and false smiling are also common responses (Scheff, 1995) as are increased facial touches and an absence of smiling (Keltner, 1995).

Embarrassment occurs when a person loses face in front of others. For example, a person who trips and falls is likely to feel embarrassed. People may also feel embarrassed when they are paid excessive attention, such as when they are recognized publicly with an award. Like shame, numerous nonverbal messages stem from embarrassment. Miller and Leary (1992) contend that the nonverbal cues that accompany embarrassment are highly recognizable and reliable. Some of these nonverbal behaviors are analogic apologies. Others may be designed to appease onlookers and/or release the tension associated with embarrassment. Such nonverbal displays include reductions in eye contact and interpersonal gaze; mirthless, fake, and silly smiles and laughter; blushing; less fluent speech; head turns and head-down positions; facial blocking or touching; and leave-taking behaviors (Cupach & Metts, 1994; Edelman, 1990; Keltner, 1995; Miller & Leary, 1992).

DISPLAY RULES

The above discussion clearly shows that people frequently express the emotions that they feel using nonverbal behaviors. However, there are times when people *manage* emotion. In these cases, the emotion a person *feels* is different than the emotion a person *shows*. The following five display rules regulate how we manage emotion:

Simulation

Simulation involves acting like you feel an emotion when no such emotion is present (Andersen & Landgraf, 1985; Shennum & Bugental, 1982). Examples include smiling without experiencing happiness, expressing guilt when you have no remorse, or showing surprise when you fully expected an event to occur (i.e., a surprise party). Children learn to simulate emotions as early as infancy. For example, young children sometimes pretend to cry to get attention. This skill is refined as children grow older and learn rules of social appropriateness. People typically simulate emotions to conform to politeness rituals and situational appropriateness (i.e., pretending to be happy when a co-worker you barely know tells you he is getting married), or to get something they want (i.e., pretending to be scared so someone will comfort you).

Inhibition

Whereas simulation involves expressing an emotion when no emotion is being experienced, inhibition (or neutralization) involves the reverse process—giving the impression of having no feelings when one truly experiences emotion (Anderson & Landgraf, 1985; Ekman, 1978; Shennum & Bugental, 1982). Examples include keeping a straight face when something strikes one as funny, hiding attraction to a third party when one's spouse is present, or suppressing anger at one's boss. Children become increasingly skilled at inhibiting emotions as they move toward adolescence because impression management becomes more important. Branigan and Humphries (1969) reported that anger displays observed in nursery-school children disappear by school age. Similarly, Andersen, Andersen, and Mayton (1985) found that teachers observe dramatic reductions in emotional communication during the preteen years, particularly in sixth and seventh grade.

Intensification

Intensification involves giving the appearance of having stronger feelings than one actually has (Andersen & Landgraf, 1985; Ekman, 1978; Saarni, 1985). In contrast to simulation, however, intensification necessarily involves experiencing a milder form of the emotion than is displayed. Examples include showing more grief at a funeral than one actually feels, laughing heartily at your boss's joke when you barely think it is funny, or communicating love to a distant relative for whom one only feels slight affection. Children learn to intensify their emotional expressions fairly early. For example, children who feel mild pain may cry loudly if a caregiver is available to soothe and comfort them. Yet these same children may merely whimper if alone or in the presence of peers (O'Hair & Cody, 1994).

Deintensification

Deintensification involves giving the appearance of experiencing an emotion with less intensity than one is actually feeling (Andersen & Landgraf, 1985; Ekman, 1978; Saarni, 1993). According to Saarni (1993), deintensification appears in children's communication as early as the second year of life. Examples include children raising their voices slightly rather than yelling when angry, or teens trying to act "cool" by smiling instead of laughing at a very humorous joke. Deintensification is often used to conform to rules of social appropriateness. Imagine, for example, a person who has just received a prestigious award. Although this individual may feel extremely proud, he or she may curb expressing pride in order to appear humble. Similarly, a person might be shocked to hear about a friend's personal or relational problems (e.g., the person has committed a crime or has abused a romantic partner) but may express only mild surprise and disappointment to avoid alienating the friend.

Masking

Masking involves communicating an emotion that is entirely different than the one a person is experiencing (Andersen & Landgraf, 1985; Ekman, 1978, Saarni, 1993; Shennum & Bugental, 1982). Masking appears later in the developmental cycle than intensification or deintensification, probably because it is easier to moderate an existing emotion than to express an emotion that is very different from what one is feeling. As Saarni (1993) stated: "Figuring out how to make substitution or how to go poker-faced may require somewhat more complexity of thought and greater command of facial muscles, and it is sometimes assumed that children will demonstrate these expressive strategies somewhat later" (p. 437). Thus, inhibition, like masking, is a complex social skill that develops gradually.

CONCLUSION

In this article, we have shown that nonverbal communication is an important way of expressing emotion. When people are happy, proud, angry, fearful, sad, shamed, or embarrassed they tend to display emotion using a variety of nonverbal behaviors. Other emotions are also expressed nonverbally. For example, Marston and Hecht (see the next article) discuss the nonverbal communication of love. Sometimes, however, people do not want others to know how they feel. In these cases, they use display rules to simulate, inhibit, intensify, deintensify, or mask their internal feelings.

References

Andersen, J. F., Andersen, P. A., & Landgraf, J. (1985, May). *The development of nonverbal communication competence in childhood.* Paper presented at the annual meeting of the International Communication Association, Honolulu, HI.

Andersen, P. A., Andersen, J. F., & Mayton, S. M. (1985). The development of nonverbal communication in the classroom: Teachers' perceptions of students in grades K–12. *Communication Education, 34,* 292–307.

Barrett, K. C. (1995). A functionalist approach to shame and guilt. In J. P. Tangney & K. W. Fischer (Eds.), *Self-conscious emotions: The psychology of shame, guilt, embarrassment, and pride* (pp. 25–63). New York: Guilford.

Bavelas, J. B., Black, A., Lemery, C. R., & Mullett, J. (1986). "I *show* how you feel": Motor mimicry as a communicative act. *Journal of Personality and Social Psychology, 50,* 322–329.

Branigan, C., & Humphries, D. (1969, May 22). I see what you mean. *New Scientist, 42,* 406–408.

Canary, D. J., Spitzberg, B. H., & Semic, B. A. (1998). The experience and expression of anger in interpersonal settings. In P. A. Andersen & L. K. Guerrero (Eds.), *Handbook of communication and emotion: Research, theory, applications, and contexts* (pp. 189–213). San Diego, CA: Academic Press.

Cupach, W. R., & Metts, S. (1990). Remedial processes in embarrassing predicaments. In J. A. Anderson (Ed.), *Communication yearbook 13* (pp. 323–352). Beverly Hills, CA: Sage.

Edelman, R. J. (1990). Chronic blushing, self-consciousness, and social anxiety. *Journal of Psychopathology and Behavioral Assessment, 12,* 119–127.

Ekman, P. (1978). Facial expression. In A. W. Siegman & S. Feldstein (Eds.), *Nonverbal behavior and communication* (pp. 96–116). Hillsdale, NJ: Erlbaum.

Ekman, P., Friesen, W. V., & Ellsworth, P. (1972). *Emotion in the human face: Guidelines for research and integration of findings.* New York: Pergamon Press.

Guerrero, L. K., & Reiter, R. L. (1998). Expressing emotion: Sex differences in social skills and communicative responses to anger, sadness, and jealousy. In D. J. Canary & K. Dindia (Eds.), *Sex differences and similarities in communication* (pp. 321–350). Mahwah, NJ: Erlbaum.

Keltner, D. (1995). Signs of appeasement: Evidence for the distinct displays of embarrassment, amusement, and shame. *Journal of Personality and Social Psychology, 68,* 441–454.

Kraut, R. E., & Johnston, R. E. (1979). Social and emotional messages of smiling: An ethnological approach. *Journal of Personality and Social Psychology, 37,* 1539–1553.

Leary, M. R., & Kowalski, R. M. (1995). *Social anxiety.* New York: Guilford.

Leary, M. R., & Meadows, S. (1991). Predictors, elicitors, and concomitants of social blushing. *Journal of Personality and Social Psychology, 60,* 254–262.

Magai, C., & McFadden. S. H. (1995). *The role of emotions in social and personality development: History, theory, and research.* New York: Wiley.

Mascolo, M. F., & Fischer, K. W. (1995). Developmental transformations in appraisals for pride, shame, and guilt. In J. P. Tangney & K. W. Fischer (Eds.), *Self-conscious emotions: They psychology of shame, guilt, embarrassment, and pride* (pp. 64–113). New York: Guilford.

McCann, C. D., & Lalonde, R. N. (1993). Dysfunctional communication and depression: Social cognitive processes. *American Behavioral Scientist, 36,* 271–287.

McCroskey, J. C. (1982). Oral communication apprehension: A reconceptualization. In M. Burgoon (Ed.), *Communication yearbook 6* (pp. 136–170). Beverly Hills, CA: Sage.

Miller, R. S., & Leary, M. R. (1992). Social sources and interactive functions of emotion: The case of embarrassment. In M. S. Clark (Ed.), *Review of personality and social psychology: Vol. 14. Emotion and social behavior* (pp. 202–221). Newbury Park, CA: Sage.

Roseman, I. J., Wiest, C., & Swartz, T. S. (1994). Phenomenology, behaviors, and goals differentiate discrete emotions. *Journal of Personality and Social Psychology, 67,* 206–221.

Saarni, C. (1993). Socialization of emotion. In M. Lewis & J. M. Haviland (Eds.), *Handbook of emotions* (pp. 435–446). New York: Guilford.

Scheff, T. J. (1995). Conflict in family systems: The role of shame. In J. P. Tangney & K. W. Fischer (Eds.), *Self-conscious emotions: The psychology of shame, guilt, embarrassment, and pride* (pp. 393–442). New York: Guilford.

Segrin, C. (1998). Interpersonal communication problems associated with depression and loneliness. In P. A. Andersen & L. K. Guerrero (Eds.), *Handbook of communication and emotion: Research, theory, applications, and contexts* (pp. 215–242). San Diego, CA: Academic Press.

Shaver, P., Schwartz, J., Kirson, D., & O'Connor, C. (1987). Emotion knowledge: Further explorations of a prototype approach. *Journal of Personality and Social Psychology, 52,* 1061–1086.

Shennum, W. A., & Bugental, D. B. (1982). The development of control over affective expression in nonverbal behavior. In R. S. Feldman (Ed.), *Development of nonverbal behavior in children* (pp. 101–112). New York: Springer-Verlag.

Siegman, A. W. (1985). Expressive correlates of affective states and traits. In A. W. Siegman & S. Feldstein (Eds.), *Multichannel integrations of nonverbal behavior* (pp. 37–68). Hillsdale, NJ: Erlbaum.

Sommers, S. (1984). Reported emotions and conventions of emotionality among college students. *Journal of Personality and Social Psychology, 74,* 385–393.

Tangney, J. P. (1995). Shame and guilt in interpersonal relationships. In J. P. Tangney & K. W. Fischer (Eds.), *Self-conscious emotions: The psychology of shame, guilt, embarrassment, and pride* (pp, 114–139). New York: Guilford.

Van Hoofe, J. (1972). A comparative approach to the phylogeny of laughter and smiling. In R. A. Hinde (Ed.), *Non-verbal communication* (pp. 209–238). Cambridge, UK: Cambridge University Press.

People experience and communicate love in different ways. Marston and Hecht's work describes seven distinct "love ways." One of these love ways probably fits your style of loving. People communicate love using many different nonverbal behaviors, such as smiling, gazing, touching, dressing up for one another, and exchanging rings. Depending on your love style, you might use some of these behaviors more than others.

34

The Nonverbal Communication of Romantic Love

Peter J. Marston
Michael L. Hecht

The traditional folk wisdom about romantic love tells us of "love at first sight" or that one has "love in her eyes." Romance literature in both Western and Eastern cultures emphasizes the role of gaze and touch in courtship, sometimes suggesting that love transcends the need for talk and can be communicated entirely through nonverbal channels. Yet, the actual role of nonverbal communication in romantic relationships is a topic that has received little attention in the study of either nonverbal communication or loving relationships.

Over the last twelve years, we have conducted a series of studies examining the subjective experience and communication of romantic love

This article was written especially for *The Nonverbal Communication Reader*.

(Marston, Hecht & Robers, 1987; Marston & Hecht, 1994; Hecht, Marston & Larkey, 1994; Marston, Hecht, Manke, McDaniel & Reeder, 1998). In this chapter we will review our conception of romantic love and our approach to the study of loving relationships, and then highlight the most significant conclusions about the nonverbal communication of romantic love that have emerged in our research.

LOVE WAYS

If we have learned one thing in our study of love, it is that there is no one way of experiencing or communicating love. Feelings or behaviors that may be central to one lover's experience of love may be irrelevant to another's. For some lovers, love is a partnership where support and negotiation are key, while others experience love intuitively through feelings of warmth and nervousness.

Conceptually, we have articulated our view this way: *love is a set of interdependent thoughts, attitudes, feelings, and behaviors that vary in importance as lovers' experiences change*. This means that as lovers experience different things in their lives and in their relationship, the *importance* of the thoughts, attitudes, feelings, and behaviors that make up the love experience will change. In addition, it means that love is an *overall or holistic* impression based on more specific thoughts, attitudes, feelings, and behaviors. Therefore, there are no *particular* thoughts, attitudes, feelings, or behaviors that are necessarily common to all love experiences. Two different individuals' experience of love may share *no* common thoughts, attitudes, feelings, or behaviors, and yet each individual may recognize his or her experience *as* love.

In our research, we have identified seven common ways of loving or "love ways." The seven ways we call *collaborative love, active love, intuitive love, committed love, secure love, expressive love,* and *traditional romantic love*. Each is experienced differently. These experiences are described in the chart below.

These "love ways" are neither exhaustive nor mutually exclusive. That is, lovers may experience various combinations of these ways of loving, and there may be ways of loving not yet discovered in our research. However, our studies reveal that these seven gestalts represent the most common ways of experiencing love, accounting for the love experiences of over 90 percent of actual lovers (Marston et al., 1987). At this point, we will turn to four specific conclusions regarding the nonverbal communication of romantic love.

Experiencing the Ways of Loving

Love Way	Experience
Collaborative Love	mutual support, negotiation, associated with feelings of increased energy and intensified emotions
Active Love	doing things with the other, feelings of increased strength and confidence
Intuitive Love	a variety of physiological responses (including feelings of warmth, nervousness, and loss of appetite), communicated nonverbally, through physical contact, sex, and eye contact
Committed Love	feelings of connectedness, making a commitment, discussing the future, and spending time together
Secure Love	feelings of security, communicated by discussing intimate topics
Expressive Love	doing things for the other, by saying "I love you"
Traditional Romantic Love	feelings of being beautiful and healthy, communicated through togetherness and commitment

Nonverbal and verbal messages both play important roles in communicating romantic love. We began this chapter by noting the traditional and romantic notion that love is communicated primarily, if not entirely, through nonverbal channels. This notion does not conform to the reports of actual lovers, however. In addition to many nonverbal behaviors—such as smiling, eye contact, facial expression, and so on—lovers also reported many verbal behaviors that are important in the communication of romantic love. These include: telling the other "I love you," writing notes and letters, talking through problems, discussing the future, and talking about feelings and intimate topics. Indeed, in terms of sheer frequency, lovers report roughly equal numbers of verbal and nonverbal behaviors that communicate love in their relationships.

Note, however, that this does not mean that verbal and nonverbal communication is equally important in the experiences of *all* lovers. Some ways of experiencing love clearly emphasize nonverbal communication (most notably, intuitive love), while other ways seem to rely more heavily on verbal communication (for example, collaborative love and secure love). Thus, for particular lovers, the relative importance of verbal and nonverbal communication in their experience of love may vary greatly. Still, across all the love ways, we find an approximate balance between verbal and nonverbal communication.

A wide range of nonverbal behaviors communicate romantic love. Nonverbal behaviors used to communicate love run the entire gamut of nonverbal communication. Here is a brief summary:

> *kinesics:* sex, facial expressions, the way he/she looks at me, smiles, gazes
> *physical appearance:* the way I dress for him/her
> *proxemics:* being close, just being together
> *haptics:* touching, holding, massage, sex
> *vocalics:* the sound of his/her voice
> *chronemics:* spending time together
> *use of objects:* gifts, rings

Given the complexity of love as a subjective experience and the various ways in which given lovers experience love, it is not surprising that so many different types of nonverbal behaviors are used to communicate romantic love.

Different nonverbal behaviors communicate different aspects of love. In our more recent studies, we have examined the subjective experience and communication not of love *per se*, but of related and overlapping experiences—specifically, intimacy, passion, and commitment (Marston et al., 1998). These studies reveal that different nonverbal behaviors are used to communicate these various aspects of love.

Nonverbal behaviors commonly used to communicate intimacy include: spending time together, sex, holding, and touching. A relatively unusual combination of nonverbal behaviors also emerged as an important way of experiencing intimacy: namely, spending time together while *not* talking, a way of experiencing intimacy that we have called "quiet company."

The communication of passion is associated with some of the same nonverbal behaviors (sex, holding, and touching), but is also characterized by the use of objects traditionally associated with romance. These include: lighting candles, putting rose petals in the bed, and sending roses and other romantic gifts.

Although some lovers report holding and touching as ways of communicating commitment, there are some important nonverbal behaviors that seem to be unique to this aspect of the love experience. One of these is relational duration—that is, some lovers express their commitment through the sheer amount of time they have spent together as a couple. Another is the performance of various routine activities, such as cooking, cleaning, picking up children at school, and going to work every day. Finally, as with passion, we commonly find the use of traditional objects, in this case, the wearing of engagement or wedding rings.

Again, it is important to note that not all lovers will use all of these behaviors to communicate intimacy, passion, and commitment in their relationships. Indeed, intimacy, passion, and commitment seem to vary greatly in their importance within the subjective experience of particular lovers, and the same is true of the nonverbal behaviors used to communicate these aspects of love.

Although lovers report different sets of nonverbal behaviors used to communicate intimacy, passion, and commitment, there are significant areas of overlap. One notable area of overlap seems to be that sex is an important aspect of communicating both passion and intimacy. Another is revealed in the use of traditional objects in the communication of passion and commitment. This similarity may derive from cultural rituals of courtship which are designed to elicit passion and culminate in commitment.

Mutually satisfying combinations or enmeshments of communication behaviors are important in maintaining love relationships. Elsewhere we have presented our views concerning the maintenance of loving relationships (Marston & Hecht, 1994). We believe that what is important is how lovers' behaviors combine or enmesh with one another—how the messages and behaviors of one lover are interwoven with those of her/his partner. Here we will only comment on how these views relate to the nonverbal communication of love.

Much research in interpersonal communication supports the "symmetry hypothesis": namely, that relational dyads are most satisfied when their communication behaviors are similar or "match." The only consistent exception to this hypothesis is in the area of dominance, where it is generally assumed that complementarity leads to greater satisfaction—that is, dominant communication behaviors lead to higher satisfaction when they elicit submissive behaviors, resulting in a "fit" as opposed to a "match."

The communication of romantic love, both in verbal and nonverbal channels, does not seem to confirm this simple hypothesis. Indeed, symmetry seems less important than a mutually satisfying enmeshment. For example, if one partner *sends* love through a smile or tone of voice, then what is most important is that the other partner *receives* love through these behaviors, and not that the behaviors be reciprocated. When we look at the *total* set of behaviors used to communicate love in any given relationship, we see the value of the term "enmeshment" as these behaviors may share many complex relationships that extend beyond simple symmetry (or even complementarity). Spending time together might elicit a loving gaze that in turn might initiate sex that may lead to spending more time together.

Thus, lovers are advised to discuss not only whether or not they are "in love" with their partners, but also, more specifically, how they send and receive love in their relationship. Such discussion is probably the most productive way to both clarify and improve communication in loving relationships.

There is undoubtedly much more to be said about the role of nonverbal communication in the experience of romantic love and in the maintenance of loving relationships. Still, these four conclusions present an appropriate overview of our most significant findings to date. For further clarification, we await not only our own future research but also that of our colleagues and students.

References

Hecht, M. L., Marston, P. J. & Larkey, L. K. (1994). Love ways and relationship quality in heterosexual relationships. *Journal of Social and Personal Relationships, 11*, 25–43.

Marston, P. J. & Hecht, M. L. (1994). Love ways: An elaboration and application to relational maintenance. In D. J. Canary & L. Stafford (Eds.), *Communication and Relational Maintenance* (pp. 187–202). Orlando, FL: Academic Press.

Marston, P. J., Hecht, M. L., Manke, M., McDaniel, S. & Reeder, H. (1998). The subjective experience of intimacy, passion, and commitment in heterosexual loving relationships. *Personal Relationships, 5*, 15–30.

Marston, P. J., Hecht, M. L. & Robers, T. (1987). True love ways: The subjective experience and communication of romantic love. *Journal of Social and Personal Relationships, 4*, 387–407.

The same types of behaviors (gaze, smiling) that are used to express flirtation and seduction are also used to express friendliness. This makes it easy for people to misinterpret friendly behaviors as flirtation or seduction. Koeppel and her colleagues examined sex differences in the perception of warm, intimate nonverbal behavior. They found that men tended to perceive these nonverbal behaviors as more seductive than do women. Ratings of seductiveness also increased when the female (rather than the male) initiated the interaction.

35

Friendly? Flirting? Wrong?

Liana B. Koeppel
Yvette Montagne
Dan O'Hair
Michael J. Cody

Not long ago, the topic of flirting would produce smiles, laughter, and even sneers from audience members in communication and psychology. The pop books on "body language" had done little more than confirm in the minds of the public that nonverbal communication is a trivial area; also, the pop books of the 1980s fueled simplistic and unsubstantiated beliefs about flirting. Indeed, only months before the Clarence Thomas-Anita Hill hearings (and the rape trials of William Kennedy Smith and Mike Tyson) forced most Americans to grapple with issues of sexual harassment, male-female relations, and date-rape, Louise Lague (1990) published an article, "Flirting For the Fun of It" in *Glamour* that likened flirting to a sport: Flirting can be as satisfying as a workout for the mind, and a boost for the ego. Some of the advice included: "If you don't mean anything by it, people know you don't mean anything by it" (p. 243), and, "Flirting is pure pleasure, like eating ice cream, but unlike most indulgences, it's a pleasure that gives pleasure" (p. 300). Simplistic? Yes, and also potentially dangerous.

In 1982, the publication of Antonia Abbey's work raised the awareness that males generally construe the world in more sexual terms than do females, and indicated that as a group men were much more likely than females to judge "friendly" behavior as "seductive" or "promiscuous" behavior. Further, work by Charlene Muehlenhard (Muehlenhard, Koralewski, Andrews, & Burdick, 1986; Muehlenhard & McFall, 1981; Muehlenhard, Miller, & Burdick, 1983) was, in part, predicated on the view that some women may not be very competent in flirting effectively, and that women would benefit both from training and from understanding why certain cues were misperceived (see especially, Muehlenhard et al., 1986). The literature on flirting is no longer a laughing matter: Flirting effectiveness, flirting error, flirting misperceptions, and consequences deserve systematic study.

SEX DIFFERENCES IN PERCEPTIONS OF SEXUAL INTEREST

The examination of perceptions and misperceptions of friendly versus flirting behavior has been increasing over the last several years. Abbey's (1982, 1987) research in particular suggests that misinterpretation of a female's friendly behavior seems to be fairly common. As we have seen in recent news headlines, these misperceptions of behavior can be extremely problematic for both males and females. In addition to the legal and moral implications of sexual harassment and date rape, the examination of misperceptions in this area has important implications for such applied and theoretical areas as attraction, sex-role socialization, and relational development.

In her seminal work, Abbey (1982) examined whether males were more likely than females to misperceive females' friendliness as sexual interest. She had participants talk in a male-female dyad while other participants unobtrusively observed the interaction. Findings indicated that males were more likely to rate females as being more promiscuous and seductive. Later works by Abbey and her colleagues (Abbey, 1987; Abbey, Cozzarelli, McLaughlin, & Harnish, 1987; Abbey & Melby, 1986) further examined the role of various nonverbal cues in the perceptions and attributions of seductiveness including: distance, eye contact, touch, and clothing. Much of this research confirmed that males were more likely to perceive the interaction in more sexual terms than females. Additionally, this research indicated that females' behavior was viewed as more sexual or promiscuous than male behavior. For instance, Abbey and Melby (1986) found that female-initiated touch was perceived to be a stronger indicator of the relationship than male touch, and females' revealing clothing were rated as more seductive than males' revealing clothing (Abbey et al., 1987).

Other research further examines the differences in perceptions between male and female behavior. Shotland and Craig (1988) examined whether males and females could distinguish between friendly versus sexual behavior, as well as whether males were more likely to attribute sexual intent than females. Their results not only found that males and females could differentiate between the two types of behaviors, but also concurred with Abbey's research regarding males' perceptions of sexual intent. Saal, Johnson, and Weber (1989) investigated perceptions of sex differences in behaviors and found, in three separate studies, that men perceive less friendliness and more seductiveness.

Sigal, Gibbs, Adams, and Derfler (1988) also examined sex differences in the perception of friendly/seductive behavior in terms of eye contact, distance, tone of voice, touching and smiling. Although this study confirmed Shotland and Craig's (1988) findings that individuals could distinguish between friendly and seductive behavior, they found no differences between male and female ratings of seductiveness, which contradicts previous research. The authors suggest that they may have obtained different results because Abbey's studies did not have actors engage in typical sexual or friendly behavior, which may have resulted in cues being unclear. Additionally, Abbey and Melby (1986) and Abbey et al. (1987) utilized photographs as opposed to actual interactions. Another potential problem is that the Abbey studies did not use standardized scripts. In other words, *both* verbal and nonverbal behavior differed in the studies examining interactions. In the present study standardized scripts were used as a backdrop against which to study sex differences in perceptions of different nonverbal behaviors.

Nonverbal Behaviors Associated with Friendly, Flirtatious, and Seductive Interactions

The present study was designed to examine the perceptions of nonverbal behaviors associated with friendly, flirtatious, and seductive interactions. We first surveyed nonverbal research to determine which cues were associated with friendly, flirtatious, and seductive behaviors. We decided to focus on the nonverbal areas of kinesics (movement), haptics (touch), proxemics (distance), oculesics (eye movement), and vocalics (voice). Appropriate nonverbal cues were assigned to one of four treatments: control (or normal), friendly, flirting, or seductive interactions.

Kinesics. Body movements, particularly smiling and body posture, are seen as indicants of friendly, flirting, and seductive behaviors. Research indicates that the amount of smiling varies along a continuum: (a) a small amount of smiling for friendly behavior (Andersen, 1985; Muehlenhard et al., 1986; Sigal et al., 1988; Walsh & Hewitt, 1985), (b) medium to large amounts of smiling for flirting behavior (Coker & Burgoon, 1987; Muehlenhard et al., 1986), and (c) constant smiling in seductive interactions (Andersen, 1985; Coker & Burgoon, 1987; Muehlenhard et al., 1986; Sigal et al., 1988; Walsh & Hewitt, 1985). Friendly versus seductive behavior is also characterized by differing degrees of body relaxation—the more relaxed, the more seductive (Schwartz et al., 1983). Finally, flirting behavior is characterized by the use of childlike expressions, open mouth (pouting) and head tilting (Burgoon, Buller, & Woodall, 1989).

Haptics. The use of touch is a common form of communication, particularly in terms of indicating the nature of a relationship. Friendly behaviors are characterized by very little to no touch (Abbey & Melby, 1986; Andersen, 1985; Muehlenhard et al., 1986; Perper & Weis, 1987; Sigal et al., 1988). On the other hand, moderate amounts of touch indicate a flirtatious interaction (Abbey & Melby, 1986; Muehlenhard et al., 1986), whereas touching the hand or leg represents seductive behavior (Abbey & Melby, 1986; Andersen, 1985; Burgoon et al., 1989; Muehlenhard et al., 1986; Perper & Weis, 1987; Sigal et al., 1988). Another sign of seductive behavior is the use of clothing adjustments (i.e., playing with buttons, smoothing skirt, adjusting pants) and self-touch (Burgoon et al., 1989).

Proxemics. The amount of personal distance between interactants also varies depending on the type of interaction. The greater the amount of distance between interactants, the less seductive the interaction (Abbey & Melby, 1986; Coker & Burgoon, 1987; Muehlenhard et al., 1986; Patterson & Edinger, 1987; Perper & Weis, 1987; Schwartz, Foa, & Foa, 1983; Sigal et al., 1988). Body orientation and physical planes have also been shown to indicate different degrees of friendliness/seductiveness. Individuals who lean toward one another and who are at the same body angle are perceived as being more seductive than those individuals who lean away from each other (Andersen, 1985). Finally, flirtatious behavior is further characterized by crossing legs toward one another (Burgoon et al., 1989; Muehlenhard et al., 1986), and more face to face interaction (Burgoon et al., 1989).

Oculesics. The amount and type of eye contact/movements are also indicants of the type of interaction. Friendly behavior exhibits little to moderate eye contact, flirtatious behavior uses moderate degrees of eye contact, and seductive behaviors are characterized by constant eye contact (Abbey & Melby, 1986; Andersen, 1985; Burgoon et al., 1989; Coker & Burgoon, 1987; Muehlenhard et al., 1986; Perper & Weis, 1987; Schwartz et al., 1983; Sigal et al., 1988; Walsh & Hewitt, 1985). In addition, flirtatious behavior includes demure glances downward (Burgoon et al., 1989).

Vocalics. The use of the voice is one of the most telling indicators of the type of interaction. General friendly interactions utilize a neutral tone of voice (Muehlenhard et al., 1986; Perper & Weis, 1987; Sigal et al., 1988), are less fluent (Andersen, 1985), exhibit decreased amounts of laughter, and more silences and less warmth (Coker & Burgoon, 1987). Flirtatious behaviors utilize animated speech (Muehlenhard et al., 1986), moderate amounts of laughter (Coker & Burgoon, 1987; Perper & Weis, 1987), decreased silences/ latencies, and increased warmth and interest (Coker & Burgoon, 1987). Finally, seductive interaction is characterized by an intimate tone of voice (Coker & Burgoon, 1987; Muehlenhard et al., 1986; Perper & Weis, 1987; Sigal Wet al., 1988), increased laughter (Coker & Burgoon, 1987; Muehlenhard et al., 1986), greater fluency, less silence, and greater warmth (Andersen, 1985; Coker & Burgoon, 1987).

Method and Results Summary

Method. Eight different videotapes showing a conversation between a male and a female were shown to 339 undergraduate students who were the observers in this study. The videotaped conversations contained the same verbal communication, but the nonverbal communication and the sex of the initiator were varied. The nonverbal communication was displayed so that it was either seductive, flirtatious, friendly, or platonic, with the platonic condition showing an absence of nonverbal cues such as touch and smiling. In half of the videotapes, the male initiated the conversation. In the other half, the female initiated the conversation. After viewing one of the eight videotapes, the student observers completed questionnaires asking them to rate, among other things, how much immediacy and seductiveness the actors showed.

Results. The key findings in this study included the following. First, observers rated the conversations differently depending on the nonverbal communication they saw. When the actors stood close to each other, touched, smiled a lot, and so forth, they were seen as more flirtatious and seductive. Second, the sex of the initiator was important. Females who initiated the conversation were seen as more seductive and immediate than males who initiated the conversation. Finally, male observers tended to see all of the interactions as more seductive than did female observers.

DISCUSSION

This research on flirting and perceived seductiveness highlights several important aspects of communication and dating behavior. First, the obvious and mundane: Certain nonverbal behaviors are perceived as indicative of a seductive motive on the part of the communicator, and both male and female observers are able to discern these different levels and interpret them accordingly. However, it is also clear that males and females interpret the meanings of the behaviors differently, and that men more easily and readily infer seductive intent than other women.

The sex of the initiator played a strong role in perceptions of seductiveness. Despite the alleged progress made in male-female relationships, it still appears that when a male initiates the conversation, such initiation is apparently considered normal, and the male is not quickly judged as seductive. However, the mere act of initiating the conversation prompted female observers and (especially) male observers to rate the woman as somewhat seductive—regardless of the level of intimacy of the nonverbal display!

It also appears that male observers placed greater emphasis on who initiated the conversation, whereas females placed greater emphasis on the nonverbal displays. For example, whether the initiator was female or male, male observers rated the actor as more seductive than female observers. Female observers, however, rated (realistically, in our opinion) the male substantially less seductive in the two nonintimate interactions than in the flirting and seductive interactions—thus discriminating on the basis of the interactant's behavior.

If some individuals perceive a woman's initiation of an interaction as seductive, the entire meaning assigned to an interaction will be altered, and how the interaction (beyond the few minutes we videotaped) and relationship progresses will be intractably changed. Women, who perceive themselves to be "friendly," will act accordingly to that mindset. On the other hand, some men will view the same interaction from a "seductive/sexual" mindset and also act accordingly (presumably attempting to fulfill a "self-fulfilling prophecy"). This misperception of the intent of the interactants is likely to lead to misunderstandings about expectations of future outcomes. It may well be that men and women misinterpret initiation as interest and respond based on that misinterpretation, with outcomes varying from harmless embarrassment to serious problems, such as date or acquaintance rape.

There are implications for relational development as well. Certainly, the more closely aligned interpretations of behavior are, the more likely effective communication will occur. And certainly, appropriate interpretation of mutual flirting behavior can eventually lead to the initiation of a relationship. Flirting is, after all, an indication of some type of interest and can be the first step in a long-term relationship. However, the fact that the initiation of an interaction is perceived to be seductive (particularly when initiated by females) suggests the potential problems of jealousy and distrust. For example, if the male in a relationship perceives interaction initiation to be an expression of sexual interest, and the female initiates interaction with other males, the male may develop distrust and jealousy ultimately resulting in some form of conflict. In terms of future relational development and maintenance, it is important to effectively respond to these misinterpretations and misunderstandings.

Men and women will continue to be in situations in which they are alone together and women will continue to initiate conversations with men. It is unrealistic to expect otherwise. On the other hand, we are bombarded daily by magazines, television shows, movies, and music that perpetuate various beliefs that women want to be swept off their feet, that flirting is common fun, and/or that flirting reflects true sexual urges. It is unrealistic to expect any fundamental change in such beliefs being advocated and adopted. However, those of us who research and study nonverbal communication can play a role in advancing a more detailed understanding of the mistakes individuals make (and why), and, it is hoped, make communicators aware of how to avoid potentially serious mistakes in social relations.

References

Abbey, A. (1982). Sex differences in attributions for friendly behavior: Do males misperceive females' friendliness. *Journal of Personality and Social Psychology, 42*, 830–838.

Abbey, A. (1987). Misperceptions of friendly behavior as sexual interest: A survey of naturally occurring incidents. *Psychology of Women Quarterly, 11*, 173–194.

Abbey, A., Cozzarelli, C., McLaughlin, K., & Harnish, J. (1987). The effect of clothing and dyad sex composition on perceptions of sexual intent: Do women evaluate these cues differently. *Journal of Applied Social Psychology, 17*, 108–126.

Abbey, A., & Melby, C. (1986). The effects of nonverbal cues on gender differences in perceptions of sexual intent. *Sex Roles, 15*, 283–298.

Andersen, P. A. (1985). Nonverbal immediacy in interpersonal communication. In A. W. Siegman & S. Feldstein (Eds.), *Multichannel integrations of nonverbal behavior* (pp. 1–36). Hillsdale, NJ: Lawrence Erlbaum Associates.

Burgoon, J. K., Buller, D. B., & Woodall, W. G., (1989). *Nonverbal communication: The unspoken dialogue*. New York: Harper & Row.

Coker, D. A., & Burgoon, J. K. (1987). The nature of conversational involvement and nonverbal encoding patterns. *Human Communication Research, 13*, 463–494.

Lague, L. (1990, March). Flirting for the fun of it. *Glamour*, pp. 242, 243, 300.

Muehlenhard, C. L., Koralewski, M. A., Andrews, S. L., & Burdick, C. A. (1986). Verbal and nonverbal cues that convey interest in dating: Two studies. *Behavior Therapy, 17*, 404–419.

Muehlenhard, C. L., & McFall, R. M. (1981). Dating initiation from a woman's perspective. *Behavior Therapy, 12*, 682–691.

Muehlenhard, C. L., Miller, C. L., & Burdick, C. A. (1983). Are high-frequency daters better cue readers? Men's interpretations of women's cues as a function of dating frequency and CHI scores. *Behavior Therapy, 14*, 626–636.

Perper, T., & Weis, D. L. (1987). Projective and rejective strategies of U. S. and Canadian college women. *Journal of Sex Research, 23*, 455–480.

Saal, F. E. , Johnson, C. B., & Weber, N. (1989). Friendly or sexy? It may depend on who you ask. *Psychology of Women Quarterly, 13*, 263–276.

Schwartz, L. M., Foa, U. G., & Foa, E. B. (1983). Perceived structure of nonverbal behavior. *Journal of Personality and Social Psychology, 45*, 274–281.

Shotland, R. L., & Craig, J. M. (1988). Can men and women differentiate between friendly and sexually interested behavior? *Social Psychology Quarterly, 51*, 66–73.

Sigal, J., Gibbs, M., Adams, B., & Derfler, R. (1988). The effect of romantic and non-romantic films on perceptions of female friendly and seductive behavior. *Sex Roles, 19*, 545–554.

Walsh, D. G., & Hewitt, J. (1985). Giving men the come-on: Effect of eye-contact and smiling in a bar environment. *Perceptual and Motor Skills, 61*, 873–874.

Prager examines how people use nonverbal behavior to communicate intimacy to one another. She argues that there are three primary forms of nonverbal intimacy: (1) nonverbal involvement, (2) touch, and (2) sexual contact. Together, these three behaviors help define the nature of a relationship and the type of intimacy (emotional versus sexual) that two people share.

36

Nonverbal Behavior in Intimate Interactions

Karen J. Prager

Two soft, unmistakably feminine arms were clasped about, his neck; a warm cheek was pressed against his, and simultaneously there was the sound of a kiss . . . [and] all of him, from head to foot, was full of a strange new feeling which grew stronger and stronger . . . He wanted to dance, to talk, to run into the garden, to laugh aloud. . . . He quite forgot that he was round-shouldered and uninteresting, that he had lynx-like whiskers and an "undistinguished appearance."

—Anton Chekhov, *The Kiss*

Behavior likely plays "an underestimated role . . . in the quality of [intimate] communication" (Keeley & Hart, 1994, p. 135). Keeley and Hart defined nonverbal communication as "signs and symbols . . . that qualify as potential messages by virtue of their regular and consistent use and interpretation" (p. 136). Nonverbal behavior may contribute as much to people's intimate experiences as verbal behavior, perhaps even more.

Adapted with permission from Prager (1995), *The psychology of intimacy* (pp. 171, 179–182, 214–215). New York: The Guilford Press.

Three categories of nonverbal behavior can be labeled as intimate. First, nonverbal "involvement behaviors" include physical proximity, gaze, touch, body lean, facial expressiveness, postural openness, gesturing, head nods, and vocal cues such as intonation, speech rate, and pauses (Patterson, 1984). These are called involvement behaviors because they display attentiveness, interest, and participation in interaction. Second, touch alone can be an intimate behavior; touch seems to intensify and is also prompted by intimate experiences (Thayer, 1988). Finally, the extensive and prolonged bodily contact involved in sexual activity is a third type of intimate nonverbal behavior.

NONVERBAL INVOLVEMENT AND
THE EXPERIENCE OF INTIMACY

The impact of nonverbal involvement behavior is illustrated in the following description of two distinctly different interactions:

> An-Mei and Kathy sit across from one another at a small table in a sidewalk cafe. They each lean forward across the table as they converse, barely taking their eyes away from one another's faces. Both are smiling as they talk. Two tables away sit Rebecca and Charles. Rebecca is leaning forward and gazing at Charles, but she is not smiling. Charles sits back in his chair, does not smile, and gazes not at Rebecca but around the room or over her head.

All we know about the interactions of our four protagonists is based on the nonverbal involvement behaviors each is displaying. Despite this limitation, most of us could make reasonable inferences about the interactions based only on those behaviors. Perhaps we would guess that An-Mei and Kathy are enjoying one another's company, that each is interested in what the other has to say, and that they like one another. Similarly, using the same kind of information, we might surmise that Rebecca and Charles are not enjoying each other and that Charles is withdrawing, from Rebecca; few of us would assume that their current interaction is intimate. That such different inferences can be made about these two conversations is a testament to the potent informative value of nonverbal involvement behaviors.

Interest in nonverbal behavior arose when theorists and researchers observed its previously unacknowledged but powerful impact on communication (Argyle & Dean, 1965). According to Mehrabian (1971), this interest originated when research on meaning expanded beyond its verbal aspects (e.g., Osgood, Suci, & Tannenbaum, 1957). Researchers soon discovered how seemingly small gestures (looking away, moving away) conveyed potent messages that could override the meaning of such verbal content as "I'm not mad at you" (Bateson, Jackson, Haley, & Weakland, 1956). Research on nonverbal interaction behavior has continued efforts to identify systematic linkages between behavior, context, and people's reactions to one another. The work has been surprisingly divorced, however, from theory and research on intimate relationships.

Each nonverbal involvement behavior has a demonstrated impact on the experience of intimacy. High levels of mutual gaze have been associated with phenomena such as liking (Argyle, Ingham, Alkema, & McCallin, 1973), love (Z. Rubin, 1970), sexual involvement (Thayer & Schiff, 1975), friendship (Coutts & Schneider, 1976), and positive evaluations of interactions (Burgoon, Buller, Hale, & deTurck, 1984). Closer seating distance conveys friendship and liking (Gifford, 1991). Forward body lean conveys attentiveness and emotional involvement while backward lean communicates indifference and detachment (Mehrabian, 1969). Smiling is a universally recognized indicator of liking, although, as Patterson (1982) pointed out, it is not completely reliable. In the main, however, nonverbal involvement behaviors are associated with intimate experience, that is, with liking, attraction, and enjoyment in interactions.

Intimate nonverbal behaviors are best understood as a subset of involving behaviors, because nonverbal involvement behaviors do not *exclusively* communicate personalness. These behaviors can communicate other messages, such as dominance submission (Kleinke, 1986) and general positivity and rapport (Tickle-Degnen & Rosenthal, 1990). People can also summon them at will for impression management purposes (Patterson, 1987). In other words, not all involving interactions are intimate, but all intimate interactions are involving (assuming they are face-to-face).

TOUCH AND THE EXPERIENCE OF INTIMACY

Touch seems to greatly affect intimate experience, perhaps because it eliminates the space between people. More than any other nonverbal interaction behavior, touch may intensify experiences of intimacy (Thayer, 1986). Certain kinds of touch have been identified that may be sufficient in and of themselves to create an intimate experience (assuming they are wanted or invited). Based on daily recordings of university students' experiences with touch, Jones and Yarbrough (1985) identified three types of touch that nearly always foster intimate experience. All convey positive affect and carry a nonverbal relational message. "Inclusion touches" (e.g., shoulders or knees touching) are sustained touches that convey or draw attention to the act of being together; they are tactile statements of togetherness, usually involving lower body parts (legs, knees, hips, side-by-side hugs), and nearly always occur between lovers, spouses, or close friends rather than between family members. Sexual touches (e.g., long strokes of the hand up and down the body) express physical attraction or sexual intent; involving holding, caressing, or both, these are prolonged, involve multiple body parts, and move from one part of the body to another. A third type of touch, "affection touches" (e.g., hand on a shoulder, squeezing an arm), always communicates affection, in part because these touches are positive and in part because they do not express any other specific meaning. These affection touches express general positive regard for the other and include a wide range of behaviors.

The extent to which touch elicits intimate experience may depend on which parts of the body are touched. College students viewed face touching, for example, as more personal than handshakes, arm touches, or arms around the shoulder or waist (Burgoon, 1991). Jones and Yarbrough (1985) distinguished between "nonvulnerable" body parts (in the United States this includes hands, arms, elbows, shoulders, and upper-middle back) and "vulnerable" body parts (all others). The former are body parts that, by convention, can be touched by those with whom one does not have an intimate relationship.

Experiences of intimacy may be intensified when touch is sustained or prolonged. In some cultures, such as the United States and New Zealand, certain kinds of sustained affectionate touch (e.g., watching television while in one another's arms) occur rarely, except between lovers and spouses, even though these touches are not sexual.

Certain kinds of touch, then, may foster experiences of intimacy, particularly when they are sustained and involve vulnerable parts of the body. It is likely true as well that positive feelings and the perception of being understood, which constitute intimate experience, prompt people to touch one another.

SEXUAL INTERACTION AND THE EXPERIENCE OF INTIMACY

People commonly define sexual interactions as intimate interactions. Sprecher and McKinney (1993) note that when researchers ask people what intimacy means to them, they are likely to include sexual contact among their answers (Helgeson et al., 1987; Waring et al., 1980). Researchers commonly include sexual intimacy in typologies of intimacy (Holt, 1977; Schaefer & Olson, 1981; Tolstedt & Stokes, 1983).

There are several ways in which dyadic sexual behavior can provide intimate experiences for participants. First, intimate behavior involves sharing that which is private. Sexuality is private behavior in most of known societies on earth. Therefore, people experience the sharing of sexuality as intimate. Sprecher and McKinney (1993) noted that "all of the actions that typically occur in the sex act—being nude in front of one's partner, expressing to the partner what feels good, actually having sex, experiencing an orgasm—are considered to be very intimate self-disclosures" (p. 100). By participating in sexual activity with a particular partner, one is sharing personal, private aspects of the self that are not known to other kinds of intimate partners, such as family members and close friends. In many cultures the relative exclusiveness of sexual sharing contributes to its value as an intimate experience.

CONCLUSIONS

This article reviews studies indicating that nonverbal interaction behaviors seem to affect intimate experience. Involvement behaviors, like gaze and physical proximity, affect experiences such as liking, attraction, and emotional engagement (e.g., Kleinke, 1986). Touch further intensifies affective aspects of intimate experience (Burgoon, 1991). Some research suggests, then, that intimate behavior exerts a direct and simple effect on partners' experiences of intimacy.

Direct and simple effects, however, are the exception rather than the rule. Most research indicates that links between intimate behavior and intimate experience depend on contextual factors. Some of these contextual factors directly affect the likelihood of intimate behavior. For example, immediate contextual variables such as the nature of the occasion (Tickle-Degnen & Rosenthal, 1990), the structure of the physical setting (Wada, 1990), partners' moods (Kowalik & Gotlib, 1987), and dyad gender composition (Gifford, 1991) seem to affect nonverbal involvement behaviors in interactions.

As this review indicates, we have much to learn about intimate interactions. A few gaps in our knowledge stand out. Sexual contact, while clearly exerting a profound impact on intimate experience, is the form of nonverbal intimate behavior scholars know least about (Sprecher & McKinney, 1993). While knowledge about human sexual anatomy, physiology, and behavior has accumulated, human sexuality research has not substantially encompassed the study of human sexual experience. Sexual experiences potentially evoke not only physical pleasure and gratification but also strong emotions about the partner, about oneself and one's body, and about one's relationship with one's partner. There is reason to believe that they play an important role in establishing attachment relationships between adults (L. Rubin, 1983; Sprecher & McKinney, 1993). Sexual experiences may even maintain relationships in the face of other difficulties. In short, thére is currently a dearth of knowledge about the psychological and relational aspects of sexual interaction, which may represent a serious gap in our understanding of intimate interactions.

References

Argyle, M., & Dean, J. (1965). Eye contact, distance, and affiliation. *Sociometry, 28,* 289–304.

Argyle, M., Ingham, R., Alkema, R., & McCallin, M. (1973). The different functions of gaze. *Semiotica, 7,* 19–32.

Burgoon, J. K. (1991). Relational interpretations of touch, conversational distance, and posture, *Journal of Nonverbal Behavior, 15,* 233–259.

Burgoon, J. K., Buller, D. B., Hale, J. L., & deTurck, M. A. (1984). Relational messages associated with nonverbal behaviors. *Human Communication Research, 10,* 351–378.

Coutts, L. M., & Schneider, F. W. (1976). Affiliative conflict theory: An investigation of the intimacy equilibrium and compensation hypothesis. *Journal of Personality and Social Psychology, 34,* 1135–1142.

Gifford, R. (1991). Mapping nonverbal behavior on the interpersonal circle. *Journal of Personality and Social Psychology, 61,* 279–288.

Helgeson, V. S., Shaver, P., & Drer, M. (1987). Prototypes of intimacy and distance in same-sex and opposite-sex relationships. *Journal of Social and Personal Relationships, 4,* 195–233.

Holt, M. L. (1977). *Human intimacy in young adults: An experimental developmental scale.* Unpublished doctoral dissertation, University of Georgia.

Jones, S. E., & Yarbrough, A. E. (1985). A naturalistic study of the meanings of touch. *Communication Monographs, 52,* 19–56.

Keeley, M. P., & Hart, A. J. (1994). Nonverbal behavior in dyadic interaction. In S. W. Duck (Ed.), *Dynamics of relationships* (pp. 135–162). Thousand Oaks, CA: Sage.

Kleinke, C. L. (1986). Gaze and eye contact: A research review. *Psychological Bulletin, 100,* 78–100.

Kowalik, D. L., & Gotlib, I. H. (1987). Depression and marital interaction: Concordance between intent and perceptions of communication. *Journal of Abnormal Psychology, 96,* 127–134.

Mehrabian, A. (1969). Some referents and measures of nonverbal behavior. *Behavioral Research Methods and Instruments, 1,* 213–217.

Mehrabian, A. (1971). *Silent messages: Implicit communication of emotions and attitudes.* Belmont, CA: Wadsworth.

Osgood, C. E., Suci, G. J., & Tannenbaum, P. (1957). *The measurement of meaning.* Urbana: University of Illinois Press.

Patterson, M. L. (1982). A sequential functional model of nonverbal exchange. *Psychological Review, 89*, 231–249.

Patterson, M. L. (1984). Intimacy, social control, and nonverbal involvement: A functional approach. In V. J. Derlega (Ed.), *Communication, intimacy, and close relationships* (pp. 13–42). Beverly Hills, CA: Sage.

Patterson, M. L. (1987). Presentation and affect management functions of nonverbal involvement. *Journal of Nonverbal Behavior, 11*, 110–122.

Rubin, L. (1983). *Intimate strangers: Men and women together*. New York: Harper & Row.

Rubin, Z. (1970). Measurement of romantic love. *Journal of Personality and Social Psychology, 16*, 265–273.

Schaefer, M. T., & Olson, D. H. (1981). Assessing intimacy: The PAIR inventory. *Journal of Marital and Family Therapy, 7*, 47–60.

Sprecher, S., & McKinney, K. (1993). *Sexuality*. Newbury Park, CA: Sage.

Thayer, S. (1986). Touch: Frontier of intimacy. *Journal of Nonverbal Behavior, 10*, 7–11.

Thayer, S. (1988, March). Close encounters. *Psychology today*, pp. 30–36.

Thayer, S., & Schiff, W. (1975). Eye contact, facial expression, and the experience of time. *Journal of Social Psychology, 95*, 117–124.

Tickle-Degnen, L., & Rosenthal, R. (1990). The nature of rapport and its nonverbal correlates. *Psychological Inquiry, 1*, 285–293.

Tolstedt, B. E., & Stokes, J. P. (1983). Relation of verbal, affective, and physical intimacy to marital satisfaction. *Journal of Counseling Psychology, 30*, 573–580.

Wada, M. (1990). The effect of interpersonal distance change on nonverbal behaviors: Mediating effects of sex and intimacy levels in a dyad. *Japanese Psychological Research, 32*, 86–96.

Waring, E. M., Tillman, M. P., Frelick, L., Russell, L. & Weisz, G. (1980). Concepts of intimacy in the general population. *Journal of Nervous and Mental Disease, 168*, 471–474.

Nonverbal communication is used to bring people together and to tear people apart. Knapp discusses the specific role that nonverbal communication plays in developing and deteriorating personal relationships. He describes eight general communication dimensions that reflect more or less relational intimacy. For example, when you meet someone, communication might be difficult and awkward. Once you get to know the person, however, your nonverbal communication will probably become smooth and efficient.

37

Nonverbal Communication in Developing and Deteriorating Relations
A Conceptual Framework

Mark L. Knapp

The essence of our relationships with other people is derived from *ongoing* personal and societal expectations that influence, and are influenced by, our overt communication behavior. Although the subject of human communication in the process of relationship development has received a con-

Adapted with permission from Knapp, Dyadic relationship development. In Wiemann (Ed.) *Nonverbal interaction*, pp. 179, 192–197, copyright © 1983. Reprinted with permission of Sage Publications, Inc.

siderable amount of scholarly attention (Altman & Taylor, 1973; Berger & Calabrese, 1975; Knapp, 1978; Miller, 1976; Phillips & Metzger, 1976), this article focuses on a decidedly limited part of this process: the manifestation of nonverbal behavior during fluctuations in the degree of closeness or intimacy felt by the relationship partners.

In 1973, Altman and Taylor proposed eight "generic . . . overlapping 'dimensions' of nonverbal, environmental and verbal behaviors" (p. 129) that they felt described "behavioral changes which occur as relationships develop" (p. 135). In 1978, I (Knapp, 1978: 14–17) discussed a modified version of these dimensions in the context of changing patterns of communication during the growth and decay of relationships (see table 1). Intimacy, in the context of the model presented in table 1, refers to variations in knowledge of and/or commitment to one's relationship partner. With changes in intimacy we would expect corresponding changes in a dyad's communication behavior, which could be plotted along the eight dimensions shown in the table. The dimensions represent the content, diversity, quality, patterning, and interpretation of messages and interactions. Now let's consider the role of nonverbal behavior in the context of these eight dimensions.

NARROW-BROAD

This dimension refers to the variety of messages communicated. As intimacy increases, we would expect the participants to have an expanding number of ideas and feelings to communicate. We would also expect greater refinements of ideas and feelings previously communicated in a more general way. In order to communicate this expanding number of mes-

Table 1
General Dimensions of Communication Associated with Relationship Development

Toward More Intimacy ⟶
⟵ Toward Less Intimacy

Narrow	Broad
Stylized	Unique
Difficult	Efficient
Rigid	Flexible
Awkward	Smooth
Public	Personal
Hesitant	Spontaneous
Overt judgment suspended	Overt judgment given

sages, intimates are expected to rely on a broader range of verbal and non-verbal behaviors. New acquaintances will probably have a narrower range of message needs. Decreasing intimacy in an established relationship should bring about a decrease in the number of ideas and feelings the participants wish to communicate.

Increased breadth of nonverbal behavior may include such things as (1) a greater number of facial blends used to communicate a wider range of emotional states; (2) a greater number of vocal nuances and blends for communicating a wider range of messages; (3) less sharply dichotomous behavior—for example, "This is my territory sometimes, but at other times you can use it"; and (4) a greater amount of time spent together, which may mean more messages exchanged.

Stylized-Unique

When we first come into contact with people, our nonverbal behavior will most likely be characterized by stylized conventions that are widely understood. Our message adaptations are based on cultural or sociological information rather than personal information specific to a given individual. Gradually, however, we obtain more information about how this person is similar to or different from others we have met. Thus, uniqueness of nonverbal communication involves the adoption of a more idiosyncratic communication system adapted to the peculiar nature of the interactants.

We would expect less intimate relationships, then, to manifest the most common emblems, the most stereotyped facial expressions, and so on. Intimates, on the other hand, should develop more specialized and unique communication patterns adapted to the particular characteristics of their personalities and the relationship. The handshake in greetings and partings is an example of a stylized behavior that may change as a friendship becomes more intimate. For example, the handshake could disappear completely, change from a longer firm grip to a brief casual clasp, or be accompanied by a hug once a relationship becomes close.

Some specific nonverbal messages that illustrate the uniqueness I have been discussing were uncovered in our study of couples' personal idioms (Hopper, Knapp, & Scott, 1981). About 28 percent of the 495 private expressions and gestures reported to us by married and cohabiting couples involved nonverbal behavior. Eight categories of personal idioms were identified, but nonverbal behavior was most evident in "expressions of affection." For example, twitching of the nose was used to say "You're special" to one's partner; pulling the right earlobe and a forward movement of the hand with the thumb, first and fourth fingers extended and the second and third curled down, both meant, "I love you." One couple agreed that a twist of the wedding ring was a signal to the other that meant, "Don't you dare say (or do) that."

DIFFICULT-EFFICIENT

With increased opportunities for interaction and feedback and a high motivation to communicate effectively as feelings of intimacy increase, we would predict a gradual increase in accuracy, speed, and efficiency of communication as intimacy increases. Difficulty in communication is not absent in intimate relationships, but we would predict that new acquaintances and relationship partners experiencing a decrease in intimacy would experience the most difficulty. Kahn (1970), for example, found that "dissatisfied husbands and wives are particularly prone to misinterpreting each other's nonverbal signals" (p. 455). In this study, the dissatisfied husbands were much more likely to interpret their wives' attempts to communicate affection, happiness, and playfulness in a negative manner.

A few studies provide support for greater accuracy and efficiency accompanying greater intimacy. For example, Zuckerman and Przewuzman (1979) found parents able to decode the facial expressions of their own children better than those of their children's classmates, and German biologists Margret Schleidt and Barbara Hold are reported to have shown that blindfolded men and women can identify the perspiration odors of their spouses (*Time*, 1981). Seventy-five couples in West Germany, Japan, and Italy wore cotton T-shirts to bed for a week and avoided using deodorants or perfumes. Generally, those tested were able to sniff out the shirts worn by their mates.

Just as a familiarity with visual, olfactory, and auditory responses of one's partner will often make communication more efficient for intimates, it may occasionally engender an overconfidence that leads to periods of difficulty—periods when old assumptions are no longer valid. Similarly, we can expect occasions when people with little intimacy will be strikingly efficient communicators compared to others at this point, but we would also expect this efficiency to increase as intimacy develops.

RIGID-FLEXIBLE

As relationship partners come to know each other better, they should be able to communicate the same idea or feeling in several different ways. New acquaintances and people in relationships that are close to termination are likely to have fewer channels of communication and to maintain more consistent ways of communicating any given message.

Some of the increased options available to people in closer relationships are associated with the negotiation of signals that are unique to the relationship pair, but we also learn interchangeable signals for certain messages as a result of experiencing interaction with another person in a variety of contexts using a variety of channels. Nonverbal signals, then, provide an important reservoir of additional communication channels to use as message substitutes or equivalents. Hence, a signal for approval may expand from multiple nods accompanied by an affirmative verbal confirmation ("Yes, I agree") to any of the following: (1) a smile, (2) a single nod, (3) a silence that signals approval due to the absence of any negative verbalization, (4) raising eyebrows and smiling during an other-directed gaze, (5) a vocalized "mm" or "mmm-hmmm," (6) a movement of the head to one side similar to the gesture people use to signal a person to "go ahead," (7) an extended hug following an action that could be evaluated negatively, (8) disapproval stated verbally and vocally in an exaggerated manner and followed by a smile, and so on.

Even though intimates have the opportunity to be more flexible in their communication behavior, they may not practice as much message flexibility with some messages as with others.

AWKWARD-SMOOTH

Although some interaction partners adapt to one another's styles more quickly than others, new acquaintances are likely to display less interpersonal meshing or synchrony than they will as their relationship becomes more intimate. When established relationships become less intimate, we would expect the smoothness characteristic of a blending of interpersonal styles to become more awkward and less synchronized.

Nonverbal displays of relationship meshing may be consciously used in an effort to promote greater smoothness of interaction (see Cappella, 1982). For example, similarities of dress and ornamentation may enhance feelings of closeness and facilitate the appearance of other coordinated activity. This synchronized activity may be in one or more areas, such as posture, body movements, or speech. Both Kendon (1970) and LaFrance (1979) have linked kinesic synchronization with attention and rapport. Scheflen (1974) suggests extraordinary possibilities for body synchronization in more intimate relationships:

> One can often observe marital partners or siblings at opposite sides of
> a large room sitting in the same posture and changing their postures
> synchronously even though they are not side by side or even talking to

the same *others*. Sometimes these partners will even unconsciously extend their hands and legs toward each other or hold their hands out as if they were holding hands. (p. 60)

Speech patterns may also reveal an increasing convergence with intimacy. Giles and Powesland (1975) indicate that people sometimes accommodate their speech styles to those of others in order to enhance perceptions of similarity and to increase attraction. In some cases, the predicted smoothness of interaction associated with increased intimacy between two people may be a result of daily accommodations over an extended period of time in close proximity. These people may gradually pick up each other's linguistic and kinesic habits.

Some people may have a relatively low degree of intimacy and a high amount of smoothness or synchrony on certain limited topics. Intimates should have greater smoothness across all types of interaction. Some types of relationships may have more synchrony than others—for example, same-sex relationships may show more than opposite-sex relationships—but in each type of relationships we would expect more synchrony as the intimacy increases.

PUBLIC-PERSONAL

At first we reveal our public selves to others. Gradually, more and more of our personal or private selves is made available to our relationship partners. When relationships lose intimacy, we would expect behaviors representing our public selves to increase.

How are nonverbal behaviors associated with more personalized communication? Just as verbal self-disclosures provide information to others about our most personal thoughts, feelings, and beliefs, nonverbal behavior can also be used to open ourselves to others and to reveal previously unknown behavior. And, like verbalizations, these nonverbal revelations make us vulnerable. First, we can show our availability and permeability to another person by providing greater access to ourselves and our possessions. Access to another may take several forms: (1) increased proximity, (2) more bodily touching in general, (3) touching certain body parts inaccessible to others, (4) looking into the other's eyes for extended periods—which Rubin (1970) found to be common among engaged couples, (5) looking at another's body or specific body parts. Second, personalized communication is also manifested by the revelation of previously unknown behaviors. With increased exposure to another, we are more likely to observe behaviors that have been deliberately hidden or controlled. These may include such things as crying or picking one's toenails. Although adaptors and regulators generally receive little feedback in conversations with less intimate others, we might expect more verbalized feedback as intimacy increases—for example, "Why don't you ever look at me when I talk to you?!"

HESITANT-SPONTANEOUS

Communication with less predictable others (new acquaintances and former intimates) is likely to be cautious. Thus, the behavior we observe should show a greater degree of hesitancy. Increased intimacy, however, should bring with it increased spontaneity—a lack of observable planning.

The explicitness of a person's hesitancy or spontaneity may vary, but some possible nonverbal manifestations may include the following: (1) Whereas spontaneous gestures and movements are free-flowing, hesitancy is characterized by gestures that stop in mid-air (for example, a movement to cover the mouth with the hand, aborted at the chest) and repeatedly incomplete "stuttering" gestures, like "false start" handshakes or vocal hesitations. (2) The speed of movement is also likely to differentiate hesitant and spontaneous behavior. Hesitancy may reveal slow, deliberate movement, but sometimes this slowness is accompanied by extreme quickness, which gives the complete gesture what can best be described as a "jerky" motion. For example, hesitancy to touch another person may involve a slow, deliberate approach and a rapid withdrawal much like touching a hot stove. (3) We might also expect hesitant behavior to show more consistency—fewer changes or shifts. This would be especially true for difficult transitions, such as moving from serious, affectionate behavior to kidding. (4) Hesitancy may also be revealed by more low intensity communication (gestures closer to the body, less vocal loudness, and fewer behavioral extremes in general). (5) Body tenseness, rather than relaxation, would also seem to be characteristic of hesitant communication. (6) We might also predict that during the course of the interaction, communicators who manifest more hesitancy will also be more sensitive to intimacy violations in the areas of space, eye behavior, and touching.

Although hesitancy is less characteristic of more intimate relationships, intimates will be hesitant during the discussion of certain topics or on certain occasions. On the other hand, people who have very little intimacy associated with their relationships may be extremely spontaneous—especially if they are not very concerned about the development of the relationship.

OVERT JUDGMENT SUSPENDED-OVERT JUDGMENT GIVEN

We probably make a number of covert or secret evaluations about people during the first stages of acquaintanceship, but our uncertainty about how the other will respond and the limited scope of these conversations tends to depress the number of overt evaluations. Too much of inappropriate praise may be perceived as insincere; too much or inappropriate criticism may provoke immediate dislike. Evaluations that occur during the formative period of a relationship are more likely to be general and positive when they do occur. In one study, both distressed and satisfied married couples provided more negative evaluations of each other than they did when interacting with unknown others (Birchler, 1972). Although positive and negative feedback are probably much less inhibited in more intimate relationships, suspended judgments are likely to return as intimacy decreases. With decreasing intimacy the motivation for giving positive feedback is decreased and the participants may eventually want to avoid the inevitable conflict brought on by negative evaluations, so, in time, those are avoided as well.

The nonverbal behaviors associated with this dimension are those signalling approval, disapproval or evaluation. Almost any nonverbal signal associated with dramatic shifts in the intimacy level of established relationships will be interpreted as evaluative. A "neutral" facial expression may be perceived as "cold," "uninvolved," or "uncaring" during a period of distress for a relationship that was previously perceived as very close. Even stereotypical signals of liking—for example, "Don't give me that feigned interest approach!"—may be perceived negatively during periods of decreasing intimacy. In time, participants who feel intimacy decreasing will even avoid commentary on such behavior in order to avoid the predictable argument over whether the expression was feigned or genuine.

Naturally, intimates do not offer overt evaluations about all that they could. Evaluations are normally avoided in what are known to be emotionally sensitive areas. In some areas, overt evaluations are absent because the evaluation has become implicit for the relationship partners (for example, "You don't need to laugh at all my witty remarks, because I know you evaluate me positively in that area"). Eventually, the relationship partners will operate within an acceptable range of overt evaluations that will be less than the highest level achieved or achievable.

CONCLUSION

As important as nonverbal communication is for understanding the way people communicate at different stages of relationship development, a full understanding of the process must also examine verbal behavior. It is often the case that nonverbal signals are best understood in a context in which the verbal behavior is also known. Although many of our verbal and nonverbal behaviors are influenced by the nature of our relationships with other people, overlapping factors—such as age, cultural background, gender and situation will surely exert their influence as well. Nevertheless, there is considerable satisfaction derived from the process of trying to connect a few pieces within this complex communication mosaic.

References

Altman, L. and Taylor, D. (1973). *Social penetration: The development of interpersonal relationships*. New York: Holt, Rinehart & Winston.

Berger, C. R., and Calabrese, R. J. (1975). Some explorations in initial interactions and beyond: Toward a developmental theory of interpersonal communication. *Human Communication Research, 1*, 99–112.

Birchler, G. R. (1972). *Differential patterns of instrumental affiliative behavior as a function of degree of marital distress and level of intimacy*. Unpublished doctoral dissertation, University of Oregon.

Giles, H., and Powesland, P. F. (1975). *Speech style and social evaluation*. New York: Academic Press.

Rubin, Z. (1970). The measurement of romantic love. *Journal of Personality and Social Psychology, 16*, 265–272.

Scheflen, A. E. (1974). *How behavior means*. Garden City, NY: Doubleday.

Time. (1981, November 30). Nose knows more ways than one, p. 87.

Zuckerman, M., and Przewuzman, S. J. (1979). Decoding and encoding facial expressions in preschool-age children. *Environmental Psychology and Nonverbal Behavior, 3*, 147–163.

—Section B—

POWER, PERSUASION, AND DECEPTION

Think about the people you know who are powerful. Do they carry themselves in a certain way? Do they have commanding voices? Are they in control of space and the environment? Chances are that the people you thought about use nonverbal communication to help them convey an air of power. When people persuade you to do something, they might also use certain nonverbal behaviors. For example, your best friend might touch your arm and ask you to "please help." Or you might tell a group of children to "stop and look both ways" in a firm, authoritative voice that causes them to stop in their tracks before going after that ball that rolled across the street. When you are attempting to persuade others in situations such as these, it is likely that you will use both nonverbal and verbal messages to try to get your point across.

What about when you try to deceive others? The research shows that nonverbal communication also plays a crucial role in sending and receiving deceptive messages. When you were a child, your parents might have told you to "look them straight in the eye" when you were trying to get away with a lie. At first, their strategy might have worked. You may have been intimidated and looked away. After a while though, you probably came to expect that your parents would ask you to look them in the eye, so you were prepared to give them full eye contact while you deceived them. This example shows that people strategically manipulate nonverbal cues when they are trying to deceive others. It also shows that people who are trying to detect deception will look at nonverbal cues to try and figure out if you are lying or not.

Whether we are trying to display power, persuade others, or deceive others, nonverbal behaviors play a crucial role in the communication process. In all of these cases, nonverbal communication can be used to try to influence others or to manage information in a particular way. In fact, the term *power* typically refers to a person's ability to influence others. Power is also related to *dominance* and *status*, although these three concepts are somewhat different from one another. Dominance generally refers to a communication style. Dominant people are able to control conversations and make decisions effectively. Therefore, they are often in leadership roles. Status refers to someone's position in a hierarchy. The CEO of a large company, for example, has much higher status than a middle manager. Notice that status is based on position rather than on any specific personality traits. Whether people have power, dominance, status, or all three of these, they are likely to use a number of nonverbal behaviors that distinguish them from more submissive, lower-status individuals. In addition, other people treat those of high power and status differently than they treat those with less power.

When people try to persuade others, they often use both verbal and nonverbal behaviors. Power might come into play here as well, since powerful people might not have to exert much effort to get others to do something for them. For example, if your boss asked you to clean up the lounge area at your workplace, you would probably just go ahead and do it. If a colleague asked you to do the same thing, you might be more resistant. As the readings in this section will show, a large array of nonverbal behaviors have been found to be effective in the persuasion process. Segrin's chapter summarizes a substantial body of literature on *compliance gaining*. When people try to gain compliance, they are trying to get someone to do something for them or to comply with a request. The overwhelming conclusion of Segrin's review is that nonverbal messages play a small but significant role in the persuasion process. Buller and Street discuss persuasion within the context of physician-patient relationships. Their review shows that people may reap health benefits when their physicians are successful in persuading them to change their lifestyles or to stick to a particular medical treatment.

The readings in this section also illustrate that nonverbal communication is essential to understanding the deception process. Research shows that people are not very effective lie detectors. Most of us are misled by cues that have nothing to do with successful detection. We all have *stereotypes* of liars as shifty eyed, fast talking, and so forth. We also have stereotypes of truthful people; they look us straight in the eye, deliver their messages forcefully, give adequate detail, and so forth. Good deceivers use these stereotypes against you to create a false impression. As the reading by Buller and Aune suggests, deceivers try to manage their behaviors by being pleasant and looking truthful.

One of the best ways to detect deception is to look for *deviations* or irregularities. These deviations occur in a number of ways. First, when you know people well, you can judge if their presentation differs from their normal style. You might know that Katie is usually very animated and expressive. If she becomes withdrawn, you might become suspicious of her. Second, even when you don't know people well, you can see if their behavior pattern differs from the way most people typically behave. For example, deception may be occurring if a salesperson talks in a higher-pitched voice at a faster rate than normal. Third, you can see if two or more channels of nonverbal communication differ from each other. Perhaps the person's facial cues are relaxed, but her or his posture is constantly shifting. You should also keep in mind that there is no perfect strategy for detecting deception. In fact, the research suggests that people only detect deception about half the time, even when they know that the person they are talking to could be lying to them. Hopefully, the readings in this section will help you to better understand how nonverbal cues work with verbal communication to deceive others, as well as to send messages of power and persuasion.

Power plays an important role in most relationships, particularly in business organizations. Andersen and Bowman discuss the nonverbal cues of power in professional relationships. The article reviews research on nonverbal displays of power in organizations.

38

Positions of Power
Nonverbal Influence in Organizational Communication

Peter A. Andersen
Linda L. Bowman

Traditional organizational communication textbooks rarely mention non-verbal communication. Laudably, a few texts present such a discussion but generally without much concern for its theoretical or practical importance (Goldhaber, 1974; Huseman, Lahiff, & Hatfield, 1976; Koehler, Anatol, & Applbaum, 1981). Traditional organizational network research also lacks nonverbal data (Albrecht & Ropp, 1982). Even the new critical and inter-pretive research that focuses on communication, messages, relationships, and meaning has systematically excluded nonverbal communication. Recently, researchers and theorists have called for studying conversa-tion, discussion, discourse, enthymatic structure, language, language-in-action, metaphors, speech, stories, talk, and vocabulary with scarcely a mention of nonverbal communication (cf. Deetz, 1982; Fairhurst, Greene, & Snavely, 1984; Jablin, 1984; Ragan, 1983; Riggs, 1983; Tompkins &

This article was written especially for *The Nonverbal Communication Reader.*

Cheney, 1985; Trujillo, 1983). Occasionally, researchers deign to recognize nonverbal behavior. For example, Tompkins and Cheney (1985) suggested that monitoring and dispensing rewards to subordinates are nonverbal much of the time but they fail to develop any theory, research strategies, or recommendations as a result. The present article is consistent with the position taken by Albrecht and Ropp (1982) who contended that, "For the communication researcher, verbal and nonverbal behaviors of interactants provide core data for analysis" (p. 168).

THE POWER DOMAIN

The power construct has been studied under a variety of labels that generally reference the same domain of communication including: assertiveness, authority, control, coercion, compliance, dominance, power, social influence, and status. *Power* typically refers to the ability to influence others to do what one wants (Berger, 1985; Henley, 1977; Patterson, 1983). *Status* references one's position in society which generally contributes to power and dominance (Henley, 1977; Patterson, 1983). *Dominance* refers to one's relative position of power in relation to other's (Duran, Jensen, Prisbell, & Rosoff, 1979; Patterson, 1983). We view these terms as referencing a single dimension of interpersonal behavior often labeled *control* (Burgoon & Hale, 1984; Duran et al., 1979). Next, the various codes of nonverbal communication will be systematically examined to demonstrate the critical role played by nonverbal communication in organizational power.

PHYSICAL APPEARANCE

A person's physical appearance communicates at the outset of every interaction and conveys power primarily through attire and physical size. Attire creates first impressions by communicating a number of simultaneous messages. Fowles (1974) maintained, "Our clothes broadcast our sex, our rank, and our up-to-dateness" (p. 348). Formal dress has been found to be an indicant of increased power and control (Brown, 1965; Bickman, 1974; Mehrabian, 1976; Molloy, 1976; Morris, 1977). Mehrabian (1976) asserted that people who select formal dress are tapping the dominance dimension, which may explain why this style of dress persists in the business setting, despite some relaxation of formal dress requirements characteristic of corporations in the past. The suit, in particular, is a symbol of dominance in the organization (Mehrabian, 1976). Molloy, in his bestselling book, "Dress for Success," asserted that most authority is transmitted by dark suits. He also claimed that the pinstripe is the most authoritative pattern and that an expensive conservative tie is a vital suit accessory for it symbolizes respectability and responsibility, although no evidence for his assertions are provided (Molloy, 1976).

A uniform is a unique form of dress in that it both conceals and reveals status within the group while suppressing other status cues (Joseph & Alex, 1972). The uniform is a certificate of legitimacy and can elicit conformity if it symbolizes authoritative power, as in the case of guard or police uniforms. In a study by Bickman (1974), people more often complied with requests made by an experimenter dressed as a guard than one dressed as a civilian or milkman. Although a uniform affords the wearer a certain authority at times, organization members who work in uniforms generally have lower status than individuals who work in street clothes (Koehler et al., 1981).

High status dress simultaneously creates perceptions of power and induces conformity. Lefkowitz, Blake, and Mouton (1955) found that when a high status person violated a law, there was a significant increase in the rate of violation by others. Knowles (1973) reported passersby resisted penetrating the boundaries of an interacting social group when the group members wore higher status attire. In an experiment in an uncrowded college library, students fled more rapidly when space was invaded by a well-dressed man than by a casually dressed man (Barash, 1973). Although dress provides a channel for expressing individuality, conformity is usually rewarded in a business organization (Scheflen, 1972). Mehrabian (1976) argued that conservative and traditional business dress developed because such attire implied status, respectability, permanence, and trustworthiness. It may be that variation in dress is negatively evaluated as an indicant of instability in the organization setting.

A person's height and physical size are important components of power and status (Mehrabian, 1972). This attribution may have its roots in the physical advantages that these characteristics gave our ancestors during hand to hand combat (Henley, 1977). The "height is power" phenomenon places short men and most women at a disadvantage; having to look up creates a position of deference (Henley, 1977). Increasing the appearance of physical size can increase dominance (Scheflen, 1972). "Standing tall is in itself a good way of achieving dominance" (Henley, 1977, p. 89). During a confrontation, the act of "standing over another or the more abbreviated displays of height (i.e., raising one's head or brow while looking down) have the effect of 'cutting the opponent down to size' symbolically" (Remland, 1982a, p. 84). Not surprisingly, a slumped posture or a curled up position is submissive as it creates a smaller appearance (Morris, 1977).

KINESICS

Kinesics, or communication through bodily movement, gesture, posture, and facial expression, has a reciprocal relationship with power.

Posture and Position

Kinesic postures and positions correspond to organizational postures and positions. In general, superiors are more kinesically expansive in both standing and seated positions than subordinates (Remland, 1982b). One expansive body position is the arms-akimbo position which is more frequently used when addressing a low-status person than a high-status person (Mehrabian, 1968b; Scheflen, 1972). Likewise, Scheflen (1972) noted that individuals who hook their thumbs in their belts are asserting dominance through the same expansiveness analog.

Relaxation is a power cue since higher-status individuals generally are more relaxed. This is probably due to the fact that the powerful can afford to relax, whereas the weak must remain watchful (Prisbell, 1982). Research has shown that when two strangers meet, the more relaxed is of higher status (Mehrabian, 1971; Mehrabian & Friar, 1969). Similarly, among acquaintances Mehrabian and Friar (1969) found that high-status listeners are more relaxed than low-status listeners. Remland (1981) reported that higher status individuals in organizations can behave in a more relaxed and inattentive fashion than those of lower status. The degree of reclining limb asymmetry and movement are important correlates of high status in contrast to the extremely submissive cues of bodily rigidity and symmetry, like soldiers standing at attention (Mehrabian, 1972, 1976). High-status individuals can exhibit limb asymmetry by sprawling or putting a foot up, whereas low-status individuals must sit erect (LaFrance & Mayo, 1978; Mehrabian, 1972, 1976). However, Scheflen (1972) suggests that sideways head tilts are submissive postures, whereas holding the head high signals dominance. Mehrabian and Friar (1969) found that closed, as opposed to open, arm positions are associated with higher status, at least for females. Mehrabian (1971) maintained that since standing is less relaxed than sitting, seated positions are high-status positions. Finally, people are most relaxed when interacting with a person of low status, moderately relaxed when interacting with those of equal status and least relaxed with a person of high status (Mehrabian, 1968a, 1968b, 1972).

Movement

Research demonstrates that higher-status persons have access to more locations than lower-status persons (Mehrabian, 1971). Access to managers and executive officers in most organizations is quite limited for most employees, although managers typically have access to their subordinates. Power is also a function of who goes first through a door. Typically the higher-status person precedes another through the door (Goffman, 1967) although this is confounded by age, sex, and physical size. Inconvenience displays are usually performed by lower-status persons. Morris (1977) asserts that low-ranking individuals must lower their bodies in the presence of a high-ranked person. However, it is also customary to rise in the presence of a high-status other. This kinesic contradiction may confuse subordinates but can be resolved by placing the high-status person in a seated but elevated position (such as a judge in a courtroom).

Gesture

Surprisingly little research has examined gestural concomitants of power and status. Drawings of men were judged as most subordinate, insignificant, and humble when they show hands behind the back and most powerful when gesticulating (Henley, 1977). Steepling, the gesture of touching the fingertips together in a raised position, is perceived as a confident, proud gesture allegedly associated with high-status individuals (Henley, 1977). Pointing at someone is a dominant gesture which often occurs in escalating verbal conflicts (Scheflen, 1972) and communicates disrespect for another's body (Remland, 1981). Henley (1977) suggested that gestures directing another person from a distance are a power prerogative.

Facial Expression

The face conveys emotional states and evaluations better than any other part of the body. Not surprisingly, numerous dominance and submission messages are sent via facial expressions. No simple relationship exists between status and one of the most common facial expressions, the smile. Among both primates and humans, smiling is a submissive gesture often displayed by an animal to appease a dominant aggressor. Women smile considerably more than men, a reflection of their traditionally submissive status. Kennedy and Camden (1983) found that women smiled significantly more than men when taking their speaking turn, evidently as a way to soften the blow of turn-taking as an apology or act of submission. They also found that smiling women were more likely to be interrupted than smiling men. At times, laughing or smiling can symbolize power. Remland (1982a) argued that in adversial proceedings (e.g., courtrooms, task discussions), smiling ridicules the claims of another and suggests their arguments should not be taken seriously. Likewise, sarcastic smiles and disrespectful giggles may be used by a high-status but not a low-status person.

Other facial expressions more clearly communicate power. Scheflen (1972) argued that a protruded jaw is a masculine dominance expression. Likewise, Henley (1977) maintained that the jutting chin, along with overhanging eyebrows, frowns, drawn muscles, and the unwavering stare constitute the stern face of authority. Koehler et al. (1981) mentioned a specific set of facial expressions, including the reddened face, furrowed brow, and tightened shoulders, that are commonly used by supervisors who are having difficulty refraining from berating a delinquent employee. Exaggerated facial expressions of displeasure such as boredom or disgust emphasize disagreement and disrespect for another individual (Remland, 1982a). Porter and Roberts (1976) concluded that the face is one of the two nonverbal modes of communication of most interest to organizational researchers. Since kinesic displays co-occur with talk during face to face interaction and since such displays may severely modify verbal messages, studies of talk should also examine kinesic behavior whenever possible.

OCULESICS

Eye contact or gazing is used to communicate an enormous range of messages including cues of control and power. In one study, recipients of prolonged gazes perceived the looker to be more dominant than recipients of brief gazes (Thayer, 1969). This perception may have early origins since direct gaze was a dominant act for primates in primitive societies, and continues to be a dominant act in contemporary societies (Burgoon & Saine, 1978; Cook, 1979; Ellsworth, Carlsmith, & Hensen, 1972; LaFrance & Mayo, 1978). Absence of eye contact at key moments in a conversation may signal submissiveness, especially in women. Kennedy and Camden (1983) found that, during a group discussion, women were interrupted significantly more often than men when they did not look at the turn-taker. Mehrabian (1971) claimed that frequent blinking during conversation may imply weakness and submissiveness. Two studies found that dominant people employ more gaze (Kendon & Cook, 1969; Strongman & Chapness, 1968) but Crouch and Koll (1979) failed to replicate this finding. Fromme and Beam (1974) found that high-dominant subjects moved closer when gazed at, while low-dominant subjects moved farther away, although this behavior was more pronounced in males than in females.

Social status is illustrated by who looks at whom. Argyle (1975) stated that individuals who receive gaze are perceived as the most powerful group members. Research has shown that lower-status persons are more likely to look at persons of higher status (Burroughs, Schultz, & Autrey, 1973; Exline, Ellyson, & Long, 1975; Exline & Fehr, 1979; Mehrabian, 1971; Mehrabian & Friar, 1969). This pattern is more pronounced if the high-status person shows approval (Efran, 1968; Fugita, 1974). In a study of a military organization, cadets who paid visual attention to low-status persons were rated lower in status (Exline et al., 1975). One is not obligated to look at a lower-status person and may actually lose status by doing so.

Higher-status persons look more when speaking and less when listening than lower-status persons (Exline et al., 1975; Exline & Fehr, 1979; LaFrance & Mayo, 1978; Patterson, 1983). Apparently the high-status individual has both the ability and prerogative to maintain visual attentiveness while speaking but is not obligated to reciprocate eye contact when listening. These gaze patterns during interactions may severely undercut or augment an individual's power and influence.

PROXEMICS

Communication through the use of interpersonal space, called proxemics, is a central status issue in most organizations. Indeed, Porter and Roberts (1976) suggested the way in which people at work use space to convey meaning is one of the two modes of nonverbal communication of greatest interest to organizational researchers. Most of the research on power and proxemics is quite consistent; we provide higher-status individuals with more personal space (Dean, Willis, & Hewitt, 1975; Mehrabian, 1969). Argyle (1975) reported that "the only direct connection between dominance or status and spatial behavior is the deference shown to high-status people by keeping at a distance from them" (p. 308). Moreover, as the status differential becomes greater, interaction distances increase even more (Dean et al., 1975). In organizational communication, Remland (1981) reported that high-status individuals have less accessible territory and more personal space than lower-status individuals. The prerogative to invade others' space clearly lies with people of high power and status. Eisenberg and Smith (1971) wrote that the power to defend one's own territory and the right to invade that of others are clear signs of dominance and prestige.

Another important proxemic variable is the degree of body orientation or angle between two communicators. Mehrabian (1968b) reported that standing individuals maintained a more direct shoulder orientation to a high-status addressee than to a low-status addressee. Body orientation is least direct toward women with low status and most direct toward disliked men of high status (Mehrabian, 1968a). Jorgenson (1975) found that equal status dyads assumed a significantly more direct angle of orientation than did discrepant status pairs and low-status pairs assumed a less direct angle of orientation than high-status pairs. Burgoon and Saine (1978) asserted that in group communication, the individual who is faced by most people probably has the most influence.

TACTILE COMMUNICATION

Touch, the most intimate form of nonverbal communication, has the power to repel, disgust, insult, threaten, console, reassure, love, and arouse. Tactile or haptic behavior functions as a primary indicant of power and status (Prisbell, 1982) and affects relationships within the business organization.

Power and control are communicated through the initiation of touch. Empirically, touchers have been found to be significantly more dominant than recipients of touch (Burgoon & Saine, 1978; Major, 1981; Major & Heslin, 1982; Patterson, Powell, & Lenihan, 1986). Likewise, researchers report that higher-status persons more frequently touch lower-status persons (Henley, 1977; Major & Heslin, 1982). Remland (1981) claimed that this pattern is commonly observed in organizations; superiors touch subordinates considerably more than the reverse. Other tactile behaviors can indicate dominance or submission. Scheflen (1972) stated that direct poking with the index finger is a dominant act, used as a controlling device. In contrast, a person who "cuddles" to the touch of another is perceived as submissive (Henley, 1977). Tactile patterns have been neglected as important but subtle mechanisms of organizational control.

PARALANGUAGE

The study of nonverbal elements of the voice is called paralinguistics or vocalics, and includes vocal qualities of speech such as pitch, tempo, rhythm, and resonance as well as vocal characterizers (e.g., laughing, yawning) and vocal segregates (e.g., "ah," "uh-huh").

Several studies have found that both social status and credibility can be detected from paralinguistic cues (Harms, 1961; Moe, 1972). Argyle (1975) reported that vocal characteristics associated with higher social status include clearer articulation, sharper enunciation of consonants, and more vocal intonation. One experiment found perceptions of leadership in women to increase as their speaking rates became faster (Stang, 1973). Several researchers have reported that power and status are associated with louder speaking (Mehrabian, 1972; Remland, 1982a; Scheflen, 1972). Voices with fast rate, high volume, low pitch, and full resonance carry the sound of authority. Conversely, high pitch is often associated with childlike submissiveness. In their book on organization communication, Koehler et al. (1981) stated that tone of voice is an important organizational variable. When a supervisor is a friend of a subordinate, friendly tones of voice may undermine the perceived importance of a request or command.

One vocalic behavior that has received little attention is laughing. Henley (1977) maintained that laughter is an expression subordinates exhibit to persons higher in status. However, laughing at someone in an awkward situation or laughing at a superior's *faux pas* is hardly a submissive message. Recently, studies have employed transcripts of conversation without much attention to intonation or paralanguage. Organizational power researchers would be remiss in failing to include vocalic data so easily preserved with audiotape. Since paralinguistic cues can modify, reinforce, undercut, or reverse the meaning of a verbal utterance, these cues mandate increased attention.

CHRONEMICS

Chronemics examines the use and structure of time, and the various meanings attached to it. Our culture is time-conscious; the American slogan "time is money" is indicative of how we treasure time. As with any valued item, the possession of time is correlated with power and status, and is particularly significant in the business organization.

Waiting-Time

While hardly an efficient managerial practice, the act of making a subordinate wait can be used to assert dominance. Insel and Lindgren (1978) maintained that "another psychological dimension to the distress of waiting is the effect of subordination. One who is in the position to cause another to wait has power over him. To be kept waiting implies that one's own time is less valuable than that of the one who imposes the wait" (p. 105). Waiting-time decreases as status increases, and the powerful are provided with luxurious facilities on the rare occasions when they must wait, such as airport V.I.P. lounges (Henley, 1977).

Talk-Time

Power and status also affect the amount of talk-time during an interaction. Dominant individuals will talk more (Kendon & Cook, 1969) and will hold the floor for a greater proportion of the total time than will a less dominant person (Rogers & Jones, 1975). High-status persons communicate more frequently and speak longer in group discussion (Hurwitz, Zander, & Hymovitch, 1968; Remland, 1981; Stephan, 1952; Weins, Thompson, Matarazzo, Matarazzo, & Saslow, 1965). Furthermore, when lower-status individuals do participate, their communication is usually directed toward those of higher status (Hurwitz et al., 1968).

Individuals of high status and those with dominant personalities interrupt more often (Burgoon & Saine, 1978; Henley, 1977; Rogers & Jones, 1975; Weins et al., 1965). This interruption pattern prevails in the business organization, where subordinates may not interrupt a superior and must immediately cede the floor when the superior interrupts (Henley, 1977).

Higher-status people influence the actual speech patterns of lower-status individuals. Koehler et al. (1981) claimed that subordinates' response latencies are shorter, whereas superiors may take their time in answering. Furthermore, utterance duration is affected by the relative status of an interacting dyad with the lower-status person following the lead of the high-status person (Mehrabian, 1968a). Mehrabian (1968a) argued that a subordinate who does not follow the customary low-status pattern will tend to be negatively perceived by a superior.

Initiating or terminating a conversation is a prerogative of the high-status individual (Mehrabian, 1971) who can also dictate the chronemic patterns of the interaction (Burgoon & Saine, 1978). Superiors typically will decide when a meeting will take place, the length of the interaction, and how much time is devoted to each discussion topic (Burgoon & Saine, 1978; Henley, 1977).

Work-Time

Flexibility of work schedule is associated with higher status in the organization, as it symbolizes control over time. The ability to control the time of others also leads to power. Henley (1977) stated, "some people have the power to annex other people's time, and the more they can annex, the more powerful they become; the more powerful they are, the more of others' time they can annex" (p. 49). In a business organization, the time of the high-status person is considered more valuable than that of the low-status person (Koehler et al., 1981; Remland, 1981). Higher-status individuals have the freedom to waste the time of others while at the same time to expect strict adherence to their own schedules (Burgoon & Saine, 1978; Goldhaber, 1974).

How an employee spends time determines power and status within the organization. Individuals who devote more time, especially spare time, to meetings, to committees, and to developing contacts are more likely to be influential decision makers (Koehler et al., 1981). Moreover, spending time with the boss increases a subordinate's power even further (Huseman et al., 1976).

THE ORGANIZATIONAL ENVIRONMENT

Privileged territories and executive artifacts both determine and maintain organization power. Pfeffer (1981) maintained:

> The provision of social actors with the symbols of power ratifies their power position within the organization and provides them with power because of the symbols. (p. 54)

Territories

Organizational behavior is influenced by territorial patterns that promote privilege and project power. As indicated previously, height is associated with power and status. Thus, it is not surprising that the height of an individual's territory symbolizes one's relative importance (Henley, 1977). Low chairs put a person in a subordinate position (Morris, 1977). Conversely, the top floors of high rise buildings are reserved for the executives, with the president or CEO occupying the topmost or penthouse floor (Kanter, 1979; Mehrabian, 1976).

The possession of larger space or territory is both a symbol and a prerequisite of power. Important executives usually have the largest office (Eisenberg & Smith, 1971; Goldhaber, 1974; Huseman et al., 1976; Mehrabian, 1976; Pfeffer, 1981). Quantity of space is not the only index of power; the elite have *quality* environments as well. The most desirable locations, such as offices with many windows, corner offices, or one next to the company president, signal importance within the organization (Eisenberg & Smith, 1971; Kanter, 1979; Mehrabian, 1976; Pfeffer, 1981). Status is also established by the protective quality of space. Lower status is indicated by an open work pit or cubicle made from temporary partitions of file cabinets, whereas the "real" walls of an enclosed office blocked by a receptionist's desk provides executive protection from territorial invasion (Goldhaber, 1974; Huseman et al., 1976; Kanter, 1979).

Executive privacy, while advantageous in many respects, has drawbacks. The inaccessibility of the elite results in loneliness and social isolation (Kanter, 1979; Mehrabian, 1976). Some executives may attempt to overcome isolation by taking strolls through their subordinates' domain, but their unusual presence causes subordinates to become anxious, clam up, feel they're being evaluated, and exhibit avoidance behavior (Mehrabian, 1976). Another detrimental consequence of upper-echelon isolation is that it creates barriers to vital information flow between managers and subordinates. Though Mehrabian (1976) stated that "management consultants are often amazed at how little many senior executives know about fairly significant interoffice matters" (p. 143), organizational researchers have devoted little attention to this important issue.

Group seating patterns can be manipulated to express power. Research has shown that dominant, high-status individuals select the most focal position in a group, particularly the end seat at a table (Heckel, 1973; Sommer, 1967). Highly visible positions also have been positively correlated with increased interaction (Hearn, 1957, Ward, 1968) and provide more control of interaction patterns (Burgoon & Saine, 1978; LaFrance & Mayo, 1978). Persons who occupy focal positions, such as the end seat of a table, were perceived as leaders (Ward, 1968) and were more likely to be selected foreperson of a jury in one study (Strodtbeck & Hook, 1961). Followers and individuals who wish to avoid interaction and leadership chose the least focal positions (Hare & Bales, 1963; Lott & Sommer, 1962; Sommer, 1961, 1965).

Artifacts

Long before much empirical research had been conducted on nonverbal communication, the suburban family of the 1950s knew that large houses, boats, and cars were symbols of status. In today's organization, leaders can be identified by the artifacts that accompany their status. Koehler et al. (1981) suggested that organizational status symbols include a special parking place, a high-status company car, and expensive office furnishings. The latest and most expensive pieces of office equipment are power symbols (Pfeffer, 1981), but knowing how to use them suggests a low power rating (Korda, 1983).

Considerable status revolves around possession and use of communication devices such as the telephone. Having more telephones displayed on one's desk than is necessary is a status symbol (Morris, 1977). However, high-status persons do not actually dial the telephones; someone else does that for them. Operating any mechanical device has a tinge of manual labor and a low-status flavor (Morris, 1977). In an age when the telephone is often an environmental invader, a secretary, an answering service or its mechanical equivalent increases an individual's control and dominance (Goldhaber, 1974; Kanter, 1979; Mehrabian, 1976). Indeed, when one executive secretary reaches another executive secretary, high power requires the other executive come on the line first (Morris, 1977). A top executive can manifest special status with a car phone which implies how busy and important he/she is. This is such a power symbol that one phone company markets dummy aerials for phoneless vehicles, a form of dominance mimicry (Morris, 1977).

Briefcases are another organization status symbol (Korda, 1983; Morris, 1977). Bulky briefcases are a sign of low status since subordinates usually attend to more paperwork. Allegedly, slimmer briefcases are higher in status since they only contain vital papers. No briefcase conveys most status, since when you have real power all they want is you (Korda, 1983).

Artifacts and territories are more than organizational ornaments; they function as symbols of organizational power in four ways. First, they are symbols, both to organization members and to outsiders, of the power structure of the organization. Second, individuals who can access high-status territories and possess symbolic artifacts associated with power may rise to more powerful positions in the formal power structure. Third, certain physical objects and spaces may be the actual rewards which maintain the power structure through material reinforcement. Finally, the accouterments of power may produce efficacious self-expectancies that actually predispose an individual to act in a more powerful manner.

CONCLUSION

In his recent review of social power and communication, Berger (1985) clearly summarized the position of the present article on the importance of attending to nonverbal variables in power research:

> It can be argued that these nonverbal behaviors are more significant in determining the experience of power than are variables related to verbal content. One conclusion to be drawn here is that failure to take into account nonverbal behavior in the study of communication and power relationships is to doom oneself to study the tip of a very large iceberg. (p. 483)

Hope for a communication theory of organization power will come from an examination of all types of power, formal and informal, expressed through the numerous channels of human communication, verbal and nonverbal.

References

Albrecht, T. L., & Ropp, V. A. (1982). The study of network structuring in organizations through the use of method triangulation. *Western Journal of Speech Communication, 46,* 162–178.

Andersen, J. E, Andersen, P. A., & Jensen, A. D. (1979). The measurement of nonverbal immediacy. *Journal of Applied Communication Research, 7,* 153–180.

Andersen, P. A. (1985). Nonverbal immediacy in interpersonal communication. In A. Seigman & S. Feldstein (Eds.), *Multichannel integrations of nonverbal behavior* (pp. 1–36). Hillsdale, NJ: Lawrence Erlbaum.

Andersen, J. P. (1986). Consciousness, cognition, and communication. *Western Journal of Speech Communication, 50,* 87–101.

Argyle, M. (1975). *Bodily communication.* New York: International Universities Press.

Barash, D. R. (1973). Human ethology: Personal space reiterated. *Environmental Behavior, 5,* 67–73.

Bateson, G. (1955). A theory of play and fantasy. *Psychiatric Research Reports, 2,* 39–51.

Berger, C. R. (1985). Social power and interpersonal communication. In M. L. Knapp & G. R. Miller (Eds.), *Handbook of interpersonal communication* (pp. 439–499). Beverly Hills, CA: Sage.

Bickman, L. (1974). The social power of a uniform. *Journal of Applied Social Psychology, 4,* 47–61.

Brown, R. (1965). *Social psychology.* New York: The Free Press.

Burgoon, J. K. (1985). Nonverbal signals. In M. L. Knapp & G. R. Miller (Eds.), *Handbook of interpersonal communication* (pp. 344–390). Beverly Hills, CA: Sage.

Burgoon, J. K., & Hale, J. L. (1984). The fundamental topoi of relational communication. *Communication Monographs, 51,* 193–214.

Burgoon, J. K., & Saine, T. (1978). *The unspoken dialogue: An introduction to nonverbal communication.* Boston: Houghton Mifflin.

Burroughs, W. A., Schultz, W., & Autrey, S. (1973). Quality of argument, leaders, votes, and eye contact in three person leaderless groups. *Journal of Social Psychology, 90,* 89–93.

Cook, M. (1979). Gaze and mutual gaze in social encounters. In S. Weitz (Ed.), *Nonverbal communication: Readings with commentary* (2d ed., pp. 77–86). New York: Oxford University Press.

Crouch, W. W., & Koll, M. (1979, May). *The function of eye behavior in signaling dominance and submission in dyadic interactions.* Paper presented at the Eastern Communication Association, Philadelphia, Pennsylvania.

Dean, L. M., Willis, F. N., & Hewitt, J. (1975). Initial distance among individuals equal and unequal in military rank. *Journal of Personality and Social Psychology, 32,* 294–299.

Deetz, S. A. (1982). Critical interpretative research in organizational communication. *Western Journal of Speech Communication, 46,* 131–149.

Duran, R. L., Jensen, A. D., Prisbell, M., & Rossoff, J. M. (1979, February). *The control dimension of interpersonal relationships: Conceptualization, behavioral correlates and measurement*. Paper presented at the annual meeting of the Western Speech Communication Association convention, Los Angeles.

Efran, J. S. (1968). Looking for approval: Effects on visual behavior of approbation from persons differing in importance. *Journal of Personality and Social Psychology, 10*, 21–25.

Eisenberg, A. M., & Smith, R. R. (1971). *Nonverbal communication*. New York: The Bobbs-Merrill Company.

Ellsworth, P. C., Carlsmith, J. M., & Henson, A. (1972). The stare as a stimulus of flight in human subjects. *Journal of Personality and Social Psychology, 21*, 302–311.

Exline, R. V., Ellyson, S. L., & Long, B. (1975). Visual behavior as an aspect of power role relationships. In P. Pliner, L. Krames, & T. Alloway (Eds.), *Nonverbal communication of aggression* (Vol. 2), (pp. 21–52). New York: Plenum.

Exline, R. V., & Fehr, B. J. (1979). *Person and context in interpretation of gaze behavior*. Paper presented at the Annual Convention of the American Psychological Association, New York.

Fairhurst, G. T., Green, S. G., & Snavely, B. K. (1984). Managerial control and discipline: Whips and chains. In R. N. Bostrom (Ed.), *Communication yearbook 8* (pp. 558–593). Beverly Hills, CA: Sage.

Fowles, J. (1974). Why we wear clothes, *ETC: A Review of General Semantics, 31*, 343–352.

Fromme, D. J., & Beam, D. C. (1974). Dominance and sex differences in nonverbal responses to differential eye contact. *Journal of Research in Personality, 8*, 76–87.

Fugita, S. S. (1974). Effects of anxiety and approval on visual interaction. *Journal of Personality and Social Psychology, 29*, 586–592.

Fullbright, J. W. (1966). *The arrogance of power*. New York: Vintage Books.

Goffman, E. (1967). *Interaction ritual*. Garden City, NY: Anchor Books.

Goldhaber, G. M. (1974). *Organizational communication*. Dubuque, IA: Wm. C. Brown Publishing.

Hare, A., & Bales, R. (1963). Seating position and small group interaction. *Sociometry, 26*, 480–496.

Harms, L. S. (1961). Listener judgments of status cues in speech. *Quarterly Journal of Speech, 47*, 164–168.

Hearn, G. (1957). Leadership and the spatial factor in small groups. *Journal of Abnormal and Social Psychology, 54*, 269–272.

Heckel, R. V. (1973). Leadership and voluntary seating choice. *Psychological Reports, 32*, 141–142.

Henley, N. M. (1977). *Body politics: Power, sex and nonverbal communication*. Englewood Cliffs, NJ: Prentice-Hall.

Hickson, D. J., Hinings, C. R., Lee, C. A., Schneck, R. E., & Pennings, J. M. (1971). A strategic contingencies theory of intraorganizational power. *Administrative Science Quarterly, 16*, 216–226.

Hurwitz, J. L., Zander, A. F., & Hymovitch, B. (1968). Some effects of power on the relations among group members. In Cartwright, D. & A. Zander (Eds.), *Group dynamics* (pp. 291–297). New York: Harper & Row.

Huseman, R. C., Lahiff, J. M., & Hatfield, J. D. (1976). *Interpersonal communication in organizations*. Boston: Holbrook Press.

Insel, P. M., & Lindgren, H. C. (1978). *Too close for comfort*. Englewood Cliffs, NJ: Prentice-Hall.

Jablin, F. M. (1984). Assimilating new members into organizations. In R. N. Bostrom (Ed.), *Communication yearbook 8* (pp. 594–626). Beverly Hills, CA: Sage.

Jorgenson, D. O. (1975). Field study of the relationship between status discrepancy and proxemic behavior. *Journal of Social Psychology, 97*, 173–179.

Joseph, N., & Alex, N. (1972). The uniform: A sociological perspective. *American Journal of Sociology, 77*, 719–730.

Kanter, R. M. (1979). How the top is different. In R. M. Kanter & B. A. Stein (Eds.), *Life in organizations* (pp. 20–35). New York: Basic Books.

Kendon, A., & Cook, M. (1969). The consistency of gaze patterns in social interaction. *British Journal of Psychology, 60*, 481–494.

Kennedy, C. W. & Camden, C. (1983). Interruptions and nonverbal gender differences. *Journal of Nonverbal Behavior, 8*, 91–108.

Knapp, M. L. (1983). Dyadic relationship development. In J. M. Wiemann & R. P. Harrison (Eds.), *Nonverbal interaction* (pp. 179–207). Beverly Hills, CA: Sage.

Knowles, E. S. (1973). Boundaries around group interaction: The effect of group size and member status on boundary permeability. *Journal of Personality and Social Psychology, 26*, 327–332.

Koehler, J. W., Anatol, K. W. E., & Applbaum, R. L. (1981). *Organizational communications: A behavioral perspective*. New York: Holt, Rinehart & Winston.

Korda, M. (1983). Status marks—a gold-plated thermos is a man's best friend. In A. M. Katz & V. T. Katz (Eds.), *Foundations of nonverbal communication* (pp. 164–169). Carbondale: Southern Illinois University Press.

LaFrance, J., & Mayo, C. (1978). *Moving bodies: Nonverbal communication in social relationships*. Monterey, CA: Brooks/Cole Publishing.

Lefkowitz, M., Blake, R., & Mouton, J. (1955). Status factors in pedestrian violation of traffic signals. *Journal of Abnormal and Social Psychology, 51*, 704–706.

Lott, D. F., & Sommer, R. (1962). Seating arrangements and status. *Journal of Personality and Social Psychology, 7*, 90–95.

Major, B. (1981). Gender patterns in touching behavior. In C. Mayo & N. M. Henley (Eds.), *Gender and nonverbal behavior* (pp. 15–38). New York: Springer-Verlag.

Major, B., & Heslin, R. (1982). Perceptions of cross-sex and same sex nonreciprocal touch: It is better to give than to receive. *Journal of Nonverbal Behavior, 6*, 148–162.

Mehrabian, A. (1968a). Communication without words. *Psychology Today, 2*, 52–55.

Mehrabian, A. (1968b). Inference of attitudes from the posture, orientation, and distance of a communicator. *Journal of Consulting and Clinical Psychology, 32*, 296–308.

Mehrabian, A. (1969). Significance of posture and position in the communication attitude and status relationships. *Psychological Bulletin, 71*, 359–372.

Mehrabian, A. (1971). *Silent messages*. Belmont, CA: Wadsworth Publishing.

Mehrabian, A. (1972). *Nonverbal communication.* New York: Aldine, Atherton.

Mehrabian, A. (1976). *Public places, private spaces.* New York: Basic Books.

Mehrabian, A. (1981). *Silent messages: Implicit communication of emotions and attitudes.* Belmont, CA: Wadsworth Publishing.

Mehrabian, A., & Friar, J. T. (1969). Encoding of attitude by a seated communicator via posture and position cues. *Journal of Consulting and Clinical Psychology, 33,* 330–336.

Mintzberg, H. (1983). *Power in and around organizations.* Englewood Cliffs, NJ: Prentice-Hall.

Moe, J. D. (1972). Listener judgments of status cues in speech: A replication and extension. *Speech Monographs, 39,* 144–147.

Molloy, J. T. (1976). *Dress for success.* New York: Warner Books.

Morris, D. (1977). *Manwatching: A field guide to human behavior.* New York: Harry N. Abrams.

Patterson, M. L. (1983). *Nonverbal behavior: A functional perspective.* New York: Springer-Verlag.

Patterson, M. L., Powell, J. L., & Lenihan, M. G. (1986). Touch, compliance, and interpersonal affect. *Journal of Nonverbal Behavior, 10,* 41–50.

Pfeffer, J. (1981). *Power in organizations.* Marshfield, MA: Pitman Publishing.

Porter, L., & Roberts, K. (1976). Communication in organizations. In M. Dunnette (Ed.), *Handbook of industrial and organizational psychology.* Chicago: Rand McNally.

Prisbell, M. (1982, May). *Nonverbal communication attributes of power and status in the organizational setting.* Paper presented at the annual convention of Eastern Communication Association, Hartford, CT.

Ragan, S. L. (1983). A conversational analysis of alignment talk in job interviews. In R. N. Bostrom (Ed.), *Communication yearbook 7* (pp. 502–516). Beverly Hills, CA: Sage.

Remland, M. (1981). Developing leadership skills in nonverbal communication: A situational perspective. The *Journal of Business Communication, 18,* 17–29.

Remland, M. (1982a). The implicit ad hominem fallacy: Nonverbal displays of status in argumentative discourse. *Journal of the American Forensic Association, 19,* 79–86.

Remland, M. S. (1982b, November). *Leadership impressions and nonverbal communication in a superior-subordinate interaction.* Paper presented at the annual convention of the Speech Communication Association, Louisville, KY.

Riggs, C. J. (1983). Dimensions of organizational conflict: A functional analysis of communication tactics. In R. N. Bostrom (Ed.), *Communication yearbook 7* (pp. 517–531). Beverly Hills, CA: Sage.

Rogers, W. T., & Jones, S. E. (1975). Effects of dominance tendencies on floor holding in interruption behavior in dyadic interaction. *Human Communication Research, 3,* 291–302.

Scheflen, A. E. (1972). *Body language and the social order.* Englewood Cliffs, NJ: Prentice-Hall.

Sommer, R. (1961). Leadership and group geography. *Sociometry, 24,* 99–110.

Sommer, R. (1965). Leadership and small group ecology. *Sociometry, 28,* 337–348.

Sommer, R. (1967). Small group ecology. *Psychological Bulletin, 67,* 145–151.

Stang, D. J. (1973). Effect of interaction rate on ratings of leadership and liking. *Journal of Personality and Social Psychology, 27,* 405–408.

Stephen, F. F. (1952). The relative rate of communication between members of small groups. *American Sociological Review, 17,* 428–486.

Strodtbeck, F. L., & Hook, L. H. (1961). The social dimensions of a twelve-man jury table. *Sociometry, 24,* 297–315.

Strongman, K. T., & Chapness, B. G. (1968). Dominance hierarchies and conflict in eye contact. *Acta Psychologica, 28,* 376–386.

Thayer, S. (1969). The effect of interpersonal looking duration on dominance judgments. *Journal of Social Psychology, 79,* 285–286.

Thompson, J. D. (1967). *Organizations in action.* New York: McGraw-Hill.

Tompkins, P. (1984). The functions of communication in organizations. In C. Arnold & J. Bowers (Eds.), *Handbook of rhetorical and communication theory* (pp. 649–719). New York: Allyn & Bacon.

Tompkins, P. K., & Cheney, G. (1985). Communication and unobtrusive control in contemporary organizations. In R. D. McPhee & P. K. Tompkins (Eds.), *Organizational communication: Traditional themes and new directions* (pp. 179–210). Beverly Hills: Sage.

Trujillo, N. (1983). "Performing" Mintzberg's roles: The nature of managerial communication. In L. L. Putnam & M. E. Pacanowsky (Eds.), *Communication and organizations: An interpretive approach* (pp. 73–97). Beverly Hills, CA: Sage.

Ward, C. D. (1968). Seating arrangement and leadership emergence in small discussion groups. *Journal of Social Psychology, 74,* 83–90.

Watzlawick, R., Beavin, J. M., & Jackson, D. D. (1967). *Pragmatics of human communication.* New York: W. W. Norton & Company.

Weins, A. N., Thompson, S. M., Matarazzo, J. A., Matarazzo, R. G., & Salsow, G. (1965). Interview interaction behavior of supervisors, head nurses and staff nurses. *Nursing Research, 14,* 322–329.

Segrin reviews the literature on nonverbal communication and persuasion using a meta-analysis. Meta-analysis is a method . used to summarize findings from many different studies to find out how strong a relationship is. Segrin looks at the relationship between nonverbal communication and compliance gaining, which involves trying to get someone to do something for you. The analysis shows that gaze, touch, moderately close distances, and professional clothing are all associated with successful compliance gaining.

39

The Influence of Nonverbal Behaviors in Compliance-Gaining Processes

Chris Segrin

Members of the lay public appear to have an intuitive sense for the fact that certain nonverbal behaviors can help make people more effective and influential in interpersonal interactions. Statements like "dress for success," "look him right in the eye," "reach out and touch someone," and "use a firm handshake," all suggest that the strategic use of certain nonverbal behaviors can lead to positive outcomes for those who use them.

This article was written especially for *The Nonverbal Communication Reader* and is based on research reported in Segrin (1993), The effects of nonverbal behavior on outcomes of compliance-gaining attempts. *Communication Studies, 44,* 169–187.

For many years social scientists have been studying the effectiveness of nonverbal behaviors such as touch, space, clothing, and gaze in compliance-gaining situations. Compliance gaining is an interpersonal process in which one party, the "source," attempts to get another party, "the target," to enact some desired behavior such as donating money to charity, signing a petition, quitting smoking, or loaning money to the target. To determine the effectiveness of certain nonverbal behaviors for enhancing compliance-gaining processes, a meta-analysis was conducted that summarized the findings of approximately fifty studies in this area (Segrin, 1993). Meta-analysis is a method of statistically summarizing and combining the results of multiple past studies (Hunter & Schmidt, 1990). The effects of various nonverbal behaviors on compliance-gaining effectiveness will be examined first, followed by a comparison of nonverbal and verbal tactics. Finally, several theoretical explanations for these effects will be discussed.

THE EFFECTS OF NONVERBAL BEHAVIORS ON COMPLIANCE-GAINING

Gaze

Twelve studies investigated the impact of gaze on behavioral compliance. Authors have had gazing and nongazing confederates attempt to get rides while hitchhiking (Snyder, Grether, & Keller, 1974), borrow a dime to make a phone call (Brockner, Pressman, Cabitt, & Moran, 1982), get targets to take pamphlets (Kleinke & Singer, 1979), obtain a nickel in exchange for five pennies (Ernest & Cooper, 1974), or donate money to charity (Bull & Robinson, 1981), to name but a few of the compliance situations. The average effect size representing the different compliance rates in the gaze and no-gaze conditions is $r = .23$. The statistic, r (Pearson correlation coefficient) can range from -1.0 (a very strong negative relationship) to 1.0 (a very strong positive relationship). This effect, $r = .23$, means that more gaze from the source is associated with more compliance from the target, although this relationship is not very powerful. It should be noted that gaze from a source produced greater compliance than gaze aversion in every one of the twelve studies conducted. This suggests that the effect for gaze, while not unusually powerful, is very consistent.

Touch

Thirteen studies examined the influence of touch on compliance-gaining. In virtually all of these studies confederates either touched the target lightly on the upper arm or shoulder when making the request or did not touch the target at all. Compliance-gaining outcomes have included getting subjects to return dimes that they took from a phone booth (Brockner et al., 1982; Kleinke, 1977), volunteer time for charity (Goldman, Kiyohara, & Pfannensteil, 1984), take and mail in a card (Kurklen & Kassinove, 1991), help score questionnaires (Patterson, Powell, & Lenihan, 1986), and sign a petition (Willis & Hamm, 1980). The average effect size representing the different compliance rates in the touch and no-touch conditions is $r = .21$. This means that the use of touch by a source increased compliance from the target. The effect for touch, similar to that of gaze, is not large in magnitude but is fairly consistent across the thirteen studies. It should be noted that virtually all of the studies on touch and compliance had an experimenter lightly touch the target on the upper arm or shoulder. The force with which targets are touched is no doubt an important determinant of compliance. Thus far we only know that *light* touch yields greater compliance. We do not know what happens when more forceful touch is used, such as when someone grabs someone by the collar and shakes them while making a demand, or pushes them forcefully. Also, the location of the touch has typically been restricted to the upper arm or shoulder. Touch to different areas of the human body draws radically different reactions (Heslin & Alper, 1983; Nguyen, Heslin, & Nguyen, 1975). Consequently, we do not know exactly what happens when a source touches, say, the face or leg of a source while making a request. Because of ethical constraints, we may never fully understand how forcefulness or body region of touch enhance or diminish compliance-gaining effectiveness. However, nonthreatening polite touches clearly have a positive impact.

Proxemics

Eight studies examined the influence of interpersonal distance on compliance gaining. In these studies confederates generally approached the target at a "close" distance (1–2 feet) or "far" distance (3–5 feet) when making a request. Compliance-gaining scenarios have involved getting targets to volunteer to participate in a study (Baron, 1978; Baron & Bell, 1976), sign a petition (Buller, 1987), give a nickel in exchange for five pennies (Ernest & Cooper, 1974) and complete a survey (Glick, DeMorest, & Hotze, 1988). The average effect size representing the different compliance rates in the near and far request conditions is $r = .18$. It generally appears that compliance is inversely related to the distance between the source and the target, as long as the approach is not so close as to violate or invade the target's personal space. Although it has not been explicitly studied yet, it is reasonable to assume that when a source invades a target's space, the target may react more negatively and try to get away from the source, rather than to comply with his or her request. Provided that the distance between the source and target is not too close for comfort, closer space is associated with slightly higher compliance rates.

Clothing

Nineteen studies examined the influence of targets' clothing on compliance gaining. In the 1970s researchers often had confederates making requests while dressed as a "hippie" or "deviant" versus "conventional attire" (e.g., Darley & Cooper, 1972; Raymond & Unger, 1972). Others examined the effectiveness of formal attire versus casual attire (e.g., Bull & Robinson, 1981) while others studied the impact of uniforms (e.g., Bickman, 1974, Bushman, 1984, 1988). Regardless of the particular details of the manipulation, in the abstract, all studies appear to have manipulated the "status/formality" dimension of clothing. Compliance-gaining scenarios associated with the dress manipulation have involved getting targets to sign a petition (Suedfeld, Bochner, & Matas, 1971), complete a questionnaire for the requester (Harris et al., 1983), make charitable donations (Bull & Robinson, 1981) and lend a dime to an "overparked" confederate (Bushman, 1984, 1988). The average effect size representing the different compliance rates as a function of the target's dress was $r = .16$. This indicates that the more formal or high-status the clothing, the greater the compliance rate obtained. These results suggest that advice to get dressed up in formal clothing for job interviews, sales appointments, and other persuasive encounters is well heeded. Although the effect is not very strong, well-dressed people appear to be more successful persuaders than those who are casually dressed.

COMPARISON OF NONVERBAL VERSUS VERBAL BEHAVIORS ON COMPLIANCE

The results of this meta-analysis indicate that certain nonverbal behaviors like gaze and touch can increase compliance-gaining effectiveness somewhat. But how strong are the effects of these behaviors in comparison to certain verbal strategies that are sometimes used in compliance-gaining situations? Several related meta-analyses provide some answers. For example, Allen (1991) examined the effectiveness of one- versus two-sided messages (i.e., telling just one side, or both sides of the story) in persuasive encounters. In that meta-analysis, the correlation between message-sidedness and a source's persuasiveness was $r = .04$. Dillard, Hunter, and Burgoon (1984) conducted a meta-analysis of the studies on the foot-in-the-door (i.e., make a initial small request, and then follow it up with a second larger request) and door-in-the-face (i.e., make a ridiculously large initial request that is typically refused, and then follow it with a more reasonable second request) techniques. Their results indicated that each of these tactics enhances compliance-gaining effectiveness, with effects of $r = .17$ and $.15$, respectively. A meta-analysis of the studies on the effectiveness of including supportive information with a persuasive argument yielded an effect of $r = .20$ (Stiff, 1986). A final meta-analytic study on the effectiveness of fear appeals for producing compliance in targets indicated an effect of $r = .10$ (Boster & Mongeau, 1984). In general, we can see that these various verbal compliance-gaining tactics are somewhat effective, but no more so than any of the nonverbal behaviors examined. In fact, something as simple as making eye contact appears to have a stronger impact on targets than any of these different verbal tactics.

WHY DOES THE STRATEGIC USE OF NONVERBAL BEHAVIORS INCREASE COMPLIANCE-GAINING EFFECTIVENESS?

Several communication theories are useful for explaining why these various nonverbal behaviors can make people more persuasive. For example, *expectancy violation theory* (Burgoon, 1983; Burgoon, Coker, & Coker, 1986) states that people have expectations about what are appropriate levels of behavior, e.g., gaze, touch, etc., in interpersonal situations. If a source's nonverbal behavior violates the expectations of a target, that produces arousal in the target. The target might experience this arousal positively if the source has certain qualities that make him or her attractive. For example if a famous, physically attractive, wealthy person put his or her arm around you and said, "Would you mind holding my shopping bag while I tie my shoe?" you might initially react with surprise but ultimately agree with the request. On the other hand, a target might experience a violation of expectations negatively and not comply with the request. This can happen when the source has largely unattractive qualities.

Another theory called *speech (or communication) accommodation theory* (Gallois, Giles, Jones, Cargile, & Ota, 1995; Street & Giles, 1982; Giles, Mulac, Bradac, & Johnson, 1987) explains that people may change their communication behaviors when interacting with others as a function of their attitudes toward each other. Communicators may converge toward or diverge from the style of the partner, or they may not change at all. When the behavior of a source becomes more like that of the target, the target may react positively to this "imitation" even though s/he may not even be consciously aware that it is going on. So, for example, if you smile a lot at a source and she starts to smile back at you, you may react positively to this behavioral convergence and be more favorably predisposed to agree with the requests that she makes in the course of the interaction.

Ellsworth and Langer (1976) proposed a theory of nonverbal behavior and compliance based upon arousal that is sometimes referred to as *demand theory*. They argue that nonverbal behaviors, in sufficient degree, can function as demands. For example, a direct and prolonged stare by a source may be understood as insistence for some behavioral response from the target. According to Ellsworth and Langer, this produces arousal. Individuals are assumed to have the desire to rid themselves of this uncomfortable arousal. As a result they search for a response that would do just this. Usually, complying with the implicit request serves to reduce the arousal and terminate the confrontation with the source. When my second grade teacher wanted a student to stop talking in class, she would just stare at the student. I would often find myself talking to a friend, and then look up and realize that (1) the teacher was staring at me, and (2) I was the only one in the class talking. Although this realization would make me very uncomfortable, I knew exactly what I had to do: stop talking. Just as demand theory would predict, she was able to get me to comply with her request without saying a word; the nonverbal behavior alone was sufficient.

Finally, Patterson's *sequential-functional model of nonverbal exchange* (Patterson, 1982, 1985) is also useful for understanding the effects of nonverbal behavior in compliance-gaining processes. According to this model, people bring various predisposing factors such as gender, culture, personality, and their learning history to interpersonal interactions. These predisposing factors make some people especially likely to respond to the nonverbal involvement of others. For example, other people who have had second grade teachers like mine might be especially predisposed to respond to direct eye contact from authority figures. These various predispositions can be enhanced or attenuated by our internal arousal and expectations in interpersonal interactions. According to Patterson, signs of nonverbal involvement from a source, such as touch, close space, and eye contact, might serve several different functions. In compliance-gaining situations, these functions might entail an expression of intimacy or social control. If interpreted as such, a source may respond positively to the source's nonverbal expression out of a feeling of liking for the source, or submissiveness to the source's expressed dominance.

CONCLUSION

Nonverbal behaviors such as gaze, touch, space, and clothing, when used appropriately, can clearly enhance the effectiveness and persuasiveness of sources in compliance-gaining situations. The effects for these behaviors are not terrifically strong. However, they are consistent and reliable. Given how easy it is to implement these "strategies" in persuasive encounters, sources would appear to have little to lose by consciously managing and employing things like eye contact, light touch, and formal attire. A comparison of verbal and nonverbal strategies in compliance-gaining situations indicates that the effects for nonverbal behaviors are every bit as strong, and in some cases stronger, than those of the verbal tactics. Finally, several different communication theories can be used to explain why these nonverbal behaviors work the way they do in compliance-gaining contexts. While none of these theories can comprehensively explain why nonverbal behaviors enhance compliance-gaining processes in all cases, each gives us a useful account for at least some instances of effective persuasion, aided by the use of nonverbal behaviors. When it comes to trying to get others to do what you want, how you say it (nonverbally) is every bit important as what you say.

References

Allen, M. (1991). Meta-analysis comparing the persuasiveness of one-sided and two-sided messages. *Western Journal of Speech Communication, 55,* 390–404.

Baron, R. A. (1978). Invasions of personal space and helping: Mediating effects of invaders' apparent need. *Journal of Experimental Social Psychology, 14,* 304–312.

Baron, R. A., & Bell, P. A. (1976). Physical distance and helping: Some unexpected benefits of "crowding in" on others. *Journal of Applied Social Psychology, 6,* 95–104.

Bickman, L. (1974). The social power of a uniform. *Journal of Applied Social Psychology, 4,* 47–61.

Boster, F. J., & Mongeau, P. (1984). Fear-arousing persuasive messages. In R. N. Bostrom (Ed.), *Communication yearbook* (Vol. 8, pp. 330–375). Beverly Hills: Sage.

Brockner, J., Pressman, B., Cabitt, J., & Moran, P. (1982). Nonverbal intimacy, sex, and compliance: A field study. *Journal of Nonverbal Behavior, 6,* 253–258.

Bull, R., & Robinson, G. R. (1981). The influences of eye-gaze, style of dress, and locality on the amounts of money donated to a charity. *Human Relations, 34,* 895–905.

Buller, D. B. (1987), Communication apprehension and reactions to proxemic violations. *Journal of Nonverbal Behavior, 11,* 13–25.

Burgoon, J. K. (1983). Nonverbal violations of expectations. In J. M. Wiemann & R. P. Harrison (Eds.), *Nonverbal interaction* (pp. 77–111). Beverly Hills: Sage.

Burgoon, J. K., Coker, D. A., & Coker, R. A. (1986). Communicative effects of gaze behavior: A test of two contrasting explanations. *Human Communication Research, 12,* 495–524.

Bushman, B. J. (1984). Perceived symbols of authority and their influence on compliance. *Journal of Applied Social Psychology, 14,* 501–508.

Bushman, B. J. (1988). The effects of apparel on compliance: A field experiment with a female authority figure. *Personality and Social Psychology Bulletin, 14,* 459–467.

Darley, J. M., & Cooper, J. (1972). The "clean for Gene" phenomenon: The effect of students' appearance on political campaigning. *Journal of Applied Social Psychology, 2,* 24–33.

Dillard, J. P., Hunter, J. E., & Burgoon, M. (1984). Sequential request persuasive strategies: Meta-analysis of foot-in-the-door and door-in-the-face. *Human Communication Research, 10,* 461–488.

Ellsworth, P. C., & Langer, E. J. (1976). Staring and approach: An interpretation of the stare as a nonspecific activator. *Journal of Personality and Social Psychology, 33,* 117–122.

Ernest, R. C., & Cooper, R. E. (1974). "Hey Mister, do you have any change?": Two real world studies of proxemic effects on compliance with a mundane request. *Personality and Social Psychology Bulletin, 1,* 158–159.

Gallois, C., Giles, H., Jones, E., Cargile, A. C., & Ota, H. (1995). Accommodating intercultural encounters: Elaborations and extensions. In R. L. Wiseman (Ed.), *Intercultural communication theory* (pp. 115–147). Thousand Oaks, CA: Sage.

Giles, H., Mulac, A., Bradac, J. J., & Johnson, P. (1987). Speech accommodation theory: The first decade and beyond. In M. McLaughlin (Ed.), *Communication yearbook* (Vol. 10, pp. 13–48).

Glick, P., DeMorest, J. A., & Hotze, C. A. (1988). Keeping your distance: Group membership, personal space, and requests for small favors. *Journal of Applied Social Psychology, 18,* 315–330.

Goldman, M., Kiyohara, O., & Pfannensteil, D. A. (1984). Interpersonal touch, social labeling, and the foot-in-the-door effect. *The Journal of Social Psychology, 125,* 143–147.

Harris, M. B., James, J., Chavez, J., Fuller, M. L., Kent, S., Massanari, C., Moore, C., & Walsh, F. (1983). Clothing: Communication, compliance, and choice. *Journal of Applied Social Psychology, 13,* 88–97.

Heslin, R., & Alper, T. (1983). Touch: A bonding gesture. In J. M. Wiemann & R. P. Harrison (Eds.), *Nonverbal interaction* (pp. 47–75). Beverly Hills, CA: Sage.

Hunter, J. E., & Schmidt, F. L. (1990). *Methods of meta-analysis.* Newbury Park, CA: Sage.

Kleinke, C. L. (1977). Compliance to requests made by gazing and touching experimenters in field settings. *Journal of Experimental Social Psychology, 13,* 218–223.

Kleinke, C. L., & Singer, D. A. (1979). Influence of gaze on compliance with demanding and conciliatory requests in a field setting. *Personality and Social Psychology Bulletin, 5,* 386–390.

Kurklen, R., & Kassinove, H. (1991). Effects of profanity, touch, and subjects' religiosity on perceptions of a psychologist and behavioral compliance. *The Journal of Social Psychology, 131,* 899–901.

Nguyen, T., Heslin, R., & Nguyen, M. L. (1975). The meanings of touch: Sex differences. *Journal of Communication, 25,* 92–103.

Patterson, M. L. (1982). A sequential functional model of nonverbal exchange. *Psychological Review, 89,* 231–249.

Patterson, M. L. (1985). The evolution of a functional model of nonverbal exchange: A personal perspective. In R. L. Street & J. N. Cappella (Eds.), *Sequence and pattern in communicative behaviors* (pp. 190–205). London: Edward Arnold.

Patterson, M. L., Powell, J. L., & Lenihan, M. G. (1986). Touch, compliance, and interpersonal affect. *Journal of Nonverbal Behavior, 10,* 41–50.

Raymond, B. J., & Unger, R. K. (1972). "The apparel oft proclaims the man": Cooperation with deviant and conventional youths. *The Journal of Social Psychology, 87,* 75–82.

Segrin, C. (1993). The effects of nonverbal behavior on outcomes of compliance-gaining attempts. *Communication Studies, 44,* 169–187.

Snyder, M., Grether, J., & Keller, K. (1974). Staring and compliance: A field experiment on hitchhiking. *Journal of Applied Social Psychology, 4,* 165–170.

Stiff, J. B. (1986). Cognitive processing of persuasive message cues: A meta-analytic review of the effects of supporting information on attitudes. *Communication Monographs, 53,* 75–89.

Street, R. L., Jr., & Giles, H. (1982). Speech accommodation theory: A social cognitive approach to language and speech behavior. In M. Roloff & C. Berger (Eds.), *Social cognition and communication* (pp. 193–226). Beverly Hills, CA: Sage.

Suedfeld, P., Bochner, S., & Matas, C. (1971). Petitioners' attire and petition signing by peace demonstrators: A field experiment. *Journal of Applied Social Psychology, 1,* 278–283.

Willis, F. N., & Hamm, H. K. (1980). The use of interpersonal touch in securing compliance. *Journal of Nonverbal Behavior, 5,* 49–55.

APPENDIX
STUDIES INCLUDED IN THE META-ANALYSIS

Baron, R. A. (1978). Invasions of personal space and helping: Mediating effects of invaders' apparent need. *Journal of Experimental Social Psychology, 14,* 304–312.

Baron, R. A., & Bell, P. A. (1976). Physical distance and helping: Some unexpected benefits of "crowding in" on others. *Journal of Applied Social Psychology, 6,* 95–104.

Bickman, L. (1971). The effect of social status on the honesty of others. *The Journal of Social Psychology, 85,* 87–92.

Bickman, L. (1974). The social power of a uniform. *Journal of Applied Social Psychology, 4,* 47–61.

Brockner, J., Pressman, B., Cabitt, J., & Moran, P. (1982). Nonverbal intimacy, sex, and compliance: A field study. *Journal of Nonverbal Behavior, 6,* 253–258.

Bull, R., & Robinson, G. R. (1981). The influences of eye-gaze, style of dress, and locality on the amounts of money donated to a charity. *Human Relations, 34,* 895–905.

Buller, D. B. (1987), Communication apprehension and reactions to proxemic violations. *Journal of Nonverbal Behavior, 11,* 13–25.

Burgoon, J. K., & Aho, L. (1982). Three field experiments on the effects of violations of conversational distance. *Communication Monographs, 49,* 71–88.

Bushman, B. J. (1984). Perceived symbols of authority and their influence on compliance. *Journal of Applied Social Psychology, 14,* 501–508.

Bushman, B. J. (1988). The effects of apparel on compliance: A field experiment with a female authority figure. *Personality and Social Psychology Bulletin, 14,* 459–467.

Campbell, D. E., & Lancioni, G. E. (1979). The effects of staring and pew invasions in church settings. *The Journal of Social Psychology, 108,* 19–24.

Chaikin, A. L., Derlaga, V. J., Yoder, J., & Phillips, D. (1974). The effects of appearance on compliance. *The Journal of Social Psychology, 92,* 199–200.

Darley, J. M., & Cooper, J. (1972). The "clean for Gene" phenomenon: The effect of students' appearance on political campaigning. *Journal of Applied Social Psychology, 2,* 24–33.

Ellsworth, P. C., & Langer, E. J. (1976). Staring and approach: An interpretation of the stare as a nonspecific activator. *Journal of Personality and Social Psychology, 33,* 117–122.

Ernest, R. C., & Cooper, R. E. (1974). "Hey Mister, do you have any change?": Two real world studies of proxemic effects on compliance with a mundane request. *Personality and Social Psychology Bulletin, 1,* 158–159.

Glick, P., DeMorest, J. A., & Hotze, C. A. (1988). Keeping your distance: Group membership, personal space, and requests for small favors. *Journal of Applied Social Psychology, 18,* 315–330.

Goldman, M., Kiyohara, O., & Pfannensteil, D. A. (1984). Interpersonal touch, social labeling, and the foot-in-the-door effect. *The Journal of Social Psychology, 125,* 143–147.

Greene, L. R. (1976). Effects of field dependence on affective reactions and compliance in dyadic interactions. *Journal of Personality and Social Psychology, 34,* 569–577.

Harris, M. B., James, J., Chavez, J., Fuller, M. L., Kent, S., Massanari, C., Moore, C., & Walsh, F. (1983). Clothing: Communication, compliance, and choice. *Journal of Applied Social Psychology, 13,* 88–97.

Hornik, J. (1992a). Effects of physical contact on customers' shopping time behavior. *Marketing Letters, 3,* 49–55.

Hornik, J. (1992b). Tactile stimulation and consumer response. *Journal of Consumer Research, 19,* 449–458.

Judd, N., Bull, R. H. C., & Gahagan, D. (1975). The effects of clothing style upon the reactions of a stranger. *Social Behavior and Personality, 3,* 225–227.

Keasey, C. B., & Keasey, C. T. (1973). Petition signing in a naturalistic setting. *The Journal of Social Psychology, 89,* 313–314.

Kleinke, C. L. (1977). Compliance to requests made by gazing and touching experimenters in field settings. *Journal of Experimental Social Psychology, 9,* 218–223.

Kleinke, C. L. (1980). Interaction between gaze and legitimacy of request on compliance in a field setting. *Journal of Nonverbal Behavior, 5,* 3–12.

Kleinke, C. L., & Singer, D. A. (1979). Influence of gaze on compliance with demanding and conciliatory requests in a field setting. *Personality and Social Psychology Bulletin, 5,* 386–390.

Kroll, H. W., & Moren, D. K. (1977). Effect of appearance in requests for help in libraries. *Psychological Reports, 40,* 129–130.

Kurklen, R., & Kassinove, H. (1991). Effects of profanity, touch, and subjects' religiosity on perceptions of a psychologist and behavioral compliance. *The Journal of Social Psychology, 131,* 899–901.

McGovern, J. L., & Holmes, D. S. (1976). Influence of sex and dress on cooperation: An instance of "person" chauvinism. *Journal of Applied Social Psychology, 6,* 206–210.

Morgan, W. G. (1973). Situational specificity in altruistic behavior. *Representative Research in Social Psychology, 4,* 56–66.

Patterson, M. L., Powell, J. L., & Lenihan, M. G. (1986). Touch, compliance, and interpersonal affect. *Journal of Nonverbal Behavior, 10,* 41–50.

Raymond, B. J., & Unger, R. K. (1972). "The apparel oft proclaims the man": Cooperation with deviant and conventional youths. *The Journal of Social Psychology, 87,* 75–82.

Smith, D. E., Gier, J. A., & Willis, F. N. (1982). Interpersonal touch and compliance with a marketing request. *Basic and Applied Social Psychology, 3,* 35–38.

Snyder, M., Grether, J., & Keller, K. (1974). Staring and compliance: A field experiment on hitchhiking. *Journal of Applied Social Psychology, 4,* 165–170.

Suedfeld, P., Bochner, S., & Matas, C. (1971). Petitioners' attire and petition signing by peace demonstrators: A field experiment. *Journal of Applied Social Psychology, 1,* 278–283.

Valentine, M. E. (1980). The attenuating influence of gaze upon the bystander intervention effect. *The Journal of Social Psychology, 111,* 197–203.

Walker, M., Harriman, S., & Costello, S. (1980). The influence of appearance on compliance with a request. *The Journal of Social Psychology, 112,* 159–160.

Walsh, E. J. (1977). Petition signing in town and on campus. *The Journal of Social Psychology, 102,* 323–324.

Wasserman, T., & Kassinove, H. (1976). Effects of type of recommendation, attire, and perceived expertise on parental compliance. *The Journal of Social Psychology, 99,* 43–50.

Willis, F. N., & Hamm, H. K. (1980). The use of interpersonal touch in securing compliance. *Journal of Nonverbal Behavior, 5,* 49–55.

Considerable research on health communication has focused on how physicians can persuade their patients to take better care of themselves and to follow treatment recommendations. Buller and Street examine ways that physicians can use nonverbal communication to be more persuasive in the context of interactions with their patients.

40

Persuasion in Physican-Patient Relations

David B. Buller
Richard L. Street, Jr.

In medical consultations, the primary concern in the realm of persuasion is to motivate patients to adhere to treatment recommendations. Persuasion is largely a function of verbal communication; however, there are several ways in which nonverbal communication enhances persuasion. Four that seem relevant are projecting an image of authority, power, and credibility, signaling intimacy, communicating expectations, and reinforcing, rewarding, or punishing behavior (Burgoon, Buller, & Woodall, 1989).

AUTHORITY, POWER, AND CREDIBILITY OF PHYSICIAN

The physician's image vis-à-vis authority, power, and credibility has been a concern in research on medical consultations. We have speculated that a common communicative pattern in physician-patient interaction relates to the exercise of dominance or control (Buller & Street, 1991; Street & Buller, 1987; Street & Wiemann, 1987). Several studies have supported this contention by revealing that physicians exercise more control in medical consultations than patients. For example, physicians have been observed to initiate more nonreciprocal touch, talk for more time, engage in more interruptions, display more and longer within-turn silences, and produce fewer adaptors than patients (Friedman, 1979; Kaplan et al., 1989; Street & Buller, 1987). In essence, physicians communicate social power by having unquestioned access to the patient's body, controlling communicative exchanges, and regulating the degree of interaction involvement (Pendleton, 1983; West, 1984).

Another nonverbal cue that may reflect authority and control are the uniforms worn by physicians (i.e., the white lab coat). Research in other contexts shows that uniforms denote status and control of resources and signal the ability to bestow favors or to punish others (Burgoon et al., 1989). People are highly conditioned to react to symbols of authority, especially uniforms. In a series of studies, Bickman (1971a, 1974a, 1974b) showed that a man dressed in a nondescript guard's uniform gained more compliance with small requests from passers-by on the street than did a man dressed in civilian clothes or a milkman's uniform. In two other studies, Bickman (1971b, 1974a) demonstrated that high status civilian clothing—suits and ties for men, dresses and coats for women—also increased compliance. Environmental trappings of the medical profession also contribute to authority and power (Friedman, 1979). The medical office setting, with its antiseptic and medicinal smells, specialized instruments, examination table, and other accoutrements, conveys an air of medical authority (Friedman, 1979). Furthermore, that the consultation takes place within the physician's environment provides the physician with greater rights to structure and control the interaction (Burgoon et al., 1989).

This authority and communicative control can result in greater adherence to treatments. Hall et al. (1981) reported that more dominance in physicians' speech was associated with more compliance, and Hall et al. (1988) concluded from their meta-analysis that a less authoritarian profile is detrimental to compliance. It appears that physicians are permitted and perhaps expected to exert some authority and control in the medical consultation (Street & Buller, 1987) and such behavior can improve compliance (Davis, 1968). Kaplan et al. (1989), however, recently found that when physicians exerted more conversational control, their patients were less healthy at follow-up. Interestingly, we also found that physicians were more likely to display nonverbal dominance when talking with patients under 30 years of age rather than with older patients (Street & Buller, 1988). Perhaps physicians may have more negative attitudes toward younger patients; or younger patients may be healthier, see the physician for more routine illnesses, or be more task-oriented during the consultation.

By exercising authority and control, physicians risk less favorable evaluations by patients (Inui & Carter, 1985). Hall et al. (1985) reported that more dominant physicians produced more patient negativity in terms of anger, anxiety, sympathy, probability of return, and satisfaction with care. Bertakis et al. (1991) found a similar negative relationship between dominance and satisfaction and found evidence that physicians' domination of speaking time was most damaging to patients' satisfaction.

EXPRESSING NEGATIVE AFFECT

Essentially, the same pattern emerges when one examines the expression of negative affect by the physician. Several studies showed that when physicians communicate negative affect, patients comply more with treatment recommendations and their health is better at follow-up. For example, Hall et al. (1981) discovered that anger and anxiety in the physician's voice was related to greater patient compliance. Kaplan et al. (1989) reported that the expression of negative affect by the physician (i.e., tension, anxiety, strain, self-consciousness, frustration, impatience) was associated with better health at a follow-up visit, but the expression of positive affect was not. Negative affect may be punishing and may motivate patients to please the physician by following treatment directives. Negative affect also may communicate concern or that the malady is more health-threatening, thereby increasing patients' motivation to adhere. In Hall et al.'s (1981) study, patients were most contented when physicians communicated more negative affect. Another notable finding in Kaplan et al.'s (1989) study was that the expression of negative affect by both the physician and patient reduced the symptoms that the patient experienced during chemotherapy for cancer. The sharing of negative affect, also witnessed in Hall et al.'s study (1981), may serve a cathartic function to reduce stress and anxieties associated with the medical condition and treatment procedures.

EXERCISING CONTROL IN INTERPERSONAL RELATIONSHIPS

Effective use of authority and control to increase adherence may depend on physicians creating a favorable relationship with the patient

(Inui & Carter, 1985). Hall et al. (1981) reported that patients reacted more positively when physicians communicated negative feelings vocally but positive feelings verbally. A positive relationship between the physician and patient may permit physicians to exercise more authority in order to achieve compliance. Also, in medical consultations reflecting more affiliation, patients may require less explanation to adhere to treatment directives. In general, intimacy increases obligations to accommodate requests from others due to the expectation that friends exchange favors and fulfill others' needs; therefore, people require less elaborate reasons for accommodating requests from friends than strangers (Roloff, 1987; Roloff, Janiszewski, McGrath, Burns, & Manrai, 1988). Research in other interpersonal contexts shows that many affiliation cues, such as increased gaze, conversational proximity, touch, open body orientation, smiling, nodding, and gesturing increase compliance (Baron & Bell, 1976; Edinger & Patterson, 1983; Ellsworth & Langer, 1976; Kleinke, 1977, 1980; Konecni, Libuser, Morton, & Ebbesen, 1975; LaCrosse, 1975; McGinley, LeFevre, & McGinley, 1975). The best conclusion, from the data on physician-patient interaction, is that affiliative cues do not directly enhance compliance. Rather, they create a context in which more aggressive attempts can be made by the physician to control the patient's behavior without the patient becoming hostile and resistant to these attempts.

PATIENT EXPECTATIONS

Finally, compliance is enhanced when physicians deal directly with patient expectations for treatment (Inui & Carter, 1985). Friedman (1979) contended that nonverbal communication is instrumental in setting patient expectations. Research from other settings such as the classroom and the experimental laboratory confirms the role of vocal and kinesic cues in creating expectations (Rosenthal, 1976, 1985; Rosenthal & Jacobson, 1968). However, to date no experiments have directly addressed how nonverbal communication actually affects patient expectations in medical consultations. Friedman (1979) forwarded the interesting thesis that nonverbal communication can create placebo effects in patients by transmitting positive expectations by the physician about the treatment's success. That is, nonverbal communication raises patient expectations for successful treatment and these psychological expectations in part improve the patient's health. Conversely, negative expectations can interfere with treatment success. This remains a novel, unstudied suggestion in the medical consultation. Certainly, the evidence of expectancy effects from classroom and laboratory settings (e.g., students whose teachers expected them to perform better did so) certainly imply that expectations could affect medical treatment and that the nonverbal behavior of the physician may be particularly instrumental in setting expectations (Rosenthal, 1976, 1985).

Table 1 summarizes recommendations that arise from our discussion of the role of nonverbal communication in medical consultations. Nonverbal communication is vital to the creation and maintenance of the relationship between the physician and patient, especially in communicating mutual affiliation and concern. Physicians should be affiliative with patients, expressing immediacy, attentiveness, encouragement, and concern. Affiliation engenders satisfaction and trust, improving the information exchange and permitting the physician to exercise some control over the patient's behavior. Patients also must bear some responsibility for creating an affiliative relationship with the patient. By matching physician's affiliative behavior, a more positive relationship will emerge. Physicians and patients also should exchange emotional reactions through vocal and facial expressions. Emotional content is important for accurate diagnosis as well as creating effective physician-patient relationships. Nonverbal communication plays a more supporting role in message comprehension and persuasion. Physicians should use nonverbal cues to focus patient attention, enhance understanding, and aid recall. Nonverbal cues also communicate authority, power, and competence in the medical consultation. Medical uniforms and equipment can lend an air of power and credibility to the physician. Affiliative behaviors also provide a sympathetic context in which physicians can more aggressively seek patient compliance. On the other side of the conversation, patients should not be overawed by the physician's authority, power, and expertise. Patients should exercise some control in the conversation, as achieving a mutually acceptable level of control in the medical consultation is just as important as a mutually acceptable level of affiliation. Physicians need to be aware that some patients expect and concede greater control to physicians, whereas others will retain greater control over their own behavior and treatment. Being sensitive and adaptable to different needs of patients will increase physicians' success. Finally, nonverbal communication may set expectations for patient behavior and treatment success that affect patients' motivations to adhere and their subsequent health.

Recommendations for Effective Nonverbal Communication in Physician-Patient Relationships

Persuasive Function	Recommendations For Physicians	Recommendations For Patients
Displaying authority, power, and credibility	Use authority, power, and credibility wisely to affect change	Exert a moderate amount of conversational control
	Establish moderate amounts of authority, power and credibility through controlling communicative exchanges, wearing medical uniforms, and manipulating the medical environment	
Expressing negative affect	Do not avoid anger and anxiety per se; use them carefully to motivate adherence	Express negative emotions concerning health and treatment
Exercising control	Establish a positive relationship with the patient before attempting to exercise authority and communicating negative affect	
Setting expectations	Be aware that vocal and kinesic cues can affect patient's expectations about how to communicate with the physician	
	Positive expectations for treatment success may function as a placebo	

References

Andersen, J. F. (1979). The relationship between teacher immediacy and teaching effectiveness. In B. Ruben (Ed.), *Communication yearbook 3* (pp. 543–560). New Brunswick, NJ: Transaction Books.

Andersen, J. F., Norton, R. W., & Nussbaum, J. F. (1981). Three investigations exploring relationships between perceived teacher communication behaviors and student learning. *Communication Education, 30,* 377–392.

Baron, R. A., & Bell, P. A. (1976). Physical distance and helping: Some unexpected benefits of "crowding in" on others. *Journal of Applied Social Psychology, 6,* 95–104.

Bensing, J. (1991). Doctor-patient communication and the quality of care. *Social Science and Medicine, 32,* 1301–1310.

Bertakis, K. D., Roter, D., & Putnam, S. M. (1991). The relationship of physician medical interview style to patient satisfaction. *Journal of Family Practice, 32,* 175–181.

Bickman, L. (1971a). Effect of different uniforms on obedience in field situations. *Proceedings of the 79th Annual American Psychological Association Convention, 359–360.*

Bickman, L. (1971b). The effect of social status on the honesty of others. *Journal of Social Psychology, 85,* 87–92.

Bickman, L. (1974a). The social power of a uniform. *Journal of Applied Social Psychology, 4,* 47–61.

Bickman, L. (1974b). Social roles and uniforms. Clothes make the person. *Psychology Today, 7,* 48–51.

Blanck, P. D., Rosenthal, R., & Vannicelli, M. (1986). Talking to and about patients: The therapist's tone of voice. In P. D. Blanck, R. Buck, & R. Rosenthal (Eds.), *Nonverbal communication in the clinical context* (pp. 99–143). University Park: The Pennsylvania State University Press.

Buller, M. K., & Buller, D. B. (1987). Physician communication and patient satisfaction. *Journal of Health and Social Behavior, 11,* 269–290.

Buller, D. B., & Street, R. L., Jr. (1991). The role of communication in patients' evaluations of health care and compliance decisions. *Southern Communication Journal, 56,* 230–237.

Burgoon, J. K., Buller, D. B., & Woodall, W. G. (1989). *Nonverbal communication: The unspoken dialogue.* New York: Harper & Row.

Burgoon, J. K., & Hale, J. L. (1984). The fundamental topic of relational communication. *Communication Monographs, 51,* 193–214.

Coker, D. A., & Burgoon, J. K. (1986). The nature of conversational involvement and nonverbal encoding patterns. *Human Communication Research, 13,* 463–494.

Davis, M. (1968). Variation in patients' compliance with doctors' advice: An empirical analysis of patterns of interaction. *American Journal of Public Health, 58,* 274–288.

DiMatteo, M. R., Friedman, H. S., & Taranta, A. (1979). Sensitivity to bodily nonverbal communication as a factor in practitioner-patient rapport. *Journal of Nonverbal Communication, 4,* 18–26.

DiMatteo, M. R., Prince, L. M., & Hays, R. (1986). Nonverbal communication in the medical context: The physician-patient relationship. In P. D. Blanck, R. Buck, & R. Rosenthal (Eds.), *Nonverbal communication in the clinical context* (pp. 74–98). University Park: The Pennsylvania State University Press.

Duck, S. (1988). *Relating to others*. Chicago: Dorsey Press.

Duker, S. (1974). *Time compressed speech: An anthology and bibliography* (Vol. 3). Metuchen, NJ: Scarecrow Press.

Edinger, J. A., & Patterson, M. L. (1983). Nonverbal involvement and social control. *Psychological Bulletin, 93*, 30–56.

Ekman, P. (1971). Universal and cultural differences in facial expressions of emotion. In J. K. Cole (Ed.), *Nebraska symposium on motivation* (pp. 207–283). Lincoln: University of Nebraska Press.

Ellsworth, P. C., & Langer, E. J. (1976). Staring and approach: An interpretation of the stare as a nonspecific activator. *Journal of Personality and Social Psychology, 33*, 117–122.

Friedman, H. S., (1979). Nonverbal communication between patients and medical practitioners. *Journal of Social Issues, 35*, 82–99.

Friedman, H. S., DiMatteo, M. R., & Taranta, A. (1980). A study of the relationship between individual differences in nonverbal expressiveness and factors of personality and social interaction. *Journal of Research in Personality, 14*, 351–364.

Geiselman, R. E., & Crawley, J. M. (1983). Incidental processing of speaker characteristics: Voice as connotative information. *Journal of Verbal Learning and Verbal Behavior, 22*, 15–23.

Giles, H., & Smith, P. M. (1979). Accommodation theory: Optimal levels of convergence. In H. Giles & R. St. Clair (Eds.), *Language and social psychology* (pp. 45–65). Baltimore: University Park.

Hadjistavropoulos, H. D., Ross, M. A., & von Baeyer, C. L. (1990). Are physicians' ratings of pain affected by patients' physical attractiveness? *Social Science and Medicine, 31*, 69–72.

Hall, J. A., Roter, D. L., & Katz, N. R. (1987). Task versus socioemotional behaviors in physicians. *Medical Care, 25*, 399–412.

Hall, J. A., Roter, D. L., & Katz, N. R. (1988). Meta-analysis of correlates of provider behavior in medical encounters. *Medical Care, 26*, 657–675.

Hall, J. A., Roter, D. L., & Rand, C. S. (1981). Communication of affect between patient and physician. *Journal of Health and Social Behavior, 22*, 18–30.

Harrigan, J. A. (1985). Self-touching as an indicator of underlying affect and language processes. *Social Science and Medicine, 20*, 1161–1168.

Harrigan, J. A., Kues, J. R., & Weber, J. G. (1986). Impressions of hand movements: Self-touching and gestures. *Perceptual and Motor Skills, 63*, 503–516.

Harrigan, J. A., Oxman, T. E., & Rosenthal, R. (1985). Rapport expressed through nonverbal behavior. *Journal of Nonverbal Behavior, 9*, 95–110.

Harrigan, J. A., & Rosenthal, R. (1983). Physicians' head and body positions as determinants of perceived rapport. *Journal of Applied Social Psychology, 13*, 496–509.

Harrigan, J. A., & Rosenthal, R. (1986). Nonverbal aspects of empathy and rapport in physician-patient interaction. In P. D. Blanck, R. Buck, & R. Rosenthal

(Eds.), *Nonverbal communication in the clinical context* (pp. 36–73). University Park: The Pennsylvania State University Press.

Harrigan, J. A., Weber, J. G., & Kues, J. R. (1986). Attributions of self-touching performed in spontaneous and posed modes. *Journal of Social and Clinical Psychology, 4,* 433–446.

Hollandsworth, J. G., Jr., Kazelskis, R., Stevens, J., & Dressel, M. E. (1979). Relative contributions of verbal, articulative, and nonverbal communication to employment decisions in the job interview setting. *Personnel Psychology, 32,* 359–367.

Inui, T. S., & Carter, W. B. (1985). Problems and prospects for health services research on provider-patient communication. *Medical Care, 23,* 521–538.

Johnson, B. S. (1965). The meaning of touch in nursing. *Nursing Outlook, 13,* 59–60.

Kaplan, S. H., Greenfield, S., & Ware, J. E. (1989). Assessing the effects of physician-patient interactions on the outcomes of chronic disease. *Medical Care, 27,* S110–S127.

Kazdin, A. E., & Klock, J. (1973). The effect of nonverbal teacher approval on student attentive behavior. *Journal of Applied Behavior Analysis, 6,* 643–654.

Kenny, D. A. (1979). *Correlation and causality.* New York: Wiley.

Kleinfeld, J. S. (1973). Effects of nonverbally communicated personal warmth on intelligence test performance of Indian and Eskimo adolescents. *Journal of Social Psychology, 91,* 149–150.

Kleinfeld, J. S. (1974). Effects of nonverbal warmth on learning of Eskimo and white children. *Journal of Social Psychology, 92,* 3–9.

Kleinke, C. L. (1977). Compliance to requests made by gazing and touching experimenters in field settings. *Journal of Experimental Social Psychology, 13,* 218–223.

Kleinke, C. L. (1980). Interaction between gaze and legitimacy of request on compliance in a field setting. *Journal of Nonverbal Behavior, 5,* 3–12.

Konecni, V. J., Libuser, L., Morton, H., & Ebbesen, E. B. (1975). Effects of a violation of personal space on escape and helping responses. *Journal of Experimental Social Psychology, 11,* 288–299.

LaBarbera, P., & MacLachlan, J. (1979). Time compressed speech in radio advertising. *Journal of Marketing, 43,* 30–36.

LaCrosse, M. B. (1975). Nonverbal behavior and perceived counselor attractiveness and persuasiveness. *Journal of Counseling Psychology, 22,* 563–566.

Larsen, K. M., & Smith, C. K. (1981). Assessment of nonverbal communication in the patient-physician interview. *The Journal of Family Practice, 12,* 481–488.

McGinley, H., LeFevre, R., & McGinley, P. (1975). The influence of a communicator's body position on opinion change in others. *Journal of Personality and Social Psychology, 31,* 686–690.

McMahan, E. M. (1976). Nonverbal communication as a function of attribution in impression formation. *Communication Monographs, 43,* 287–294.

Mehrabian, A. (1967). Orientation behaviors and nonverbal attitude communication. *Journal of Communication, 17,* 324–332.

Milmoe, S., Rosenthal, R., Blane, H. T., Chafetz, M. E., & Wolf, I. (1967). The doctor's voice: Postdictor of successful referral of alcoholic patients. *Journal of Abnormal Psychology, 72,* 78–84.

Morris, D. (1977). *Man watching: A field guide to human behavior.* New York: Abrams.

Navarre, D. (1982). Posture sharing in dyadic interaction. *American Journal of Dance Therapy, 5,* 28–42.

Noller, P. (1985). Video primacy—a further look. *Journal of Nonverbal Behavior, 9,* 28–47.

Oster, H., & Ekman, P. (1978). Facial behavior in child development. In W. A. Collins (Ed.), *Minnesota symposium on child psychology* (pp. 231–276). Hillsdale, NJ: Lawrence Erlbaum Associates.

Patterson, M. L. (1983). *Nonverbal behavior: A functional perspective.* New York: SpringerVerlag.

Pendleton, D. (1983). Doctor-patient communication: A review. In D. Pendleton & J. Hasler (Eds.), *Doctor-patient communication* (pp. 5–53). London: Academic Press.

Richmond, V. P., Gorham, J. S., & McCroskey, J. C. (1986). The relationships between selected immediacy behavior and cognitive learning. In M. McLaughlin (Ed.), *Communication yearbook 10* (pp. 574–590). Beverly Hills, CA: Sage.

Riseborough, M. G. (1981). Physiographic gestures as decoding facilitators: Three experiments exploring a neglected facet of communication. *Journal of Nonverbal Behavior, 5,* 172–183.

Rogers, W. T. (1978). The contribution of kinesic illustrators toward the comprehension of verbal behavior within utterances. *Human Communication Research, 5,* 54–62.

Roloff, M. E. (1987). Communication and reciprocity within intimate relationships. In M. E. Roloff & G. R. Miller (Eds.), *Interpersonal processes: New directions in communication research* (pp. 11–38). Beverly Hills, CA: Sage.

Roloff, M. E., Janiszewski, C. A., McGrath, M. A., Burns, C. S., & Manrai, L. A. (1988). Acquiring resources from intimates: When obligation substitutes for persuasion. *Human Communication Research, 14,* 364–396.

Rosenthal, R. (1976). *Experimenter effects in behavioral research* (enlarged ed.). New York: Irvington.

Rosenthal, R. (1985). Nonverbal cues in the mediation of interpersonal expectancy effects. In R. L. Street, Jr. & J. N. Cappella (Eds.), *Sequence and pattern in communicative behavior* (pp. 85–102). London: Edward Arnold.

Rosenthal, R., & Jacobson, L. (1968). *Pygmalion in the classroom: Teacher expectation and pupils' intellectual development.* New York: Holt, Rinehart & Winston.

Stiles, W. B. (1989). Evaluating medical interview process components: Null correlations with outcomes may be misleading. *Medical Care, 27,* 212–220.

Street, R. L., Jr. (1982). Evaluation of noncontent speech accommodation. *Language and Communication, 2,* 13–31.

Street, R. L., Jr. (1990). Communication in medical consultations: A review essay. *Quarterly Journal of Speech, 76,* 315–357.

Street, R. L., Jr., Brady, R. M., & Putman, W. B. (1983). The influence of speech rate stereotypes and rate similarity on listeners' evaluations of speakers. *Journal of Language and Social Psychology, 2*, 37–56.

Street, R. L., Jr., & Buller, D. B. (1987). Nonverbal response patterns in physician-patient interactions: A functional analysis. *Journal of Nonverbal Behavior, 11*, 234–253.

Street, R. L., Jr., & Buller, D. B. (1988). Patients' characteristics affecting physician-patient nonverbal communication. *Human Communication Research, 15*, 60–90.

Street, R. L., Jr., & Wiemann, J. (1987). Patients' satisfaction with physicians' interpersonal involvement, expressiveness, and dominance. *Communication Yearbook, 10*, 591–612.

Waitzkin, H. (1990). On studying the discourse of medical encounters: A critique of quantitative and qualitative methods and a proposal for reasonable compromise. *Medical Care, 28*, 473–487.

West, C. (1984). *Routine complications: Troubles with the talk between doctors and patients*. Bloomington: University of Indiana Press.

Woodall, W. G., & Folger, J. P. (1981). Encoding specificity and nonverbal cue context: An expansion of episodic memory research. *Communication Monographs, 48*, 39–53.

Woodall, W. G., & Folger, J. P. (1985). Nonverbal cue context and episodic memory: On the availability and endurance of nonverbal behaviors as retrieval cues. *Communication Monographs, 52*, 319–333.

Goleman explains how to tell when someone is lying to you. The chapter describes the most common clues to lying and then describes the best lie detectors. Finally, Goleman discusses sex differences in lie detection.

41

Can You Tell When Someone Is Lying to You?

Daniel Goleman

"I liked her . . . because of the way she immediately put everyone at their rest," a high-pitched, almost whiny male voice says on the tape I'm listening to. His words are pressured, slurred. He pauses for an instant, then continues, "*Umm* . . . there was little tension between people . . . between everybody in the house. *Uh* . . . she, *um*, she has a lot of good . . ."

I don't trust this guy; I don't believe him. He's lying about this woman. I'm sure of it. Something in the way he insists that she put people at their ease, that there was no tension. Why bring it up, then? Then there's the way he pauses before each rush of words. He's tense. I can hear it in his voice. He's *pretending* to like her.

I check the words "pretending to like" on my scoring sheet just as another man's voice—this one speaking in neutral tones—announces "Number 20" in a series of statements about people. Then, after a few seconds' pause, the previous voice speaks again, now describing someone else:

"In many ways she remains, she remains very much like, you know, very much like a child, and *uh* . . . in a nice way, though, not *um* . . . and yet in some way somehow has matured emotionally so that you. . . ."

He's more relaxed this time. His voice is pitched lower, and the pace of his words is slower. I think he's telling the truth this time, I mark "Likes."

"Number 21," the announcer says.

I am taking a tape-recorded test of the ability to detect lies, in which people describe someone they know, but in some instances purposely misrepresent their feelings about that person. In the last five years, a group of researchers under the tutelage of social psychologist Robert Rosenthal at Harvard University has given hundreds of subjects tests of this sort in an effort to determine how people maneuver on the morass of distortions and lies that can be glimpsed beneath the surface of our social lives.

The Rosenthal group's professional interest in lying stems less from concern about moral issues than from a longstanding fascination with nonverbal messages and the otherwise hidden realities that they convey. Unlike philosophers and theologians, the researchers are not particularly interested in making ethical distinctions, in sorting out great from small lies. They are more interested in studying the little lies and insincerities that are often necessary to smooth interactions in our everyday lives.

Rosenthal and his colleagues have looked long and without flinching at what makes people good liars and good lie detectors. More precisely, their research has suggested answers to a number of intriguing questions that nobody has investigated very thoroughly in the past: How do children learn to tell and detect lies? Are there any reliable signs that a person is lying? What kinds of people are best at detecting lies? Are there sex differences in the ability to spot lies? Is skill in lie detection a social advantage or a liability? One further question has been largely ignored by researchers: What are the ethics of studying the process of deception?

Much of the research on these issues has been done by two Rosenthal protégés: Miron Zuckerman and Bella DePaulo. Both had participated in Rosenthal's earlier studies of empathy, which they investigated chiefly by using the so-called PONS test (Profile of Nonverbal Sensitivity). That test assesses how well a person can interpret nonverbal messages. It consists of a series of videotapes of a young woman expressing feelings ranging from motherly love to hatred. The direct message is muffled, so the viewers have to detect it from nonverbal cues.

The PONS gets at empathy because the young woman tries to portray the emotion as best she can. From this test it was fairly easy for the Rosenthal group to derive methods of studying sensitivity to attempted deception.

The search for clues to lies is ancient. A papyrus dating back to 900 B.C. bears this description of a liar: "He does not answer questions, or gives evasive answers; he speaks nonsense, rubs the great toe along the ground, and shivers; he rubs the roots of the hair with his fingers."

Contemporary research shows that people have not changed much in their perception of liars and lying. Certain kinds of behavior, much like that described almost 3,000 years ago, regularly make human beings suspect that others are lying to them. Among the responses often taken to be signs of dishonesty are smiling, stammering, fidgeting, vagueness, long pauses in speaking, and answers that seem too quick, too short, too long, or too elaborate. According to DePaulo and her colleagues, "Any deviation from a humdrum response, whether in the direction of overplay or an underplay, can serve to signal fraudulence."

Unfortunately, the signal is very likely to be misleading. When Robert Krauss, a social psychologist at Columbia University, and his coresearchers compared the signs that observers used to detect lies with the behavior that actually accompanied lies, they found that most of the presumed clues did not correlate with deception. In a study by Robert Kraut at Cornell, subjects interpreted the same behavior as a sign of truth or falsehood, depending on how suspicious the observer was to begin with. If a subject was primed to expect a lie, he would take a long pause as confirmation that the speaker was lying. An observer who was led to trust the speaker took the identical hesitation as evidence of truth.

It is no wonder, therefore, that when DePaulo, Zuckerman, and Rosenthal reviewed nearly 50 studies of people as lie detectors, they concluded that detecting a lie is not as easy as we might think. As a matter of fact, there are no foolproof signs of lying.

CLUES TO LYING

But some signs are at least more reliable than others. Research shows that voice pitch is a more dependable indicator than facial expression—thus confirming the wisdom of the artist who depicted justice as wearing a blindfold.

Oddly enough, however, not many people seem to recognize that the ears are better than the eyes at distinguishing truth from falsehood. When Krauss asked subjects to name the signs they relied on to uncover lies, not one person mentioned the human voice. DePaulo's subjects revealed a similar ignorance. She asked 251 college students, "If you wanted to know whether someone was lying to you, do you think you could tell better by telephone or in person, or could you tell about as well either way?" Of the

251, the vast majority—220—said that a face-to-face meeting would be best. Only seven made the correct choice, the telephone. The conclusion is that if you're going to tell a lie, you're better off face-to-face. If you suspect one, you'll do better over the telephone. (See "Getting the Phone's Number," *Psychology Today*, April 1982).

In all, the results of more than 20 studies point to the value of words—particularly the tone in which they are spoken—as clues to lie detection. On the basis of these findings, DePaulo speculated that "people might be helped in their lie-detection attempt by a little hint," the hint being, "Pay particular attention to the tone of voice." To test her speculation, she and her colleagues asked college students to watch a videotape of people describing acquaintances and to figure out which ones were lying about liking or disliking them.

A quarter of the students were told to pay particular attention to what the speakers said, another quarter to how they said it, and another to how the speakers looked. The rest were left to their own devices. Those told to note with special care how the words were said did the best at detecting lies.

The result may surprise some readers, since it is reasonable to presume that people can readily control their tone of voice and use it to mislead. The available evidence though, suggests otherwise. For one thing, because of the acoustics of the skull, the voice we hear as we speak does not sound the same to us as to our listeners. This may explain the almost universal reaction of dismay when people first hear their recorded voices. On tape, people hear inflections and tonal qualities that leak their feelings but are unnoticed by them as they speak. As a matter of fact, clinicians have long recognized the leaky nature of tone of voice, and often rely on it for clues to a patient's true feelings.

None of this means that nonverbal cues are useless for unmasking liars; quite the contrary. It is a commonplace that the body yields clues to a person's true feelings. Deception research shows that different kinds of body language provide better clues to deception than others. Constructing a speculative hierarchy of "leaky channels," the Rosenthal group put discrepancies between two channels of communication (a smiling face with an angry voice, perhaps) at the top of the list as the leakiest. Next came fleeting body movements or facial expressions, tone of voice, the body in general, and lastly, the face. Initially, the ordering of the leakage hierarchy was an educated guess, since no one had ever compared more than two of the channels for leakage at any one time. Later, the researchers demonstrated that their speculations were consistent with their results.

A discrepancy, the Rosenthal group proposed, is the leakiest of channels because it involves two modes of communication that are hard to control simultaneously. A liar might be very careful in how he phrased his lie, might even remember, say, to smile in its support, but might not be skillful enough to control the anger in his voice. That discrepancy could tip off an alert observer. Discrepancies, of course, are typical of irony, sarcasm, and humor—but those are intended. Discrepancies during the telling of a lie are unintentional leaks.

A bit less revealing, or leaky, are micro-lapses that take the form of brief, unintended changes, such as a muted hand movement or a fleeting smile.

It was face expert Paul Ekman (see "The 7,000 Faces of Dr. Ekman, *Psychology Today*, February 1981) and his colleague Wallace Friesen who first suggested why the face should be the least leaky nonverbal channel—and thus the best liar. A person's ability to deceive, they proposed, varies with the "sending capacity" of the channel that is used. The greater that channel's sending capacity—that is, the more messages it can send, the more quickly it can send them, and the more visible they are—then the more deceptive the channel can be. The face, Ekman and Friesen argue, has maximal sending capacity. Therefore, it is especially well equipped to tell lies, and provides the least reliable cues for someone trying to detect lies. By contrast, the body is less controllable, slower, and less obvious. Its reduced sending capacity makes lying with the body difficult, but it also makes the body a leaky channel: Gestures and other body movements (for example, fidgeting or other signs of nervousness) often betray deceit.

On the whole, unpremeditated lies probably are more easily detected than planned lies, DePaulo suggests, because of the advantage rehearsal gives. Planning a lie ahead of time makes the liar less likely to have to pause for words and more free to control tone of voice and other potential leaks. Suspicions may make a person more easily misled—particularly if he relies on looking the liar in the eye and focuses on the liar's demeanor. Such overattentiveness to the face (which leaks less) could interfere with noting leaky cues, such as tone of voice.

GOOD LIE DETECTORS

Dozens of studies suggest that most people just aren't very good at detecting deception. Another conclusion that emerges from this research is that the ability to recognize a lie does not necessarily carry with it the ability to say what the liar's true feelings may be.

Yet another basic fact is that some people are skilled at identifying certain kinds of deception but are easily fooled by other kinds. The Rosenthal group distinguishes between "sugar-coated" lies, in which positive feelings mask negative ones, and "vinegar-coated" lies, in which feigned negative feelings hide true positive ones. Their research method is by now familiar. They had volunteers tell sugar-coated lies by describing people they disliked as though they like them; vinegar-coated lies were descriptions of people whom the volunteers liked, rendered as though they disliked them. The volunteers watched videotapes of one another and tried to guess whether or not a given description was a lie. Those who proved to be clever at detecting sugar-coated lies were not particularly good at recognizing vinegar-coated ones, and vice versa.

One characteristic often found in good lie detectors has been labeled "social participation," a more or less self-explanatory term referring to people who are outgoing, friendly, and active in many social groups. In general, these people are "interaction specialists"—good communicators who seem to follow the credo that interactions go most smoothly when people are straightforward in what they say and do. Perhaps for that very reason, they are particularly sensitive to lies. Not surprisingly, such people often tend to be poor liars themselves.

Another characteristic of good lie detectors is social anxiety, as measured by a questionnaire devised by David Lykken at the University of Minnesota that requires respondents to choose between pairs of unpleasant alternatives. In each pair, one choice is social, involving other people, and one is not. An example: hearing someone comment on how strangely you are dressed, versus cleaning out a cesspool. The socially anxious more often choose to endure the nonsocial pain. The uneasiness and sensitivity these people experience in social situations seems to alert them to signs that they are being lied to. They are good at sending their own true feelings, but poor at telling lies, possibly because of timidity at the prospect of being caught in a lie.

One much-studied trait that might well seem related to lie detection turns out not to be: Machiavellianism. People high in this trait (as measured on a scale designed by Richard Christie of Columbia University) are not particularly adept at detecting other people's falsehoods. However, their belief that others are manipulatable, and their willingness to take advantage of this vulnerability, help make Machiavellians devious enough to lie with great success and little regret.

ARE WOMEN TOO POLITE?

When the Rosenthal group began to study deception, they were in for a surprise. Earlier research had shown overwhelmingly that women are far superior to men at reading nonverbal messages. When asked to say what feeling a tone of voice or a gesture reflected, women were right much more often than men were. But Rosenthal and his colleagues discovered that women's empathy seemed to fail them when they were asked to decode leaks. The more leaky a tone of voice, the more discrepant a message; the more furtive a look, the less well women did in interpreting it. Men showed just the opposite pattern: As communications became more leaky and deception more blatant, the men's accuracy in detecting lies improved relative to the women's. The sex difference showed up when Rosenthal and DePaulo studied 242 high-school and college students. The method the researchers used was to administer a whole battery of tests designed to assess the leakage hierarchy, the rank-ordering of clues to deception described above. The pattern was clear. Women were far better than men at reading the face. But their advantage decreased steadily as they confronted more leaky channels, including hand gestures and the tone of voice.

"Women," say Rosenthal and DePaulo, "may be more polite than men in their decoding of nonverbal cues." In the researchers' view, noticing leaks is a form of "eavesdropping," and paying attention to a person's slips and leaks is therefore tantamount to rudeness.

To Rosenthal and DePaulo, it seemed possible that women might be penalized more than men for being too perceptive at reading leaks, and so might learn to ignore them. The first step the researchers took to test this idea was to devise a study that would show whether either sex pays a social penalty for detecting deception.

At the high school where the researchers had given the leakage hierarchy test, they asked teachers to rate the students who had taken it on popularity with their own and with the opposite sex, and on their degree of "social understanding." When the ratings were compared with leakage detection, there was a strong (though not statistically significant) trend for social effectiveness to go along with insensitivity to the leakier channels. "There are indications," DePaulo and Rosenthal conclude, "that eavesdropping skill may not be as socially beneficial as skill decoding less 'leaky' channels." That is, social life may run more smoothly for those who politely ignore other people's obvious leaks. Rosenthal and DePaulo assume that this is especially true for women, in keeping with the "standards of politeness and social smoothing-over" that are part of the traditional woman's role.

Oddly, the high-school students themselves did not seem to find eavesdropping damaging to their social lives. When asked to rate the quality of their relations with both sexes, the students' evaluations did not correlate at all with sensitivity to leaks. Indeed, there was a tendency for those good at detecting leaks to be more pleased with their social life. "For our younger students," Rosenthal and DePaulo observe, "skill at eavesdropping on increasingly leaky channels was associated with increasingly better social relationships, as they perceived these relationships."

But the high-school students may have been deluding themselves. When the same survey was done with college students, the pattern was reversed: Skill at eavesdropping on leaks was associated with increasingly poor social relationships, as the students perceived them. "Perhaps," Rosenthal and DePaulo comment, "those students have learned, as have the younger students' teachers, that it may not be beneficial to social relationships to be an effective eavesdropper on leaked nonverbal cues." With maturity, it would seem, comes discretion.

Rosenthal and DePaulo soon found some support for their idea that society rewards women more than men for this kind of discretion. They had already observed that their female subjects gave more credence to the face, the least leaky channel, than male subjects did. When the researchers compared the women's ratings of their social life with the degree to which they gave primacy to the face, a telling piece of evidence emerged. The more attention women paid to the face, the better they considered their relationships, particularly with men. Rosenthal and DePaulo think it may be that "women are reinforced with better opposite-sex relationships when they attend to the better-controlled channels and learn to avoid eavesdropping on the more poorly controlled, more leaky channels."

While the facts are clear, there are differences in what they seem to say about women's social motives. One reading of women's greater "politeness" could be that it signifies a submissive role vis-à-vis men. This interpretation irks some researchers on nonverbal messages. One of these is Professor Judith Hall, who was once a graduate student of Rosenthal's and collaborator on much of his empathy research.

"The theory," says Hall, "is that the woman confronts the leaky cues and says to herself, maybe unconsciously, 'Oh my God, I'm in deep trouble if I respond to this accurately.' Whereas it may have nothing to do with their response to leakiness per se, or with being accommodating. It's just that this skill has little importance in social intelligence, it's not that crucial in daily life. Social life works by ignoring little social lies. Women seem wiser to this than men. It seems to me that the profile of women as a group of interpreters of social cues is one of 'savvyness'—being good at what's useful and not so good at something that isn't so useful."

In an article in the *Annals of the New York Academy of Sciences*, DePaulo makes a similar point with the question, "Are we better off seeing right through a person's true underlying feelings or might we sometimes do better not to see what another person does not want us to know?" In the case of deception that might do us harm, she notes, the ability to detect lies is obviously an asset. And in professions such as psychiatry or police work, such sensitivity is particularly useful. In everyday life, this is not necessarily so.

"It seems," writes DePaulo, "that what children are learning as they grow older, probably through socialization, is politely to read what other people want them to read, and not what they really felt. The polite mode of decoding is probably an easier way of dealing with interpersonal information than a more probing and skeptical style would be . . . People who begin to doubt external appearances are first of all going to experience more uncertainty; they may also feel guilt about their suspiciousness and lack of trust; and finally they might find out something about the other person's feelings toward them that they might be much happier not to know. The person who knows when deception is occurring and who knows what other people are feeling has a more accurate grasp of what the interpersonal world is really like. But in some ways, under some circumstances, maybe being good at understanding social and interpersonal cues is just no good at all."

What DePaulo writes echoes what Erving Goffman pointed out years ago: Most situations call for overlooking social lies; it is tactless and ungraceful to call our family, friends, and associates on them. Or as Judith Hall paraphrases Goffman, "You can be too smart socially. Smooth interaction requires that people not notice or comment on every little lapse in decorum, or every little bit of insincerity. Social life works by ignoring little social lies."

This study compared the behavior of intimates, friends, and strangers during deceptive and truthful conversations. Buller and Aune found that strangers showed more arousal and negative affect than friends or intimates. Friends and intimates, in contrast, seemed to monitor their behavior more carefully during deception by controlling arousal and negative affect. This study shows that friends and intimates sometimes strategically try to control their behavior when they are deceiving, which can make it difficult to detect deception.

42

Nonverbal Cues to Deception among Intimates, Friends, and Strangers

David B. Buller
R. Kelly Aune

Research into behavioral cues to deception has linked several types of behavior with deceptive intent. Recent meta-analyses and summaries provide some of the best evidence on the cues related to deception (DePaulo, Stone, and Lassiter, 1985) (Kraut, 1980; Zuckerman, DePaulo, & Rosenthal, 1981; Zuckerman & Driver, 1985). Zuckerman and Driver report that 58% of the behaviors examined in two or more of the studies they meta-analyzed reliably distinguished truthtellers from liars. Further,

Adapted from Buller & Aune (1987), Nonverbal cues to deception among intimates, friends, and strangers, *Journal of Nonverbal Behavior* 11(4), 269–276, 285–290. Copyright © 1987 by Human Sciences Press.

a number of additional experiments not included in the meta-analyses provided evidence of recurrent patterns in deceivers' behavior.

Buller and Burgoon (1994) argue that the behaviors which distinguish truthtellers from liars can be characterized as either strategic or nonstrategic. According to Buller and Burgoon, strategic nonverbal behaviors are encoded to reduce the deceiver's responsibility for the deceptive statement and to avoid the negative consequences of detection. Buller and Burgoon identify four classes of strategic nonverbal behaviors: (a)uncertainty and vagueness, (b) nonimmediacy, reticence, and withdrawal, (c) disassociation, and (d) image-protecting behavior.

In contrast, some nonverbal behaviors inadvertently leak the deceiver's deceptive intent. Buller and Burgoon's notion of nonstrategic leakage behaviors incorporates a substantial portion of Ekman and Friesen's (1969) leakage hypothesis and Zuckerman et al.'s (1981) four-factor theory of deception behavior. Nonstrategic cues leak information about arousal and nervousness and negative emotional reactions which often occur when the communicator deceives. Another cognitive change which often results in nonstrategic deception cues is an increased cognitive effort directed at controlling the strategic behaviors and masking the cues of anxiety and negative affect. As Zuckerman et al. argue, this increased effort can produce mixed or inconsistent messages which create an incompetent presentation.

From Buller and Burgoon's (1994) review, nonverbal cues appear to play the most significant role in two classes of strategic behavior—nonimmediacy, reticence, and withdrawal behaviors and image-protecting behaviors—and in two classes of nonstrategic leakage—arousal and nervousness cues and negative affect cues. In contrast, uncertainty and vagueness, disassociation, and incompetent communication performances are comprised largely of verbal cues and therefore were not investigated in this experiment.

NONIMMEDIACY, RETICENCE, AND WITHDRAWAL

Nonverbally, deceivers appear to indicate nonimmediacy, reticence, and withdrawal through the use of shorter replies, more pauses, and longer response latencies (Baskett & Freedle, 1974; deTurck & Miller, 1985; Feldman, Devin-Sheehan, & Allen, 1978; Knapp, Hart, & Dennis, 1974; Krauss, Geller, & Olson, 1976; Kraut, 1978; Mehrabian, 1971; Motley, 1974). Similarly, Mehrabian (1972) and Knapp et al. (1974) report that liars decrease the frequency and duration of glances, decrease forward body lean, and increase distance. The overriding result of these studies is that deceivers become more withdrawn and inaccessible to their conversational partners, perhaps in an effort to hinder surveillance and probing by a suspicious partner. Zuckerman, DeFrank, Hall, Larrance, and Rosenthal (1979) found that deceptive answers do in fact create impressions of less personal involvement. In the verbal domain, Kuiken (1981) reported that deceivers use more nonimmediate language when they fabricate a reply, and the Zuckerman and Driver (1985) meta-analysis supports the use of verbal nonimmediacy by liars.

This conclusion, however, has not always been supported. Studies have showed that some liars increased, some decreased, and some alternated between increasing and decreasing their reaction time (English, 1926; Marston, 1920) and one study (Matarazzo, Wiens, Jackson, & Manaugh, 1970) found the topic influenced whether liars gave shorter or longer answers and had shorter or longer response latencies. Further, some experiments failed to find gaze differences between liars and truthtellers (Matarazzo et al., 1970; McClintock & Hunt, 1975) or found increased eye contact from liars (Riggio & Friedman, 1983). DePaulo et al. (1985a) have claimed that liars do not avert their eyes any more than truthtellers do. However, the weight of the findings appears to support the following hypothesis:

H1: Deceivers will display more nonverbal behaviors indicative of nonimmediacy, reticence, and withdrawal than truthtellers.

IMAGE-PROTECTION

The notion of image-protecting behavior was first suggested by DePaulo et al. (1985a). These authors speculate that a major objective of deceivers is to protect their image. Deceivers do so by displaying innocuous conversational behaviors such as nodding, smiling, and refraining from interruptions. Presumably, such behaviors deflect attention away from the deceiver by maintaining a positive demeanor. In fact, evidence of a more pleasant demeanor by deceivers is mixed. A few experiments have found that liars do encode more smiling, nodding, and pleasant faces, particularly if they are not anxious (e.g., Ekman, Friesen & Scherer, 1976; Mehrabian, 1971, 1972); however, more studies find the opposite pattern or no differences in these behaviors (e.g., Bennett, 1978; Ekman & Friesen, 1974; Feldman et al., 1978; Hocking & Leathers, 1980; Kraut, 1978; Mehrabian, 1972; Zuckerman et al., 1981). Finally, the meta-analyses generally conclude that smiling decreases when a communicator deceives. While these results do not make it clear what deceivers do to protect their image, it is an appealing hypothesis that deserves further investigation:

H2: Deceivers will display more nonverbal behaviors designed to protect their image (i.e., project a positive demeanor) than truthtellers.

AROUSAL AND NERVOUSNESS

That deception induces arousal is one of the more consistently cited propositions in the deception literature. It is a major component in Ekman and Friesen's (1969) leakage hypothesis and Zuckerman et al.'s (1981) four-factor theory about behaviors emitted during deception. These researchers propose that arousal is "leaked" by the actions of deceivers. This leakage, however, is moderated by the extent to which actors can monitor and exercise control over particular communication channels, resulting in a leakage hierarchy among the channels of nonverbal communication. Deceivers are least likely to display arousal cues in the face and most likely to display them in the body and voice (DePaulo et al., 1985; DePaulo, Zuckerman, & Rosenthal, 1980; Ekman & Friesen, 1969, 1974; Zuckerman & Driver, 1985).

The research on arousal-linked deception cues generally supports the leakage hierarchy. The meta-analyses, as well as experiments not included in them (Berrien & Huntington, 1943; Clark, 1975; Ekman et al., 1976; Ekman, Friesen, O'Sullivan & Scherer, 1980; Hocking & Leathers, 1980; Knapp et al., 1974; McClintock & Hunt, 1975; Mehrabian, 1971; O'Hair, Cody, & McLaughlin, 1981; Riggio & Friedman, 1983; Streeter, Krauss, Geller, Olson, & Apple, 1977), have found that liars engage in more blinking, pupil dilation or instability, self- and object-manipulations, higher pitch, vocal nervousness, more speech errors and hesitations, more word repetitions, and less gesturing. Research has been mixed on whether liars engage in more or less postural shifting; random leg, foot, and head movement; gestural activity; and other bodily indicators of nervousness (cf. Ekman & Friesen, 1974; Ekman et al., 1976; Knapp et al., 1974; Hocking & Leathers, 1980; Mehrabian, 1972). It may be that liars attempt to suppress bodily activity to mask their anxiety. Alternatively, the lesser gestural animation and bodily movement together may be indicative of less involvement and commitment to what one is saying. Either way, the net result is often stiff, restrained trunk and limb positions indicative of tension.

H3: Deceivers will display more nonverbal behaviors indicative of arousal and nervousness than truthtellers.

NEGATIVE AFFECT

Ekman and Friesen (1969) and Zuckerman et al. (1981) also believe that deception is an unpleasant experience for most communicators. Consequently, one of the clues to deception that may be leaked is negative affect. As already noted, some experiments report that deceivers smile less and display fewer positive head nods. Thus, deceivers may be revealing a state of negative affect by failing to give positive feedback to their conversational partners. The reduction in gaze reported in some studies (e.g., Knapp et al., 1974) may be a further indication of liars experiencing unpleasant emotional states, which they attempt to mask by closing off the visual channel. In sum, while only a few studies have focused directly on negative affect, the data tend to support such displays as one by-product of deception:

> H4: Deceivers will display more nonverbal behaviors indicative of negative affect than truthtellers.

It is apparent from the foregoing discussion that some nonverbal cues, particularly smiling and head nodding, can serve multiple functions in a deceptive conversation. For instance, smiling and head nodding may decrease when deceivers experience negative affect; however, smiling and head nodding may increase as deceivers attempt to present a positive image. Also, smiling may function as an immediacy cue, although Buller and Burgoon (1994) did not include it in their nonimmediacy classification. As an immediacy cue, smiling may decrease during deception. The multifunctional nature of some of the nonverbal cues makes predictions about specific cues difficult. Therefore, general hypotheses about the display of nonimmediacy, image-protecting, arousal, and negative affect cues were formulated in this study.

RELATIONSHIP TYPE

Although there appears to be some consensus in this research, several important issues remain unexplored that could modify the conclusions on the nonverbal cues to deception. One issue is whether the cues identified in previous research—research which has examined almost exclusively deception among strangers—are generalizable to deceiving relational partners such as friends and intimates. Three factors may alter the nature of deception when communicators deceive friends and intimates: (1) deceivers' belief that relational partners can detect deceit better than strangers due to their greater familiarity with the communicators (Buller,

1987; McCornack & Parks, 1985), (2) deceivers' increased concern about the negative consequences if deceit is detected by the relational partners (Buller, 1987; Ekman, 1985), and (3) deceivers' prior experience deceiving the relational partners. Therefore, this study also compares the deceptive behavior of strangers, friends, and intimate partners.

Method and Results Summary

Method. Students were recruited from undergraduate courses and asked to bring a friend and an intimate partner with them to a research laboratory where they were joined by a stranger. Student participants were then asked to conduct three interviews—one with their friend, one with their intimate partner, and one with the stranger. Thus, the friends, intimate partners, and strangers were the "interviewees." The order of these interviews were varied so that some participants interviewed the stranger first, others interviewed the intimate partner first, and still others interviewed the friend first. A total of 130 interviews were videotaped. Prior to each interview, some of the interviewees were told to lie in response to the questions, whereas others were told to be completely truthful. Later, undergraduate students were trained to code the nonverbal behaviors that the interviewers and interviewees displayed during the interactions.

Results. Results from statistical analyses produced the following results. As predicted by Hypothesis 1, strangers signalled more nonimmediacy when deceiving by encoding fewer forward leans. Deceiving friends and intimates, however, became more immediate as the interview progressed by increasing gaze. There was no support for Hypothesis 2: Deceivers did not engage in more image-protecting behavior than truthtellers. In contrast to Hypothesis 3, results showed that arousal cues were less apparent in deceivers than in truthtellers. The only nonverbal behavior that showed more arousal for deceivers was chair twisting. Furthermore, these results imply that deceivers monitored and controlled nonverbal arousal cues so that they would look more credible. As the interviews progressed, deceivers showed more evidence of behavior control. The results associated with Hypothesis 4 showed that strangers were less vocally pleasant when deceiving than when telling the truth. However, friends and intimate partners did not express less vocal pleasantness when deceiving than when truthtelling.

DISCUSSION

The findings supported the hypothesized increase in nonimmediacy and negative affect cues during deception. However, the predicted increase in arousal cues was only weakly supported and deceivers did not engage in image-protecting behaviors. Deceivers communicated nonimmediacy through a lack of forward lean and increased gaze avoidance. The possibility also exists that some deceivers exhibited nonimmediacy by gazing at the target only when the target was not gazing at them. This behavior may have been an attempt to monitor the targets' responses to the deceptive source without engaging in eye contact. Conversely, one-sided gazing could be unsuccessful attempts by deceivers to make eye contact and increase immediacy with the target.

In this experiment, negative affect was leaked by deceptive strangers via their vocal cues, rather than via the facial cues assessed by the general pleasantness measure. Not only does this result support the proposition that deceivers experience negative affect during deception, it also conforms with predictions made from the leakage hierarchy. Namely, the voice has a lower sending capacity than the face and therefore is more likely to leak negative affect (Buller & Burgoon, 1994; DePaulo et al., 1985a; Ekman & Friesen, 1969; Zuckerman et al., 1981; Zuckerman & Driver, 1985).

The hypothesized increase in arousal cues due to deception was only evident in the frequency of chair twisting by all sources. Deception did increase the number of brief head and face adaptors by strangers and vocal activity by intimates; however, the more dominant trend was a general decrease in arousal cues by deceivers, resulting in a more rigid, inhibited nonverbal display. Deceivers exhibited fewer adaptors, were less animated, and encoded less vocal activity.

The results did not support the prediction that deceivers would strategically encode a positive demeanor. Deceivers did not increase their rate of head nodding, head shaking, and general pleasantness. It may be premature to dismiss the appealing notion that deceivers attempt to project a positive image to their targets, given the paucity of research on this dimension. Further, in this study friends were slightly more positive vocally, perhaps indicating that deceivers create a positive image via positive vocal cues as well as positive facial cues.

More important than the foregoing effects of deception was the variation in nonverbal deception cues across relationship type and time. All of the main effects of deception on the nonverbal cues were overridden by interactions with relational history. Reviewing these interactions, it appears that strangers displayed more nonverbal cues to deception than either friends or intimates. Specifically, strangers were most nonimmediate, displayed more arousal cues in the body (chair twisting, face and head adaptors, and general animation), and expressed greater negative affect vocally when deceiving. In contrast, friends and intimates were more immediate, indicated less arousal (only displaying chair twisting and vocal activity), and did not leak negative affect when deceiving.

Earlier, three factors were identified that might alter the deception cues emitted by strangers, friends, and intimates: (1) belief that intimates and friends are better able to detect deceit, (2) increased concern for negative consequences of detection by friends and intimates, and (3) prior experience deceiving friends and intimates. All three of these factors suggested that friends and intimates might attempt to monitor and control their nonverbal presentation more than strangers, although the concern for negative consequences might produce a curvilinear trend with friends being most controlled.

In this study relational partners did attempt to monitor and control their arousal and negative affect cues more than strangers. There are, however, two qualifications to this conclusion. First, strangers seemed to monitor and control some of their arousal cues, but they were not as successful as relational partners in masking as many arousal cues. Second, friends and intimates were not able to mask successfully all deception cues. Chair twisting was not controlled well by friends or intimates. Intimates did reduce their frequency of chair twisting late in the deceptive conversations, but they leaked arousal by displaying greater vocal activity throughout the conversations. This last finding may indicate that a compensation effect occurs which deceivers attempt to mask deception cues. That is, when a deceiver controls one set of cues, arousal and negative affect are leaked by other cues.

In conclusion, the experiment supported the prediction that deceivers display nonverbal behaviors signalling nonimmediacy, negative affect, and arousal; however, the type of relationship made a difference. Friends and intimates may monitor and control deception cues more than strangers. This study has added additional complexity to the deception picture. The data challenge deception researchers to move beyond studies which examine merely strangers and to investigate both strategic and nonstrategic deception behaviors.

References

Baskett, G., & Greedle, R. O. (1974). Aspects of language pragmatics and the social perception of lying. *Journal of Psycholinguistic Research, 3*, 112–131.

Bennett, R. (1978, April). Micromoments, *Human Behavior*, 34–35.

Berrien, F. K., & Huntington, G. H. (1943). An exploratory study of pupillary responses during deception. *Journal of Experimental Psychology, 32*, 4443–4449.

Buller, D. B. (1987). *Deception among intimates, friends, and strangers: Attributional biases due to relationship development*. Paper presented to the annual meeting of the Speech Communication Association, Boston.

Buller, D. B., & Burgoon, J. K. (1994). Deception: Strategic and nonstrategic communication. In J. A. Daly and J. M. Wiemann (Eds.), *Strategic interpersonal communication* (pp. 191–223). Hillsdale, NJ: Erlbaum.

Clark, W. R. (1975). *A comparison of pupillary response, heart rate, and GSR during deception*. Paper presented at the annual meeting of the Midwestern Psychological Association, Chicago.

DePaulo, B. M., Stone, J. I., & Lassiter, G. D. (1985) Deceiving and detecting deceit. In B. R. Schlenker (Ed.), *The self and social life* (pp. 323–370). New York: McGraw-Hill.

DePaulo, B. M., Zuckerman, M., & Rosenthal, R. (1980). Detecting deception: Modality effects. In L. Wheeler (Ed.), *Review of personality and social psychology* (pp. 125–162). Beverly Hills, CA: Sage.

deTurck, M. A., & Miller, G. R. (1985). Deception and arousal: Isolating the behavioral correlates of deception. *Human Communication Research, 12*, 181–202.

Ekman, P. (1985). *Telling lies: Clues to deceit in the marketplace, politics, and marriage*. New York: Norton.

Ekman, P., & Friesen, W. V. (1969). Nonverbal leakage and clues to deception. *Psychiatry, 32*, 88–105.

Ekman, P., & Friesen, W. V. (1974). Detecting deception from the body or face. *Journal of Personality and Social Psychology, 29*, 288–298.

Ekman, P., Friesen, W. V., O'Sullivan, M., & Scherer, K. (1980). Relative importance of face, body and speech in judgments of personality and affect. *Journal of Personality and Social Psychology, 38*, 270–277.

Ekman, P., Friesen, W. V., & Scherer, K. (1976). Body movement and voice pitch in deceptive interaction. *Semiotica, 16*, 23–27.

English, H. B. (1926). Reaction-time symptoms of deception. *American Journal of Psychology, 37*, 428–429.

Feldman, R. S., Devin-Sheehan, L., & Allen, V. L. (1978). Nonverbal cues as indicators of verbal dissembling. *American Educational Research Journal, 15*, 217–231.

Hocking, J. E., & Leathers, D. G. (1980). Nonverbal indicators of deception: A new theoretical perspective. *Communication Monographs, 47*, 119–131.

Knapp, M. L., Hart, R. P., & Dennis, H. S. (1974). An exploration of deception as a communication construct. *Human Communication Research, 1*, 15–29.

Krauss, R. M., Geller, V., & Olson, C. (1976). *Modalities and cues in the detection of deception*. Paper presented at the annual meeting of the American Psychological Association, Washington, DC.

Kraut, R. (1978). Verbal and nonverbal cues in the perception of lying. *Journal of Personality and Social Psychology, 36*, 380–391.

Kraut, R. (1980). Humans as lie detectors: Some second thoughts. *Journal of Communication, 30*, 209–216.

Marston, W. M. (1920). Reaction-time symptoms of deception. *Journal of Experimental Psychology, 3*, 72–87.

Matarazzo, J. D., Wiens, A. N., Jackson, R. H., & Manaugh, T. S. (1970). Interviewee speech behavior under conditions of endogenously-present and exogenously-induced motivational states. *Journal of Clinical Psychology, 26*, 141–148.

McClintock, C. C., & Hunt, R. G. (1975). Nonverbal indicators of affect and deception in an interview setting. *Journal of Applied Social Psychology, 5*, 54–67.

McCornack, S. A., & Parks, M. R. (1985). Deception detection and relationship development: The other side of trust. In M. L. McLaughlin (Ed.), *Communication Yearbook 9* (pp. 377–389). Beverly Hills: Sage.

Mehrabian, A. (1971). Nonverbal betrayal of feeling. *Journal of Experimental Research in Personality, 5,* 64–73.

Mehrabian, A. (1972). *Nonverbal Communication.* Chicago: Aldine.

Motley, M. T. (1974). Acoustic correlates of lies. *Western Speech, 38,* 81–87.

O'Hair, H. D., Cody, M. J., & McLaughlin, M. L. (1981). Prepared lies, spontaneous lies, Machiavellianism, and nonverbal communication. *Human Communication Research, 7,* 325–339.

Riggio, R. E., & Friedman, H. S. (1983). Individual differences and cues to deception. *Journal of Personality and Social Psychology, 45,* 899–915.

Streeter, L. A., Krauss, R. M., Geller, V., Olson, C., & Apple, W. (1977). Pitch changes during attempted deception. *Journal of Personality and Social Psychology, 35,* 345–350.

Zuckerman, M., DeFrank, R. S., Hall, J. A., Larrance, D. T., & Rosenthal, R. (1979). Facial and vocal cues of deception and honesty. *Journal of Experimental Social Psychology, 15,* 378–396.

Zuckerman, M., DePaulo, B. M., & Rosenthal, R. (1981). Verbal and nonverbal communication of deception. In L. Berkowitz (Ed.), *Advances in experimental social psychology* (Vol. 14, pp. 1–59). New York: Academic Press.

Zuckerman, M., & Driver, R. E. (1985). Telling lies: Verbal and nonverbal correlates of deception. In A. W. Siegman & S. Feldstein (Eds.), *Multichannel integrations of nonverbal behavior* (pp. 129–148). Hillsdale, NJ: Erlbaum.

—Section C—

CREATING IMPRESSIONS AND MANAGING INTERACTION

Knowing how to start, manage, and end conversations is an art form. Can you think of times when you were in a conversation with someone and the interaction was awkward? Maybe your partner kept interrupting you. Or maybe when your partner paused you thought that he or she was done speaking, only to find that you both started talking at the same time. Have you ever had trouble initiating a conversation with someone you don't know very well? Perhaps you weren't sure how to approach a romantic interest or a potential friend. Sometimes we also have trouble ending conversations. You can probably think of times when you wanted to get off the phone and your partner kept talking, or when you wanted to leave someone's home at the end of the party and you were detained. Leave-taking, which refers to the behaviors you engage in when you are trying to end conversations, can be tricky. People try to leave the interaction without appearing rude.

In this section, you will learn more about the specific types of behaviors that people use to initiate, regulate, and end conversations. The first reading in this section focuses on a very specific situation—how people manage interactions in enclosed spaces like elevators. Imagine walking into an elevator that has four occupants already in it. Would you speak to them at length or would you just acknowledge them and then look away? Zuckerman and his colleagues conducted an experiment that shows that you would probably engage in "civil inattention." This means that you would politely agree not to interact with one another. Civil inattention is a good example of how nonverbal behaviors (such as diverted gaze) can be used to manage interaction when we don't want to be rude, but we don't want to start a conversation with someone either.

In initial encounters, stereotypes and expectations also play an important role. You may have read about the "self-fulfilling prophecy" before. The self-fulfilling prophecy means that if you expect someone to act a certain way, your treatment of that person might actually cause them to act in a way that confirms your expectations. For example, if you hear that

377

one of your professors is gruff and unapproachable, you might approach that professor in a defensive manner. The professor might feel uncomfortable because of your defensive approach, causing her or him to appear unapproachable. Manusov's chapter in this section discusses how expectations and cultural stereotypes can impact our initial encounters with people from other cultures.

People use nonverbal communication to say "hello" and to beckon people to come close. In Axtell's chapter you will see that numerous different body movements can be used to greet and beckon people. If you go to different places around the world, these greeting and beckoning gestures change. What means "hello" in one culture might be an obscene gesture in another. Therefore, it is important to know the nonverbal language of a culture before you start gesturing.

Rules also guide how we regulate or manage interaction during the conversation itself. Wiemann and Knapp tell us that in order for the conversation to run smoothly, people must have clear speaking and listening turns. Imagine a conversation where both people were speaking and listening at the same time. It would be hard to make sense of such a conversation. In this section of the reader, you will learn that there are many different nonverbal cues that regulate speaking and listening turns. For example, you might lean forward and open your mouth slightly when you want to speak, or you might sit back in your chair nodding, smiling, and saying "uh huh" when you want your partner to continue speaking.

Finally, the O'Leary and Gallois chapter describes how people also use a variety of different nonverbal cues to end conversations. These leave-taking behaviors include averted gaze, looking at a watch, taking a step backward, arranging your backpack, and so forth. These types of cues provide subtle, and sometimes not so subtle, clues that you want to end the interaction. A competent communicator will pick up on these nonverbal cues and let the conversation end rather than extending it. Knowing the art of initiating, regulating, and ending conversations is indeed an important nonverbal skill.

How do people manage interaction when they are in enclosed places (like elevators) with strangers? Zuckerman, Miserandino, and Bernieri explain a phenomenon called "civil inattention." Civil inattention occurs when two people are together in a space, notice each other, and agree not to pay attention to each other. The process, which was first discussed by Erving Goffman, shows how the environment, space, and gaze can work together to set up a situation where people manage interaction by politely deciding not to interact.

43

Civil Inattention Exists—in Elevators

*Miron Zuckerman
Marianne Miserandino
Frank Bernieri*

According to Goffman (1963), "civil inattention" is a behavioral ritual enacted when two or more persons are mutually present but not involved in any form of interaction. This ritual involves the exchange of glances between the persons in question followed by gaze aversion. The function of the glance is to acknowledge each other's presence; the subsequent aversion of gaze serves to assure the other person that he or she is not an object of curiosity or attention. By enacting this ritual, "the individual implies

Adapted with permission from Zuckerman et al., Civil inattention exists—in elevators. *Personality and Social Psychology Bulletin, 9*, (41), 578–586, copyright © 1983. Reprinted by permission of Sage Publications, Inc., that he has no reason to suspect the intention of the others present and no reason to fear the others, be hostile to them, or wish to avoid them" (Goffman, 1963, p. 84). The two possible violations of civil inattention are an open stare, indicating a search for information as well as a reaction to this information; or a complete gaze aversion, indicating that the other person is not worthy of even minimal attention.

Goffman (1963) proposed that civil inattention is likely to occur when pedestrians encounter one another on the street. When separated by a distance of about eight feet, the pedestrians eye each other and then cast their eyes down until they pass, "a kind of dimming of the lights" (p. 84). Surprisingly, it was not until recently that a series of studies by Cary (1978a) examined this ritual. Unexpectedly, the results failed to support predictions derived from Goffman's model. Specifically, two film studies of naturally occurring behavior showed that people did not avoid or use less direct gaze when passing another person. A third study indicated that behavior consistent with the rule of civil inattention—looking and then looking away—was rated less favorably than behaviors inconsistent with civil inattention—a continuous stare, and no looking followed by a sudden look. In a fourth study, confederates found that pedestrians on the street neither lowered their heads nor averted their gaze as they approached and passed them.

Cary suggested that the rule of civil inattention may not apply to the population of students participating in his studies; or that civil inattention could be conveyed by more subtle cues than those examined in these studies—for example, eyeblinks or facial microexpressions (see Ekman & Friesen, 1975). It is also possible, of course, that the rule of civil inattention does not exist—at least not for pedestrian passing.

Actually, there is a good reason why pedestrians can easily break the rule of civil inattention. First, it takes very little time for two people to close an eight foot distance while walking toward one another. Second, after the pedestrians pass one another, they are not likely to meet again. Thus both the duration and the likelihood of punishment (embarrassment, difficulty in interaction, etc.) are minimal. From this perspective, Cary's failure to find support for civil inattention appears less surprising. On the other hand, civil inattention may exert greater influence on visual behavior in settings other than those he has examined.

One setting that appears particularly suitable for circumstances leading to Goffman's description of civil inattention is the elevator. During an elevator ride, passengers share a limited amount of space usually without being involved in any interaction. Also, unlike pedestrians on the street, they are forced to remain in proximity, at least for the duration of the ride. Consequently, the need arises to acknowledge the presence of others without turning them into targets of attention. In short, it appears probable that at the beginning of an elevator ride there will be an exchange of glances followed by gaze aversion lasting the length of the ride.

The present series of studies was designed to examine the existence of civil inattention in elevators. Two complementary procedures were used: observation of natural behavior in Study 1 and controlled experimental manipulation in Studies 2 and 3. In Study 1, experimenter-observers recorded the frequency of glances they received as well as the latency and length of the first glance during elevator rides. In Studies 2 and 3, confederates behaved in a manner consistent or inconsistent with the rule of civil inattention; the effects of these behavioral patterns on other riders' impressions of the confederate as well as of the ride were measured.

STUDY 1

Method

The visual behavior of 320 elevator riders was observed by two experimenters, one male and one female. Half of the subjects were males and half females; half were observed in elevators of a downtown department store or office building, and half in elevators of a large apartment building serving the university and its medical school; finally, half of the subjects were already in the elevator when the experimenter arrived and entered (Enter condition) whereas the other half met a waiting experimenter as they themselves entered the elevator (Wait condition) x 2 (sex of subject) x 2 (location: downtown or university) x 2 (experimental condition: Enter/Wait) factorial design with 20 subjects in each cell. Only single elevator riders were observed.

The experimenters trained extensively to standardize the procedure for observations, timing, and recording of the data. Only looks that were oriented toward the experimenters' face or upper body were recorded, looks that were oriented toward the experimenters' feet did not count. The experimenters used two stopwatches, one to record the latency and the other to record the length of the subject's first look. Stopwatches were held in the experimenters' pockets and could not be heard. Timing of latency started when either the subject or the experimenter crossed the threshold of the elevator door. During the ride, the experimenters maintained neutral expressions and directed their gaze somewhat away from the subject. Thus they were able to observe the subject without staring at him or her.

On completion of a trial, the experimenter recorded the number of glances received from the subject, latency and length of first glance, location and length of the ride (first recorded as number of floors and later translated into time units), and the estimated age and sex of the subject.

Results and Discussion

The elevator rides ranged in length from 10 to 29 seconds, with a mean of 16.1 seconds. Within this time span, 50.3% of the subjects looked at the confederate once, 25% looked twice, 10.0% looked three times, and 4.1% looked four or five times; 10.6% did not look at all. It can be seen that, in general, subjects let very little time pass before looking at the experimenter (median latency=.56 sec.); in fact, latency of 73% of all first looks was less than 1 second. Similarly, first looks were short (median length=.35 sec.); 88% of all first looks lasted less than 1 second.

Overall, the above results are consistent with predictions of the civil inattention rule. The only exception was that a substantial number of subjects engaged in more than one glance. Although the duration of these additional glances was not recorded, they did not seem longer or different in any other way (e.g., direction, the accompanying facial expression) when compared to the first glance. Perhaps some of the subjects needed to renew their acknowledgement of the confederate as the ride progressed; a second glance may also be a ritualized display of interest in the other person.[1] Consistent with this latter notion, Cary (1978b) reported that the occurrence of mutual glances predicted the initiation of conversation between two strangers.

The extent to which people tend to follow the rule of civil inattention may be influenced by other variables. In the present study we were able to examine effects of sex of experimenter, sex of subject, location of observation, and experimental condition. These four variables served as between-subjects factors in three separate analyses of variance; number of looks, latency of first look, and length of first look served as the dependent variables.[2]

Analysis of the number of looks showed that subjects glanced more at an experimenter who entered the elevator than at an experimenter who waited for them; perhaps the waiting experimenter was perceived as part of the situation, whereas the entering experimenter was considered an intrusion deserving more visual notice. Females looked more at a male experimenter and less at a female experimenter in the university apartment building relative to the downtown location; males showed the opposite pattern, thus looks were relatively more common between mixed-sex pairs at the university building than downtown. This finding may simply indicate greater interest in the opposite sex at the university.

Latency of first look was greater in the downtown location than at the university building. This difference may indicate a greater reluctance to accord recognition to others at the more public downtown location. In addition, the Enter condition induced greater latency when experimenter and subject were of mixed sex, whereas the Wait condition induced greater latency when experimenter and subjects were of the same sex. We are not sure how to interpret this interaction.

The first look lasted longer when the experimenter was male rather than female, when subjects were males rather than females, and when subjects and experimenter were of same sex. It appears as if the rule of only a brief glance is more relaxed when the looker or the person looked at is male or if same-sex pairs are involved. Finally, the university building induced longer looks than the downtown location. This latter result is consistent with the previously reported finding of shorter latency at the university, indicating a stronger tendency to create contact with others at this location.

None of the effects reported above was predicted and some are hard to interpret. Furthermore, the obtained differences between the single male and single female experimenters may be due to other factors besides gender, and the same may be true for differences between the university and the downtown location. Thus the only possible inference at this point is that there may be systematic variation in the enactment of civil inattention. It should be noted, however, that the absolute magnitude of this variation was very small. That is, these results do not suggest any exceptions to the general rule of civil inattention.

If civil inattention is the customary and expected behavior in elevators, people should look unfavorably on those who choose not to practice it. Furthermore, infraction of the rule may lead not only to negative impressions regarding the violators but to negative impressions regarding the elevator ride itself. These predictions were examined in Studies 2 and 3.

STUDIES 2 AND 3

Method

Study 2 was designed to examine subjects' reactions to violations of the rule of civil inattention. Study 3 was an exact replication, conducted two years later with different experimenters and a different subject population.

Subjects (144 in Study 2 and 240 in Study 3) were single riders in elevators in university buildings. Half were males and half were females; half were run with a male confederate and half with a female confederate; as in Study 1, the confederate either entered an elevator already occupied by a subject (Enter condition) or waited in the elevator until a subject entered (Wait condition). During the ride, the confederate behaved in a manner that was either consistent or inconsistent with the civil inattention rule. In the former case, he or she glanced at the subject as soon as the two met and then avoided eye contact for the rest of the ride (Glance condition); in the latter case, the confederate either avoided eye contact (Ignore condition) or stared at the subject (Stare condition) for the duration of the ride. It should be noted that compared to Study 1, the confederate's body orientation in the Ignore condition was further away from the subject, reducing any possibility of eye contact. Equal numbers of subjects were assigned to the Ignore, Glance and Stare conditions. Thus, the experimental design consisted of a 2 (sex of subject) x 2 (sex of confederate) x 2 (Enter/Wait condition) x 3 (Ignore/Glance/ Stare) factorial. There were six subjects in each cell in Study 2 and 10 subjects in each cell in Study 3.

Subjects' reactions to the manipulation of civil inattention were measured by an experimenter who was unaware of the condition to which a specific subject was assigned. This experimenter waited at ground or other exit floors and administered a short questionnaire to every person leaving the elevator in the company of the confederate. Specifically, subjects were asked to fill out a short questionnaire as part of a survey about reactions to elevator rides. The questionnaire consisted of three items, each answered on a 9-point scale: (1) Did you have a pleasant ride? 1=ride was extremely unpleasant, 9=ride was extremely pleasant. If there was another person with you in the elevator—what was your overall impression of him or her? (2a) 1=person was extremely impolite, 9=person was extremely polite; (2b) 1=person was extremely unpleasant, 9=person was extremely pleasant. On completion of the questionnaire, the subjects were thanked for their participation.

Results

Responses to each question were examined in an analysis of variance with sex of subject, sex of confederate, Wait/Enter conditions, Ignore/Glance/Stare conditions, and Study 2/Study 3 as the between-subjects factors. For each question, the mean scores associated with the three experimental conditions, F of the contrast between behavior consistent with civil inattention (Glance condition) and behaviors inconsistent with civil inattention (Ignore and Stare conditions) and the d, or effect size associated with this contrast were analyzed. It was evident that violations of civil inattention were rated less favorably than behavior consistent with civil inattention. Not surprisingly the magnitude of this effect was almost twice as large for ratings of the violators (how polite and how pleasant was the confederate) than for ratings of the ride (how pleasant was the ride).

The difference between the Glance and Ignore conditions for ratings of the ride only approached significance, $F(1,224)=3.36$, $p <.07$, whereas all other differences were significant. It appears that the two violations of the rule of civil inattention were frowned on equally.

Of the 45 possible interactions between the manipulation of civil inattention and other variables, only two were significant and thus could have been due to chance alone.

GENERAL DISCUSSION

The present series of studies provides strong support for the existence of civil inattention. Study 1 showed that about half of all elevator riders tended to eye a fellow passenger briefly at the beginning of the ride and subsequently avoid contact for the remainder of the ride. Of the riders, 35% added to the initial look one or two glances, indicating perhaps a renewal of acknowledgement or a certain interest in the other person. Studies 2 and 3 indicated that behaviors inconsistent with the rule of civil inattention—continuous gaze aversion or continuous stare—were rated less favorably than behaviors consistent with the civil inattention rule—a glance followed by gaze aversion. The fact that gaze aversion and staring were equally unwelcome is of particular importance, since there have been previous reports indicating that staring alone can be negatively interpreted by subjects. Specifically, Ellsworth, Carlsmith, and Henson (1972) in a field study composed of five experiments, found that subjects exposed to a continuous stare moved away from the person staring faster than did those exposed to a fleeting glance. However, the setting in the Ellsworth et al. (1972) study was not particularly appropriate for the enactment of the civil inattention ritual. Consequently, it was found that an Ignore manipulation in Experiment 5 (a condition labeled incongruous because the confederate was engaged in an unusual activity) did not produce more negative reactions than the fleeting glance. In short, the relatively negative reactions to both gaze aversion and staring in the present experiment indicate that the normative behavior in an elevator must have two components—acknowledgment of another's presence followed by a withdrawal of attention.

It could be argued that the pattern of behavior that was found reflects situational demands rather than the ritual of civil inattention. Specifically, one glances at another passenger in order to orient oneself in the confined space of an elevator, but one does not stare so as to avoid intruding on another's personal space. However, an explanation of glancing in terms of orientation in space cannot account for the lower pleasantness and politeness rating obtained in the Ignore condition. If anything, the person who does not glance may be considered more polite, since he or she avoids exploration of space so as not to inconvenience the other passenger. Staring, on the other hand, can certainly be conceptualized as an intrusion, but this is almost identical to Goffman's explanation of gaze aversion. According to his model, people do not stare at an individual so as to avoid an expression of too much curiosity. Stated differently, staring is avoided so that the other person's privacy is maintained and his or her personal space not violated. Thus civil inattention consists of acknowledging the other's presence without making him or her an object of inquiry.

Once the existence of civil inattention is established, it is interesting to speculate on variations and exceptions to the rule. For example, it was found in Study 1 that about a third of the subjects looked more than once at the confederate. It is possible then, that elevator riders would not react negatively to a small increase in the number of glances given them. Furthermore, although the most frequent behavioral pattern observed in the elevator involved an initial glance followed by gaze aversion, this temporal order may not be that important. Thus riders on elevators may rate aversion followed by a glance more favorably than continuous gaze aversion or staring, although perhaps less favorably than a glance followed by gaze aversion. One may also wonder about the point at which staring becomes aversive. Perhaps longer and/or more frequent looks than the single glance practiced in the present study will not be rated unfavorably. Of course, there must be a point where the interest shown by longer and/or more frequent looks is no longer welcome. However, the temporal location of this point is unknown to us.

Civil inattention may also be modified by the size of the group that is involved. It is possible that in groups consisting of three or more persons, there is less need to acknowledge any particular person's presence. Thus diffusion of responsibility, anonymity, and practical difficulties (one can look at only so many people) may lead to a shift from civil inattention to complete inattention in public places (e.g., crowded elevators, waiting lines, subways).

The visual behavior of civil inattention may be replaced or modified by other forms of nonverbal displays. For example, a person standing adjacent to a fellow rider in an elevator cannot establish eye contact, and yet the small distance between the pair and the "cooperative posture" (the two standing side by side) may already suggest some kind of acknowledgement. Finally, the extent to which civil inattention is expected and practiced may vary across cultures. Perhaps in cultures mandating close physical contact among interactants, civil inattention would be considered a cold and relatively impolite behavior; conversely, there may be cultures in which civil inattention implies too much intimacy between strangers.

Notes

[1] This possibility was suggested to us by Mark S. Lay, whose help is gratefully acknowledged.

[2] Analysis of covariance, with estimated age of subjects and length of ride as covariates, were also performed. However, neither covariate was related to any of the dependent variables. Specifically, of six partial correlations (all independent variables, sex of experimenter, sex of subject, and so on were held constant), only the correlation between length of ride and number of looks approached significance, $r = .10$, $< .10$. Consequently, the covariance analyses did not change any of the results obtained by the analyses of variance.

References

Cary, M. S. (1978a). Does civil inattention exist in pedestrian passing? *Journal of Personality and Social Psychology, 36,* 1185–1193.

Cary, M. S. (1978b). The role of gaze in the initiation of conversation. *Social Psychology, 41,* 269–271.

Ekman, P., & Friesen, W. F. (1975). *Unmasking the face: A guide to recognizing emotions from facial expressions.* Englewood Cliffs, NJ: Prentice-Hall.

Ellsworth, P. C., Carlsmith, J. M., & Henson, A. (1972). The stare as a stimulus of flight in human subjects: A series of field experiments. *Journal of Personality and Social Psychology, 21,* 802–811.

Goffman, E. (1963). *Behavior in public places.* New York: Free Press.

Rosenthal, R. (1978). Combining results of independent studies. *Psychological Bulletin, 85,* 185–193.

When you meet someone from a different culture, you might have certain stereotypes and expectations about how they will behave. Do you think that the stereotypes and expectations you hold about their culture will influence how you manage interaction? Manusov's study attempts to answer this question. She found that stereotypes do indeed affect what people see and how they behave during conversations with someone from a different culture. However, people often re-evaluate their stereotypical views if a person acts in ways that violate cultural stereotypes.

44

Stereotypes and Nonverbal Cues
Showing How We Feel about Others during Cross-Cultural Interactions

Valerie Manusov

> There's nothing the world loves more than a ready-made description which they can hang onto a [hu]man, and so save themselves all trouble in the future.
>
> —W. Somerset Maugham

Fewer things intrigue and repel people as much as stereotypes. In part because of the belief that stereotypes influence many of our interactions, and because their effects may often be prejudicial, most of us try to understand why we often stereotype one another and what effects that stereo-

This article was written especially for *The Nonverbal Communication Reader* and is based on a study by Manusov, Winchatz, & Manning (1997), Acting out our minds: Incorporating behavior into models of stereotype-based expectations for cross-cultural interactions. *Communication Monographs, 64*, 119–139.

typing has on those we categorize. This article tries to help in this understanding.

Stereotypes are a type of "knowledge structure" that creates expectations for others' behavior and character. For example, if we think that people who are from a particular culture are likely to be friendly, we assume that the person with whom we are going to interact will also be friendly. As well, we tend to explain another's behaviors in a manner consistent with our expectancies if such an explanation is possible (Yee & Eccles, 1988). We're also likely to make more favorable judgments if the person behaves in ways that are consistent with how we thought he or she would act (Vrij & Winkel, 1992).

While stereotypes are often incorrect, and almost always less complex than how we think about our own group members, they still seem to help us by providing a way to make sense of the world around us. Indeed, Macrae, Milne, and Bodenhausen (1994) said that "[i]n our long journey from the primordial soup to intellectual hegemony, we seem to have evolved an inferential system that actively sustains stereotype-based modes of thought" (p. 45). While they may lessen the degree to which we are accurate in our explanations and judgments and make it difficult for others to "escape" the stereotypes, our expectancies do help us to interact with others largely because they provide a way to explain and predict what will occur.

We do not just judge others by our stereotypes, however. We also make evaluations and respond to others based on how they act when we are with them. In fact, people may abandon, or at least modify, their expectations in the face of information that personalizes another (i.e., makes the person with whom we are interacting appear to be an individual rather than a member of a particular group; Fiske & Neuberg, 1990; Jussim, 1990). So, if people act more favorably than we expected someone from their culture to act (e.g., they smile more or sit at a comfortable distance), we are likely to judge them based, at least in part, on the positive interaction we had with them rather than on our stereotypes.

Stereotypes or expectancies, then, can affect how we think about members of a stereotyped group, but we are also influenced by how people actually behave. Our stereotypes may also impact how *we* act with someone from another group. For example, we are likely to behave more immediate or involved (e.g., spending more time together, being more verbally engaged in the conversation, acting less hesitant, and using a friendlier voice) with groups we know well and/or like versus those we do not (Berger, 1986; Manusov & Hegde, 1993; Word, Zanna, & Cooper, 1974). Thus, not only do stereotypes mean that we think in certain ways about our interactions with people from distinct groups, stereotypes may also lead us to act in a particular manner with them. Moreover, our behavior may lead others to act differently with us because of how we act with them (Rosenthal & Rubin, 1978; but see Swann, 1987).

In sum, research on the interplay between stereotypes, evaluations, and behaviors points to the following three conclusions: (1) stereotype-based expectancies are tied to judgments of a conversational partner (i.e., if we think that certain things are likely to happen, those thoughts will affect how we judge another person); (2) judgments are also associated with conversational partners' behaviors (i.e., we make evaluations of people based on the behaviors they use when talking to us); and (3) expectancies correlate with behaviors in cross-cultural or cross-racial exchanges (i.e., we act in ways that are influenced by the stereotypes we have for another person; as well, if we act in ways affected by our stereotypes, we may be changing how our conversational partner acts in response). The present study set out to test these conclusions further.

METHOD

Participants in this study included two groups of students from a large northwestern university. One group, the U.S. participants, came from various speech communication classes. The second group, the international participants, were recruited from a range of organizations on campus created for students from other countries. One U.S. participant was paired with one international participant for each interaction.

The sixty-six pairs of participants were told that the study was designed to explore the behaviors used when members of diverse cultures are first getting to know one another. Participants completed brief questionnaires designed to gain information about their degree of knowledge and their attitude toward their partners' culture. This was how "stereotypes" were assessed for this study. The pair members were then brought together to a room where they were videotaped during a ten-minute conversation. Afterwards, they completed a questionnaire asking about the degree to which the conversation met their expectations, the degree to which it was enjoyable, and their assessment of their partners.

After the study was over, a group of trained nonverbal communication students watched the videotapes for certain behaviors. Behaviors were measured across the first five minutes and then again for the second five minutes, because (1) cues reflecting expectations may be more likely to occur early in the interaction, (2) cues change as people feel more or less comfortable in interactions, and (3) evaluations may differ depending on the timing of certain behaviors. The behaviors are listed in table 1. The degree to which the partners' behaviors were similar to one another's was

Table 1
Behavioral Scales Used for Rating Conversation Cues

Immediacy Cues

facially unpleasant [1] to facially pleasant [7]
vocally unpleasant [1] to vocally pleasant [7]
no head nodding [1] to frequent nodding [7]
indirect body orientation [1] to direct body orientation [7]
silent [1] to talkative [7]
no gaze at partner [1] to high gaze at partner [7]
many speech errors/disfluencies [1] to few speech errors/disfluencies [7]
lean away from partner [1] to lean toward partner [7]
didn't follow-up on partner's conversation [1] followed-up on partner's conversation [7]

Composure Cues

many adaptors [1] to few adaptors [7]
tense posture [1] to relaxed posture [7]
high shifting [1] to low chair shifts [7]

Verbal Bias

language biased toward own culture [1] to language not biased toward own culture [7]
leading questions [1] to open questions [7]

---

also rated on the following seven-point scale: from (1) "were not at all similar" to (7) "were very similar." Similarity/congruence ratings were conducted for three face cues (facial expression, orientation, and eye behavior), four kinesic behaviors (amount of gestures, body movements, body orientation, and lean/posture), and three paralinguistic cues (vocal tone, speech rate, and vocal loudness).

RESULTS

Evaluations Based on Stereotypes

Although previous research has found that people's stereotypes will affect how they judge others, this study only found limited support for this belief (i.e., stereotypes didn't have many effects on how people were judged after a conversation). Specifically, there was only one significant result for the U.S. sample: The more positive people were about people from the culture with which they interacted, the better their judgments of the conversation they had with their partner.

Evaluations Based on Interaction Behavior

How people acted during an interaction was *much* more likely to affect the judgments their partners made about them. As can be seen in Table 2, there were a number of specific relationships between how people acted and the ways in which they were judged after the conversation. This occurred for both groups and included individual behaviors and the degree of behavioral similarity/congruence.

Table 2
Significant Relationships between Behaviors and Evaluations

	Behaviors	**Judgment**
U.S. Sample	Vocal congruence	Conv. enjoyment
	Relaxed posture, facial expression congruence, vocal congruence, and kinesic congruence	Emotional stability
	Immediacy, following up, lean away, relaxed posture, and vocal congruence	Extraversion
International	Immediacy and head nods	Conv. enjoyment
Sample	Lean incongruence	Agreeableness
	Following up and body orientation	Culturedness
	Direct body orientation and gaze	Emotional stability
	Following up, lean discongruence, and facial orientation congruence	Extraversion

Effects of Stereotypes on Behaviors

There was some evidence that the stereotypes people had for one another affected their own behavior and, ultimately, how their conversational partners acted. Specifically for the U.S. sample, more positive attitudes were related to more direct body orientation during the entire interaction and with more gaze in the initial five minutes of the conversation. For the international sample, more positive attitudes were linked with *less* gaze, showing some small behavioral reflections of the attitudes related to stereotypes.

The U.S. sample's reported knowledge of the other culture was also linked with the international sample's use of fewer head nods in the second five minutes of the conversation. The international sample's reported knowledge was tied to the U.S. sample's gaze, due to more gaze at time one and less gaze at time two, suggesting that each group was picking up and responding, at least in a small way, to the expectations or stereotypes of the other group.

CONCLUSIONS

The present study aimed to examine possible ways in which stereotype-based expectancies worked within models of cross-cultural interactions. What was found was that expectancies, and the degree to which people believed their expectations were met, had some, but limited, links with evaluations of the interaction and interaction partners. The behaviors people used, on the other hand, were related to evaluations more consistently. Stereotypes or expectancies *were* associated with certain behaviors used during the interaction, however, highlighting their role in conversational dynamics. In general, the behaviors linked to one's own expectancies occurred in the initial five minutes of the interaction; the cues tied to a partner's expectancies tended to come later. The assumption is that people do not necessarily respond right away to others' cues. Rather, the behaviors follow from (are created by) a partner's earlier actions.

From these results, and previous investigations, a "directive/emergent" model integrating stereotype-based expectancies, behaviors, and evaluations can be proposed. Stereotypes or expectancies appear to have possible, although weak, "directive" connections with one's own (particularly initial) behaviors, and, to a lesser extent, with evaluations. That is, what people bring with them to a conversation with a person from another culture will have at least some impact on what they see and how they behave. "Emergent" interaction behaviors (i.e., the behaviors people actually use in interactions), on the other hand, appear to have quite a strong link with how people judge a conversation and their partners; in other words, people have the chance to alter the evaluations others make of them and, potentially, of other people in their group.

Thus, much of what is likely to occur when people from different groups interact is built from within the interaction itself. Importantly, however, *in cases where expectancies are more pronounced or when circumstances dictate greater weight to holding onto expectations, the more direct influence of stereotypes will likely prove more potent.* To the extent that expectancies play a more pronounced role in interactions, however, the effects of emergent behaviors will likely decrease. These ideas are yet to be tested.

References

Berger, C. R. (1986). Social cognition and intergroup communication. In W. Gudykunst (Ed.), *Intergroup communication* (pp. 51–61). Baltimore: Edward Arnold.

Fiske, S. T., & Neuberg, S. L. (1990). A continuum of impression formation, from category-based to individuating processes: Influences of information and motivation on attention and interpretation. In M. P. Zanna (Ed.), *Advances in experimental social psychology* (Vol. 23, pp. 1–74). San Diego, CA: Academic Press.

Jussim, L. (1990). Social reality and social problems: The role of expectancies. *Journal of Social Issues, 46,* 9–34.

Macrae, C. N., Milne, A. B., & Bodenhausen, G. V. (1994). Stereotypes as energy-saving devices: A peek inside the cognitive toolbox. *Journal of Personality and Social Psychology, 66,* 37–47.

Manusov, V., & Hegde, R. (1993). Communicative outcomes of stereotype-based expectancies in cross-cultural dyads. *Communication Quarterly, 41,* 338–354.

Manusov, V., Winchatz, M. R., & Manning, L. M. (1997). Acting out our minds: Incorporating behavior into models of stereotype-based expectancies for cross-cultural interactions. *Communication Monographs, 64,* 119–139.

Rosenthal, R., & Rubin, D. B. (1978). Interpersonal expectancy effects: The first 345 studies. *Behavioral and Brain Sciences, 3,* 377–415.

Swann, W. B. (1987). Identity negotiation: Where two roads meet. *Journal of Personality and Social Psychology, 53,* 1038–1051.

Vrij, A., & Winkel, F. W. (1992). Crosscultural police-citizen interactions: The influence of race, beliefs, and nonverbal communication on impression formation. *Journal of Applied Social Psychology, 22,* 1546–1559.

Word, C. O., Zanna, M. P., & Cooper, J. (1974). The nonverbal mediation of self-fulfilling prophecies in interracial interaction. *Journal of Experimental Social Psychology, 10,* 109–120.

Yee, D. K., & Eccles, J. S. (1988). Parent perceptions and attributions for children's math achievements. *Sex Roles, 19,* 317–333.

What do you do when you say "hello" or beckon someone to come closer? Do you think that people in other cultures use the same nonverbal behaviors to greet and beckon people that you do? If you do, Axtell would tell you to think again. In this article, Axtell reviews how people across the globe use different types of nonverbal behaviors to initiate interaction with one another. Many of his observations are similar to those found by anthropologists and psychologists who have studied cultural variation in gestures.

45

Initiating Interaction
Greetings and Beckonings across the World

Roger E. Axtell

Are greetings important? Consider this:

Item: In January 1994, a simple handshake was the subject of great deliberation and discussion between two world leaders and U.S. president Bill Clinton. The occasion was the history-making accord between Palestinian leader Yasir Arafat and Israeli prime minister Yitzak Rabin. According to news reports, considerable discussion occurred over if, when, and how the two leaders should shake hands at the press announcement. Rabin was reticent, but Arafat was eager. Rabin reportedly agreed when Arafat assured him there would be no kissing of cheeks. Even then, via international television, the world

Adapted from Axtell (1998), *Gestures: Do's and taboos of body language around the world*. Reprinted by permission of John Wiley & Sons, Inc.

witnessed as Arafat made the first move with his outstretched hand and Rabin exhibited momentary hesitation.

Like most of us, I learned the protocol of handshaking from my parents.

"When you shake hands," my father used to growl at me, "be sure you give 'em a good, firm grip. Also, look 'em straight in the eye."

Little did I realize that in other parts of the world fathers were teaching their sons and daughters something entirely different.

Figure 1   A man from India greeting a Westerner with a *namaste.*

For example, fathers in India were instructing their children in the *namaste* (figure 1), where the hands are placed in a praying position, about chest high, accompanied by a slight bow. With this gesture, you are saying, in effect, "I pray to the God in you." It also means "thank you" and "I'm sorry." In Thailand, this same gentle and gracious gesture is called the *wai.* Don't get carried away and lift the pressed hands above the head, however, or it could be construed as an insult.

The exact origins of both the handshake and *namaste* are unclear. Citizens of the Roman empire greeted each other with a hand-and-forearm clasp, but some anthropologists believe our handshake of today may be only a couple hundred years old.

Whatever the genesis, the intent seems clear. Whether it's the outstretched hand or the palms pressed together, each signal suggests openness and a clear sign that the greeter is not carrying a weapon.

Some believe the hug or embrace originally had a similar purpose: the assurance that no weapons were hidden beneath the flowing robes worn from the time of the Egyptians through the Middle Ages.

Another sign of openness when we greet one another involves the eyes and forehead. Anthropologists point out that when humans greet, regardless of our nationality or race, we all open our eyes wider than normal and wrinkle our foreheads. Since the eyebrows move upward, this is often referred to as the "eyebrow flash." Both motions appear to be instinctive and signal openness and are, therefore, a form of greeting.

There are other more exotic forms of greetings as well. In the Middle East, the older generation can still be seen giving the *salaam*. In this signal, the right hand sweeps upward, first touching the heart, then the forehead, and finally up and outward, perhaps with a slight nod of the head (figure 2). The words that accompany this greeting are *salaam alaykum*, meaning, appropriately, "Peace be with you."

Figure 2   The *salaam*, a Middle Eastern greeting.

The Hollywood movie industry popularized the stereotype of a tall, bronze-skinned American Indian standing with palm upraised, saying "How." As every American schoolchild knows, that was the way all Native Americans greeted the palefaced settlers. At least that is what Hollywood would have us believe. True or not, it is a fact that communication between different tribes of Native Americans and the first white explorers was solely through sign language. Therefore, the simple, raised palm as a form of greeting was critical to the exploration and opening of the U.S. West.

Greetings can also convey secret messages. On my last trip to the Mediterranean area, I was told that in many countries there, a greeting among homosexual men is to shake hands in a very specific and hidden manner: with the middle finger folded down into the palm.

Greetings can be downright physical, too, to the point you may want to wear a football helmet and shoulder pads. Eskimos greet each other by banging the other party with a hand either on the head or shoulders. Polynesian men who are strangers welcome each other by embracing and then rubbing each other's back.

The Maori tribespeople in New Zealand choose even today to greet each other with a gesture that seems to epitomize closeness and friendship:

Figure 3   The Maori greeting.

they rub noses (figure 3). The Eskimos use this same gesture, but with more personal meaning.

Some East African tribes greet each other by spitting at each other's feet. And for perhaps the most unusual and mysterious greeting, Tibetan tribesmen are said to greet each other quite warmly by *sticking out their tongues* at each other.

Let's return to the more familiar gesture of greeting, the handshake. While *my* father was drilling me with "Firm handshake, direct eye contact," fathers in the Middle East were instructing their sons, "When you shake hands, a *gentle* grip is appropriate. Don't grip the hand firmly. A firm grip suggests aggression." And in places like Japan and Korea, fathers were not only advocating "Yes, gentle, not firm" but were adding "and try to avoid direct eye contact. Staring at someone is intimidating and disrespectful."

Among North Americans and many Europeans, gripping a limp hand is distasteful. They liken it to being weak and effeminate. A simile often used is that it is like "grasping a dead fish."

Some people believe Americans go too far in the other direction, however. Prince Charles of England, who must be a connoisseur on greetings by now, has complained of the finger-crunching grip of the Americans. "Especially Texans," he adds.

Handshakes can be either "gentle," "firm," or "Texan." But there is more than just hand pressure involved in the business of shaking hands.

In northern Europe, you are most likely to receive a curt, firm, one pump handshake. Also, women and children there will customarily extend their hand in greeting, whereas in parts of North America and in the Far East, women will only occasionally take that initiative. The same is true for children.

In Islamic countries, it is forbidden for unrelated men to touch women, so men should never offer to shake hands with women there. West African male friends will often add a snappy finish to a handshake as follows: as they release the grip, each middle finger is pressed together and then snapped abruptly into the fleshy pad below the thumb.

The French seem to be the most "handshakingest" of all. Visitors remark on how the French seem to shake hands when greeting, when departing, when returning . . . and repeat the custom each morning of every day, no matter if the relationship is business or social. Author Peter Mayle, in his engaging book *A Year in Provence*, explains that if a Frenchman happens to have soiled hands he will offer his forearm in greeting, or if he is holding packages he will even extend a little finger to be grasped.

In South America, Bolivians win the title of "Greatest Greeters." Whenever two friends meet and chat, their greeting usually includes a handshake and a hearty clap on the back.

Psychologists regard the handshake as one of the most powerful of all tactile contacts, so maybe there's something to be learned from the French and the Bolivians.

In southern Europe and Central and South America, the handshake will usually be warmer and probably a bit longer, frequently accompanied by the left hand touching the other person's forearm, elbow, or even lapel.

A version popular in American politics is to shake hands using the free hand to cover the grip. On the scale of warmth of a greeting, this gesture supposedly adds several degrees of closeness and implied unity.

In Russia, good male friends, especially among the older generation, will start with a strong, firm handshake and then continue forward into the so-called bear hug so often identified with that country. But, just to demonstrate that common customs do not necessarily cross common boundaries, neighboring Finns firmly reject bear hugging. "Don't do it here," they warn. "We don't hug or kiss or have bodily contact with strangers as the Russians do."

In Latin American countries, the hug is called the *abrazo,* which means "embrace." It is often accompanied by a couple of hearty claps on the back (figure 4). Most North Americans, northern Europeans, and Asians find any such touching or hugging very uncomfortable.

My first encounter with the Latin *abrazo* occurred in the airport at Buenos Aires, Argentina, when I was very new to this game of gestures and greetings. There to meet me, arms outstretched, was the manager of our local company. "My God," I thought, "that man is going to hug me!" My life seemed to pass before my eyes. Walking forward stiffly, I forgot that one must move

Figure 4
Un abrazo (embrace).

the head either right or left. We ended up smashing noses.

Now let us turn to that most courtly of all greetings, the bow. Veteran travelers to Japan counsel, "When you visit Japan, keep your shoes shined at all times, since everyone will be looking at them a lot when bowing." I am often asked, "Should a North American or European bow to a Japanese?" No, it is not absolutely necessary, but a slight bow demonstrates that you respect their customs. And in Japan, where style and grace and courteousness are revered, this simple act would surely be noted, appreciated, and probably remembered. Think about the subtle psychology of this and all gestures. Do we expect other cultures to adopt our customs, or are we willing to adopt theirs? This might translate to how business or even foreign relations are to be conducted. Do we compromise or force our associate to deal only on our terms? You may not have time to learn a language, but taking time to learn the "signals" can make you a powerful communicator.

Western businesspeople stationed in Japan know this and take pains to carefully emulate the Japanese. But they also joke among themselves: "You know you've stayed in Japan too long when you have a telephone conversation and find yourself bowing into the telephone." (See figure 5.)

Figure 5

Many Westerners view the bow as an act of subservience, but in Japan that would be completely wrong. For the Japanese a bow signals respect and humility, two qualities coveted throughout Asia.

Westerners face many handicaps in trying to learn the complete art of Japanese bowing because there is so much hidden meaning in every dip and bob. For example:

• *Who bows first?*

• *How low does one bow?*

• *When do we shake hands?*

• *When do we exchange business cards.*

The answers are as follows:

Who bows first? And how low?

The operative word is *rank*. The shortcut for this lesson is simply to remember "The higher the rank of the person facing you, the lower you bow." In Japanese society, it is extremely important, especially in business, to know the rank of people with whom you come in contact. The same applies to the rank of your company For example, the middle-level manager in a large powerful company outranks a department head from a smaller, less important company.

Therefore, who bows first and lowest? Answer: The person of lower rank bows first and lowest.

When do we shake hands?

The answer is complicated by the fact that many Japanese, especially those who travel abroad on business, are quickly adopting Western ways. As a result, our respective learning curves may collide midway. We may bow in respect to their practices, while they may simultaneously stick out their hand. They may even give a *firm* grip and add direct eye contact because they've been told that's how Westerners do it.

When do we exchange business cards?

Called *meishi* in Japanese, business cards are very important. The business card is more than a convenience. It represents one's personal identity, one's label, shingle, sign, rank, and name tag—all in one. (Incidentally, take care when listing your title on the card; make certain it is clear and accurate, neither overblown nor obscure. Also, have all the information printed in Japanese on the reverse side, preferably with the same quality printing on both sides lest you imply their language is second class.) In Japan, greetings and business cards go together like *sake* and rice. When exchanging business cards in Japan, the proper etiquette is:

- Exchange cards at the very first stages of an introduction.
- Present (and receive) the card with *both hands*. Grasp the card between thumbs and forefingers, with the lettering facing the recipient. Accompany all this with a slight bow. (See figure 6.)
- Each recipient then takes several seconds to study the name, title, company name, and address before continuing.
- Now . . . shake hands and bow a few more times.
- Some final words of advice: Treat business cards with respect. The card is, after all, a symbol of that person's very identity. Avoid writing notes on it, at least in front of the other person. Avoid carrying your cards or putting their card in your

Figure 6   In Japan, always present and receive business cards with both hands.

hip pocket—you are, obviously, then *sitting* on the cards. After receiving the other person's card, place it respectfully on the table in front of you. And, speaking of wrong signals, I've seen one bored American businessperson take the Japanese person's card and absentmindedly *pick his teeth* with it!

In his informative book *Japanese Etiquette & Ethics in Business* (Passport Books, 1987), author Boye DeMente advises, "The lower the bow and the longer one holds the position, the stronger is the indication of respect, gratitude, sincerity, obeisance, humility, contriteness, etc." DeMente explains there are three degrees of bowing:

1. The informal bow (about 15 degrees, with the hands at the side), which is used for all casual occasions between people of all ranks;

2. The formal bow (30 degrees) with palms on knees, and often bobbing up and down; and

3. The formal or "highest form of salutation," which is rarely used and is reserved for the imperial family. (So we won't detail it here!)

As a final reminder of the importance of rank in Japan, they actually joke among themselves that when playing golf it is customary to tee off in accordance with the level of their respective salaries.

Elsewhere in Asia, in places like Taiwan, Hong Kong, Singapore, and mainland China, the bow is much less common. In those places, the conventional handshake is the customary form of greeting. You might detect a slight—very slight—bob of the head, but that's all.

Turning to other parts of the world, here are two more variations on the custom of shaking hands. In East Africa, friends shake hands with more of a casual light slap to each other's palm followed quickly by a cupping and grasping of fingers. And in Mexico, especially outside the metropolitan area of Mexico City, friends will greet with a conventional shaking of hands but then slip the palm upward and grasp each other's thumb.

A word of caution about the Thai *wai,* the Indian *namaste,* and Japanese bowing. While it is important to know, to practice, and to respect these forms of greetings, many people in the societies in which these greetings are practiced have traveled abroad and may have adopted the handshake as the lingua franca of physical greeting. Wherever you travel, the handshake may greet you. Nevertheless, be prepared to demonstrate your knowledge and respect for the local customs as well. This show of respect will be appreciated.

We now turn to *beckoning gestures*. The way people beckon one another around the world can be almost as diverse as the way we greet and bid farewell to one another. (See figure 7.)

Think about this commonplace situation for a moment: If you are seated in a restaurant and you wish to attract the attention of the waiter or waitress, what do you do? The odds are that whatever gesture you customarily use may be interpreted as strange or even rude in some other part of the globe.

In the following discussion, we review a series of common beckoning gestures and where they are popular, along with explanations of *other* meanings each gesture may have in other parts of the world.

Figure 7   Beckoning

In the United States, the common gesture for getting someone's attention, as when calling a waiter, is to raise a hand (with the index finger raised) about head high, or a little higher (figure 8). It probably stems from our first experiences in school, where we are taught simply to raise our hand in order to get the teacher's attention. There are many variations. This gesture could be considered rude in some countries, like Japan, where pointing the finger at anyone is considered impolite. In places like Germany, this signal also means "two," because two fingers (one finger and a thumb) are being held upright. So an American might be signaling in this fashion and then saying

Figure 8   The most common beckoning gesture in the United States.

"Waiter—some water, please," and a German waiter would bring two glasses of water.

Another beckoning or attention-getting motion common in the United States is simply to raise the hand and with the full, open palm wave the hand back and forth to attract attention.

The trouble with this motion is that in, say, Europe it could be interpreted as signaling "no." So, an American could be trying to get the attention of the waiter to come to his table and the waiter, seeing the gesture, says to himself: "That fellow is signaling 'no' to me. I guess he doesn't need me."

Also in America, a person might curl the index finger in and out to signal "come here."

In countries as widespread as the former Yugoslavia and Malaysia, that gesture is used only for calling *animals*. Therefore, using it to beckon a human would be terribly impolite.

In Indonesia and Australia, it is also used for beckoning "ladies of the night."

Figure 9   A beckoning gesture used in many European and Latin American countries.

Throughout much of Europe and in many Latin American countries the preferred gesture for signaling "come over here" is to extend the arm, hand out, palm down, and then make a scratching motion with the fingers (figure 9).

North Americans do not customarily use this gesture and may consider it uncomfortable, effeminate, or puzzling.

If not done properly, in some European countries, particularly Italy and Greece, this gesture might be confused with one used to signal "good-bye." In that case, though, while the palm faces down, the fingers are *waggled* up and down as opposed to making an inward, scratching motion.

In France, the preferred way to call a waiter to your table is simply to catch his eye and then perhaps nod the head backward quickly.

In Colombia, one way to get a waiter's attention is to clap the hands lightly.

In China, to beckon a waiter to refill your tea, simply turn your empty cup upside down in its saucer. If the teapot is empty, turn its lid upside down. These gestures have no significance at all in most other countries.

In Spain, Mexico, Haiti, and a sprinkling of other countries, when calling a waiter, restaurant patrons can be heard issuing a noise with the lips, something like "hssssst," or "pssssst." Another variation is to *snap the fingers*. But guidebooks caution that while this may be done by some local inhabitants, it is often considered impolite if done by visitors.

On one of my visits to Brazil, my group was seated in a fine restaurant with waiters scurrying busily around us, so I used the opportunity to ask my dinner companions, "What is the preferred way to get a waiter's attention in Brazil?" "Oh, we don't ever gesture or signal to get a waiter's attention," was the answer of my rather refined host. "In a fine restaurant, you should never have to call the waiter—he should hover so closely near your side that all you have to do is raise your head upward and whisper your wishes."

In Mexico I discovered perhaps a most unique way of beckoning a waiter. In some parts of the country they purse and pucker the lips and make a kissing noise with the lips. I would, however, in other countries urge you to exercise extreme caution in using this signal!

Try using this category of gestures to start your own investigation of various signals around the world. When you are visiting another country and being hosted by local nationals at dinner, just ask, "What is the customary way to beckon a waiter here?" It is an easy way to slip into a discussion of different gestures used around the world. And you may even discover a new beckoning gesture.

In order for conversations to run smoothly and efficiently, people have developed rules or norms for turn-taking. Have you ever been in a group interaction where people kept interrupting each other or everyone sat in silence waiting for someone else to speak? Turn-taking rules help prevent this from happening by signalling when people want control of the floor and when they want others to speak. In this classic article, Wiemann and Knapp discuss a variety of nonverbal cues that help people manage interaction through efficient turn-taking.

46

Turn-Taking in Conversations

John M. Wiemann
Mark L. Knapp

The mechanisms by which people take turns speaking in a conversation are both spoken and nonverbal, open and subconscious.

A child of five enters a room where his mother and another woman are talking. The child tugs on his mother's skirt for attention and, without waiting for her to respond, he begins talking to her. The mother becomes irritated and scolds the child for interrupting while she is talking.

Adapted from Wiemann & Knapp (1975), Turn-taking in conversations. *Journal of Communication, 25*, 75–92. Permission from Oxford University Press.

Five college students are sitting in a dorm room talking. One of the five students has been talking for about ten minutes when another member of the group says, "Jim, why don't you shut up! I can't get a word in edgewise."

In each of the preceding stories, the central figure is guilty of violating a communicative norm in our culture. And in each case, the response was in the form of a reprimand. At least two explanations account for the reprimands given to the central figures in the stories: (a) they did not provide for a smooth transition of the speaking turn from one person to the next, and (b) they forced a definition of the situation that the other interactants present were not willing to accept. The nature of this conversational "turn-taking" or "floor apportionment" will be the focus of this essay.

This leads to an important aspect of rule-governed interaction behavior: *the manner in which specific rules are employed provides us with information about the nature of the relationship between the interactants.* This seems to underline the importance of interaction rules: they directly impinge on each interactant's presented self. For example, interruptions or inattention may convey disrespect and "must be avoided unless the implied disrespect is an accepted part of the relationship" (Goffman, 1967, p. 36).

Unlike other societal rules (e.g., criminal laws), interaction rules are seldom specified, and consequently the actions they govern are usually carried out unthinkingly. For the most part, it is only when a rule is broken that the interactants become aware that something is amiss with the interaction, and attention is then usually directed away from the content of the conversation and toward putting the interaction back on the right track (Goffman, 1967). Thus, in the earlier examples, the interactants interrupted their partners to remind the offenders of two existing rules: (a) one person speaks at a time, and (b) speaker-changes should reoccur (Speier, 1972). One result of the sanctioning action might have been embarrassment for *all* present—a culturally undesirable state of affairs and a rule violation in its own right.

The way interaction is regulated in an elementary school classroom is an example of what we have been discussing. When children enter first grade, they are often told they must raise their hands before speaking. The rule is: "You may not speak unless the teacher gives you permission." The symbol by which the rule is implemented—by which permission is requested and gained—is the upraised hand. New students may be given some amount of time in which to learn the rule. Note that learning the rule and learning the symbol to implement the rule are, for all practical purposes, one and the same thing. During the learning period, violations of the rule are corrected, but tolerated. The assumption is that the children are not yet part of the school-culture. After a certain period, the teacher decides that all of the first graders have had enough time to become acculturated—that is, they have had enough time to learn the rules. Now when the hand-raising rule is violated, the children are likely to be punished; disrespect and disregard for the school-culture is assumed.

This rather ordinary example illustrates that people often rely on conformity to interaction rules—particularly turn-taking rules—for information about an individual's relationship with or orientation towards a group or individual. Speier states this same point more strongly:

> Cultural competence in using conversational procedures in social interaction not only displays adequate social membership among participants in the culture, but more deeply, *it provides a procedural basis for the ongoing organization of that culture* when members confront and deal with one another daily (Speier, 1972, p. 398, emphasis in original).

The conversational procedures Speier is concerned with are the turn-taking phenomena.

In order to communicate successfully, an interactant must understand and subscribe to the interaction rules of his or her culture. The violation of interaction rules provides us with information about an individual's orientation toward his or her fellow interactants.

With the exception of people in classrooms or those attending formal meetings, individuals usually devote little conscious time to deciding who will speak. In our culture we have no formal system for determining who will speak at "informal" gatherings. In other words, there is no cultural norm that states, for example, that when adults are sitting around the dinner table, the person sitting on the north side of the table will speak first and thereafter the speaking turn will rotate in a clockwise direction.

Yet we often evaluate our interactions in terms of the allocation of speaking roles. A person who dominates a conversation is often judged a "boor" (particularly if the "judge"—the other interactant—had something to say and did not get the opportunity). The person who constantly interrupts is judged "rude." Thus, it may be embarrassing and rude to tell the boor to give someone else a chance to speak.

In spite of this seeming paradox, there are numerous encounters in which the need to interrupt someone else to get the floor does not confront us. If interactants need not resort to violence—either verbal or physical—to get the floor, how do they decide who will speak and who will listen? In other words, how are the numerous interaction rules governing the respect of the speaker implemented?

The behavior by which an exchange of speaking turns is accomplished will be referred to here as the turn-taking mechanism. While a number of studies have dealt with various behaviors which may be part of the turn-taking mechanism, only Duncan (1970, 1972, 1973) has dealt directly with it in its entirety. Taking an inductive approach, Duncan observed interactions, and then described the behavior that accompanied speaking-role changes.

Duncan (1972, 1973) posits three rules operating during successful exchanges of the speaking turn: (1) turn-yielding cues, which are used by speakers to signal that they are concluding their remarks and that the auditors can take the floor; (2) suppression of speaking-turn claims, which are exhibited by speakers in conjunction with turn-yielding cues, when they intend to maintain their speaking turn; and (3) back channel cues, which are displayed by the auditors to indicate that they do not wish the floor, even though the speaker is displaying yielding cues.

Turn-yielding. The rule for turn-yielding states that the auditor may take his or her speaking turn when the speaker emits any one of a number of verbal or nonverbal turn-yielding cues. The display of a turn-yielding cue does not require the auditor to take the floor; he or she may remain silent or reinforce the speaker with a back channel cue. The absence of simultaneous turns (i.e., both participants in the conversation claiming the speaking turn at the same time) during the exchange of speaking roles is considered a successful exchange. If the turn-taking mechanism is operating properly, the auditor will take his or her turn in response to a turn-yielding cue emitted by the speaker, and the speaker will immediately yield his or her turn.

Suppression of speaking-turn claims. This cue serves to maintain the turn for the speaker by counteracting any turn-yielding cues emitted simultaneously. It consists of "one or both of the speaker's hands being engaged in gesticulation" (Duncan, 1973, p. 38). Self- and object-adaptors, such as scratching oneself or arranging one's clothing, do not function as claim suppressors.

Back channel cues. These cues, exhibited by the auditor, are related to various speaker signals, either within-turn signals (Duncan, 1973) or turn-yielding cues. In relation to turn-yielding cues, they serve to signal the speaker that the auditor does not wish to take the speaking role (Yngve, 1970).

Turn-requesting. Personal experience tells us that participants in a conversation are not at the mercy of the speaker, in spite of the interaction rules. To account for this, Wiemann (1973) proposed that a turn-requesting rule exists, and that auditors employ such a rule to let the speaker know that they want the floor without violating the respect due the speaker because he or she is the speaker.

Turn-requesting consists of display of one or more of a number of verbal or nonverbal cues, such as gaze and forward lean, by the auditor. If the turn-taking mechanism is functioning correctly, the speaker should relinquish the speaking role upon completion of the thought unit he or she is communicating at the time the request is made.

Weimann (1973) took a more deductive approach than Duncan in studying the floor yielding and requesting aspects of the turn-taking mechanism. A review of literature, observation in a number of different settings, and introspection led to the construction of two analysis systems, one for verbal behavior and one for nonverbal behavior (see table 1).

The verbal behaviors that played a role in turn-yielding were (in order of incidence): completions, interrogative requests, and buffers.

The only nonverbal behavior that seemed to play a role in turn-yielding was other-directed gaze. An analysis of the time spent in other-directed gazes indicated that speakers steadily increased the amount of time spent looking at the auditor as their speaking turn approached completion. This phenomenon was also noted by Kendon (1967). Other nonverbal behaviors observed, including the termination gestures specified by Duncan (1970), seemed to play little or no role in the turn-yielding of these subjects.

Verbal turn-requesting behavior included (again, in order of occurrence): simultaneous talking, buffers, reinforcers, interrogative requests, and stutter starts.

Nonverbal turn-requesting behavior included other-directed gazes and head nods. While the other nonverbal behaviors included in the study were emitted by the auditors, they seemed to play little or no role in turn-requesting for these subjects.

Since the nonverbal channel is often more subtle than the verbal, speakers can be expected to make more use of it. Probably the most frequently occurring nonverbal yielding behavior is auditor-directed gazes. The percentage of time spent by the speaker looking at the face of the auditor increases steadily as the speaking turn approaches finality from 61 percent in the first third of the interaction episode to 83 percent in the final third. Conversely, the percentage of time the auditor spends looking at the speaker increases from the first third to the second third of the interaction episode, and then drops off in the final third. It seems that other-directed gazes function more as a turn-yielding device than as a turn-requesting device, but they can function as both.

Table 1

Behavioral Analysis Categories for the Turn-Taking Mechanism

Nonverbal	*Verbal*
1. **Other-directed gazes**. The amount of time spent looking at the facial area around the eyes of the other person.	1. **Interrogative request**. A question specifically directed to the other dyad member.
2. **Smiles**. A positive facial expression marked by upturned corners of the mouth (as opposed to a straight or down-turned mouth)	2. **Completion**. The completion of a declarative "statement" with no attempt being made by the speaker to continue.
3. **Reclining angle**. When that plane defined by a line from the communicator's shoulders to his hips is away from the vertical plane, such that the communicator is leaning backward to some degree.	3. **Buffers**. Short words or phrases which are "content-free," more or less stereotypical, and which either precede or follow substantive statements (e.g., "but uh," "you know," "or something," "um," "well," and "uh-well").
4. **Forward-leaning angle**. When that plane defined by a line from the communicator's shoulders to his hips is away from the vertical plane, such that the communicator is bending forward at the waist.	4. **Interruption**. The attempt to assume the speaking role before it has been relinquished by the current speaker.
5. **Gesticulations**. Hand and arm movements (excluding self-manipulations), including side-to-side, forward-back, and up-and-down movements (e.g., an up-raised and pointed index finger).	5. **Simultaneous talking**. Speaking by both interactants at the same time. (This includes simultaneous turns, where both speakers attempt to hold the floor at the same time.)
6. **Head nods**. Cyclical up-and-down movements of the head.	6. **Stutter starts**. Short words (including nonfluencies) or phrases repeated with increasing frequency by one interactant while the other interactant holds the speaking role (e.g., "I . . . I . . . I . . . I think we should vote now.")
	7. **Reinforcers**. Words that provide feedback to the speaker, but do not necessarily attempt to gain the speaking role for the interactant emitting them. Short questions asking for clarification are coded in this category. (Examples include: "Yeah," "yes," and "um-hm.")

The role that gesticulations play in the turn-taking mechanism is not entirely clear. Duncan (1970, 1972, 1973) reports that his subjects used gesticulations as turn-yielding signals. On the other hand, Wiemann (1973) found a very low incidence of gesticulations—too low to draw any meaningful conclusions. A number of factors may account for low incidence of gesticulations in some situations. The setting may encourage interactants to tone down their behaviors—not just gesticulations, but all overt behaviors. Also, the topic may or may not encourage excited or animated behavior.

The role that shifts of posture play in the turn-taking mechanism is unclear. The available data—which are unconvincing—suggest that it plays no role at all. However, Kendon (1970) and our own natural-state observations argue against this interpretation. People do not really sit still in their seats for an appreciable length of time. Auditors may be reclining for a time and then, as they prepare to take the speaking role, move to an upright position or even to a forward-leaning position. Likewise, speakers at times "punctuate" their yielding of the floor by leaning back in their chairs as they finish their utterances.

Head nodding appears to play a major role in turn-requesting, while having little or no significance in turn-yielding. Speakers do not systematically increase the amount of nodding as the episode progresses. On the other hand, there is a dramatic increase in nodding by the auditor.

The rapidity of the head nods and whether or not they are accompanied by any verbal behavior seems to determine how speakers interpret them. Closely placed, successive nods, and nods that accompany short, rapid-fire reinforcers (e.g., "yeah, yeah") or buffers (e.g., "uh, uh"), constitute requests for the floor by the auditor. On the other hand, nods that serve as responses to a request for feedback from the speaker seem to be interpreted by the speaker as support for his maintaining the floor.

Both nodding and other-directed gazes appear to be important to the turn-taking mechanism because of the dual role they play. These behaviors indicate support for and interest in the other interactant when they are displayed by one member of the dyad. They also provide both the speaker and the auditor with a means of either yielding or requesting the floor. Their supportive nature "softens" the terms of the exchange. The nodding auditor is signaling the speaker his or her agreement and reinforcement at the same time the request is being made; the respect of the speaking role is maintained because, in effect, the auditor is letting the speaker know that there is no threat or disrespect intended by the takeover of the floor. In like manner, the speaker can use nodding and auditor-directed gazes to inform the auditor that he or she is looking for feedback and that he is receiving the auditor's messages. All this can be accomplished without interrupting the flow of the "conversation."

While primarily yielding cues, gesticulations may also be used by auditors to signal in a rather dramatic way their desire to get the floor. An example of this use of gesticulation is the pointed and raised index finger—usually accompanied by an open mouth, poised to speak, or other such behavior that is similar to school-trained hand-raising.

Other nonverbal cues not yet specifically studied, but whose co-occurrence with reinforcers (see table 1) might influence the interpretation of reinforcers, include a deep inspiration of breath immediately before the reinforcer is uttered and the holding open of the mouth for a brief period before the reinforcer is uttered (Wiemann, 1973).

The line of thinking developed here suggests that a "grammar" of dyadic interaction exists. This is not to imply that there is any relationship between this grammar and that proposed for spoken languages. Rather, the term "grammar," as used here, implies the existence of a structure of interaction. By correctly applying the rules of this structure, interactants can accurately express their relationship to the other interactants without interrupting the flow of the content of the conversation.

Argyle (1969, 1972) has suggested that social competence can be studied much as motor skills are, with similar implications. If the components of "successful" interaction can be isolated, they can be analyzed and taught. Argyle lists four components of social competence: (1) perceptual sensitivity, (2) basic interaction skills, (3) rewardingness, and (4) poise (Argyle, 1972). While all of these come into play even in something so elementary as negotiating the speaking turn, basic interaction skills seem to be at the heart of the matter: "To be socially competent it is necessary to be able to establish a smoothly meshing pattern of interaction with other people" (Argyle, p. 78).

Turn-taking in conversations not only helps us apportion the floor, but also serves a symbolic function of helping the interactants to define their relationship. The way in which this ritual is managed by one interactant will affect the judgments made about him or her by the other interactant. Thus, research may show that it is the management of the small, unnoticed, ritualistic behaviors that has the greatest effect upon our attributions about others; it may be these behaviors that determine whether or not we are successful interactants.

References

Argyle, M. (1969). *Social interaction*. Chicago, Aldine Atherton.

Argyle, M. (1972). *The psychology of interpersonal behavior* (2nd ed.). Baltimore: Penguin.

Duncan, S. (1970). Toward a grammar for floor apportionment: A system approach to face-to-face interaction. In *Proceedings of the Second Annual Environmen-*

tal Design Research Association Conference. Philadelphia: Environmental Design Research Association.

Duncan, S. (1972). Some signals and rules for taking speaking turns in conversations. *Journal of Personality and Social Psychology, 23*, 283–292.

Duncan, S. (1973). Toward a grammar for dyadic conversation. *Semiotica, 9*, 29–46.

Goffman, E. (1967). *Interaction ritual*. Garden City, NY: Doubleday Anchor.

Kendon, A. (1967). Some functions of gaze-direction in social interaction. *Acta Psychologica, 26*, 22–63.

Kendon, A. (1970). Movement coordination in social interaction: Some examples described. *Acta Psychologica, 32*, 101–125.

Kendon, A. (1972). Some relationships between body motion and speech: An analysis of an example. In A. W. Seigman & B. Pope (Eds.), *Studies in dyadic communication*. Elmsford, NY: Pergamon Press.

Speier, M. (1973). *How to observe face-to-face communication: A sociological introduction*. Pacific Palisades, CA: Goodyear.

Speier, M. (1972). Some conversational problems for interactional analysis. In D. Sudnow (Ed.), *Studies in social interaction*. New York: Free Press.

Wiemann, J. M. (1973). An exploratory study of turn-taking in conversations: Verbal and Nonverbal behavior. Unpublished M.S. thesis, Purdue University.

Yngve, V. H. On getting a word in edgewise. In M. A. Campbell et al., (Eds.), *Papers From the Sixth Regional Meeting, Chicago Linguistics Society*. Chicago: Dept. of Linguistics, U. of Chicago.

Can you remember a time when you wanted to end a conversation and your partner didn't get the hint? Chances are that you engaged in a number of leave-taking behaviors, such as taking a step back, looking away, and nodding rapidly. In this article, O'Leary and Gallois examine leave-taking behaviors by examining the last ten conversational turns in interactions between friends and strangers.

47

The Last Ten Turns in Conversations between Friends and Strangers

Maria J. O'Leary
Cynthia Gallois

There has been considerable interest in recent years in the temporal structure of face-to-face interactions, in particular, the ways in which an interactional phase or episode is signalled. A number of studies (Gallois & Markel, 1975; Jaffe & Feldstein, 1970; Prebor, 1972) have identified differences in temporal aspects of speech at the beginning, middle, and end of conversations; other researchers have also studied the nonvocal behavior associated with particular phases of an interaction (e.g., Kendon & Ferber, 1973; Knapp, Hart, Friedrich, & Schulman, 1973) and the signals which exist

From O'Leary & Gallois (1985), The last ten turns: Behavior and Sequencing in friends and stranger's conversation endings, *Journal of Nonverbal Behavior, 9*, 8–27. This version of the paper has been shortened and edited with permission from the authors.

within these larger phases to exchange the floor (Duncan & Fiske, 1977; LaFrance & Mayo, 1976; Markel, 1975) or mark an episode change (Erickson, 1975). The focus of this study was the sequence of behaviors, both verbal and nonverbal, which differentiate the end of an interaction from the rest. The unit of analysis chosen was the conversation turn.

Goffman (1971) postulated that the greeting phase of a face-to-face interaction functions to affirm the existence of a previous relationship and to fix the roles of interactants, while the ending " . . . must bring the encounter to an unambiguous close, sum up the consequences of the encounter for the relationship, and bolster the relationship for the anticipated period of no contact" (p. 79). Schegloff (1968) suggested a sequence in the types of statements used to begin telephone conversations. Krivonos and Knapp (1975) found a similar sequence, and also described nonverbal behaviors commonly associated with greetings, as did Kendon (1976).

Research on interactional endings or "leave-taking" has pointed out the importance of a sequence of signals in negotiating the close of an encounter. Schegloff and Sacks (1973) conceptualized the problems of ending a conversation as one of halting the turn-taking mechanism. They proposed the application of a recognized terminal exchange, such as "goodbye—goodbye," as a solution to this problem, but only when it is part of a properly initiated closing section. In any case, the whole end of the interaction must be negotiated, and the partners must signal their acceptance of each stage of the close if the turn-taking mechanism is to halt.

In an extension of their earlier work on conversational endings, Albert and Kessler (1978) described a sequence of characteristic verbal statements: first summary statements, or a selective restatement of part of the history of the encounter, followed by (second) justification statements, or reasons for ending the encounter; third, positive statements, to end the interaction on a positive note, followed by (fourth), continuity statements, which affirm the underlying relationship despite termination; and, finally, fifth, well-wishing statements, indicating a concern about the other person's future well-being. Albert and Kessler studied unstructured telephone conversations between friends and strangers and confirmed the existence of this sequence. One aim of the present study was to determine whether this same sequence of verbal behavior exists in face-to-face interactions.

Nonverbal behavior, as well as words, forms an integral part of the process of ending a conversation. For example, Kendon (1976) observed a behavioral pattern of departure that includes stepping backwards, then stepping back into the group, and finally walking away. Lockard, Allen, Schiele, and Wiemar (1978) also found that unequal weight stances and weight shifts, along with breaking of eye contact and hand gestures, indicated imminent departure. This work and Erickson's (1975) finding that postural shifts are associated with a change in topic indicate the importance of proxemic change as a signal in intention to depart.

Knapp et al. (1973) attempted to isolate the verbal and nonverbal components of leave-taking. They found that the most frequently occurring behaviors, breaking eye contact, smiling, major nodding movements, major leg movements, forward lean, and leverage positions (such as putting one's hands in a position that will help him or her get up from a chair), peaked in frequency in the 15 seconds prior to standing, while orientation of the subject in the direction of proposed exit occurred most frequently during the final stage, as the subject left the room.

The work reported here all suggests the existence of regular patterns of behavior, both verbal and nonverbal, which occur at the end of an interaction. These behaviors serve to distinguish the end from earlier phases and to reinforce the relationship between interactants. In the present study, the verbal and nonverbal behavior in the last ten turns of two-person conversations were chosen for study and were compared to behavior in the ten middlemost turns. It was hypothesized that the sequence of statements in conversation endings, as proposed by Albert and Kessler (1978), would consist of summary statements, followed by justification, positive, continuity, and finally well-wishing statements. We added three elements to this sequence derived from Knapp et al. (1973): information statements, verbalizations, and questions. We also predicted that nonverbal behaviors, including breaking of eye contact (or looking away from the partner), smiling, nodding, and proxemic change, would be more frequent in the end than the middle phase of face-to-face interactions.

Finally, maintenance of the relationship appears to be an important feature of endings. Some previous research has found that friends engage in more affiliative behavior than strangers at the ends of interactions (e.g., Summerfield & Lake, 1977), while other studies have found the opposite (e.g., Albert & Kessler, 1978). Therefore, while it was expected that conversational endings between friends would differ from those between strangers, no specific predictions were made.

Method and Results Summary

Method: Twenty female pairs consisting of undergraduate psychology students participated in this research. Ten of these pairs were strangers. The other 10 were friends. All pairs were videotaped as they engaged in conversations about abortion as a social issue. One member of the pair was told that she was to go to another room to complete a different task immediately after the conversation about abortion was completed. The average length of the conversations was eight minutes. Two sections of the conversation were analyzed: the middle ten turns and the last ten turns. The verbal and nonverbal behavior used during these turns was coded using the categories in Tables 1 and 2.

Results: This study showed that the typical sequence of verbal communication during leave-taking was information statements followed by summary statements, questions, and verbalizations. In terms of nonverbal behavior, four behaviors occurred more during the last ten turns than the middle ten turns. These leave-taking behaviors were: (1) leverage and forward lean, (2) smiling, (3) gesturing, and (4) looking away. Results also showed that during leave-taking, friends looked away more and used more grooming behavior than did strangers. In contrast, strangers nodded more during conversational endings than did friends.

Table 1

Categories of Verbal Behavior Used in Data Analysis

Category	Example	Definition
Information	"I think . . .," "Uh, huh, I also think. . . ."	gives opinion or suggestion, sometimes along with an indication of agreement
Question	"How do you feel?"	asks a question of partner
Verbalization	"Hm-mm;" "Uh-huh"	single words or sounds in response to partner, sometimes including agreement
Summary statement	"So we've decided that. . . ."	statement of all or part of prior verbal or emotional content
Continuity statement	"See you later"	any acknowledgment of future meetings
Justification	"We seem to be finished."	statement of reason for ending the encounter
Well-wishing statement	"Take care" "Good-bye"	statement of concern about partner's future well-being

---

Table 2
Categories of Nonverbal Behavior Used in Data Analysis

Category	Definition
Looking	
at	eyes and nose pointed at partner's face
away	eyes and nose pointed away from partner's face
Head Movement	
shaking	movement from side to side
nodding	movement up and down
Arm/Hand Movement	
gesture	movement accompanying own speech
grooming	touching of own body (to stroke or groom)
leveraging	hands placed on arms of chair in a manner that would assist rising from chair
Facial Expression	
smile	raising or upturning of the corners of the mouth
Trunk Movement	
leaning forward	movement of trunk forward 30° or more from previous position
leaning backward	movement of trunk back 30° or more from previous position
standing	rising from a sitting to standing position
Leg Movement	any movement of legs resulting in a significant change in posture, e.g., uncrossing
Orientation (while standing)	
door	trunk oriented in direction of door

DISCUSSION

The results of this study shed further light on the verbal and nonverbal behavior which both distinguishes the ending phase of a conversation from the rest and aids in the negotiation of the closing. The analysis of verbal behavior supported Albert and Kessler's (1978) study and indicated that the statement types suggested by Knapp et al. (1973) combine with them as predicted. Within the ending phase, information statements were followed by summary statements, which were followed in turn by questions, verbalization, justification, continuity, and well-wishing statements. Thus verbal behavior appeared to fall into two phases: one in which the conversation topic was ended (information, summary, some questions and verbalizations), and a second which ended the interaction itself, as well as signaled that the relationship would resume (justification, continuity, and well-wishing).

The results also indicated the occurrence of distinctive nonverbal behaviors at the end of conversations. There was a marked increase in mutual smiling, together with leverage and forward lean by the subject who was about to depart. The change in nonverbal behaviors, which Knapp et al. (1973) also found, suggests that they too play an important role in signalling the end of turn-taking, and thus of the conversation.

Smiling is a well-recognized signal of support and affiliation (Knapp et al., 1973; Mehrabian & Ksionzky, 1972) and its mutual occurrence within one turn was noted by Duncan, Brunner, and Fiske (1979). Within conversational endings, smiling may affirm the existence of a relationship that transcends physical presence. In addition, although forward leans have been associated with affiliation (Mehrabian, 1971), Knapp et al. noted their second function of signalling inaccessibility. When leveraging and forward lean occur in the same turn, as they did in the present study, they provide a strong signal of imminent departure. It appears, then, that behaviors which identify the ending phase of a conversation may sometimes serve a dual purpose. Most of the behaviors distinguishing the end section are associated in some way with signalling support and affiliation. At the same time however, they may, along with looking away, which is often associated with lower affiliation, and standing and turning away, which clearly indicate departure, function to signal inaccessibility.

A sequence of nonverbal behaviors was suggested by the results of this study: smiling by both subjects, hand gesture by the subject who would remain, hand gesture by the subject who would depart, looking away by both subjects, leverage/lean forward by the departing subject, head nodding by the subject who would stay, and grooming by the departing subject. These results, however, must be interpreted cautiously, as discrepancies existed in the placement of several behaviors. Mutual smiling regularly preceded all other behaviors. Hand gesture by the departing subject usually followed gestures by the subject who would remain and preceded mutual looking away. On the other hand, the placement of the remaining behaviors was found to vary somewhat.

Finally, the nonverbal behavior in the ending phase of the conversations differed depending on whether the interactants were friends or strangers. First, conversations between friends showed more activity than those between strangers, a result similar to those of Summerfield and Lake (1977). In addition, three behavioral clusters—more looking away by both partners, more grooming by the departing partner, and fewer head nods by the partner who would remain—characterized conversations by friends. Thus, friends appeared to make more use of signals of inaccessibility by breaking gaze more frequently and by giving fewer signals to continue the conversation (head nods), as well as by grooming in preparation for departure. Friends may have felt the need for a more definite end to the conversation, while strangers were more concerned to end their first interaction on a positive note. At the same time, friends appeared to make specific appointments with their continuity statements, while strangers used vaguer statements, such as "See you later"; thus it was clear to friends that the relationship would continue. Nonetheless, there were no significant differences between friends and strangers in the types of statements used, only in the nonverbal behavior.

The fact that this study, like those of Albert and Kessler (1978), Knapp et al. (1973), and Summerfield and Lake (1977), failed to find outstanding differences between the conversations of friends and strangers, reflects the wide scope of norms about conversational endings. Certain behavioral regularities seem to be present in the end phase of conversations across a number of situations and levels of acquaintance. Our subjects were relatively casual friends, who in some cases had known each other for only a few months. Close friends might have behaved differently. Still, when the literature as a whole is considered, similar results have appeared in studies of face-to-face and telephone conversations, with formal interview and informal settings, between friends and strangers of equal and unequal status, and with artificially induced or naturally occurring termination. Our results, along with those of previous research, give evidence for the importance of both a verbal and a nonverbal sequence of signals, which may be to some extent interchangeable in smoothly negotiating the last few turns.

References

Albert, S., & Kessler, S. (1978). Ending social encounters. *Journal of Experimental Social Psychology*, 14, 541–553.

Duncan, S., Jr., & Fiske, D. W. (1977). *Face-to-face interaction: Research, methods, and theory*. Hillsdale, NJ: Lawrence Erlbaum.

Erickson, F. (1975). One function of proxemic shifts in face-to-face interaction. In A. Kendon, R. Harris, & M. R. Key (Eds.), *Organization of behavior in face-to-face interactions*. The Hague: Mouton.

Gallois, C., & Markel, N. N. (1975). Turn-taking: Social personality and conversational style. *Journal of Personality and Social Psychology*, 31, 1134–1140.

Goffman, E. (1971). *Relations in public*. New York: Basic Books.

Jaffe, J., & Feldstein, S. (1970). *Rhythms of dialogue*. New York: Academic Press.

Kendon, A. (1976). The F-formation system: The Spatial organization of social encounters. *Man-Environment Systems, 6*, 291–296.

Kendon, A., & Ferber, A. (1973). A description of some human greetings. In R. P. Michael & J. H. Cook (Eds.), *Comparative ecology and behavior of primates*. London: Academic Press.

Knapp, M., Hart, R., Friedrich, G., & Shulman, G. (1973). The rhetoric of goodbye: Verbal and nonverbal correlates of human leave-taking. *Speech Monographs, 40,* 182–198.

Krivonos, P. D., & Knapp, M. L. (1975). Initiating communication: What do you say when you say Hello? *Central States Speech Journal, 26,* 115–125.

La France, M., & Mayo, C. (1976). Racial differences in gaze behavior during conversations: Two systematic observational studies. *Journal of Personality and Social Psychology, 33,* 547–552.

Lockard, J. S., Allen, D. J., Schiele, B. J., & Wiemar, M. J. (1978). Human postural signals: Stance, weight-shifts, and social distance as intention movements to depart. *Animal Behavior, 26,* 219–224.

Markel, N. N. (1975). Coverbal behavior associated with conversation turns. In A. Kendon, R. Harris, & M. R. Ken (Eds.), *Organization of behavior in face-to-face interaction.* The Hague: Mouton.

Mehrabian, A. (1971). Verbal and nonverbal interaction of strangers in a waiting situation. *Journal of Experimental Research in Personality, 5,* 127–138.

Mehrabian, A., & Ksionzky, S. (1972). Some determiners of social interaction. *Sociometry, 35,* 588–609.

Prebor, L. D. (1972). *The natural history of a conversation.* Unpublished doctoral dissertation, University of Florida.

Schegloff, E. A. (1968). Sequencing in conversational openings. *American Anthropologist, 70,* 1075–1095.

Schegloff, E. A., & Sacks, H. (1973). Opening up closings. *Semiotica, 8,* 289–327.

Summerfield, A. B., & Lake, J. A. (1977). Non-verbal and verbal behaviors associated with parting. *British Journal of Psychology, 68,* 133–136.

PART IV

Contemporary Nonverbal Theories of Message Exchange

So far, this reader has focused on the types (or codes) of nonverbal communication and the various functions that nonverbal communication serves in your life. As you have seen, nonverbal behaviors can help you express emotion and intimacy, persuade or deceive others, and manage interactions more effectively. However, it is not enough to just look at how *one* person uses nonverbal communication. To really understand nonverbal communication as a process, you must understand how one person's behavior affects another person's behavior. From this perspective, nonverbal communication can be thought of as a series of moves and countermoves, with each move having an impact on the exchange of messages.

Since the mid-1970s, communication researchers have been very interested in explaining why people react in particular ways to the nonverbal behavior of others. Specifically, researchers have been interested in a process called *nonverbal adaptation*, whereby one person changes her or his behavior so that it is more or less similar to the partner's behavior. When people change their behavior to become more similar, *reciprocity* or *convergence* has occurred. When people change their behavior to become less similar, *compensation* or *divergence* has occurred.

Researchers have looked at how these patterns of reciprocity and compensation occur in response to increases or decreases in *immediacy* or *involvement*. Immediacy cues include behaviors such as touch, smiling, and close distance. These cues increase physical or psychological closeness, signal availability for communication, and send messages of interpersonal warmth. Similarly, *involvement* cues, which also include behaviors such as touch and close distances, show that people are actively engaged in a conversation with you. Other immediacy or involvement behaviors include forward lean, direct body orientation, and gaze, to name a few. What happens when your friend decreases immediacy by acting cold or distant? How do you respond? What do you do when your romantic interest unexpectedly acts especially warm and flirtatious toward you? The theories discussed in this final section of the reader attempt to answer these and other important questions.

Giles and Wadleigh discuss the basic concepts and ideas related to communication accommodation theory. This theory shows how you accommodate the behavior of others by becoming more similar to them (convergence) or more dissimilar from them (divergence).

48

Accommodating Nonverbally

Howard Giles
Paul Mark Wadleigh

Consider some backpackers gathering at the end of the day in a European youth hostel (Giles & Noels, 1997). These travelers come from all over the world and include Scandinavians, Americans, Chinese, Italians, Germans, Thai, and New Zealanders. In a common room, they come together to prepare their meals, discuss adventures, share impressions of foreign sites, and offer advice on where to go and whom to avoid. How will they communicate (and in what language[s])? Will the Germans slouch in their chairs when they speak with the Americans? Will the Americans sit up straight? Will everyone line up to use the shower in an orderly and patient fashion? Or will there be (what will look to some) a mad dash and jostling as everyone races to feel clean and fresh?

Consider instances of interaction within the same culture. How does a fifteen-year-old behave when visiting an elderly relative or a much younger cousin? How does a male gang member relate to a female police

This article was written especially for *The Nonverbal Communication Reader.*

425

officer who interviews him? How does he approach a rival gang member in the street? Who changes their behavior to accommodate whom? The answers, of course, depend on the relationship between the communicators as well as their individual motives and desires. Other important "intergroup" encounters suggest a relational power differential, such as that between a freshman and a middle-aged teaching assistant, an applicant and a job interviewer, or a supplicant and a loan officer. When people come together, do they give some and move toward each other, do they attempt to remain resolutely true to themselves, or do they emphasize their distinctivenesses by increasing communicative distances? Do they swing between these options (like a communicative pendulum within an encounter), or do they achieve all these goals simultaneously? How do others react to such chameleon-like behavior? Communication accommodation theory (CAT) provides a wide-ranging framework to predict and explain the answers to such questions.

A BRIEF BACKDROP

CAT developed in the early 1970s as a means of exploring the above questions (Giles, 1973; Giles, Taylor, & Bourhis, 1973). Initially, CAT focused much of its attention on how and why speakers shift their accents toward and away from one another—a vocal, nonverbal dimension of considerable social meaning (see Ryan, Giles, & Bradac, 1994). Since then, the nonverbal (as well as verbal and discursive) parameters of the theory have widened enormously. As its name implies, CAT now lends itself to being a general interpersonal communication theory. It has been utilized in an array of applied situations (e.g., occupational, medical, legal, and media), has been studied in a number of languages, and has been invoked to explain long-term dialect shifts in urban and rural communities (Trudgill, 1986) as well as why minority languages survive or die away (e.g., Leets & Giles, 1995). Many renditions (and revisions) of the theory have been crafted in formal, propositional terms, and the theory has also been represented visually in a model (see, for example, Giles, Mulac, Bradac, & Johnson, 1987; Gallois, Giles, Jones, Cargile, & Ota, 1995). Here, however, we provide a basic description of the theory to illustrate CAT's power and appeal as an explanation for patterns of nonverbal behavior.

CONVERGENCE AND DIVERGENCE

Convergence

Convergence can be defined as a strategy whereby individuals adapt their communication so that their visual, vocal, and/or verbal behavior becomes more similar to their partner's behavior. These communicative behaviors include facial expression, gaze, features, postures, proxemics, touch, gait, smiling, speech rate, and pitch. Typically, convergence improves the effectiveness of communication episodes. The premise is that the more nonverbally similar we are to our partner, the more he or she will like and/or respect us, and the more social rewards, including compliance (see Buller & Aune, 1988), will be garnered as a consequence. Convergence is associated with favorable evaluations (e.g., Gregory, Dagan, & Webster, 1997) if the accommodative intent is perceived favorably and not as, for example, mimicry or patronizing (cf. Simard, Taylor, & Giles, 1976).

Convergence can occur within a power motif between the communicators. Depending on the relative social status of those involved, converging can be upward or downward. For instance, the convergence of a student adopting his renowned professor's faster speech rate would be labeled and perceived as "upward," whereas assuming one's gardner's ethnic accent might be construed as "downward." In tandem, the extent of convergence can, of course, be partial or full. Moving toward that professor's 100 words per minute by means of matching it exactly would be "full" convergence, whereas a shift to only 75 would be "partial" (Street, 1982).

CAT proposes that convergence reflects a communicator's need for social integration with another (or their group). As such, it is a reflection of an individual's desire for social approval. This process of social identification is also evident in music. Some British popstars use an "American" brogue in their singing to accommodate audiences in the United States. A recent study showed that on his popular American TV talk show, Larry King changed the pitch of his voice as a function of his guests' status (e.g., he would converge more toward President Clinton than toward former Vice-President Dan Quayle). Conversely, guests of lower status would accommodate more to Larry King than he would to them (Gregory & Webster, 1996). Relatedly, Bourhis (1991) found that English was the language most often converged to in government offices in New Brunswick, Canada, even though French speakers were the majority and even when French speakers were communicating with an English-speaking subordinate employee.

Accommodation is usually directed toward those of greater rather than lesser power—hence, convergence is often uni-directional (see Giles, Bourhis, & Taylor, 1977). In accord with traditional sex-role theory, it has been found that females converge to the gaze patterns of males, but not so much the opposite (Mulac, Studley, Wiemann, & Bradac, 1987). Indeed, the more a male endorses a masculine sex-role ideology, the less likely he is (as CAT would predict) to converge toward women (Fitzpatrick, Mulac, & Dindia, 1995). This also underscores another important issue: whether the convergence is symmetrical in nature or asymmetrical (see Gallois & Giles, 1998). With symmetrical patterns, both people converge. With asymmetrical patterns, only one person converges.

The desire to make oneself intelligible, predictable, and comprehensible often leads to convergence, particularly with people whom the accommodator respects or who hold significant social rewards. This is not to suggest that needs for social approval and integration are the only primary motives for interpersonal convergence. The need to express empathy (to, say, a trauma victim) may also mediate convergent tendencies. Yet convergence in compassionate circumstances—and especially when disastrous consequences are shared (e.g., an economic recession, a local ferry disaster, a bombing raid)—can soon dissipate once the tragedy's impact pales. In fact, accommodation can sometimes be unhelpful, as when familial security and empathy encourages over-dependence and a lack of autonomy (see Williams, Giles, Coupland, Dalby, & Manasse, 1990).

Divergence

Divergence refers to the way in which communicators accentuate perceived nonverbal (and other) differences between themselves and others. Like convergence, it can take many forms (e.g., full vs. partial, upward vs. downward, and symmetrical vs. asymmetrical). The motives for divergence can include personal disdain for another (including habits, mannerisms, dress, arguments, etc.) and the emphasis of a valued group identity (see Giles & Johnson, 1981; Pittam, 1996). For instance, it has been shown that some African-American schoolchildren will adopt Black features in their voice patterns (and presumably ethnically distinctive nonverbals, such as gestures and gait) when they become aware and proud of their cultural identity—as do certain singers wishing to emphasize their ethnic heritages (e.g., Yaeger-Dror, 1991). In this vein, some readers may recall the 1961 movie, *The Sound of Music*, set in Europe during World War II. Therein, and depicting a supposedly true event, the von Trapp family performed a concert in which they deliberately sang an Austrian song ("Edelweiss") to a mixed audience comprised of the local (Austrian) community and German Nazis. Its function was clearly to differentiate themselves from the latter and to rally the former group's sense of national identity and vigor. Empirical studies have shown that the mere maintenance of nonverbal styles and, especially, divergence are generally evaluated negatively by recipients—as emerged for the Nazis in this famous musical. Presumably, being the target of divergence is an indication that you are not deserving of the diverger's liking or respect, a feeling that does not endear one to the convergently deficient.

It is critical to highlight that divergence (or lack of convergence) is not always a personally directed, communicative tactic. According to intergroup theory (see, for example, Giles & Coupland, 1992; Tajfel, 1978), the behaviors may reflect a valued dimension of one's identity and not be intended to be personally insulting or rude. Communicative parameters such as accent, gestures, and gait are often valued symbols of ingroup identity for ethnic (and other social) groups (Cargile, Giles, & Clément, 1996). What is perceived negatively as divergence or rebellion by outgroup members may be perceived positively as convergence by ingroup members (Doise, Sinclair, & Bourhis, 1976).

As with convergence, divergence's motivational origins need not always be affective and allied to facework as in the maintenance or creation of a positive personal or group identity. Rather, it can sometimes function more cognitively so as to facilitate the coordination of communication. As an example, slowing down one's speech rate considerably may be strategically employed to induce another to bring their intolerably (and "machine gun-like") fast speech rate down to a more conversationally comfortable level. In this instance, the initial divergence need not be devalued by the recipient but, perhaps, appreciated as fostering comprehensibility.

FURTHER DISTINCTIONS

Thus far, we have focused implicitly on "objective" accommodation. That is, actual behaviors that can be reliably measured and coded. However, the examination of accommodative phenomena need not be restricted to the behavioral level, but can also include an appraisal of the intentions of communicators and perceptions of receivers. These latter two levels are termed psychological and subjective accommodations, respectively (see Thakerar, Giles, & Cheshire, 1982).

In the case of psychological accommodation, a communicator's intention is often consistent with the actual behavior, but this need not always be the case. For example, one of our American backpackers may innocently and "helpfully" decide to adopt an Italian accent and expressive gestures with one of the Italian students. However, these nonverbals may be way off the mark. Such miscues have been documented with some parents' misguided attempts to sound and move like their adolescent children (Platt &

Weber, 1984). In such cases, the actual behavior is interpreted as "over-accommodative" at best or divergent at worst!

Subjective accommodation is when the receiver interprets the communication to have been convergent or divergent. Again, this may or may not correspond with objectively measured behaviors. To use the above incident again, the Italian recipient may not be familiar enough with American English to even have been aware that such an attempt was made. Psychologically, convergence was intended, but neither objectively nor subjectively accomplished. Such mismatches (and others) are the breeding ground for miscommunication.

The differences between objective, psychological, and subjective accommodation suggest that interactants have some notion of the optimal level of accommodation required (Giles & Smith, 1979). That is, communicators have beliefs and expectations that act as guidelines for what is appropriate and acceptable accommodative behavior in particular situations. For instance, people tend to have preconceived notions about how outgroup members will behave in certain social encounters (Gallois & Pittam, 1996). Americans may expect that Italians are generally more emotional and outgoing. The American backpacker (above) runs the risk of offending the travel-weary Italian, who may interpret the former now as boisterous and intrusive. It could be said that the American was overaccommodating the Italian (see Coupland, Coupland, Giles, & Henwood, 1988). Note that the Italian may now have a new stereotype of how Americans communicate. If the Italian's stereotype of Americans was of a relatively more reserved demeanor, then the Italian could conceivably be offended at the American's failure to behave according to expectations. Either way, a communication faux pas resulted and convergence was not optimally achieved. CAT contends that people do not like being accommodated fully on all conceivable communicative dimensions. Complete convergence implies that one's communicative identity (and hence persona) is not unique and immutable.

Another stereotype—turning now to the nonverbal dimension of dress style—is the classic example of the "Texas tycoon" and the similar "Southern gentleman." This garb is represented in the media as a cowboy hat and multi-yoked suit with pearl snap buttons for the Texan and a planter's hat, white suit, and string tie for the southern gentleman. Molloy (1975), a business consultant advising on matters of nonverbal communication, claims that it is a tragic mistake for anyone not actually native to an area to assume such regional and cultural trappings. Even amongst natives who sport such attire, it is considered an emblem of nativity and is not to be appropriated by immigrants. The same can be said for regional accents in the southern United States, with the difference that over time an individual's accent can often shift to resemble that of the adopted home area, and this is ultimately welcomed (if it is even noticed). Consider the Americanization of Bob Hope, Cary Grant, Mel Gibson, and Ted Koppel, or the Britification of Billy Idol, T. S. Eliot, and Winston Churchill.

The distinctions, then, between psychological, subjective, and objective accommodation are at the sociopsychological heartland of CAT in the following ways. First, people tend to assume they are moving communicatively toward where they believe others are. Interestingly, the seminal study by Bell (1982) showed just this in the context of New Zealand radio announcers. The same announcers read the same news but at different points in the day to different radio station audiences. The stations had presumed audiences of different socioeconomic strata. The announcers then accommodated their reading pronunciations toward that of the accents of their anticipated listeners. However, this trajectory may not lead to where others actually are or where others believe themselves to be; another important issue. For example, some older hospital patients mismanage their downward convergent attempts by assuming any woman in hospital garb entering their room is a nurse, and not a doctor. Indeed, a fair proportion of socially active and cognitively alert elderly informants in a recent study claimed that they had been the recipients of patronization (e.g., slow talk, "over"-smiling, excessive touching) which they mostly found demeaning (Giles, Fox, & Smith, 1993). Interestingly, these respondents claimed that other elderly people were more the recipients of such patronizing stances than they were themselves!

Second, the coupling of psychological convergence with objective divergence is an interesting phenomenon we termed "speech complementarity." For instance, Hogg (1985) found, in his taped discussion sessions, that male students adopted more masculine-sounding voices when talking to females. Although "divergent" in terms of measured responses, the males here may have been aiming for a nonverbal stance that symbolized their male identity and appeal. Interestingly, and in parallel, it has been found that American women sound more "feminine" (e.g., having a higher and more variable pitch and softer voices)—and hence perhaps more seductive—when talking to an intimate, as opposed to an unknown, male over the telephone (Montepare & Vega, 1988). Indeed, and in accord with the notion that we embrace multiple goals in interaction, it has been argued that a fine meshing of physician convergence on the one hand (e.g., matching the patient's nonverbal style), and complementarity on the other (e.g., the physician underscoring her medical expertise) is essential for patient satisfaction and compliance with health regimes (see Street, 1991).

Third, and conversely, dissociating from another psychologically can be managed by converging toward where the other is communicatively. For instance, Woolard (1989) invoked the etiquette of an "accommodation norm" in Catalonia in the early 1980s, which was that "Catalan should be spoken only between Catalans." Shortly thereafter, when the status of Catalan increased dramatically, Castillians began accommodating (and seeking approval) by speaking Catalan (not without some degree of effort). They were often responded to in Castillian! This behavior (at least in objective terms) underscores the belief that Catalan boundaries should and could not be broached; Castillians would be pushed back accommodatively (and divergently in a psychological sense) into their own communicative territory.

This last point brings up the concept of "underaccommodation." Many young adults claim that their interactions with older people are unsatisfactory. One of the main reasons they report such situations difficult to manage is the elders' apparent lack of attention to the young's communicative needs. This is manifested variously but includes an over-attention to the elder's life situation and painful self-disclosures (Williams & Giles, 1996), a tendency which is even more apparent, surprisingly perhaps, in Eastern societies such as Korea, Hong Kong, and China than in Western societies (Williams et al., 1997). Not being seen to converge, for example, by lack of smiles, body lean, gaze aversion, and so forth, has predictably detrimental effects on the recipients' attributions, evaluations, and subsequent conversational involvements.

EPILOGUE

We have seen that through convergence we generally indicate closeness; through divergence, we generally imply degrees of social distance. That said, we now have some appreciation of the many contextual and relational caveats that accompany these principles. We have also seen that interactants have: expectations regarding optimal levels of convergence (and probably divergence); expectations that may be based on stereotypes about outgroup members; norms for intergroup interactions; and guidelines for situationally acceptable behavior. Individuals' nonverbal (and other) choices may correspond with their intentions and with listeners' interpretations, but there is oftentimes a mismatch between these aspects of accommodation, which can sometimes have the potential for misattribution and miscommunication. The CAT perspective shows that communication is often not so much about the exchange of referential information as it is about social connectedness and the negotiation of social identities.

Space has precluded an in-depth discussion of many other issues addressed by CAT, such as the accommodative strategies of attuning to another's interpretive competence, conversational needs, and level of interpersonal control (see Jones, Gallois, Callan, & Barker, in press). In addition, we have not been able to highlight other potent symbols of non-verbal divergence and convergence that can be vividly illustrated through dress and hair styles, tattoos, facial accouterments (e.g., earrings), cosmetics, visible family possessions (e.g., cars, fine art), graffiti, and so forth.

We also did not explore the potency of our theoretical stance over others (but for discussions of some advantages of CAT over other relevant social cognitive and intercultural frameworks, see Street & Giles [1982] and Gallois et al. [1995], respectively). Yet CAT theorists have been eager to reach out hands to other related paradigms in sociolinguistics, communication science, and cognitive psychology (Coupland & Giles, 1988; Giles, Coupland, & Coupland, 1991). CAT has been heralded as practical and useful in communication skills training (including the nonverbal) in industry (Sparks & Callan, 1992). Arguably, CAT has received most of its research attention during the last quarter century in bilingual, dialect, and discursive circles. Hopefully, this essay will go some way toward matching this in nonverbal domains so we can move ultimately to a comprehensive analysis of CAT constructs and processes across the complex interplay of verbal and nonverbal dynamics.

References

Bell, A. (1982). Radio: The style of news language. *Journal of Communication, 32,* 150–164.

Bourhis, R. Y. (1991). Organizational communication and accommodation: Toward some conceptual and empirical links. In H. Giles, J. Coupland, & N. Coupland (Eds.), *Contexts of accommodation* (pp. 270–303). Cambridge, UK: Cambridge University Press.

Buller, D. B., & Aune, R. K. (1988). The effects of vocalics and nonverbal sensitivity on compliance: A speech accommodation theory of explanation. *Human Communication Research, 14,* 301–332.

Cargile, A., Giles, H., & Clément, R. (1996). The role of language in ethnic conflict. In J. Gittler (Ed.), *Conflict knowledge and conflict resolution* (pp. 189–208). Greenwich: JAI Press.

Coupland, N., Coupland, J., Giles, H., & Henwood, K. (1988). Accommodating the elderly: Invoking and extending a theory. *Language in Society, 17,* 1–41.

Coupland, N., & Giles, H. (Eds.) (1988). Communication accommodation: Recent developments. *Special Double Issue of Language and Communication, 8,* 175–327.

Doise, W., Sinclair, A., & Bourhis, R. Y. (1976). Evaluation of accent convergence and divergence and competitive intergroup situations. *British Journal of Social and Clinical Psychology, 15,* 247–252.

Fitzpatrick, M. A., Mulac, A., & Dindia, K. (1995). Gender-preferential language use in spouse and stranger interaction. *Journal of Language and Social Psychology, 14,* 18–39.

Gallois, C., & Callan, V. J. (1988). Communication accommodation and the proto-typical speaker: Predicting evaluations of status and solidarity. *Language and Communication, 8,* 271–283.

Gallois, C., & Giles, H. (1998). Accommodating mutual influence. In M. Palmer (Ed.), *Mutual influence. in interpersonal communication: Theory and research in cognition, affect, and behavior* (pp. 135–162). New York: Ablex.

Gallois, C., Giles, H., Jones, E., Cargile, A. C., & Ota, H. (1995). Accommodating intercultural encounters. In R. Wiseman (Ed.), *Intercultural communication theory* (International and Intercultural Communication Annual, Vol. 19) (pp. 115–147). Thousand Oaks: Sage.

Gallois, C., & Pittam, J. (1996). Communication attitudes and accommodation in Australia: A culturally diverse English-dominant context. *International Journal of Psycholinguistics, 12,* 193–212.

Giles, H. (1973). Accent mobility: A model and some data. *Anthropological Linguistics, 15,* 87–109.

Giles, H., Bourhis, R. Y., & Taylor, D. M. (1977). Toward a theory of language in ethnic group relations. In H. Giles (Ed.), *Language and intergroup relations* (pp. 307–348). London: Academic Press.

Giles, H., & Coupland, N. (1992). *Language: Contexts and consequences.* Pacific Grove, CA: Brooks/Cole.

Giles, H., Coupland, J., & Coupland, N. (Eds.) (1991). *Contexts of accommodation: Developments in applied sociolinguistics.* New York: Cambridge University Press.

Giles, H., Fox, S., & Smith, E. (1993). Patronizing the elderly: Intergenerational evaluations. *Research in Language and Social Interaction, 26,* 129–149.

Giles, H., & Johnson, P. (1981). The role of language in ethnic group relations. In J. C. Turner & H. Giles (Eds.), *Intergroup Behavior* (pp. 199–243). Oxford: Blackwell.

Giles, H., Mulac, A., Bradac, J. J., & Johnson, P. (1987). Speech accommodation theory: The next decade and beyond. In M. McLaughlin (Ed.), *Communication Yearbook* (pp. 13–48). Newbury Park: Sage.

Giles, H., & Noels, K. A. (1997). Communication accommodation in intercultural encounters. In J. Martin, T. Nakayama, & L. Flores (Eds.), *Readings in cultural contexts* (pp. 139–149). Mountain View: Mayfield.

Giles, H., & Smith, P. M. (1979). Accommodation theory: Optimal levels of convergence. In H. Giles & R. St. Clair (Eds.), *Language and social psychology* (pp. 45–65). Oxford: Blackwell.

Giles, H., Taylor, D. M., & Bourhis, R. Y. (1973). Towards a theory of interpersonal accommodation through language: Some Canadian data. *Language in Society, 2,* 177–192.

Gregory, S. W., Dagan, K., & Webster, S. (1997). Evaluating the relation of vocal accommodation in conversation partners' fundamental frequencies to perceptions of communication quality. *Journal of Nonverbal Behavior, 21,* 23–43.

Gregory, S. W., & Webster, S. (1996). A nonverbal signal in voices of interview partners effectively predicts communication accommodation and social status predictions. *Journal of Personality and Social Psychology, 70,* 1231–1240.

Hogg, M. (1985). Masculine and feminine speech in dyads and groups: A study of speech style and gender salience. *Journal of Language and Social Psychology, 4,* 99–112.

Jones, E., Gallois, C., Callan, V., & Barker, M. (in press). Strategies of accommodation: Development of a coding system for conversational interaction. *Journal of Language & Social Psychology.*

Leets, L., & Giles, H. (1995). Intergroup cognitions and communication climates: New dimensions of minority language maintenance. In W. Fase, K. Jaspaert, & S. Kroon (Eds.), *The state of minority languages: International perspectives on survival and decline* (pp. 37–74). Lisse: Swets & Zeitlinger.

Molloy, J. T. (1975). *Dress for success.* New York: Wyden.

Montepare, J. M., & Vega, C. (1988). Women's vocal reactions to intimate and casual male friends. *Personality and Social Psychology Bulletin, 14,* 103–112.

Mulac, A., Studley, L. B., Wiemann, J., & Bradac, J. J. (1987). Male/female gaze in same-sex and mixed-sex dyads: Gender linked differences and mutual influence. *Human Communication Research, 13,* 323–343.

Pittam, J. (1996). *Voice in social interaction.* Thousand Oaks: Sage.

Platt, J., & Weber, H. (1984). Speech convergence miscarried: An investigation into inappropriate accommodation theories. *International Journal of the Sociology of Language, 46,* 131–146.

Ryan, E. B., Giles, H., & Bradac, J. J. (1994) (Eds.). Recent studies in language attitudes. *Language and Communication, 14,* 211–312.

Simard, L., Taylor, D., & Giles, H. (1976). Attribution processes and interpersonal accommodation in a bilingual setting. *Language and Speech, 19,* 374–387.

Sparks, B., & Callan, V. J. (1992). Communication and the service encounter: The value of convergence. *International Journal of Hospitality Management, 11,* 213–224.

Street, R. L. (1985). Participant-observer differences in speech evaluation. Journal of *Language and Social Psychology, 4,* 125–130.

Street, R. L., & Giles, H. (1982). Speech accommodation theory: A social cognitive approach to language and speech behavior. In M. Roloff & C. R. Berger (Eds.), *Social cognition and communication* (pp. 198–226). Beverly Hills, CA: Sage.

Tajfel, H. (1978). *Differentiation between social groups.* London: Academic Press.

Thakerar, J. N., Giles, H., & Cheshire, J. (1982). Psychological and linguistic parameters of speech accommodation theory. In C. Fraser & K. R. Scherer (Eds.), *Advances in the social psychology of language* (pp. 205–255). Cambridge, UK: Cambridge University Press.

Trudgill, P. (1986). *Dialects in contact.* Oxford: Blackwell.

Williams, A., & Giles, H. (1996). Intergenerational satisfaction-dissatisfaction: Young adults' accounts. *Human Communication Research, 23,* 220–250.

Williams, A., Giles, H., Coupland, N., Dalby, M. & Manasse, H. (1990). The communicative contexts of elderly social support and health: A theoretical model. *Health Communication, 2,* 123–143.

Williams, A., Ota, H., Giles, H., Pierson, H. D., Gallois, C., Ng, S. H., Lim, T-S., Ryan, E. B., Somera, L., Maher, J., & Harwood, J. (1997). Young peoples' beliefs about intergenerational communication: An initial cross-cultural comparison. *Communication Research, 24,* 370–393.

Woolard, K. A. (1989). *Double talk: Bilingualism and the politics of ethnicity in Catalonia*. Stanford, CA: Stanford University Press.

Yaeger-Dror, M. (1991). Linguistic evidence for social psychological attitudes: Hypercorrection or (r)1 by singers from a Mizrahi background. *Language and Communication, 11,* 309–331.

*This article describes Burgoon's expectancy violations theory. Accord-
ing to this theory, you are likely to respond differently to your partner's
increase or decrease in intimacy depending on whether you think
your partner is "rewarding" or "unrewarding." Other factors affecting how people respond to increases and decreases in intimacy
behavior (such as someone standing close to you) are discussed.*

49

Expectancy Violations Theory

Kory Floyd
Artemio Ramirez, Jr.
Judee K. Burgoon

Chris loves her parents dearly, but she used to dread when they would
come to visit. Her father would constantly compare Chris to her older
brother, while her mother was always nagging her to get married and start
having babies. Spending time with her parents always left Chris feeling
resentful, defensive, and depressed. The last time they were in town, however, they did nothing but praise her accomplishments and remark on how
proud they are of her. Chris was so pleasantly surprised by this change in
her parents' behavior that she is actually looking forward to their next
visit. She feels that her relationship with them has improved dramatically.

This article was written especially for *The Nonverbal Communication Reader.*

It's almost as if they are closer now than if her parents had been agreeable all along. But how can that be?

In an effort to understand situations like this, Judee Burgoon and colleagues (Burgoon, 1978; Burgoon & Hale, 1988; Burgoon & Jones, 1976; Burgoon, Walther, & Baesler, 1992) developed expectancy violations theory (EVT). Prior to the introduction of EVT, many communication scholars assumed that it was always best for people to act the way others expected them to act. It was commonly believed that violating others' expectations would routinely produce negative outcomes. EVT presented a different idea, however. It suggests that, under certain circumstances, we can actually produce more positive outcomes by behaving in unexpected ways than by doing what others expect. Recall that Chris's parents behaved very unexpectedly during their most recent visit; however, their unexpected behaviors actually improved their relationship with Chris, rather than harming it.

Although EVT was originally proposed as a way to explain responses to personal space violations, it has since been refined and expanded to apply to a number of verbal and nonverbal behaviors. Our goal in this chapter is to explain the principles of EVT and to provide examples of how its ideas apply to several everyday behaviors. We begin by discussing the key concepts of EVT, including *expectancies, expectancy violations, violation valence,* and *communicator reward*.

EXPECTANCIES AND EXPECTANCY VIOLATIONS

Whether we realize it or not, we have a number of expectancies about our own and others' behaviors. Some of our expectancies are *predictive*; these tell us what to expect in a given situation based on what usually occurs in that situation. For instance, a man may expect his wife to kiss him as he leaves for work because that's what she does every morning. Other expectancies are *prescriptive*; these tell us what to expect in a given situation based on what is appropriate or desired. For example, a man may expect his wife to kiss him as he leaves for work because that's what married people are supposed to do. Whatever form our expectancies take, they help guide our behaviors in a number of ways. When walking through a crosswalk, we expect motorists to stop and wait, and we trust that they will do so. We expect retailers to give us change when we pay too much for an item, and we bring it to their attention if they don't. When we go to the dentist, fly on an airplane, or take a college course, we expect to deal with people who have the training and experience they need to do their jobs effectively.

Where do our expectations come from? They come from several sources, according to EVT. Many are based on characteristics of the individuals we deal with, such as their age, their sex, their ethnic background, physical appearance, and personality. For instance, we often expect women to be more nurturing and emotionally expressive than men, or we may expect someone in a suit to be more articulate than someone in a t-shirt and cut-offs. Moreover, several studies of nonverbal communication have demonstrated cultural differences in such behaviors as touch and eye contact; thus, we might expect people from southern Europe or Latin America to touch us more than people from Asia or Scandinavia.

Our expectations also come from characteristics of particular relationships we have with other people, such as our level of familiarity with them, how close we feel to them, what our experiences with them have been, our relative status, and the type of relationship we have. We generally expect our close friends and romantic partners to be more affectionate, to self-disclose more, to touch us more, and to stand closer to us than strangers. We are also expected, in many instances, to behave differently when we're talking with a superior than with a peer or a subordinate. For instance, superiors often have the "right" to initiate touch, to interrupt, and to control the flow of conversation whereas we would consider these behaviors inappropriate for a subordinate.

The third major source of our expectations, according to EVT, is context. We can think about context in a few different ways. The cultural context provides several norms and customs that can shape our expectancies; for instance, people are expected to give each other more personal space in the United States than they are in the Middle East. The social context also helps us know what to expect; different behaviors are called for whether we are at a basketball game, attending a wedding, going to church, participating in a bachelor party, or sitting in class, for instance. Even the historical context influences our expectancies; in the 1950s there was an expectation that men would be breadwinners and women would be full-time housewives, whereas this traditional division of roles is far less expected today.

Characteristics of individuals, our relationships with them, and the contexts in which we interact often work together to determine what our expectations are. For the most part, people tend to behave as we expect them to; we call this *expectancy confirming* behavior. Expectancy confirming behavior largely goes unnoticed. That is, when people do what we expect, we consider their behavior to be normal and we often don't pay much attention to it. For example, when a professor arrives to class wearing appropriate attire, we may notice what he or she is wearing but we probably wouldn't think twice about whether it is appropriate or not. What we *do* tend to notice, however, is when someone does something we don't expect; we call this *expectancy violating* behavior. If a professor arrives to teach a class wearing nothing but undergarments, for instance, we would most certainly notice it! That's because, as EVT suggests, expectancy violations catch our attention and heighten our awareness of the situation. EVT predicts that our responses to such situations are largely determined by two factors: the violation valence and the communicator reward level.

VIOLATION VALENCE

Many theories would predict that any time our expectations are violated, we are likely to react negatively. This is because, for the most part, people value consistency and predictability in their lives. When unexpected events occur, therefore, they force us to admit that our predictions were wrong and they can cause us to feel uncertain about the future. EVT concedes that expectancy violations often do produce more negative outcomes than expectancy confirmations. However, it parts ways with other theories by suggesting that, under certain circumstances, expectancy violations can produce outcomes that are actually more positive than those produced by expectancy confirmations. That is, EVT recognizes that violations have a *valence* attached to them, meaning that they are sometimes considered positive and sometimes considered negative.

An example might help clarify this point. For her birthday last year, Louise wanted her husband Dan to take her to dinner at a fancy restaurant. She began dropping hints (some less subtle than others) several months in advance and was fairly certain she would be getting what she wanted. If Dan had, in fact, taken her to a fancy dinner, that would have been an expectancy confirmation and it would have made Louise happy, since that's what she wanted and what she had come to expect would happen. Suppose that Dan had given her only a birthday card and nothing more. A card is probably less desirable than a fancy dinner; therefore, this is what EVT refers to as a *negative violation*. Suppose, however, that instead of taking her to dinner, Dan had booked them both on a cruise to the Bahamas. Even though that isn't what Louise expected, it's probably more desirable than being taken out to dinner. EVT refers to this as a *positive violation*.

What determines whether an expectancy violation is positive or negative? According to EVT, we make a couple of important judgments when our expectations are violated that help us to label the experience as positive or negative. One of these judgments is about the nature of the behavior itself. Certain behaviors (e.g., being punched in the face) are quite often considered negative no matter what the situation is. Thus, when someone punches us unexpectedly, we are more likely to consider that a negative violation than a positive violation, all other things being equal. Other behaviors (e.g., being taken on a cruise) have more positive inherent meanings, and so we are more likely to consider violations involving such behaviors to be positive than negative.

It is often the case, however, that communication behaviors are ambiguous in meaning. That is, we may not immediately have a sense of whether we consider an unexpected behavior to be positive or negative. EVT predicts that in such situations, we will turn our attention to judging the reward level of the person or people who violated our expectations.

COMMUNICATOR REWARD LEVEL

Let's say you are standing at a bus stop when someone you don't know comes up and stands close enough to you to violate your personal space. This would clearly qualify as an expectancy violation, since we expect strangers to maintain a certain distance from us when we interact with them. However, is this violation positive or negative? If we look only at the nature of the behavior itself, we realize it is somewhat ambiguous; a personal space violation can signal an interest in getting to know someone, but it might also signal an attempt to dominate or intimidate. According to EVT, when we cannot decide on the valence of the violation by looking only at the behavior, we think about the characteristics of the person who caused the violation, and how rewarding we consider that person to be. When the violator is someone we regard positively (that is, when we see him or her as having a high reward value), we are more likely to see the violation itself as positive. However, violations caused by people who are unrewarding to us will likely be judged as negative. Reward can come in a number of forms. Suppose the person who invaded your personal space is extremely attractive. In this case, you might be flattered that he or she stood so close to you, and you would probably consider this a positive violation. Likewise, if this person is famous, or wealthy, or powerful, or an authority figure, you would most likely consider the personal space violation to be positive. However, suppose the person smelled as though he or she had not bathed in a week. In this instance, you would probably consider the person to be unrewarding and the violation to be negative.

EFFECTS OF EXPECTANCY VIOLATIONS

According to EVT, expectancy violations cause different outcomes than expectancy confirmations. Specifically, EVT predicts that positive violations will cause more positive outcomes than confirmations, while negative violations will produce more negative outcomes than confirmations will. In one of the initial tests of the theory, Burgoon (1978) examined how students responded to different levels of proximity to an interviewer. As hypothesized, the reward value of the interviewer (which Burgoon manipulated by having the interviewer provide either positive or negative feedback while talking to students) significantly affected students' perceptions of the interviewer's credibility and attractiveness. Moreover, personal space violations enacted by rewarding interviewers were favored over violations enacted by nonrewarding interviewers, as EVT would suggest.

Later, in a series of field experiments on proximity, Burgoon and Aho (1982) provided further evidence that rewarding communicators often engender the most favorable outcomes by violating, rather than confirming, personal space expectations, while nonrewarding communicators usually create the most favorable outcomes by confirming, rather than violating, personal space expectations. Other experiments testing EVT have demonstrated similar effects with respect to a number of interpersonal behaviors, including gaze (Burgoon, Manusov, Mineo, & Hale, 1985; Manusov, 1984), touch (Burgoon & Walther, 1990; Burgoon et al., 1992), immediacy and conversational involvement (Burgoon & Hale, 1988; Burgoon, Newton, Walther, & Baesler, 1989), and pleasantness (Burgoon & LePoire, 1993; Burgoon, LePoire, & Rosenthal, 1995).

Key Points of Expectancy Violations Theory

1. People develop expectations about the verbal and nonverbal communication of others.

2. Violations of these expectations are arousing and distracting, causing the receiver to pay attention to communicator, relationship, and violation characteristics and meanings.

3. Communicator reward level influences how ambiguous communication behaviors are interpreted and evaluated. Ambiguous behaviors by rewarding communicators will be judged positively while the same behaviors by unrewarding communicators will be judged negatively.

4. Violation valences are a function of (a) the evaluation of the actual behavior, (b) whether the behavior is interpreted as more positive or more negative than what we expected, and (c) how much it differs from our expectation. Positive evaluations occur when actual behaviors are more favorably evaluated than expected behaviors. When actual behaviors are less favorably evaluated than expected behaviors, negative violations occur.

5. Compared to confirming expectations, positive violations produce more favorable outcomes and negative violations produce more unfavorable ones.

Adapted from Burgoon, Stern, & Dillman (1995).

SUMMARY

Our expectations guide many of our day-to-day behaviors and give us a sense of control over our lives; consequently, we notice it when people violate them. How we evaluate and respond to unexpected behavior is largely dependent on our interpretation of the behavior itself and on our assessment of how rewarding the person is who enacted the behavior. In cases when the behavior is more desirable than what we expected, we may actually be more satisfied than if we had gotten what we expected in the first place, just as Chris feels closer to her parents now because they positively violated her expectations.

References

Burgoon, J. K. (1978). A communication model of personal space violations: Explication and an initial test. *Human Communication Research, 4*, 129–142.

Burgoon, J. K. (1991). Relational message interpretations of touch, conversational distance, and posture. *Journal of Nonverbal Behavior, 15*, 233–259.

Burgoon, J. K., & Aho, L. (1982). Three field experiments on the effects of violations of conversational distance. *Communication Monographs, 49*, 71–88.

Burgoon, J. K., & Hale, J. L. (1988). Nonverbal expectancy violations: Model elaboration and application to immediacy behaviors. *Communication Monographs, 55*, 58–79.

Burgoon, J. K., & Jones, S. B. (1976). Toward a theory of personal space expectations and their violations. *Human Communication Research, 2*, 131–146.

Burgoon, J. K., & Le Poire, B. A. (1993). Effects of communication expectancies, actual communication, and expectancy disconfirmation on evaluations of communicators and their communication behavior. *Human Communication Research, 20*, 67–96.

Burgoon, J. K., Le Poire, B. A., & Rosenthal, R. (1995). Effects of preinteraction expectancies and target communication on perceiver reciprocity and compensation in dyadic interaction. *Journal of Experimental Social Psychology, 31*, 287–321.

Burgoon, J. K., Manusov, V., Mineo, P., & Hale, J. L. (1985). Effects of eye gaze on hiring, credibility, attraction, and relational message interpretation. *Journal of Nonverbal Behavior, 9*, 133–146.

Burgoon, J. K., Newton, D. A., Walther, J. B., & Baesler, E. J. (1989). Nonverbal expectancy violations and conversational involvement. *Journal of Nonverbal Behavior, 13*, 97–119.

Burgoon, J. K., Stern, L. A., & Dillman, L. (1995). *Interpersonal adaptation: Dyadic interaction patterns*. New York: Cambridge University Press.

Burgoon, J. K., & Walther, J. B. (1990). Nonverbal expectancies and the evaluative consequences of violations. *Human Communication Research, 17*, 232–265.

Burgoon, J. K., Walther, J. B., & Baesler, E. J. (1992). Interpretations, evaluations, and consequences of interpersonal touch. *Human Communication Research, 19*, 237–263.

Manusov, V. L. (1984). *Nonverbal violations of expectations theory: A test of gaze behavior*. Unpublished master's thesis, Michigan State University, East Lansing, MI.

Cappella discusses his discrepancy-arousal theory. According to this theory, if your partner's behavior is discrepant from what you expect, you will likely feel arousal in the form of cognitive activation. If this arousal is moderate and pleasant, you will likely approach your partner. However, if the arousal change is high and unpleasant, you will likely avoid your partner.

50

Explaining Face-to-Face Interaction
Discrepancy-Arousal Theory

Joseph N. Cappella

Much of my research over the past twenty years has been directed at crafting explanations of the patterns of interaction between people in conversations. These explanations have focused on the how and the why of conversational partners' influences on one another's vocal and kinesic behaviors. I have called these effects mutual influence (Cappella, 1981) or adaptation (Cappella, Palmer, & Donzella, 1991) and have focused not only on adults' interactions but also childrens' and infants'.

Explanations about "how and why" are really attempts to offer a theory about partners' influences in interaction. Theories are answers to puzzles and paradoxes. In the end, if a theory is a good one, it should help us understand the puzzles and paradoxes and it should be successful in predicting future examples of partners' influences on one another.

This article was written especially for *The Nonverbal Communication Reader.*

One of the puzzles that has concerned me about human face-to-face interaction is the problem of automatic mutual influence. By this, I mean that in interaction people make subtle, automatic adjustments to one another's behavior and often are not aware of doing so. For example, the speed and tempo of conversation tends to be contagious (toward more similarity) while violations of personal space norms are compensatory (toward more separation or distancing). I have tried to give an explanation for this puzzle with a theory called "discrepancy-arousal" (Cappella & Greene, 1982). Although it is impossible to explore all the details of this explanation, the rest of this essay will sketch its main points and the research that gave rise to the theory.

MUTUAL INFLUENCE

Mutual influence is arguably the essential characteristic of every interpersonal interaction. Despite its centrality, this process is a subtle one, often not readily recognized by the participants or observers. However, the research supports three conclusions about the influences partners have on one another's behaviors. These three conclusions are discussed next.

Mutual Influence Is Pervasive

Many different behaviors are involved in mutual influence (Cappella, 1981, 1991). These behaviors are as different as fundamental frequency of voice (i.e., pitch) and self-disclosure of personal information. For example, Krause, Steimer, Sanger-Alt, and Wagner (1989) found that when a depressed and non-depressed person interact imitation of facial emotion resulted with the depressed person's facial displays having greater impact on the non-depressed than the reverse. Cappella and Planalp (1981) observed that partners tended to match their speech tempos while interacting. Besides these two, many other behaviors are influential and are the objects of influence when partners interact.

Mutual Influence Occurs in the Earliest Forms of Human Interaction

Although it may not be surprising to find that children with well-developed language capacity exhibit adaptation to adult partners in vocal tempo (Street & Cappella, 1989); similar findings with the linguistically less developed are striking. Bernieri, Reznick, and Rosenthal (1988) observed greater synchrony in body movements during interactions between mothers and their fourteen-to-eighteen-month-old infants than between mothers and a different infant. The most striking findings, though, are those of Murray and Trevarthen (1985). Mothers adopted a blank facial expression while interacting with their six-to-twelve-week-old infants. In response, the infants exhibited more signs of distress, less smiling and relaxation, and less gaze toward the mother during the blank-face sequence. Being responsive is very important, even to infants. Together with an array of other data (Cappella, 1991; Field, 1987), the research suggests that adaptation occurs not only in childhood and infancy but even very early in the life of the neonate.

Mutual Influence Is Associated with Important Relational Outcomes and Individual Differences

Interactions are complex exchanges of verbal, vocal, and kinesic information that have no simple or single relationship to rapport and attachment between people. However, there is accumulating evidence that some form of mutual influence between partners is positively associated with the development of secure attachment in infants, rapport between teachers and students and between doctors and their patients, and attraction between adults. Mutual influence can also discriminate satisfied from dissatisfied couples, even predicting future separation. Although mutual influence cannot be considered to be the only basis for attachment and rapport, it is an important correlate.

One study concerned students in a teaching situation. Bernieri (1988) found that judges' ratings of movement synchrony between high school students was positively associated with the students' self-reports of rapport. Even ratings of movement synchrony between infants and their mothers are positively associated with ratings of the child's positivity (Bernieri, Reznick, & Rosenthal, 1988).

One of the more striking conclusions about mutual influence and attachment was offered by Isabella, Belsky, and van Eye (1989). Mothers and their infants were observed interacting at one, three, and nine months of age and categorized as being in synchrony or not. Pairs that were synchronous at ages one and three months tended to be securely attached to the primary caregiver at one year. Although this study does not mean that the interaction caused the attachment (since the causality could be the opposite), the results are certainly suggestive of the significance of mutual influence in infant development.

The development of positive and negative reactions in adult and infant-adult interactions is part of the basis for establishing long-term attachment and shorter-term rapport in various relationships. The relationships between infants and their caregivers, doctors and their patients, therapists and clients, teachers and students and between spouses are established, grow, and dissolve in the interactions which are the bases of attachment and rapport.

IMPLICATIONS FOR THEORY

Research and observation suggest that mutual influence is a regular occurrence in human social interaction, yet the need to explain mutual influence is not obvious. First, a good explanation must encompass the range of behaviors that seem to fall under the umbrella of mutual influence. A first cut would distinguish between relatively automatic and relatively deliberate behaviors. For example, explaining why speech tempo might be contagious may take quite a different form than explanations of reciprocity of self-disclosure. As a theory, discrepancy-arousal has focused on the more automatic forms of adaptation because of both the continuities between adult and infant populations and the fact that the findings were more subtle (and less predictable) than those for the more deliberate behaviors.

Mutual influence does not always show increased similarity (sometimes called reciprocity) nor always show greater difference (sometimes called compensation). Rather, the typical form of the adaptation depends on the behavior being studied. For example, speech tempo between partners is typically reciprocal while invasions of personal space typically produce strong compensatory reactions.

A third problem is that even when the norm is contagion (for example in speech tempo), not all dyads follow it. Differences between partners could be a function of personality, relational differences, and social situational constraints (Cappella, 1981). These complexities must be accounted for by a good theory of mutual influence.

The apparent continuity of adaptive processes for more automatic behaviors across the developmental spectrum from infancy to adulthood is both a puzzling and striking conclusion. Why should adaptation occur so early in the ontogeny of the organism? What function do such processes serve? How can we explain their existence and their purpose in the development of the species?

Two lines of explanation were developed. The first focused on a theory of mutual influence between adult partners and also between infants and adult caretakers in relatively automatic behaviors manifested during social interaction. This was the discrepancy-arousal theory (Cappella & Greene, 1982). A second, and quite different, tack explored the evolutionary and biological bases for the existence of adaptation processes in the human species (Cappella, 1991). I will only discuss the discrepancy-arousal theory here.

DISCREPANCY-AROUSAL (DA) THEORY

The theory assumes that when two people interact, they have expectations about how the other person will behave and they compare these expectations to how the person is actually behaving. For example, if Molly is normally an up-tempo person when she is around me, then finding her quiet and slow spoken is unusual. This comparison is a kind of *discrepancy*.

The expected behavior is based on social situational factors, individual preferences, and experience with the partner (if any). Even though I expect Molly to be up-tempo normally, when we meet at a formal reception for a visiting dignitary, I expect her to mute her normal buoyancy. If I don't have any experience with Molly, I might be initially taken aback by her vibrancy just because it is different from what I expect of other people in general. But once I get to know her, my expectations are about her, not people in general.

Discrepancy is assumed to produce *arousal* in the form of *cognitive activation*. Most theories of cognitive activation, alerting, and attention assume that discrepancy (or its variants in terms of interruption or unusualness) is a key causal force (Mandler, 1975). If people were not alerted cognitively and emotionally by the discrepancies in their environment, they would be at risk from threats for which they were unprepared. Even though Molly may be anything but a threat, her behavior gets noticed just because it is not what I expect it to be.

In turn, cognitive activation determines the intensity and quality of a person's *affective response*. Following Berlyne (1967), activation levels are presumed to influence affective responses so that excessive changes in activation are experienced as affectively negative while low to moderate changes are experienced as affectively neutral to positive. If Molly's normal bubbly, high-tempo style was replaced by a manic, nearly pathological frenzy, an initial recognition of her increased tempo might be replaced by an aversive feeling and withdrawal from her. The affective changes, in turn, are paralleled by behavioral *avoidance* (for negative affect) and behavioral *approach* (with positive affect).

The central components of the theory are discrepancy and activation and then activation and affect. These two pieces working together produce a complex linkage that varies as a function of individual differences as well as relational factors. For example, if Molly is a long-term relational partner, I am less likely to withdraw from her even in the face of extreme discrepancies because I tolerate more from those to whom I have a commitment. Also, if I am the kind of person who finds unusual behavior and risky situations thrilling—that is, I am a sensation-seeker (Zuckerman, 1979)—I might tend to find Molly's behavior attractive rather than repulsive. These are but two of the relational and personality differences that moderate the effects of discrepancy on a person's affective response and subsequent behavioral reaction.

The theory explains the existence of both reciprocal and compensatory effects depending in part on whether the interaction produces a desire to approach or to avoid. Approach and withdrawal does not depend just on how the other person is behaving and my expectations (that is, discrepancy is not the only factor in approach and withdrawal) but rather depends upon individual differences, prior experience with the partner, relationship stage, and situational norms. For example, in neutral to mildly positive social settings with acquaintances, severe violations of personal space should be very arousing, experienced as affectively negative and result in avoidance responses and, hence, compensation. However, when the partners are intimates, the region of acceptance is widened and violations of personal space norms are experienced as affectively positive, and approach results. With a different behavior like speech tempo, very high rates of speech might be arousing but would probably have to reach extreme rates before they were experienced as affectively negative with concomitant withdrawal. Thus, the theory recognizes a variety of factors that enter into a person's consideration when reacting with approach or withdrawal responses to another's behavior.

The theory also allows for continuity between the adult and infant domains. No aspect of the theory requires linguistic skill or abstract cognitive abilities. The keys are a comparison between an expectation (sometimes called a schema, especially for infants, Stern, 1977) and an observed state. Discrepancy drives affect and approach or withdrawal. These forces can operate in infants and children as well as adults, although adults will certainly employ a much wider variety of mitigating conditions.

The theory also posits mechanisms that are relatively automatic rather than cognitive and deliberative. This is intentional. Some other theories of interaction have a lot of what I call "plumbing." The theories assume people are weighing this and that when making a decision to approach or avoid a stimulating or threatening partner. Discrepancy-arousal makes the decisions automatic, both because I believe that most of the behavioral reactions are themselves automatic and because the theory is meant to account for mutual influence in adults and children.

CONCLUSION

Discrepancy-arousal theory is but one of several explanations of mutual influence processes in social interaction that have been put forward in the past twenty years. Whichever explanatory system is ultimately successful in accounting for mutual influence, I believe that it will have certain characteristics that can be identified now. Context effects cannot be ignored. The verbal, nonverbal, and vocal behaviors that we have been discussing are noticed and attended to when they are unusual relative to some expected baseline. That expectation level must be built into any successful theory. The evidence that certain verbal, vocal, and kinesic behaviors produce various forms of arousal is too great not to insure some place for arousal (cognitive activation attention, or alerting) in a theory of mutual influence. Its place may not be as important as that hypothesized by discrepancy-arousal theory, but arousal reactions as mediators cannot be ignored.

Allow me one final point. Discrepancy-arousal theory tries to explain how mutual influence comes about through proximate causal mechanisms, or, in other words, the theory looks at what directly causes mutual influence to occur. These causal mechanisms can be cognitive, physiological, or social. But the presence of mutual influence processes in infants' interactions with their primary caretakers suggests that these patterns may be more fundamental, perhaps evolving to become part of the genetic endowment of the species (Cappella, 1991).

References

Berlyne, D. E. (1967). Arousal and reinforcement. In D. Levine (Ed.), *Nebraska Symposium on Motivation* (pp. 1–110). Lincoln: University of Nebraska Press.

Bernieri, F. J. (1988). Coordinated movement and rapport in teacher-student interactions. *Journal of Nonverbal Behavior, 12,* 120–138.

Bernieri, F. J., Reznick, J. S., & Rosenthal, R. (1988). Synchrony, pseudosynchrony, and dissynchrony: Measuring the entrainment process in mother-infant interactions. *Journal of Personality and Social Psychology, 54,* 243–253.

Cappella, J. N. (1981). Mutual influence in expressive behavior: Adult-adult and infant-adult dyadic interaction. *Psychological Bulletin, 89,* 101–132.

Cappella, J. N. (1991) The biological origins of automated patterns of human interaction. *Communication Theory, 1,* 4–35.

Cappella, J. N., & Greene, J. O. (1982). A discrepancy-arousal explanation of mutual influence in expressive behavior for adult-adult and infant-adult interaction. *Communication Monographs, 49,* 89–114.

Cappella, J. N., Palmer, M. T., & Donzella, B. (1991, May). *Individual consistency in temporal adaptations in nonverbal behavior in dyadic conversations: High and low expressive groups.* Paper presented at the annual meeting of the International Communication Association, Chicago, IL.

Cappella, J. N., & Planalp, S. (1981). Talk and silence sequences in informal conversations. Ill: Interspeaker influence. *Human Communication Research, 7,* 117–132.

Field, T. (1987). Affective and interactive disturbances in infants. In J. D. Osofsky (Ed.), *Handbook of infant development* (2nd ed., pp. 972–1007). New York: John Wiley.

Giles, H., Mulac, A., Bradac, J., & Johnson, P. (1987). Speech accommodation theory: The first decade and beyond. In M. L. McLaughlin (Ed.), *Communication Yearbook 10* (pp. 13–48). Newbury Hills, CA: Sage.

Isabella, R. A., Belsky, J., and van Eye, A. (1989) Origins of mother-infant attachment: An examination of interactional synchrony during the infant's first year. *Developmental Psychology, 25,* 12–21.

Krause, R., Steimer, E., Sanger-Alt, C., & Wagner, G. (1989). Facial expression of schizophrenic patients and their interaction partners. *Psychiatry, 52,* 1–12.

Mandler, G. M. (1975). *Mind and emotion.* New York: Wiley.

Murray, L., & Trevarthen, C. (1985). Emotional regulation of interactions between two-month-olds and their mothers. In T. M. Field & N. A. Fox (Eds.), *Social perception in infants* (pp. 177–198). Norwood, NJ: Ablex.

Stern, D. N. (1977). *A first relationship: Mother and infant.* Cambridge, MA: Harvard University Press.

Street, R. L., & Cappella, J. N. (1989). Social and linguistic factors influencing adaptation in children's speech. *Journal of Psycholinguistic Research, 18,* 497–519.

Zuckerman, M. (1979). *Sensation seeking: Beyond the optimal level of arousal.* Hillsdale, NJ: Erlbaum.

Andersen describes his cognitive valence theory. Both arousal and cognition play key roles in this theory. According to Andersen, if your partner increases immediacy in a way that leads to high levels of arousal, you will become defensive and avoid her or him. If your partner increases immediacy in a way that leads to moderate levels of arousal change, you might approach or avoid the partner, depending on factors such as the relationship, the situation, your mood, and so forth.

51

Creating Close Relationships through Nonverbal Communication
A Cognitive Valence Approach

Peter A. Andersen

The mysteries surrounding personal relationships affect all of our lives. After teaching nonverbal communication and relational communication for over twenty years, I have discovered that the mysteries I wonder about are the same ones that my students ponder. "Why do some people back off from affection while others give you affection in return?" "Why are nonverbal behaviors often more powerful than words in close relationships?" "Why do I often move too fast or too slow in my relationships?" "Why are people attracted to each other?" "Out of the thousands of relationships I have, why are only a few very close and intimate?"

This article was written especially for *The Nonverbal Communication Reader.*

To try to answer these and other mysteries of human relationships, I created cognitive valence theory (CVT). Articles and chapters about this theory have appeared in a number of places (see Andersen, 1985, 1989, 1993, 1998; Andersen & Andersen, 1984; Andersen, Guerrero, Buller, & Jorgensen, 1998). Other researchers have created parallel theories to help solve these mysteries (see Andersen & Andersen, 1984; Burgoon, Stern, & Dillman, 1995 for a discussion of these theories). Although each of these theories is a solid attempt to answer these questions, this article will focus on cognitive valence theory.

The central question posed by CVT is this: "When one person increases intimacy or immediacy, how can you explain the response of their partner?" Sometimes when you move closer to people, they move closer to you. Other times they move away. If you give someone a kiss, sometimes she or he kisses back, but other times the person moves away and avoids the kiss entirely. Eye contact is sometimes returned, but sometimes your interaction partner just looks away. Sometimes intimate disclosure leads to disclosure by your partner, but sometimes not.

Sometimes affectionate or immediate behaviors are perceived negatively by one's interaction partner. If a behavior is perceived negatively by someone, it is said to be *negatively valenced*. This is a term borrowed from physics. Negative particles repel and give off a negative charge whereas positive particles attract and give off a positive charge. Therefore, *positively valenced* behaviors are those that are perceived positively by someone.

According to CVT, the only way that relationships grow closer is by two people communicating warmth and immediacy to one another. This involves one person sending messages of warmth and intimacy, and the other person responding with similarly warm and intimate messages. Sometimes, however, our efforts to increase intimacy are negatively valenced and rebuffed; our efforts to create immediacy are met with coldness and avoidance. This is what CVT seeks to explain.

IMMEDIACY BEHAVIORS

Intimate relationships always begin with some form of immediacy behavior. Closer distances, eye contact, and touch are nonverbal immediacy behaviors—actions that decrease psychological distance, increase sensory stimulation, communicate warmth, and signal availability for interaction (Andersen, 1985). *Proxemic* immediacy behaviors, including closer distances, more direct face-to-body angles, sharing confined spaces, and communicating on the same physical plane (e.g., sitting down to talk to a child) are effective means of increasing immediacy. Increased touching, including warm handshakes, hugs, kisses, and caresses, are ways of communicating immediacy through *haptic* channels.

A number of *kinesic* behaviors, such as positive facial expressions (especially smiling), head nods, gestural animation, open rather than closed body positions, and overall bodily relaxation, have been shown to communicate immediacy. *Oculesic* or eye behavior, such as eye contact and even pupil dilation, has been shown to increase warmth and immediacy. *Vocalic* communication that is more expressive, enthusiastic, and varied is also immediacy behavior. *Chronemic* behaviors, such as spending time with another person, waiting for someone, and being on time have been found to communicate immediacy. Finally, behaviors that are matched or synchronized to your partner's behaviors have been shown to communicate warmth and immediacy (see Burgoon et al., 1995).

While most immediacy is accomplished in nonverbal channels, immediacy can also be communicated verbally (Andersen, 1989). Inclusive pronouns (such as *we* vs. *you and I*), personal forms of address (Pete vs. Dr. Andersen), disclosure of personal information, and explicit communication about the relationship (e.g., "I love you") are all ways of increasing immediacy through verbal communication.

In figure 1, the behavior column suggests that all relationships begin when one person initiates immediacy with the other. Communication always involves two people, so as indicated in the perception column, your partner must perceive that you increased immediacy for your actions to have any impact. From a communication perspective, if you smile and gaze at your partner, but your partner did not notice, it did not matter that you smiled or looked at your partner since these messages were never received (see figure 1, column 2). Immediacy behaviors, like other messages, only communicate when they are received.

AROUSAL

When someone looks at a person, touches them, or engages in any other immediacy behavior, physiological arousal, such as increased heart rate and brain temperature, occurs. Numerous studies have demonstrated the immediacy-arousal relationship (see Andersen et al., 1998, for a summary of this research). Very large increases in physiological arousal are unpleasant and aversive (see Andersen, 1989; Buller, Jorgensen, Andersen, & Guerrero, 1995; and Cappella & Greene, 1982, for summaries) and result in panic, fear, anger, and disorientation (see figure 1, arousal column). For example, being followed closely by a stranger in the middle of

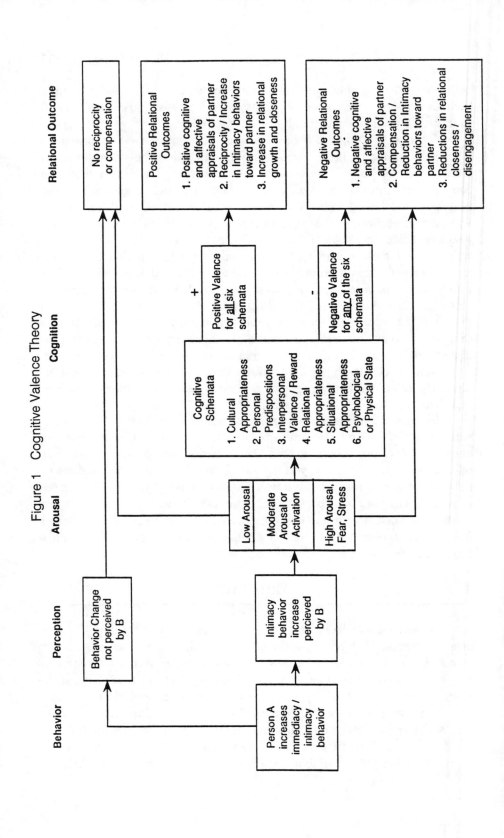

Figure 1   Cognitive Valence Theory

the night would create a very large arousal increase and cause flight-or-fight response. Very high arousal increases circumvent cognitive processes, producing an instantaneous physical response. On the other hand, low levels of arousal send nonwarning signals to the person and therefore do not result in any behavioral changes. When immediacy-induced arousal is moderate, the most complex and interesting responses emerge (Andersen, 1998; Andersen et al., 1998). These moderate arousal changes are insufficient to initiate a flight response or a panic attack, but are sufficient to stimulate cognitive processes that attempt to make sense of the immediacy-induced arousal change (see figure 1, arousal column).

COGNITIVE SCHEMATA

We all carry around social knowledge in our heads. This knowledge is both of a general nature and about our various interpersonal interactions. "Cognitive schemata" is a fancy, social scientific term for the social knowledge we all have. At the head of cognitive valence theory are cognitive schemata—the knowledge structures that help us interpret others' behavior and help us make some sense of what behaviors are appropriate for a given situation or relationship (see Andersen, 1993; Planalp, 1985). CVT incorporates six types of cognitive schemata that regulate interpersonal interaction: culture, personality, interpersonal valence, situations, state, and relationship. If *any* of these six schemata are violated, CVT predicts that the behavior will be negatively valenced and negative outcomes will occur (see figure 1, cognition column).

Culture

Our culture provides us with a set of rules regarding all forms of our behavior. Culture influences our behavior so powerfully and invisibly that it is often mistaken for human nature itself. In some cultures it is acceptable for men to kiss; in others it is not. In certain cultures it is fine to touch with the left hand; in others it is a taboo. Eye contact and staring is normal in some cultures but considered weird, intrusive, or rude in others. Immediacy behaviors must be culturally appropriate. It is important to understand the nonverbal behavior of another culture when interacting with members of that culture (see also article 1, this reader). For example, kissing the wife of a friend goodbye, while appropriate in the United States, would be highly inappropriate in an Arab culture and would bring shame on her and on you. Standing six inches away while talking, as some people from Arabic or South American countries do, would be perceived as offensive in Great Britain or the United States. Such behavior would be negatively valenced.

Personality

Humans all have different personalities, and these personality predispositions affect how we react to another person's immediacy behavior. People differ in their degree of sociability, their attitudes toward touch, their shyness, the degree to which they seek or avoid sensation, and hundreds of other traits that researchers have studied. Research on touch avoidance, for example, has shown that warm, affectionate touch is viewed positively by touch approachers but negatively by touch avoiders (see Andersen, 1999; Andersen & Leibowitz, 1978). Immediacy behaviors are not universally appreciated. Knowing your receiver is essential to avoiding inappropriate nonverbal behavior that will be negatively valenced by your interaction partner.

Interpersonal Valence

Who initiates nonverbal communication is one of the most important factors in how an individual reacts to immediate behavior. Touch from a dirty, homeless stranger versus the classmate to whom you are physically attracted, is likely to produce distinctly different responses. Interpersonal valence is positive for people we find socially or physically attractive, credible, high in status, powerful, rewarding, or similar to ourselves. When interpersonal valence is positive for an interaction partner, we tend to positively valence the partner's immediacy behaviors. When interpersonal valence is negative, we negatively valence the immediate behavior.

Situation

Not all situations are created equal. Immediacy in the classroom, boardroom, restroom, and bedroom are likely to produce completely different reactions. No communication behavior can be interpreted without considering the context or situation in which it occurred. Indeed, "out of context" means something is meaningless, misleading, or uninterpretable. Some settings are more conducive to high levels of intimacy, such as living rooms, bedrooms, or hotel rooms. Some situations are quite formal and require only minimal immediacy displays, such as handshakes and polite smiles. Sensitivity to the situation is a fundamental part of competent communication. One married woman I know dislikes being caressed or kissed in public by her husband because she dislikes "public displays of affection." Their happy marriage and three children suggest that she has no problem with private displays of affection. Excessive immediacy, even with one's closest relational partners, will lead to negative valencing of the behavior.

State

All of us have good days and bad days, emotionally and physically. While situations are the short-term external conditions in which communication occurs, states are short-term internal conditions that affect our communication. Many things affect our physical or mental state, including illness, a fight with one's boss, hunger, a bad grade, our body rhythms, a hangover, the death of an old friend, birthdays, pay raises, and many other positive and negative factors. Generally, we are receptive to immediacy when we are in positive moods and states, although sometimes we need the comfort or support that immediacy can provide during sad or distressing moments. Negative physical or emotional states generally lead to negative valencing of immediacy. A classic example of negative valencing of immediacy is a wife's response to her affectionate husband: "Not tonight, dear, I have a headache." Conversely, high immediacy is appreciated and expected when someone is in a positive state at the end of finals, the return of good health, or the achievement of personal accomplishments.

The Relationship

Perhaps the most important valencer of nonverbal immediacy is the relationship. People are easily able to classify their relationships into relational categories: friend, coworker, roommate, fiancée, best friend, acquaintance, parent, boss, and so on. Identical immediacy displays from different types of relational partners lead to highly differing reactions to the immediacy displays. In a study of excessive intimacy that I conducted, the most common reason given for believing that an immediacy display was excessively intimate was that it was inappropriate for the relationship (Andersen, 1992). This included too much touch or too much eye contact on the first date, as well as inappropriate intimacy from one's boss or coworker. Similarly, Wertin and Andersen (1996) used CVT to predict perceptions of sexual harassment and found that behavior inappropriate to the relationship was the most important factor resulting in negative valencing of the behavior. In the right relationship, almost any immediacy behavior could be appropriate; in the wrong relationship, many immediacy behaviors are inappropriate and negatively valenced.

VALENCE AND RELATIONAL OUTCOME

One of the tricky and perplexing aspects of communication and relationships is that violating *any* of these six schemata can result in negative valencing of an immediacy behavior. This is one of the reasons why we form close relationships with only a fraction of the thousands of people we meet. These reactions to immediacy displays usually occur in a fraction of a second, as our expectations are matched to the immediacy behavior.

In the last column in figure 1, the relational outcome is shown. If the immediacy behavior one observes appropriately matches the perceiver's cultural, personal, interpersonal, situational, state, and relational schemata, the behavior will be positively valenced and three positive outcomes will occur: (1) the perceiver will have positive perceptions and attitudes toward the interaction partner; (2) the perceiver will be likely to reciprocate the immediacy behaviors toward the partner by responding with intimate, warm behavior; and (3) increased closeness and relational growth will occur. If the immediacy behavior violates *any* of these six schemata, negative outcomes will likely occur, including: (1) negative perceptions and attitudes toward the interaction partner; (2) compensation, avoidance, and reductions in immediacy behavior; and (3) reductions in relational closeness and feelings of intimacy.

CONCLUSION

Cognitive valence theory is useful in explaining many diverse communication events that occur in personal relationships. It explains why intercultural communication is so difficult and why learning to tolerate seemingly strange behaviors from different cultures is important. It explains why escalating a relationship too fast will scare one's partner, resulting in compensation and withdrawal. In turn, this often leads to a desperate attempt by the escalating partner to increase immediacy, resulting in more withdrawal by one's partner. It explains why people need to be sensitive to the interpersonal situation and the state of one's partner to be competent communicators.

Immediacy behaviors are the energy and the positivity that creates closeness among all human beings. Without nonverbal immediacy displays, humans would be cold, suspicious islands who are isolated from others and experience few of the joys of human relationships. But nonverbal immediacy is like fire: It can warm the hearth, light the campground, singe one's skin, or burn down a home. It can attract or repel. The key to successful nonverbal immediacy is to be nonverbally appropriate to your partner's culture, personality, interpersonal valence, situations, state and mood, and relationship.

References

Andersen, P. A. (1985). Nonverbal immediacy in interpersonal communication. In A. W. Siegman & S. Feldman (Eds.), *Multichannel integrations of nonverbal behavior* (pp. 1–36). Hillsdale, NJ: Erlbaum.

Andersen, P. A. (1989, May). *A cognitive valence theory of intimate communication.* Paper presented at the biennial meeting of the International Network on Personal Relationships, Iowa City, IA.

Andersen, P. A. (1992, July). *Excessive intimacy: An account analysis of behaviors, cognitive schemata, affect, and relational outcomes.* Paper presented at the sixth interpersonal conference on personal relationships, Orono, ME.

Andersen, P. A. (1993). Cognitive schemata in personal relationships. In S. Duck (Ed.), *Individuals in relationships* (pp. 1–29). Newbury Park, CA: Sage.

Andersen, P. A. (1998). The cognitive valence theory of intimate communication. In M. T. Palmer & G. A. Barnett (Eds.), *Progress in communication sciences, Vol. 14: Mutual influence in interpersonal communication theory and research in cognition, affect, and behavior* (pp. 39–72). Norwood, NJ: Ablex.

Andersen, P. A. (1999). *Nonverbal communication: Forms and functions.* Mountain View, CA: Mayfield.

Andersen, P. A., & Andersen, J. F. (1984). The exchange of nonverbal intimacy: A critical review of dyadic models. *Journal of Nonverbal Behavior, 8,* 327–349.

Andersen, P. A., Guerrero, L. K., Buller, D. B., & Jorgensen, P. F. (1998). An empirical comparison of three theories of nonverbal immediacy exchange. *Human Communication Research, 24,* 501–535.

Andersen, P. A., & Leibowitz, K. (1978). The development and nature of the construct touch avoidance. *Environmental Psychology and Nonverbal Behavior, 3,* 89–106.

Buller, D. B., Jorgensen, P. F., Andersen, P. A., & Guerrero, L. K. (1995, June). *Correspondence among physiological, nonverbal, and perceptual measures of arousal.* Paper presented at the annual meeting of the International Network on Personal Relationships, Williamsburg, VA.

Burgoon, J. K., Stern, L. A., & Dillman, L. (1995). *Interpersonal adaptation: Dyadic interaction patterns.* New York: Cambridge University press.

Cappella, J. N., & Greene, J. O. (1982). A discrepancy-arousal explanation of mutual influence in expressive behavior for adult and infant-adult interactions. *Communication Monographs, 46,* 89–114.

Planalp, S. (1985). Relational schemata: A test of alternative forms of relational knowledge as guides to communication. *Human Communication Research, 12,* 3–29.

Shoffstall, V. A. (1997). After a while. In J. Canfield, M. V. Hansen, & K. Kirberger (Eds.), *Chicken soup for the teenage soul* (p. 7). Deerfield Beach, FL: Health Communications.

Wertin, L., & Andersen, P. A. (1996, February). *Cognitive schemata and perceptions of sexual harassment.* Paper presented at the annual meeting of the Western States Communication Association, Pasadena, CA.

*This article takes a look at the newest of the nonverbal adaptation
theories—interaction adaptation theory. At the heart of this theory
is the idea that we respond to our partners' behaviors based on required factors (such as biological need for sleep); expectations (including what social norms and knowledge of our partners lead us to
anticipate); and desires (including our personal preferences and what
we want from a given relationship).*

52

Converging on the Phenomenon of Interpersonal Adaptation
Interaction Adaptation Theory

Nathan Miczo
Lisa E. Allspach
Judee K. Burgoon

In our everyday interactions, we respond and adjust our behavior to one
another in a variety of ways. When we are talking to someone we may look
for eye contact, head nodding, or other indicators that our partner is
engaged and paying attention to us; when we are listening we may find
ourselves performing similar kinds of behaviors. Indeed, social interaction
would seem very awkward without these signals of attentiveness and
involvement. Researchers refer to this process of interactants responding

This article was written especially for *The Nonverbal Communication Reader.*

to and coordinating their behavior with one another as interpersonal adaptation. Evidence from domains as different as mother-infant pairs (Malatesta & Haviland, 1982; Thoman, 1975), marital (Gottman, 1993), and interviewer-interviewee interactions (Siegman & Reynolds, 1982) suggests that the ability of individuals to coordinate their behavioral patterns with one another is an essential component of successful and healthy interpersonal relationships. In this article, we will outline the principles and the elements of a recent theory that attempts to explain and predict the presence of these adaptation patterns.

Consider the following scenario:

Eric and Diana have been engaged for eight months. Their wedding is scheduled for a Saturday, a little over three months away. Today they are meeting with Reverend Billingsley for the first of five prenuptial counseling sessions. They are a little nervous because Reverend Billingsley has to evaluate their compatibility. His evaluation will be based on their individual responses to his questions as well as their interaction with each other. While they want the counseling sessions to be productive for them as a couple, they are also concerned that what they perceive as their compatibility be evident to the reverend. Reverend Billingsley wants what is best for these two young people and takes his job as a premarital counselor seriously. His job, as he sees it, is to spot potential problems that Diana and Eric may not see at the present time, so as to prepare the couple for what it really means to be "married."

Following a brief introduction and some opening questions, the reverend proposes that the couple role-play the following scenario: Eric's widowed father has had a stroke and will require in-home care indefinitely. After proposing the scenario, the reverend sits back and waits for them to begin.

Diana: (looking at Eric) What do you think we should do?
Eric: I don't want to put him in any kind of a nursing home.
Diana: What do you see as the alternative, then?
Eric: Well, I want him to be able to stay in his own house. But I don't know how we'd manage that because I know he doesn't get disability from his job and my salary isn't enough to support two households.
Diana: What are you saying?
Eric: Could we have him come and live with us? At least for a while?

Reverend Billingsley has been watching their interchange intently. At first, Diana seems hesitant and apprehensive. Her words come out slow and measured, but as the conversation progresses, Eric and Diana's exchanges have quickened in tempo and they both seem very involved in the topic and the responses of the other.

While the above scenario may not be something that any of us would have to deal with on an everyday basis, many of the underlying processes that do influence and guide our everyday communications with one another are evident in this example. Issues such as managing the impressions we make on other people, adhering to social norms and expectations for interactions, managing conversations, and achieving interactional and relational goals help us to frame how we interact with and react to our conversational partners. A recent theory that tries to take all these influences and factors into account in predicting how and why we adapt our communication to one another is interaction adaptation theory (Burgoon, Stern, & Dillman, 1995).

PRINCIPLES OF THE THEORY

Interaction adaptation theory is based on nine fundamental principles. The first of these is that we as humans are biologically predisposed to adapt our interaction patterns to one another during interactions. For example, in the above scenario, Diana is at first slow to enter the role-playing conversation about Eric's dad, but as the conversation continues, she quickly becomes caught up in the topic and Eric's responses to the imaginary situation created by the reverend. Without deliberate effort on her part, she has adapted to his communication.

A second principle guiding the theory suggests that while there is an inborn pressure to adapt to one's partner in interactions, such behavior is likely to take particular forms. Burgoon, Stern and Dillman (1995) state that "Matching and synchrony patterns should be especially common when both participants are subject to the same external influences" (p. 261). Matching refers to behavioral similarity between interactants in the most general sense. Most definitions of interaction synchrony emphasize that synchrony involves the coordination of behavior or behavioral patterns in a process of mutual influence (Bernieri, Reznick, & Rosenthal, 1988; Burgoon et al., 1995; Mathiot & Carlock, 1982). Using the above scenario, if the reverend notices that as Eric becomes more assertive and forceful about his dad living with them, Diana too becomes assertive and forceful in her misgivings about that arrangement, then the reverend has observed what would be considered matching behaviors by Diana.

Principle three of the theory asserts that while there is a natural tendency to match and synchronize with one's partner, there is also a competing, biologically driven tendency to manage the interplay between oneself and others, utilizing what are called approach and avoidance behaviors. Approach behaviors include such things as facial animation, direct body orientation, gesturing, and smiling. We typically engage in these behaviors when we are seeking out or trying to get close to another person. However, seeking out and getting close to others often entangles us in situations which we would prefer to avoid. Thus, we enact avoidance behaviors in order to distance ourselves from situations where we feel there is some danger or threat to our self. Nonverbally, avoidance behaviors can include such things as averting one's gaze when the topic of a conversation becomes too intimate, or turning away from one's partner to signal that one is no longer interested in the conversation. Verbally, it may take such forms as indirect language or changing the topic. In our example, if Diana and Eric keep playing off of each other's assertiveness and forcefulness, the simple role-playing exercise is likely to escalate into a full-blown conflict. So it is likely that either Eric or Diana, or both, will begin to engage in some kind of avoidance, or de-escalation, behaviors that will begin to bring the tone of the conversation back down to a manageable level.

According to principle four, in addition to the strong inborn pressure to adapt to others, there is also a strong social pressure to engage in matching and reciprocal behaviors. Gouldner's (1960) norm of reciprocity posits that social life is maintained through contingent social exchanges. That is, we will act toward others as others act toward us. To go back to our example, when Diana and Eric first arrived for their session, it is very likely that the reverend set the tone for how the session would go by greeting them with a smile and extending his hand. The social norm of politeness would dictate that Eric and Diana respond in kind.

The fifth principle of the theory of interaction adaptation states that both reciprocity and compensation can function as communicative messages. As a communication message, reciprocity refers to a pattern in which one partner responds to the other's behavior with behaviors that are either similar, in the same direction, or functionally equivalent (Burgoon et al., 1995; Ross, Cheyne, & Lollis, 1988; Street, 1988). Responding to an intimate touch with an intimate smile would be an example of reciprocating with an act that has the same functional meaning (intimacy). When one partner responds to the behavior of the other with behaviors that are dissimilar, in the opposite direction, or functionally nonequivalent, then the partner is engaging in compensation (Burgoon et al., 1995; Street, 1988). In our example, as the role-playing scenario has progressed, Diana and Eric have begun reciprocating each other's forcefulness and assertiveness. In order to avoid a conflict, one of them is going to have to consciously enact some kind of compensatory behavior that sends a clear message to the other. Eric may soften his tone or drop his head, or Diana may smile or lower her gaze. The behavior is functioning to let the partner know that the person is attempting to alter the communication pattern.

In any given communicative situation, according to principle six, an individual's ability to adapt will be limited by such things as individual differences, behavioral tendencies, and cultural influences. While in our example the reverend extended his hand to the couple upon meeting them, if Eric and Diana had been from a culture where bowing was the norm, they may have been put off or startled by the reverend's behavior. In such an instance, the reverend's behavior could have a negative impact on how much Diana and Eric feel compelled to adapt to the reverend in the session.

The biological, social and psychological forces that influence us to adapt, principle seven argues, cause us to enact predominantly matching, reciprocal and synchronous behaviors. To go back to the role-playing scenario, suppose that Diana has engaged in the first compensatory move by averting her gaze. Eric may now feel pressure to reciprocate with a de-escalation behavior of his own, such as softening his tone. If he fails to match Diana's initial compensatory move, she may make another attempt. However, if her repeated attempts fail, it is very likely that she will re-synchronize with Eric by resuming her own assertiveness and forcefulness.

Principle eight allows that a variety of factors influence the adaptation that occurs in any given communication situation. For example, it may become evident to the reverend halfway through the role-playing scenario that Diana is no longer responding in a reciprocal fashion to Eric's comments. This might occur for any one of a number of reasons: a headache, a distraction, a mood change, a disagreement with something Eric said, or an attempt to "lighten up" the conversation.

Finally, principle nine states that sets of adaptation behaviors be considered from a global level, rather than focusing on individual cues, in an effort to detect the presence of actual adaptation to the partner as opposed to simple behavioral change. At issue here might be the question of how Reverend Billingsley is going to determine whether Diana's nonreciprocation is a response to Eric, or to some other environmental factor, including her own internal state. The theory states that one has to look at more than just a single nonverbal cue in order to make these determinations. Thus, the reverend may notice that Diana has averted her eyes, but gaze aversion by itself will not provide conclusive evidence regarding her adaptation patterns. If he notices that she averts her eyes and clutches her stomach, he may conclude that she has a stomach ache; but if he notices that she averts her eyes and frowns, while shaking her head slightly, he may conclude that her behavior is a direct response to Eric. Interaction adaptation theory is concerned with the direct responses of one interactant to another, rather than the responses of either partner to environmental factors.

ELEMENTS OF THE THEORY

Earlier theories of interpersonal adaptation often failed to take into account the vast number of factors that influence dynamic interactions, and, as a result, they suffered from rather restricted applicability. On the other hand, in attempting to build a theory that can more accurately capture the enmeshed, fluid orchestrations of interaction patterns, one is faced with the daunting task of trying to determine what variables are more important than others and when. Interaction adaptation theory (IAT) holds that many of these variables can be covered with the following three concepts: requirements (R), expectations (E), and desires (D). Simply stated, IAT accounts for the fact that individuals enter an interaction with a set of requirements, expectations, and desires that will heavily influence their initial interaction behavior. Accordingly, let us examine each one of these concepts in turn.

Requirements primarily refer to biological factors which possess the potential to interfere with normal, ongoing interaction. For example, if you are extremely hungry or extremely tired, you may not be able to concentrate on your partner, and this lack of attentiveness may disrupt adaptation patterns. Another factor that has the potential to disrupt interaction is arousal, or anxiety. Arousal management "concerns a person's requirement to maintain control over his or her emotional and expressive states, to feel comfortable, and to prevent overstimulation" (Burgoon, Allspach, & Miczo, 1997, p. 5). Although there are some people who experience chronic anxiety, there are certain social situations that are particularly conducive to creating arousal. Job interviews and oral presentations are two examples of situations where the need to manage anxiety may override other factors. A common element in many of these situations is that they entail some sort of evaluation by someone else.

Expectations "refer to what is anticipated, based on social norms, social prescriptions, or individuated knowledge of the other's behavior, and include the general communication functions or goals operative in the situation" (Burgoon et al., 1995, p. 265). There is considerable evidence that people expect interactions with others to be fairly pleasant and moderately involved (Burgoon & Le Poire, 1993; Gendrin & Honeycutt, 1988; Hilton & Darley, 1985). This is especially true for interactions between strangers, including strangers from different cultures (Burgoon et al., 1997). In addition to these general social norms, people also form and hold expectations based on their past experience with their interaction partner and/or the context within which the interaction is taking place. Societies and cultures also tacitly shape what general goals and behavior patterns are likely to prevail: A business transaction is usually associated with influence goals;

a birthday celebration with relational solidarity, emotional expression, and recreational goals. Any or a combination of these influences may feed into the expectations people hold when they enter an interaction.

Desires encompass the broad category of personal preferences and objectives and are often indistinguishable from personalized goals. This notion of goals emphasizes both the general and specific outcomes that individuals hope to attain in the interaction. One such goal that is particularly pertinent in interactions between strangers is the desire to present oneself in a favorable manner (Goffman, 1959). Other goals include such things as managing the conversation effectively, avoiding embarrassment, maintaining a friendly relationship, and minimizing conflict. In addition, as in the case of expectations, people may have very situation-specific goals that will frame the entire course of the interaction, such as asking someone for a date or asking their boss for a raise. Desires, together with requirements and expectations, form the frame for each interaction.

IAT does not suggest that these R, E, and D elements are independent of one another. Rather, all three combine to produce an interactional position (IP). It is this IP that represents the behavioral stance an individual will take with respect to an upcoming or ongoing interaction. Further, each participant in the interaction possesses an IP. Going back to our example of the prenuptial counseling session, one might try to guess what the IP of the participants might be. Given the evaluative component of the situation, it is likely that both Eric and Diana will be anxious about the session. Thus, managing arousal will be a concern for them. Additionally, they may have general expectations about the session as well as specific expectations regarding Reverend Billingsley, based on what they may have heard from other couples they know who have attended such sessions. Finally, they may have the goal of wanting to come across as compatible. Reverend Billingsley is unlikely to be highly anxious about the session, so his concern for managing anxiety would be low. However, he may expect that the young couple will be nervous and that they will be trying hard to make a good impression on him. Thus, he may have the goal of putting the couple at ease, while at the same time pursuing the goal of accurately assessing their compatibility.

The final element of the theory concerns the actual behavior of the interactants (A). IAT argues that the discrepancy between a person's IP and her or his partner's A will be predictive of either reciprocity or compensation, depending upon the valences, or evaluations, of the IP and A. If the actual behavior is desirable (i.e., positively valenced) and exceeds the IP, then one would predict reciprocity. For example, if a person expects and desires that his or her interaction partner will be fairly pleasant, and then the partner is even more pleasant than was expected, the theory predicts that the person will reciprocate by becoming more pleasant him- or herself.

When the IP exceeds the A (i.e., A falls short of the IP), then one would predict compensation. If a person expected and desired a pleasant partner, but the partner was unpleasant, the person would be expected to compensate by becoming more pleasant him- or herself. Thus, although in both cases the person becomes more pleasant, in the one case the behavior decreases the distance between the interactants, while in the other case it increases that distance. Put differently, change should be in the direction of whichever is more positively valued, the A or the IP. Let us return to our example with Eric and Diana to demonstrate.

As they enter the reverend's office, Eric and Diana are somewhat nervous and unsure of what exactly to expect, but very much want the session to go well. If this is true, how would their "state of mind" translate into nonverbal behavior? Their posture may be somewhat rigid and stiff; vocally, they may exhibit disfluencies and hesitancies; they may also engage in "adaptor behavior" designed to alleviate anxiety, such as twirling one's hair, biting one's nails, or playing with a pencil. Having anticipated this kind of IP for the young couple, the reverend may strategically use his behavior to put them at ease: He may smile and exude warmth; he may speak with a calm and relaxing voice; he may sit forward to show his attentiveness to the couple. Given that these behaviors are positively valenced for the couple, the theory would predict that they would reciprocate, bringing the IPs and the As of the interactants closer together. The couple's nervousness would begin to dissipate and they would become more involved in the session.

The above example suggests that the reverend expects that the couple would be nervous and uncertain, trying hard to come across favorably and being respectful. For the reverend, those are positively valenced behaviors. But what if Eric and Diana had behaved very differently? What if they entered his office seeming overconfident and somewhat arrogant, acting as if they knew what was coming and weren't that concerned with his opinion? Given the reverend's IP for the interaction, the couple would be engaging in actual behavior that was negatively valenced. In that case, the theory would predict that the reverend would engage in compensation; that is, rather than trying to put the couple at ease, he may become more reserved and authoritative, attempting to send the message to the couple that they should take the session more seriously.

CONCLUSION

In this article, we have attempted to present an emerging theory of interpersonal adaptation. Interaction adaptation theory has the potential to predict patterns of reciprocity and compensation across a wide array of nonverbal behaviors and behavioral sets, based on the goals and expectations of interactants. These predictions are important insofar as they suggest to us the probable outcome of an interaction. That is, if we have some knowledge or understanding of our partner's interaction position, based on a profile of his or her goals and expectations, then we can adjust our own behavior in order to elicit the desired outcome. Research from a variety of domains has shown that the ability of people to adapt to one another predicts such outcomes as infant development (Malatesta & Haviland, 1982; Thoman, 1975), marital satisfaction (Gottman, 1993), and interviewing situations (Siegman & Reynolds, 1982). Thus, theories that explain this most subtle and powerful role of communication not only have important implications for counselors, physicians, and others whose work depends on establishing rapport and eliciting reciprocity, they are also important to us in the conduct of our daily lives.

References

Bernieri, F. J., Reznick, J. S., & Rosenthal, R. (1988). Synchrony, pseudosynchrony, and dissynchrony: Measuring the entrainment process in mother-infant interactions. *Journal of Personality and Social Psychology, 54*, 243–253.

Burgoon, J. K., Allspach, L. E., & Miczo, N. (1997, February). *Needs, expectancies, goals and initial interaction: A view from interaction adaptation theory.* Paper presented to the annual meeting the Western States Communication Association, Monterey, CA.

Burgoon, J. K., & Le Poire, B. A. (1993). Effects of communication expectancies, actual communication, and expectancy disconfirmation on evaluations of communicators and their communication behavior. *Human Communication Research, 20*, 75–107.

Burgoon, J. K., Stern, L. A., & Dillman, L. (1995). *Interpersonal adaptation: Dyadic interaction patterns.* New York: Cambridge University Press.

Gendrin, D. M., & Honeycutt, J. M. (1988, November). *The relationship between self-reported affinity-seeking competence and nonverbal immediacy behaviors among strangers and acquaintances.* Paper presented to the annual meeting of the Speech Communication Association, New Orleans, LA.

Goffman, E. (1959). *The presentation of self in everyday life.* New York: Doubleday.

Gottman, J. M. (1993). The roles of conflict engagement, escalation, and avoidance in marital interaction: A longitudinal view of five types of couples. *Journal of Consulting and Clinical Psychology, 61*, 6–15.

Gouldner, A. W. (1960). The norm of reciprocity: A preliminary statement. *American Sociological Review, 25*, 161–178.

Hilton, J. L., & Darley, J. M. (1985). Constructing other persons: A limit on the effect. *Journal of Experimental Psychology, 21*, 1–18.

Malatesta, C. Z., & Haviland, J. M. (1982). Learning display rules: The socialization of emotion expression in infancy. *Child Development, 53*, 991–1003.

Mathiot, M., & Carlock, E. (1982). On operationalizing the notion of rhythm in social behavior. In M. Davis (Ed.), *Interaction rhythms: Periodicity in communicative behavior* (pp. 175–194). New York: Human Sciences Press.

Ross, H. S., Cheyne, J. A., & Lollis, S. P. (1988). Defining and studying reciprocity in young children. In S. Duck (Ed.), *Handbook of personal relationships* (pp. 143–60). Chichester: John Wiley & Sons.

Siegman, A. W., & Reynolds, M. (1982). Interviewer-interviewee nonverbal communications: An interactional approach. In M. Davis (Ed.), *Interaction rhythms: Periodicity in communicative behavior* (pp. 249–276). New York: Human Sciences Press.

Street, Jr., R. L. (1988). Communication style: Considerations for measuring consistency, reciprocity, and compensation. In C. H. Tardy (Ed.), *A handbook for the study of human communication: Methods and instruments for observing, measuring, and assessing communication processes* (pp. 139–161). New Jersey: Ablex Publishing .

Thoman, E. B. (1975). The role of the infant in the early transfer of information. *Biological Psychiatry, 10*, 161–169.